Credo Credit Crisis

Critical Perspectives on Theory, Culture and Politics

Critical Perspectives on Theory, Culture and Politics is an interdisciplinary series, developed in partnership with the Centre for Critical and Cultural Theory, which is based in the School of English, Communication and Philosophy at Cardiff University, UK. The series focuses on innovative research produced at the interface between critical theory and cultural studies. In recent years much work in cultural studies has increasingly moved away from directly critical-theoretical concerns. One of the aims of this series is to foster a renewed dialogue between cultural studies and critical and cultural theory in its rich, multiple dimensions.

Series editors:

Glenn Jordan, Visiting Research Fellow, Cardiff School of Journalism, Media and Cultural Studies, Cardiff University. Former Director of Butetown History & Arts Centre.

Laurent Milesi, Tenured Professor of English Literature and Critical Theory, Shanghai Jiao Tong University. Former Chair of the Centre for Critical and Cultural Theory, Cardiff University.

Radhika Mohanram, Professor of English and Critical and Cultural Theory, Cardiff University.

Chris Norris, Distinguished Research Professor, Cardiff University.

Chris Weedon, Professor Emerita and Honorary Chair, Centre for Critical and Cultural Theory, Cardiff University.

Titles in the series:

Culture Control Critique: Allegories of Reading the Present, Frida Beckman

Prometheanism: Technology, Digital Culture and Human Obsolescence, Günther Anders and Christopher John Müller, translated by Christopher John Müller

Creole in the Archive: Imagery, Presence and the Location of the Caribbean Figure, Roshini Kempadoo

The Attention Economy: Labour, Time, and Power in Cognitive Capitalism, Claudio Celis

Performative Contradiction and the Romanian Revolution, Jolan Bogdan

Chinese Subjectivities and the Beijing Olympics, Gladys Pak Lei Chong

The Extreme in Contemporary Culture: States of Vulnerability, Pramod K. Nayar

Superpositions: Laruelle and the Humanities, edited by Rocco Gangle and Julius Greve

Credo Credit Crisis: Speculations on Faith and Money, edited by Laurent Milesi, Christopher John Müller and Aidan Tynan

Materialities of Sex in a Time of HIV: The Promise of Vaginal Microbicides, Annette-Carina van der Zaag (forthcoming)

Refusing to Share: The Cultural Politics of Settler Colonialism in Palestine, Marcelo Svirsky and Ronnen Ben-Arie (forthcoming)

Affective Connections: Towards a New Materialist Politics of Sympathy, Dorota Golańska (forthcoming)

Homemaking: Radical Nostalgia and the Construction of a South Asian Diaspora, Anindya Raychaudhuri (forthcoming)

Partitions and Their Afterlives: Violence, Memories, Living, edited by Radhika Mohanram and Anindya Raychaudhuri (forthcoming)

Contested Borders: Queer Politics and Cultural Translation in Contemporary Francophone Writing from the Maghreb, William J. Spurlin (forthcoming)

Credo Credit Crisis

Speculations on Faith and Money

Edited by Laurent Milesi,
Christopher John Müller and Aidan Tynan

ROWMAN &
LITTLEFIELD
INTERNATIONAL
London • New York

Published by Rowman & Littlefield International Ltd
Unit A, Whitacre Mews, 26–34 Stannary Street, London SE11 4AB
www.rowmaninternational.com

Rowman & Littlefield International Ltd. is an affiliate of Rowman & Littlefield
4501 Forbes Boulevard, Suite 200, Lanham, Maryland 20706, USA
With additional offices in Boulder, New York, Toronto (Canada), and Plymouth (UK)
www.rowman.com

British Library Cataloguing in Publication Data
A catalogue record for this book is available from the British Library

ISBN: HB 978-1-78348-380-8
PB 978-1-78348-381-5

Library of Congress Cataloging-in-Publication Data Available

ISBN 978-1-78348-380-8 (cloth: alk. paper)
ISBN 978-1-78348-381-5 (pbk.: alk. paper)
ISBN 978-1-78348-382-2 (electronic)

∞™ The paper used in this publication meets the minimum requirements of American National Standard for Information Sciences – Permanence of Paper for Printed Library Materials, ANSI/NISO Z39.48–1992.

Printed in the United States of America

Contents

Acknowledgements ix

Introduction: Speculative exchange: Between religion and economics 1
Aidan Tynan and Christopher John Müller

SECTION ONE: MODERNITY AND THE TRAJECTORIES OF SOVEREIGNTY 19

1 The ascendancy of finance: Toward a concept of Seignioral power 21
Joseph Vogl

2 Hobbes, sovereign power and money 39
Peter R. Sedgwick

3 'Accelerator despite Itself': Credo, crisis, *Katechon* 65
Arthur Bradley

SECTION TWO: THE LIVING SOUL OF MONEY 85

4 The Bank of England in ruins: Photography, money and the law of equivalence 87
Christopher John Müller and Ian Wiblin

5 Seeing is believing: Looking at the gold standard 129
Nicky Marsh

6 Universal Shylockery: Money and morality in *The Merchant of Venice* 149
Simon Critchley and Tom McCarthy

7 'We are all prostitutes': Crisis and libidinal economy 169
Benjamin Noys

8 The materiality of belief: On the real death of Mammon 185
Hollis Phelps

SECTION THREE: SPECULATION AND CRITIQUE **209**

9 Impotent signs: Money, speculative subjectivity and the ontological proof 211
Aidan Tynan

10 Speculation upon speculation; or, a contribution to the critique of philosophical economy 239
Josh Robinson

11 Believing in deconstruction 271
Laurent Milesi

SECTION FOUR: FUTURE REVELATIONS **301**

12 Credit and investment: A matter of faith 303
Philip Goodchild

13 How do we know we have a future? 333
Richard Dienst

Index 349

Notes on contributors 361

Acknowledgements

The fruitful discussions and exchanges that led us to embark on this editorial project began as early as 2007, in the wake of the 'Theory, Faith, Culture' international conference organised by the Centre for Critical and Cultural Theory at Cardiff University. One year after, the onset of a long, global economic recession, first with the advent of the so-called credit crunch, was to give this collective venture its current reorientation and its suggestive title.

We would like to thank our colleagues at the School for English, Communication and Philosophy at Cardiff University for all their thoughts, comments and support throughout the genesis and long development of this book. In particular, Angus McBlane deserves special mention as his early input was instrumental in its overall trajectory. Chris Weedon has provided invaluable assistance at various key stages throughout, and we would also like to express our gratitude to the external reviewers for their insightful suggestions for improvements. We also wish to record our special thanks to Mareile Pfannebecker for her stylish translation of the original German essay by Joseph Vogl. Finally, we would like to thank Simon Critchley and Tom McCarthy for granting permission to include their essay, first published in *Diacritics* 34.1 (2004): 2–17, in the present volume.

Introduction

Speculative exchange: Between religion and economics

Aidan Tynan and Christopher John Müller

To say that we are living in a time of crisis would seem a trivial observation. Crisis is the very medium of contemporary social reality. Yet we tend to experience crisis not as anything meaningful, as the element of a larger narrative, but merely as shock, a disruption to the smooth running of our lives. The crises that afflict us can be grouped under three main headings: ecological, religious and economic. This book focuses on the last two of these. Its goal is to isolate the links between religious and economic life as something that secular modernity has rendered largely unconscious in the course of its development. The religious and economic crises of the twenty-first century, for which the September 11 terrorist attacks and the 2007–08 subprime mortgage crash may function as the most potent representatives, can be understood in terms of a 'return of the repressed' relating to these submerged links.

The acknowledgement of the religious nature of capitalism defined much of the most significant nineteenth and early twentieth-century social thought from Georg Simmel and Karl Marx to Max Weber and Walter Benjamin. For these thinkers, capitalism emerged amid the transformations of religious tradition characteristic of modernity. The economic could not be understood in the absence of a conception of modernity as an age of spiritual crisis. This is an approach that needs to be revived today. The chapters to follow pursue new frameworks for understanding contemporary experience by approaching the religious and the economic as fundamentally intertwining realities. Wherever we see religious or economic life in crisis today, whether this is in the form of violent fundamentalism or the volatility of financial markets, it is in some crucial sense the same crisis at work.

The 2007–08 credit crunch and the debt crises that have come in its wake bear witness to a *fundamental disturbance in our faith in money.*

Money has always been an object of belief, something in which to place trust. While economists often speak in a quasi-theological register about money and markets, they assume this to be a rhetorical or metaphorical strategy. We maintain, however, that money is the religious core of contemporary experience and that the rationality of modern economic discourse is essentially incapable of grasping this fact. The public sphere has thus been colonized by forms of religious conviction that cannot recognize themselves as such. Meanwhile, secular modernity presupposes a segregation of religious sentiment within a private sphere in a way that renders many public avowals of faith incomprehensible and threatening.

What this volume offers is neither a theological response to the economic turmoil of recent years nor a critique of the blind faith in economic orthodoxy that led to it but an attempt to excavate a new *speculative* space freed from the traditional demarcation that generally separates the religious from the economic. The notion of speculation suggests, on the one hand, a thought freed from its relationships to empirical reality, a thought redoubled in the mirror of its self-contemplation. The financial speculator is today regarded as an embodiment of sheer greed, but this is not a merely economic greed. Rather, it is an indulgence in the pure autopoesis of thought itself, a thought that generates thought, just as money generates money.

On the other hand, speculation is that which also frees us from the prison of our own forms of thought and experience, allowing us to conceive of a reality greater than the one in which we find ourselves. Recent years have seen the appearance of a large and varied body of work grouped under the label 'speculative realism' that has sought to orient philosophy and theory away from a concern with language and signification, or more precisely with the closed circuit between subject and object, in an effort to return thought to a speculative engagement with mind-independent reality.[1] The present book engages the idea of speculation in a different though not unrelated way by suggesting the possibility of an 'exchange' between religious and economic thought. Speculation may generate a speculative object such as 'god' or 'money' and thereby imprison us, or it may shatter the mirror of self-contemplation.

John Maynard Keynes, in a now-famous passage from the history of economics, distinguished speculation as 'the activity of forecasting the psychology of the market' from enterprise as 'the activity of forecasting the prospective yield of assets over their whole life'.[2] Speculation thus relates to an ungrounded, almost irrational, sense of possibility, which Keynes attributes to 'animal spirits' rather than to prudent calculation. Speculative thought, likewise, operates according to the attractions of something incalculable and unknowable in advance. The task of thinking, we claim, thus involves taking risks similar to those faced by the market speculator. Thinking must free itself from expectations of a 'yield'. In this sense, thinking mimics a certain religious impulse to be free of worldly attachments. The 'speculator' today is half philosopher and half priest.

Most discourse still presumes a clear-cut distinction between the secular and the sacred. An act of physical violence committed on the streets of Paris or Berlin is regarded as purely religious, while an act of financial violence committed in a boardroom is considered purely economic. Politics, especially the politics of the liberal left, often finds itself trapped between these two domains, unable to intervene in either for fear of overstepping its bounds or getting its hands too dirty. According to liberal doctrine, the institutions of the secular state demand that religious conviction remain a private affair, while the politicization of religious discourse is felt to be a dangerous retreat from the grand project of secularization. But the classical sociological theory that modernization and secularization necessarily go hand in hand now no longer appears tenable, even if many today still cling to it.[3]

Many of the contributions to follow draw on a body of continental philosophy that has witnessed a return to religion in a speculative sense. Twentieth-century philosophy from Martin Heidegger, Emmanuel Levinas and Georges Bataille to Jacques Derrida, Jacques Lacan and Gilles Deleuze has worked with religious concepts in a speculative space halfway between religion and atheism. This kind of work can ultimately be related back to Friedrich Nietzsche's contention that the death of God does not necessarily mean the death of religious attitudes. Religious belief can persist in a world defined by secularism and atheism, and within a subjectivity that sees itself as belonging wholly to this world. The economic faith in money is a perfect example of this persistence, but it is perhaps only when this faith is challenged by the crisis that we start to see it for what it is.

What has come in the past couple of decades to be called the 'post-secular' is an attempt to conceptualize the persistence of religion within the context of secular modernity. While secularization remains the official narrative of the West, what we call secular can in no way be understood as the simple absence of religion from public discourse and politics. This situation is increasingly a social reality, but how we should understand it has come to be a matter of intense theoretical debate. Derrida has offered us the provocative notion of 'religion without religion', the idea that a structure of faith is operative within all forms of experience to the extent that experience contains a fundamentally enigmatic kernel. The obscure heart of finite subjectivity resists the revelations of knowledge yet does not, for all that, contain any transcendent truth that would align it with religion in the traditional sense. The boundaries of the religious thus need to be rethought and expanded accordingly. As John D. Caputo puts it,

> [t]he religious sense of life awakens when we lose our bearings and let go, when we find ourselves brought up against something that exceeds our powers, that overpowers us and knocks us off our hinges, something impossible vis-à-vis our limited potencies.[4]

Gianni Vattimo's idea of a non-dogmatic, post-metaphysical 'weak thought' occupies very similar ground to Derrida and Caputo's work.[5]

In a different register, Jacques Lacan – whose thought often contained crucial theological dimensions – argued that 'the true formula for atheism is not *God is dead* . . . [but] *God is unconscious*'.[6] What he means is that subjectivity is capable of disavowing its beliefs, so that belief may remain effective at an unconscious level. Gilles Deleuze and Félix Guattari's notorious *Anti-Oedipus* uses this very point against psychoanalysis by claiming that the latter tends to legitimate the privatized, bourgeois individual of modern capitalism:

> psychoanalysis . . . fills the following function: causing beliefs to survive even after repudiation; causing those who no longer believe in anything to continue believing; reconstituting a private territory for them, a private Urstaat, a private capital (dreams as capital, said Freud).[7]

Many of the key strands of the continental philosophical tradition from Kant and Nietzsche through to Heidegger to French structuralism and poststructuralism have offered contemporary theoretical discourse the means to engage with the strange co-existence of religion, atheism and secularism characteristic of late twentieth- and early twenty-first-century experience. The decade following the September 11 attacks saw a proliferation of such work including some truly landmark edited collections featuring major philosophers, theologians and social theorists.[8] Likewise, a new debate on the radical potentials of political theology has been led by some of Europe and America's key thinkers.[9]

The failure of secularism to supplant religion can be regarded as one of the most urgent topics for theoretical discourse in the twenty-first century. However, it is not sufficient to assume a secular or atheist position and then ask: why is religion still with us? For the faithful, the answer will be self-evident, while for the rest the question will simply be unanswerable. This is why the various 'God vs. science' debates of recent years appear so interminable and sterile. The only way to engage with the clash of religious and secular world views is from the perspective of religion in crisis. Indeed, the notion of a theology of crisis has for this very reason been a key component of twentieth-century theology. That a failure of transcendence is central to religious experience is a consistent theme of neo-orthodox and radical theology from Karl Barth to Thomas Altizer.

The phrase 'crisis of religion' can mean different things, of course. In one sense, it designates the simple fact that Western liberal society has, since the 1960s, been witnessing a decline of institutional religious authority. Private religious faith has undergone a historically unprecedented dilution in line with the secularization paradigm. At the same time, the secular state appears increasingly menaced by outbursts of 'excessive' religious conviction in the public sphere, notably in the form of Islamist extremism. One cannot help but see some complementarity, here, between declining personal religious convictions and religion's power as a threat to public order and liberal values.

The contributions gathered here take some important cues from the post-secular problematic in contemporary theory, but they combine these concerns with elements related to what, since the financial crash of 2008, has emerged as our new economic condition of austerity, indebtedness and precariousness. While some important volumes by Philip Goodchild, whose work is featured in this book, have gone a long way towards developing a theoretically rigorous account of the intersection of religion and capitalism in the twenty-first century, this is a topic that demands much more widespread attention. This is because what we have witnessed since 2008 is not only a transformation of economics and politics but a whole new distribution of life, a new existential condition characterized by permanent crisis or 'crisis ordinariness', to borrow an expression from Lauren Berlant.[10] As Žižek has put it,

> After decades of the welfare state, when cutbacks were relatively limited and came with the promise that things would soon return to normal, we are now entering a period in which a kind of economic state of emergency is becoming permanent: turning into a constant, a way of life.[11]

Maurizio Lazzarato identifies this situation with a new regime of indebtedness: 'Everyone is a "debtor", accountable to and guilty before capital. Capital has become the Great Creditor, the Universal Creditor'.[12] We maintain that this condition is essentially a *spiritual* one to the extent that the spiritual dimension is what calls forth rituals and symbols. Anthropologists in particular have long grasped money's ritualistic and symbolic elements. Mary Douglas, following Marcel Mauss, writes that

> [t]he metaphor of money admirably sums up what we want to assert of ritual. Money provides a fixed, external, recognisable sign for what would be confused, contradictable operations; ritual makes visible external signs

> of internal states. Money mediates transactions; ritual mediates experience, including social experience. Money provides a standard for measuring worth; ritual standardises situations, and so helps to evaluate them. Money makes a link between the present and the future, so does ritual. The more we reflect on the richness of the metaphor, the more it becomes clear that this is no metaphor. Money is only an extreme and specialised type of ritual.[13]

But today, money seems on the verge of losing its ritual power, and this is why it is being marshalled through new technocratic and authoritarian structures of unprecedented reach. Money is increasingly a source of disruption and uncertain futures; its exact sign-value is increasingly confused, recognizable only by a few specialists and sometimes not at all. The precariousness of money as a ritual mediator is often used today to legitimate protectionist state intervention in the form of bank bailouts and similar measures. The idea that money will somehow stop working is the stuff of our most apocalyptic nightmares and seemingly excuses the worst reversions of the liberal democratic state to its authoritarian roots (as when, for example, the military had to intervene to prevent people from withdrawing money from banks during the Cypriot crisis of 2012). Money may allow access to the continuity of time and a belief in the future – it is the very medium of stability and reproducibility. But when the economic system threatens to break down, the religious problem surges back into the world with renewed force and money becomes medium and object of a lost or empty faith.

AUTOMATIC FAITH

Secular liberal society represents not so much a waning of faith's 'passionate intensity', to adopt Yeats's phrase, but its automation by capitalism, its integration into a system that believes *on our behalf* and does so ever more effectively for that reason. The secular state demands a kind of faith without which civil society would not be able to function at all. *We call this faith money*, and in capitalist society its operations involve largely self-regulating systems of signs that are more or less abstracted from material reality, more or less purged of the passion of the individual believer. That we disavow this faith, or that the use of money does not in any way require from us any personal conscious avowal of it, does not diminish money's efficacy. Yet money – as contract, bond or promise of value – remains an object of faith nevertheless.

We must understand carefully how capitalism's relationship to religion is different to that of prior economic systems. Anthropologist David Graeber's remarkable genealogy of our current debt crises draws on the role religion has played in the formation of economic institutions throughout history. Graeber goes so far as to argue that 'all the major world religions . . . arose amidst intense arguments about the role of money and the market in human life'.[14] In what sense should modern capitalism be regarded as religious in particular, however? The most famous answer to this question came from Max Weber's 1904–5 essay *The Protestant Ethic and the Spirit of Capitalism*. There, Weber argues that ascetic Protestantism provides an ethical sanction to money-making activity since the latter stresses not hedonism and the spontaneous enjoyment of life but prudence and restraint. More recently, Derrida has observed that, in a capitalist society, 'everything depends on the act of faith'.[15] The credit offered to us by money as a pure symbol or 'fiduciary' sign is the *credo* of capitalist society, but this is a sign freed from the metaphysics of the referent, thus possessing infinite speculative possibility.

The theological role of the capitalist form of money is that it believes for us, as long as we use it, and in turn leaves the individual to believe whatever he or she may wish. In this sense, capitalism becomes one of the conditions of atheism *but is not itself atheist*. This would seem to be the crucial point. As Philip Goodchild puts it in his ground-breaking work *Theology of Money*:

> Just as the independent order of nature is the basis for the science separate from faith, and so the theoretical condition for atheism, the independent sphere of the market is the practical condition for atheism. While it is possible to imagine a godless universe in theory, it is impossible to live without effective distribution. Therefore, it is only when a self-ordering system of distribution is achieved that atheism becomes a live option.[16]

And yet, on the impersonal level of economic markets and global financial operations, money appears curiously vulnerable to the waxing and waning of faith. Money is thus key to making sense of how our post-secular society is a curious combination of faith and faithlessness. This is what justifies a theological critique of capital.

When money becomes synonymous with debt, which it must do to ensure the continued expansion of capitalism, it takes on an increasingly religious character, as Goodchild explains:

> a market based on debt money is an immanent system of credits and liabilities, of debts and obligations, and it is capable of unlimited growth. It ensures participation and cohesion, with promises of wealth and threats of exclusion, through a system of social obligations. Debt takes over the roles of religion in economic life.[17]

The essential difference, however, between the economic and the religious spheres, and what allows these spheres to appear separate in modern society, is that economic faith is largely unconscious. Indeed, as soon as economists start using quasi-theological terms such as faith, belief, trust, confidence and so on, it is usually an indicator that a crisis is afoot and that something which should have remained unconscious is now conscious. In addition, there is no theology, no dogma attached to money in capitalism; we are free to buy and sell as we wish. In this sense, capitalism is a purely 'cultic' religion, as Benjamin wrote in a remarkable fragment titled *Capitalism as Religion*: 'Capitalism is a pure religious cult, perhaps the most extreme there ever was. Within it everything only has meaning in direct relation to the cult: it knows no special dogma, no theology'.[18] Money believes for us, without the intervention of dogma, but only as long as we use it. This is why Benjamin says that the capitalist religion is one of constant worship and ceremony, an unbroken 'feast day' in the form of continuous consumption.

Capitalism, then, tends to render the historical links between money and religion *unconscious* as a necessary part of its functioning. The becoming unconscious of money's religious character is part of the genealogy of our present economic circumstances. Central, here, is the continuity between debt and guilt or sin. Graeber argues that medieval Chinese Buddhism was important for the rise of finance and the market because of the overt economic role of monasteries, which would be used to store money paid by the faithful in an attempt to eliminate 'karmic debt', the sins accumulated in past lives. The treasuries of Buddhist monasteries became 'the world's first genuine forms of concentrated finance capital'.[19] For prior ages, the sacrificial logic inherent to money would have been more apparent than it is for us today. Media theorist Sybille Krämer observes that

> the power of money to enable the peaceful transfer of goods from those who have them to others who do not derives from the sacrificial character of payment. The desired object is only acquired through a renunciation. Acquisitions mediated by money function as acts of self-denial. This is precisely the same functional logic that motivated the practice of holy sacrifice.[20]

This idea was perhaps first recognized by Nietzsche, whose genealogy of morality exploited terminological ambiguities of the German word *Schuld*, which can mean guilt, blame or debt. For Nietzsche, all ideas of conscience and moral duty originate in the creditor-debtor relationship. But the sense of guilt only becomes innate once the size of the debt renders it unpayable in principle. Religious ideas of original sin, the fallenness of nature and the infinite judgement of God arise when payment becomes futile, when the creditor is of a qualitatively different order to the debtor.

Graeber traces this idea to early Sanskrit religious literature written as far back as 1500 BC.[21] In these texts, debt, sin and guilt are often treated as synonymous. Indeed, Geoffrey Ingham argues that 'in all Indo-European languages, words for "debt" are synonymous with those for "sin" or "guilt"'.[22] This suggests that money originates from the sense that we *owe* others, and ultimately some big Other – the universe itself – for our very existence. The ability of the state to be a representation on Earth of divine or cosmic authority grants it the power to guarantee the efficacy of money and the right to demand taxes. As Marx once wrote, 'Public credit becomes the *credo* of capital. And with the rise of national debt-making, lack of faith in the national debt takes the place of the sin against the Holy Ghost, for which there is no forgiveness'.[23] But the state cannot eliminate the central contradiction at the heart of the relationship between money, debt, guilt and religion: to pay off one's primordial debt to the cosmos is strictly impossible as there can be no conceivable equivalence between the cosmos and the self that feels guilt. The debt is fundamentally infinite, unpayable. Many religious traditions not only feature this contradiction but are built upon it.

For Nietzsche, however, Christianity is unique for the kind of solution it offers in the form of the sacrifice of Christ, in which God attempts to pay Himself back via man:

> *Christianity's* stroke of genius: none other than God sacrificing himself for man's debt, none other than God paying himself back, God as the only one able to redeem man from what, to man himself, has become irredeemable – the creditor sacrificing himself for his debtor, out of love (would you credit it? –), out of *love* for his debtor![24]

God's self-sacrifice provides the asceticism necessary for the capitalist logic of accumulation, but it also includes God and man within the same circle of infinite debt. God Himself becomes guilty at the same time as He offers redemption. That Christianity provides a concrete figure (Christ crucified) for the management of infinite debt leads to a certain form of atheism because it suggests that God becomes man and dies. That the finitude of man is required for God to 'pay Himself back' is perhaps the first truly atheistic idea, and it is a profoundly Christian one even as it secretes atheism.

But capitalism may be said to prevent or arrest the atheist trajectory that Christianity initiates. Capitalism emerges, in this sense, as the last religion, the final refuge of belief and of a God who is, finally, unprofanable. As Giorgio Agamben writes, in an important reflection on Benjamin's 'Capitalism as Religion' fragment,

> Capitalism, in pushing to the extreme a tendency already present in Christianity, generalizes in every domain the structure of separation that defines religion. Where sacrifice once marked the passage from the profane to the

> sacred and from the sacred to the profane, there is now a single, multiform, ceaseless process of separation that assails every thing. . . . This process is entirely indifferent to the caesura between sacred and profane, between divine and human. . . . An absolute profanation without remainder now coincides with an equally vacuous and total consecration. . . . If to profane means to return to common use that which has been removed to the sphere of the sacred, the capitalist religion in its extreme phase aims at creating something absolutely unprofanable.[25]

Capitalism becomes the religion of modernity by making the profane and the sacred overlap. This does not mean eliminating the distinction between sacred and profane, but by rendering the distinction a matter of complete indifference to the operations of capital. If, as Benjamin argues, the capitalist religion needs no dogma or theology, then the only way of combating capitalism's total consecration is to provide the very theology it is lacking. A theology of capitalism would, then, automatically be a critique.

Section One: Modernity and the Trajectories of Sovereignty brings together three pieces that track the transformation of the nature of politics and power accompanying the so-called secularization of the West and the related rise of a world financial system. Joseph Vogl's analysis of the rise of the early banking system shows how sovereignty, defined as the minimization of dependency, finds itself intertwined with and even dependent on the rise of financial institutions to which the regent finds himself indebted. Already in early modern theories of the state, the complex fiscal arrangements in which the sovereign needs to enter to enact power are isolated as the sites of a peculiar political pathology. The levy on coinage called the seigniorage, which was payable directly to the sovereign, leads to the institution of territorially bound methods of payment and the entwinement of the state with private merchant banks operating on international markets. Thus, the formation of private finance capital begins to undermine the very sovereignty the system seeks to promote. Vogl tracks the emergence of a particular type of power that 'cannot be described via political structures, nor via economic strategies'. Political sovereignty is shown to be rooted in 'sovereign debt', and with this analysis Vogl begins to isolate the contours of 'seigniorial power' and shed a foreboding light on a domain of sovereignty of its own kind that is set apart from the state and challenges its authority.

Peter Sedgwick's chapter picks up on this theme of sovereignty through debt, and thus dependency and disempowerment. The fantasy of 'taking back control' which dominates current political discourse leads Sedgwick back to Thomas Hobbes's treatment of the sources of sovereign power in the seventeenth century. Engaging with Agamben, Foucault and Schmitt, Sedgwick discusses how the paradigms of secular liberalism and biopolitics assume power against the horizon of a better future derived from religious discourse. This leads him to a close analysis of the purportedly 'pre-liberal' biopolitics at work in Hobbes's *Leviathan* which brings out the complicity of the text's secular and religious aspects with modern economic and scientific discourse. Understood in these terms, Hobbes's articulation of sovereign power prefigures the full-blown biopolitics that emerges in tandem with scientific-economic liberalism in the eighteenth century. The Hobbesian and modern biopolitical states have in common the fact that they conceive of government as calculating, predicting and managing the desires, propensities and drives of citizens' bodies rather than ruling over their souls. Sedgwick argues that sovereign power is always already sovereign consumption. As such, it feeds on a faith in the unifying function of money that is endlessly undone by the fractious growth of a global economy.

Arthur Bradley's chapter contemplates how impending catastrophe shapes political sovereignty by offering a new reading of Carl Schmitt's political theology. To do so, Bradley turns to Schmitt's enigmatic figure of the Katechon, 'a mysterious delaying power', which defers the demise of empires. Bradley delineates how this mysterious figure of restraint is introduced in Paul's Letters to the Thessalonians as 'a temporary stopgap' between historical time (the time that remains) and eschatological time (the time of the end), a concept which helps explain why a Christian ought to obey a worldly sovereign even though destruction may visit this sovereignty at any point. Christian political theology begins to subtly transform this figure into a permanent fixture 'in an interregnum that now stretches outwards toward infinity', meaning that the very force of ruin to be restrained becomes the very foundation of sovereignty itself. It is in this articulation of 'a sovereign beastliness' in the Pauline letters that Bradley recognizes a central motif of Schmitt's political theology and a precursor of the modern paradigm of security (in political, military or financial terms) that needs to enshrine as the basis of its sovereignty the very insecurity it seeks to stave off. In doing so, he opens us to speculation on a world in which the very act of restraint accelerates us towards future doom.

Section Two: The Living Soul of Money opens by picking up on this vision of ruin. In Müller and Wiblin's chapter, Joseph Michael Gandy's painting *The Bank of England in Ruins* acts as a catalyst for a speculation on the 'void', 'inalienable otherness' and necessary 'insecurity' of money that enables it to function as a mediator of value. By pioneering the state-backed bank note which ultimately led to the concept of national debt and the monetization of the marketplace, the Bank is said to enshrine the inalienable otherness of money. As such, the Bank is used as the site for a reflection on how the spiritualization of monetary value leads to the gradual technologization of monetary infrastructures. Inspired by Gandy's painting, Wiblin's photographic engagements are produced on ruined film and as such they facilitate contemplation on how money is both a miracle and a machine. The trajectory of pictorial representation – from painting to silver-based photographic film to digital image – is mobilized to expose an inherent technological corruption that is ever more powerfully amplifying the ruinous force of speculation that money harnesses. German Media theory and the thought of Simmel, Benjamin, David Wills and Goodchild are the main coordinates of this speculation on the inherently artificial 'life' with which money animates all aspects of our lives to maintain a ruinous, automatic faith, no longer in need of any believers.

Following on from this reflection on the gradual dematerialization of money, Nicky Marsh's chapter provides a close-up view on a decisive moment in post-war American history by providing a visual history of the end of the gold standard. On the 15th of August 1971 President Richard Nixon terminated the international exchange agreements and severed the link of the dollar to the gold standard. This act, part of a range of measures referred to as the Nixon Shock, led to widespread cultural anxieties about the substitution of gold with a counterfeit and mere paper. Marsh's chapter responds to the multifaceted visual and artistic representations of this decisive event to complicate the prevailing cultural narratives attached to it. While the ending of the Bretton Woods agreement is often presented as an event that encapsulates the post-modern, in which the end of the gold standard comes to stand for a crisis in meaning and intensification of money's alienation, Marsh presents a more subtle reading. Her analyses of the art of Andy Warhol and a wider range of visual representations suggest that these cultural anxieties were not in fact connected to a loss of meaning, but to the emergence of a new kind of real: the emergence of a market fundamentalism. While returning to the record of visual material from this time, Marsh also addresses some of the theoretical assumptions which literary studies have broadly followed while conceptualizing money.

Simon Critchley and Tom McCarthy return to the intersection of money and debt to track the crucial intersection between debt and moral guilt in continental thought. They build on a reading of Nietzsche, who posits morality as a relationship of credit and debt, in which punishment is enacted not because the criminal is responsible for his crime, but because the culprit needs to pay back the crime through corporeal or psychological pain. They go on to read Shakespeare's *The Merchant of Venice* as one of the primal scenes of continental thought on the nature of the relationship between money, credit and debt – Marx, Nietzsche, Freud, Heidegger, Levinas and Derrida – but also as an essay in the genealogy of morals in its own right. The spiritualization of morality in which an infinite guilt sets the ground for moral reasoning in the form of a debt to be repaid psychologically, through self-censuring gestures, is linked to the double economy which Shakespeare's play exposes. In this system, man becomes transformed into money (our credit rating) and money is literally incorporated into him, for when Shylock asks for Antonio's flesh he enacts 'the essence of credit'.

Moving on from this, Benjamin Noys broaches the question of libidinal economy, sexual desire and the body as the 'living currency' of capitalism and the source from which it derives its value. The trajectory of thought mobilized here sees in the liberation and transvaluation of sexual desire the means to overcome capitalism, and Noys's chapter shows how this gesture of thought is precariously advanced against the backdrop of Marx's controversial analogy of crude communism to a system of 'universal prostitution' (and thus the ultimate image of the capitalist commodification of the body). Noys tracks the development of the concept of 'living currency' in the work of Pierre Klossowski, Jean-François Lyotard and the French activist group Tiqqun to show how it is used to indicate a possibility of resistance coded as a reversal from capitalist sexualization into a new collective body. In doing so, Noys analyses some problematic tensions in such theologically inspired vitalism to isolate and confront us with a 'real impasse in the capacity to engage with sexuality as a political site'.

Hollis Phelps mobilizes the main ideas gathered in this section – money as a material and social object and debt as a lived experience – to respond to Goodchild's argument that the world financial crisis signified the 'death of Mammon', but that this event will take decades to sink in and transform our relationship to money. Phelps turns to the thought of Benjamin, Nietzsche, Graeber and Lazzarato to think through the implications of Goodchild's diagnosis and suggest that the rise of consumer credit and the connected experience of being in debt is in danger of concealing the more fundamental sense in which money itself is the origin of debt. Through a reading of the emotional investment that money channels and forces us to excerpt, Phelps shows that the pressures of being in debt, although not immediately attractive in their own right, also act as promises of salvation. It is from this platform that Phelps returns to Goodchild's suggestion that Mammon has died to argue that this death can begin to have a transformative effect only when it is translated into 'a solidarity against debt', a solidarity which necessarily entails a shift in our material practices pertaining to money.

Section Three: Speculation and Critique opens with Aidan Tynan's chapter which develops a conception of speculative subjectivity through a reading of key texts from the history of philosophy on the relationship between God and money. If money is a speculative object, an object compelling belief and disbelief, then what are the subjective modes that accompany it? He argues that since the development of economics as a scientific discipline, we have lost sight of money's ontology, of what it is and how it is. Whereas philosophy in prior times had been very much attuned to such economic questions, twentieth-century philosophy remains largely silent on them. Tynan analyses the writings of Kant, Hegel, Marx and Deleuze and Guattari so as to argue that an engagement with money's ontology is necessary in order to dispel money's power and to reveal its essence as an impotent sign. Just as modern philosophy attempted to separate speculative subjectivity from God, something similar must happen today with respect to the speculative object of money.

Josh Robinson situates the 'Speculative Turn' in continental thought and its relationship to the philosophical labour of thinking in a more general crisis rooted in the decline of the economic productivity of labour. Robinson isolates the mediating presence of the very social and economic processes of valorization that the current investment in pure metaphysical speculation on the real or absolute seeks to transcend while demarcating itself against the 'decreasing returns' of Marxist, psychoanalytic and post-structuralist registers of thought. In the course of a detailed engagement with Quentin Meillassoux's *After Finitude*, Robinson pierces the surface of the financial metaphors that are mobilized in the emerging speculative approaches to expose deep-rooted and unresolved tensions in the conceptualization of the relationship between labour and speculation. While responding to Meillassoux's reading of Hegel's definition of how labour translates into thought, Robinson argues that the speculative gesture in contemporary thought is in danger of entangling itself in a paralytic oppositional logic according to which labour and speculation are set against one another – a logic that is widely deployed to explain the 2008 Financial Crisis – missing their intertwining and mutual implication. Robinson begins to trace a path out of this impasse, by arguing that rather than opposing speculation to the labour of critique, a more radical reading of Marx can provide a means to reinvigorate the attempt to transcend the correlative limitations of instrumental reason. In doing so, Robinson forcefully suggests that speculation does not require the abandonment of critique, but its renewal.

Laurent Milesi's chapter concludes this section with a detailed reading of the question of faith, idiom and an awareness of a generalizable principle of convertibility at work in the linguistic sign and currency that features in the work of Jacques Derrida. Milesi repositions some major motifs of Derrida's thought – 'the gift', 'the experience of the impossible', 'the untranslatable' and 'the fiduciary bond' at work in religion and finance in the light of examples of Derrida's 'ante-primal' idiom and textual motifs: the *cru*, the *coup de don*, unbinding (*déliaison*) and *fiancé* (fiding, fidence). The major textual focus of Milesi's chapter is Derrida's essay 'Faith and Knowledge', which shows the intimate complicity between religion and technics (faith as automatic, spontaneous, before rational justification) as it deals with the 'return of the religious' and the rise of fundamentalism in the 1990s. The various strands of deconstruction's privileged insight into the common foundations and mechanisms underpinning religion and economics are tied together in the concluding sections of the chapter, where Milesi probes the relevance of Derrida's more specific reflections on the symbolic nature of money-as-sign, a *pharmakon* of sorts torn between guarantee and threat.

Section Four: Future Revelations completes this volume by collecting two pieces that look ahead into the world growing out of the 2007/8 world financial crisis. Philip Goodchild confronts us with the certainty that one day capitalism will come to an end, even if it endures as long as the sun, only to provoke us into contemplating whether capitalism, as a collective illusion that guides conduct within a broader ecological, economic and psychological reality, has in fact ended already. To draw out the stakes involved in these questions, his chapter proceeds by identifying a discrepancy between knowledge and belief when it comes to the future, a discrepancy which might be seen to have eroded the very foundation of capitalism itself. In the course of this analysis, Goodchild exposes the contradiction between the law that demands the repayment of debt and the grace which has the authority to forgive debts, the contradiction that became so starkly visible in the action of the central banks in the wake of the world financial crisis. The chapter explains how the temporal nature of economic life can be understood only in terms of moral and religious categories, in contrast to the secular fiction of a market. Faith is shown to be a universal condition of human life, rooted in its orientation towards the future; yet it is here that Goodchild also locates the seat of crisis today, for an empiricist faith focused on knowledge and predictability has been replaced by an apocalyptic faith in which central banks act as redeemers. Once the basic tenet that all debts must be repaid is undermined in this manner, we are arrested in a discrepancy of knowledge and faith that can only lead to instability and potential catastrophe.

Richard Dienst uses the very discrepancy between knowledge and belief to ask how we know that we have a future at all. Through engagement with a long philosophical tradition, Dienst elaborates that knowledge happens in the present tense, as our sense of certainty falls away as soon as we venture into the past and the future. Current repudiation of the future, Dienst suggests, has little to do with old philosophical debates, but rather with a crisis in futurity which traverses structures of government and feeling. Our very 'world picture' is one that presents itself as being in crisis. Dienst turns to the 'apparently simple act' of navigating a newspaper, in his case a Sunday edition of The *New York Times* (20 April 2014) to isolate wherein this crisis consists. The paper's discussions of Thomas Piketty's *Capital in the Twenty-First Century* and its profile of Paul Kingsnorth, one of the authors of the manifesto *Uncivilisation*, are the focus of his analysis. Echoing Jameson's famous analysis, Dienst responds by noting that we are getting better at imagining the ruin of the planet, while losing the feeling of regret about the permanence of capital's dominion. And it is to Jameson's thought that Dienst turns in conclusion to outline a response to this impasse and ask if the question of the future can still be posed at all, and where such questioning might happen. In doing so, he forcefully reiterates the challenge to which the present volume seeks to respond to by approaching the current crisis in capitalism as a crisis of faith.

NOTES

1. See *The Speculative Turn: Continental Materialism and Realism*, ed. Levi Bryant, Nick Srnicek and Graham Harman (Melbourne: re.press, 2011).
2. John Maynard Keynes, *The General Theory of Employment, Interest, and Money* (London: Macmillan, 1936), 158.
3. Steve Bruce, *Secularization: In Defence of an Unfashionable Theory* (Oxford: Oxford University Press, 2011).
4. John D. Caputo, *On Religion* (London: Routledge, 2001), 13.
5. Gianni Vattimo, *After Christianity*, trans. Luca D'Isanto (New York: Columbia University Press, 2002), 20.
6. Jacques Lacan, *The Four Fundamental Concepts of Psychoanalysis*, trans. Alan Sheridan, ed. Jacques Alain-Miller (New York: Norton, 1977), 59.
7. Gilles Deleuze and Félix Guattari, *Anti-Oedipus: Capitalism and Schizophrenia*, trans. Robert Hurley, Mark Seem and Helen R. Lane (Minneapolis: University of Minnesota Press, 1983), 314.
8. See *Political Theologies: Public Relations in a Post-Secular World*, ed. Hent de Vries and Lawrence E. Sullivan (New York: Fordham University Press, 2006); *Religion: Beyond a Concept*, ed. Hent de Vries (New York: Fordham University Press, 2008).

9. Alain Badiou, *Saint Paul: The Foundation of Universalism*, trans. Ray Brassier (Stanford, CA: Stanford University Press, 2003); Giorgio Agamben, *The Kingdom and the Glory: For a Theological Genealogy of Economy and Government*, trans. Lorenzo Chiesa with Matteo Mandarini (Stanford, CA: Stanford University Press, 2011); *Theology and the Political: The New Debate*, ed. Creston Davis, John Milbank and Slavoj Žižek (Durham, NC: Duke University Press, 2005).

10. Lauren Berlant, *Cruel Optimism* (Durham, NC: Duke University Press, 2011), 10.

11. Slavoj Žižek, 'A Permanent Economic Emergency', *New Left Review* 64 (July–August 2010): 87.

12. Maurizio Lazzarato, *The Making of the Indebted Man: An Essay on the Neoliberal Condition*, trans. Joshua David Jordan (Amsterdam: Semiotext(e), 2011), 7.

13. Mary Douglas, *Purity and Danger: An Analysis of Concepts of Pollution and Taboo* (London: Routledge, 1966), 86.

14. David Graeber, *Debt: The First 5,000 Years* (New York: Melville House, 2011), 80.

15. Jacques Derrida, *Given Time: I. Counterfeit Money*, trans. Peggy Kamuf (Chicago: The University of Chicago Press, 1992), 124.

16. Phillip Goodchild, *Theology of Money* (Durham, NC: Duke University Press, 2009), xiii.

17. Goodchild, *Theology of Money*, xiv.

18. Walter Benjamin, 'Capitalism as Religion', in *The Frankfurt School on Religion: Key Writings by the Major Thinkers*, ed. Eduardo Mendieta (New York: Routledge, 2005), 259.

19. Graeber, *Debt*, 262–63.

20. Sybille Krämer, *Media, Messenger, Transmission: An Approach to Media Philosophy*, trans. Anthony Enns (Amsterdam: Amsterdam University Press, 2015), 110.

21. Graeber, *Debt*, 80.

22. Quoted in Graeber, *Debt*, 59.

23. Karl Marx, *Capital: A Critique of Political Economy, Volume One*, trans. Ben Fowkes (Middlesex: Penguin, 1976), 919.

24. Friedrich Nietzsche, *On the Genealogy of Morality*, ed. Keith Ansell-Pearson, trans. Carol Diethe (Cambridge: Cambridge University Press, 2007), 63.

25. Giorgio Agamben, *Profanations*, trans. Jeff Fort (New York: Zone, 2007), 81–82.

BIBLIOGRAPHY

AGAMBEN, Giorgio. *The Kingdom and the Glory: For a Theological Genealogy of Economy and Government*. Translated by Lorenzo Chiesa with Matteo Mandarini. Stanford, CA: Stanford University Press, 2011.

AGAMBEN, Giorgio. *Profanations*. Translated by Jeff Fort. New York: Zone, 2007.

BADIOU, Alain. *Saint Paul: The Foundation of Universalism*. Translated by Ray Brassier. Stanford, CA: Stanford University Press, 2003.
BENJAMIN, Walter. 'Capitalism as Religion'. In *The Frankfurt School on Religion: Key Writings by the Major Thinkers*. Edited by Eduardo Mendieta. New York: Routledge, 2005, 259–62.
BERLANT, Lauren. *Cruel Optimism*. Durham, NC: Duke University Press, 2011.
BRUCE, Steve. *Secularization: In Defence of an Unfashionable Theory*. Oxford: Oxford University Press, 2011.
BRYANT, Levi, Nick SRNICEK and Graham HARMAN (eds.). *The Speculative Turn: Continental Materialism and Realism*. Melbourne: re.press, 2011.
CAPUTO, John D. *On Religion*. London: Routledge, 2001.
DAVIS, Creston, John MILBANK and Slavoj ŽIŽEK (eds.). *Theology and the Political: The New Debate*. Durham, NC: Duke University Press, 2005.
DELEUZE, Gilles and Félix GUATTARI. *Anti-Oedipus: Capitalism and Schizophrenia*. Translated by Robert Hurley, Mark Seem and Helen R. Lane. Minneapolis: University of Minnesota Press, 1983.
DERRIDA, Jacques. *Given Time: I. Counterfeit Money*. Translated by Peggy Kamuf. Chicago: University of Chicago Press, 1992.
DE VRIES, Hent (ed.). *Religion: Beyond a Concept*. New York: Fordham, 2008.
DE VRIES, Hent and Lawrence E. SULLIVAN (eds.). *Political Theologies: Public Relations in a Post-Secular World*. New York: Fordham, 2006.
DOUGLAS, Mary. *Purity and Danger: An Analysis of Concepts of Pollution and Taboo*. London: Routledge, 1966.
GOODCHILD, Philip. *Theology of Money*. Durham, NC: Duke University Press, 2009.
GRAEBER, David. *Debt: The First 5,000 Years*. New York: Melville House, 2011.
KEYNES, John Maynard. *The General Theory of Employment, Interest, and Money*. London: Macmillan, 1936.
KRÄMER, Sybille. *Media, Messenger, Transmission: An Approach to Media Philosophy*. Translated by Anthony Enns. Amsterdam: Amsterdam University Press, 2015.
LACAN, Jacques. *The Four Fundamental Concepts of Psychoanalysis*. Translated by Alan Sheridan. Edited by Jacques Alain-Miller. New York: Norton, 1977.
LAZZARATO, Maurizio. *The Making of the Indebted Man: An Essay on the Neoliberal Condition*. Translated by Joshua David Jordan. Amsterdam: Semiotext(e), 2011.
MARX, Karl. *Capital: A Critique of Political Economy, Volume One*. Translated by Ben Fowkes. Middlesex: Penguin, 1976.
NIETZSCHE, Friedrich. *On the Genealogy of Morality*. Edited by Keith Ansell-Pearson. Translated by Carol Diethe. Cambridge: Cambridge University Press, 2007.
VATTIMO, Gianni. *After Christianity*. Translated by Luca D'Isanto. New York: Columbia University Press, 2002.
ŽIŽEK, Slavoj. 'A Permanent Economic Emergency'. *New Left Review* 64 (July–August 2010): 85–95.

Section one

MODERNITY AND THE TRAJECTORIES OF SOVEREIGNTY

Chapter 1

The ascendancy of finance

Toward a concept of Seignioral power

Joseph Vogl

Translated by Mareile Pfannebecker

At the end of the seventeenth century, in the era of the emerging political economy, a touching story set in the mid-sixteenth century was making the rounds. It referred to the fate of Emperor Charles V and his bourgeois financiers. One version went something like this: On his travels, Charles V once made a stop at Augsburg. The Fuggers, known for their fabulous wealth, showed their deference to the emperor with spectacular hospitality; a bundle of cinnamon sticks, a spice that was then one of the most expensive commodities, was hung in a fireplace. After the emperor had been shown a promissory note for a very significant sum, signed by himself, it was burnt just as the cinnamon sticks were ignited. They were now spreading 'a fragrance and light, which were the sweeter and the more pleasant to the emperor, as by them he saw himself freed from a debt; which, given his financial situation, he could only have paid with difficulty and which was, in this way, elegantly offered as a gift'.

This anecdote, put into circulation by French art theorist André Félibien in 1685, is probably strictly apocryphal; that it is nonetheless significant becomes apparent in its correspondence to a number of related episodes.[1] Similar tales are told of merchants from Genoa or Antwerp; the sums of money vary considerably, but every time, the story ends with the burning of the imperial promissory note.[2] However reconciliatory this circulation of offerings to the benefit of the imperial coffers may appear, the spectacular gesture and the cancellation of the prince's debt are merely the surface of these stories. Félibien's anecdote, in particular, presents an involvement of the financier with the sovereign, the dissolution of which tends towards the tragi-comical.

Aside from the fact that the anecdote is fitting for a time in which the bankruptcies of the Habsburgs were proverbial, it presents a scene in which prince and finance dynasty change position in a surprising manner. In the first instance, it evokes all those borrowed sums, from bribes for the imperial election to the cost of his military campaigns that put Charles V in the debt to the Fuggers and others. Meanwhile, the pyrotechnical turn reverses the political order. Burning cinnamon sticks demonstrates luxury and unproductive wastefulness; the burnt bill of exchange marks an early modern liquidation of debts, and thus the simple fact that the sovereign no longer owes credit. In the patrician abode, the emperor is confronted, in the same measure, with the display of courtly luxury and the reminder of his insolvency and his unfulfilled obligation – a move that must appal the sovereign. Sovereignty understood as a measure for the minimization of dependency, as the manifestation of self-unity and as the embodiment of the final authority renders the trader's gift an act of usurpation.[3] The merchants' gift suspends all reciprocity; it interrupts the circle of gift and return of the gift and marks a decisive asymmetry. While seventeenth-century doctrines of sovereignty position the prince and his treasury as the ultimate creditor, the burnt promissory note itself claims the role of ultimate, but significantly, private creditor in the relationship between prince and finance capital.[4] Something is given to the emperor that was not his; he receives nothing, which is what he owns. This is the precarious resolution of the situation: in the Augsburg scene of Félibien's narration, the sovereign is made once more what he already was, that is, the ruler of the Holy Roman emperor by the grace of capital. The interest in this little tale lies in how the generous performance of the financier provokes a referential confusion about where and in whom the position of sovereign power will be embodied.

The anecdote also reflects the difficult condition of public households in the Renaissance and their entanglement with contemporary finance capital. It articulates an irritation already apparent in the writing of early modern theories of state and sovereignty by Jean Bodin, Cardin Le Bret or Charles Loyseau. For however much these theories strain to convert a multitude of authorities and privileges into a unified political format and to define 'the absolute and perpetual power of a commonwealth', the settling of fiscal questions takes up a precarious place within them.[5] On the one hand, coinage prerogative, tax collection and public budget are claimed as essential markers of sovereignty.[6] On the other hand, they differ from other privileges of sovereignty – such as legislation, supreme judicial power, the right to pardon and others – in that they lead into a controversial and murky area made up by unclear responsibilities, peculiar considerations, complex decisions, uncomfortable commitments. Questions of coinage, for example, point to a sphere of activity where trade in offices, intervention of lease-holders, informants and hangers-on of all kinds threaten the erosion of sovereign state power.[7] The levying of long-term tributes conjures up conflicts with bourgeois property rights as well as concerns about the independence of princely households.[8] Finally, the negotiation of a state budget on the basis of credit is accompanied by a horror of its own kind – the absolute limit of absolute power comes into view. The cycle of loan and debt servicing caused by credit – an evil that Bodin saw to originate with Francis I – becomes the embodiment of political pathology. It signifies the 'fever' of statecraft, the 'ruin' of the prince; it marks the place where sovereignty's monopoly on power is undermined by economic dependency.[9]

Evidently, national finance raises a subject that challenges the theoretical development of early modern doctrines on sovereignty in a particular manner; it provokes more than one inconsistency and comes up against incompatibilities with the unified format of sovereign power. There is a noticeable resistance of objects that makes the theoretical text hesitate, and that testifies to their difficult fit within the concept of the sovereign who embodies the state. It shows an early concern about a sensitive sacrifice of sovereign privileges. These difficulties appear to be due to the fact that the fiscal complex presents a key motive for the consolidation of early modern state power, and at the same time marks its limits or fault lines. Fiscal matters take up a critical position that resists resolution within a homogenous idea of the political. Three basic elements – the idea of the treasury [*Fiskus*],[10] the state of coinage politics and the role of public debt – will show how early modern finance emerges in close correspondence to political tasks, how along with this a strategic field of a different quality emerges and how this field appears as a politico-economic zone of indifference, which cannot be accommodated within current concepts of political power.

First. Roman law already made the *fiscus*, the 'purse' or 'coffers', subject to complex differentiations that reflected the relation between imperial private fortune and state assets. At stake were questions concerning the rightful property of the treasury, legal limitation periods, inalienability, relations between the treasury and the immortal unity of the empire. The treasury becomes a strange object, the classification of which remains debated, unclear or riddled with exceptions. So, as Otto von Gierke notes, in the Roman Empire the *fiscus Caesaris*, the emperor's private treasury, is consolidated with the *aerarium* of the *res publica,* the state assets; in a certain sense it is nationalized, and yet it remains subject to the rules of procedure under private law. Yet it is precisely by its own nationalization that the treasury models itself on an idea of personhood under private law and thus introduces a strange doubling in the form of imperial power. While the state as such 'elevates itself ever more decisively above all law, the state as fiscal entity, as treasury, subjects itself to the law, and goes as private entity among private persons'. At the same time, the private position of the treasury was compromised by a whole sequence of exceptions, which again mark a tension between private and public in the treasury itself. In some ways it remained unclear who or what – *res publica*, emperor or private person – was acting in the name of the treasury.[11]

In the modern era, the steadfast link between treasury and state is demonstrable; nonetheless, wavering regulations of this kind persisted. For example, fiscal law is understood as emerging from imperial power, the *summum imperium*, and as part of sovereignty, *superioritas*. The treasury is in itself a mark of sovereignty and can be attributed to all sovereign authorities – princes, states, free cities – in the same measure. The bearer of rights to national assets coincides with the subject of national jurisdiction; the treasury overlaps with the person of the sovereign. Yet, it is in its impulse of sovereignty that the treasury takes the form of an independent, 'personified fund' or asset. It becomes, as Giercke notes, an immortal and abstract 'creature of terminology', a 'fictive legal personality', which survives its changing representatives. It faces the sovereign as a sign of sovereignty and binds him to specific duties – for example, the prohibition of the disposal of national assets.[12] The treasury takes up an eccentric position and remains, as a defining instance of sovereignty, beyond the sovereign grasp.

Where the treasury is positioned in contradistinction to the ruler as a private person, but also to the sovereign as bearer of national jurisdiction, a distinction is also introduced in the fiscal realm itself. Here, some areas (like coinage rights) are unequivocally assigned to the sovereign authority of an inalienable and indivisible power of the state; others (like mining and tolls) are subject to bare property laws – a peculiar combination or confusion between sovereign jurisdiction and private law. The division between legal transactions of state and plain business is provoked by the instance of the treasury, yet made problematic at the same time. Items relating to the treasury somehow belong to the jurisdiction of the sovereign but cannot finally be isolated from the activity of private business.[13] Bodin still renders public domains and national assets as bound to the status of the sovereign; accordingly, they are 'sacred, inviolable and inalienable' (*saint, sacré, et inalienable*); nonetheless, fiscal authority cannot be immediately claimed as a marker of sovereignty, if it refers to public assets as well as to the prince's private property.[14] And when, in the seventeenth century, the maxim 'that only the sovereign prince has the right to a treasury' has established itself, it is just this prerogative that is immediately bound up with limiting commitments and liabilities.[15]

One might say: attempts to frame the problem of sovereignty in a monolithic way are pervaded by resistances that go back to fiscal matters and the problem of the fiscal objects related to them. On the one hand, the treasury is allotted a domain of authority by virtue of essential marks of sovereignty. On the other hand, this domain immediately divides into distinct private and public tasks; it cannot, or can only under great conceptual strain, be associated with the unified form of sovereignty. On the one hand, the treasury takes shape as an impersonal, ahistorical and non-transferable entity, a quasi-sacred object, which, like the sovereign, is placed above the law and marks, as 'soul of the state', a sphere of supra-personal continuity. On the other hand, the treasury creates an independent legal personality, wherewith a tension between sovereign jurisdiction and the 'sacred' domain of finance unfolds: the quasi-infinite duration of sovereignty is made dependent on the quasi-infinite duration of the treasury. In this way, a process has been completed which, as Ernst Kantorowicz notes, a decidedly secular entity like the treasury is awarded the ability to represent the invincible aspects of prince and state.[16] At the same time, cracks become apparent in the concept of sovereign power: treasury [*Fiskus*] or finance appears as the scene on which political power, business transactions and private citizenship are peculiarly intertwined. Before this backdrop, the special status of the early modern treasury is clearly marked by the way in which it coincides with the arcane domain of sovereignty and yet establishes its particular arena of agency and power.

Second. Similar rifts and interferences are recognizable in an unquestionable sovereign fiscal power, the coinage prerogative. Until the early modern period, coin and monetary functions – like measures and weights in general – were understood as the property of the regent, which secured a large share of the prince's income. Beside the notorious manipulation of coins and coin renovations, this was insured by the levying of the seigniorage, which was due to the minting authority and was extracted as a sort of tax. Profit from coinage and production cost made up the difference between the nominal value and the cost of the metal of the coins in circulation. The coinage prerogative included the determination of the legal market value, dictated the conditions of circulation and set the confines for private business transactions such as the trade in precious metals. In the mints, usually set up as private enterprises that were awarded privileges, the production of money as the transformation of commodities, or rather, raw materials, into legal tender was determined by a close interlacing of business and princely interests. This is not to say that the seigniorage was one isolated privilege developed in connection to monopoly-like production sites. The relation to sovereign statehood rather lies in the fact that the prince standardized the units of measure circulating in his territories and authenticated the reference value. And, until the sixteenth century, the fiscal levying of monetary duties meant that the arbitrary act of sovereign power – represented as *valor impositus* impressed on the coins as the nominal value – signified the legitimation of that other power. The coin is the sovereign's stage; his name or minted portrait shows that the coin is 'entirely subjected to the authority of the prince, who prescribes its material, form, rate, weight and price according to his own pleasure'.[17] The funding of the treasury began the mechanisms of early modern monetary circulation as well as the institution of territorially bound methods of payment.

In this combination of factors, an impressive interlacing of political rulership and private gain has taken place. A situation ensued in which acts of sovereignty lead to the development of early money- and finance markets and unleashed a double momentum. One part is set into motion by the sovereign coinage prerogative. While cash of all kinds circulated unhindered across state borders, the methods of payment fixed via the coinage prerogative were only valid within the realm in question. This meant that in a given territory, the rate of foreign coins was not determined according to the nominal value of the originating country (metal cost plus seigniorage), but according to the metal value of the coin in question; the exchange rate thus was the result of a transaction where foreign coins relate to legal tender as commodity. This situation makes sense as a contingent effect of emergent statehood in the Renaissance and was caused by acts of sovereignty, that is, by the territorial standardization of the coinage system.

The second part of this discussion pertains to business practices in operation with the *merchant bankers*[18] since the thirteenth century. Their objects were bills of exchange, a prominent process for cashless payment transactions that facilitated the transfer of money from one location to another or the taking up of a loan in one place that could be repaid elsewhere. Of course, these transfers were usually linked to an exchange of currency; and in this way, mechanisms were set in motion, in which sovereign decrees and private business contracts systematically and efficiently worked upon each other. When, for example, a merchant banker bought a bill of exchange for a specified sum, with which the initiator of the exchange wanted to fund a deal at another location, then the price was fixed according to a rate calculated by the relation of local currency at its nominal value and foreign coins at their metal value (and therefore deducting the seigniorage). The sum was calculated according to the local legal rate of the coins. Yet the sum was only due at the destination of the transaction, and there it would again be calculated according to the local exchange rate, that is, in the legal tender (and therefore including the attached seigniorage). The merchant banker thus profited by the equivalent of the seigniorage of foreign coins. This profit, however, would only ensue, if the exchange trade went into the next round, and the sum of the bill of exchange was transferred back to the original location, where now the seigniorage of the original currency was added. Economic historians have called this the 'seigniorage effect': the correlation between exchange rate in the traffic of bills of exchange and the legal rate in the exchange of cash meant that, with every deal at a location where the seigniorage was levied, the merchant banker profited according to the difference between the two.[19] In this way, under the banner of sovereign privilege, a basic form of capitalist enrichment established itself.

Two aspects of this phenomenon are remarkable. First, there is a notable intertwining of private and political powers. The prince's seigniorage facilitates private gain; at the same time the practice of the exchange trade indirectly secures the independence of princely privilege in financial matters. While the sovereign's minting rights relate to territory and guarantee fiscal income, the exchange trade constitutes an international currency system and promotes the formation of private finance capital.[20] Second, the circulation of money in early modernity is accordingly characterized by the opposite currents of nationalization and privatization of money markets. The transformation of private goods into legal tender is opposed by the cashless 'minting' in the exchange traffic. Along with the seigniorage, the trade in bills of exchange privatized public currency.[21] The monetization of European business transactions in the early modern period therefore cannot be explained by a juxtaposition of state structures and economic dynamics. The political pole of the coinage prerogative is defined by the interlinking of public and private agents and their operations. Conversely, private business practice does not amount to an atomized market, but a tissue of exchange processes structured by monopolies developing as a direct consequence of princely prerogatives. Before this horizon, coordinated capitalization processes unfold which concern private wealth (the merchant banker), public finance and sovereign power in equal measure. The very form of money represents a private-public relationship. All these aspects can be situated in a framework of general historical developments, in which – somewhat paradoxically – the expansion of sovereign power unfolded alongside a divestiture of public functions.

This brings us to the third and final aspect. Since the Hundred Years' War, there had been a vehement expansion of fiscal debt; furthermore, the beginnings of public debt were bound up with the double concern over how royal houses might become reliable debtors and how the finances of the treasury could be secured in the long term. Dynastic succession did not guarantee the acceptance of the debts of a predecessor; conversely, the acquisition of monetary means in emergencies and war was ever uncertain. Funding via the raising of taxes and duties took the shape of extraordinary emergency confiscations, which could often only be enforced against resistance. An exception were perhaps the city societies; their burghers with their private properties warranted for public debt and ensured that the cities thus attained the character of abstract, 'infinite' legal personalities – across changing governments.[22]

In the sixteenth century, at the latest, a process began that contemporaries already recognized, for example in the financial politics of Francis I (the French king who lost a ruinous campaign for the emperor's crown to Carl V). Three elements of this process are commonly noted. First, interest-bearing loans were used not only for extraordinary expenses during times of war but also for the funding of running costs – which led to the formation of finance consortia. Second, payable interest was funded by indirect taxes on consumer goods like meat, fish and wine. Third, finance management was centralized; the income from royal dominions and the tax income were consolidated in a unified treasury. Here we can trace the emergence of a tax- or financial state, marked by a peculiar turn: what was once an exception, that is, the confiscation in national emergency and war, has now become interior 'budgetary needs of administration'.[23] With the link between national debt and tax levy, the diktat of *necessitas* is installed at the centre of the administrative architecture.

This brings about two principal consequences. On the one hand, the increasingly steady demand for extraordinary capital must be recognized as the driving force behind the formation of early modern states and their administrative apparatuses. One might put it in this way: before a sovereign and 'infinite power of state' was acknowledged in principle, it was preceded by the idea of 'infinite debt' in public finance.[24] The national loan desired a debtor who would answer for his or her debts and survive them. National debt is the arch scene of modern state machines: fiscal debt can be seen as one of the prerequisites to the securing of national sovereignty. Sovereign debt precedes political sovereignty.

On the other hand, this form of national financing has mobilized the power of private capital. The institutionalization of public debt has shown itself the richest source of private wealth.[25] What is at stake is not so much the individual instances of symbioses and alliances between regent and trade capital, like the one that bound Augsburg's Fuggers to the Habsburg emperor Carl V in a crescent from their rise to the fall of both. Rather, there was a significant process under way, in which the antagonisms between political structures and money capital as such collapsed. Emerging from these circumstances were the most aggressive figures of early modern capital power, as are recorded in most detail in the example of North Italian city-states.

For example, as early as 1148, the Republic of Genoa was forced to take up loans, and their creditors united in societies, which, in lieu of the payment of interest, were accorded the administration of various tax revenues. In 1407, a number of these societies were united in the Casa di San Giorgio, the House of St George, which provided credit to the government of Genoa until the eighteenth century. In this way, a consortium of private creditors was at the same time directly incorporated into the administration of the Genoese republic. Traders claimed positions of political administration; they controlled government incomes, state credit and public finance. The Casa was allotted tax monopolies, mortgaged state property, ran army and navy, waged wars and agreed contracts; it was awarded jurisdiction, colonies and sovereignty over dominions. In this way, Genoa became 'the capitalist city par excellence', and the Casa was regarded as 'true state within the state'.[26] By the mid-fifteenth century, the Casa had already become the most powerful financial institution in the Western world. Genoese bankers transferred returns from trade with goods into government bonds, and in the sixteenth century they entered an alliance with Spain, pushed German traders out of the credit business with that nation, organized the transport of Spanish silver to Northern Italy, financed Spanish troops in the Netherlands and dominated the money markets on fairs in Lyon, Besancon and Antwerp. The entanglement of socialized debt and privatized state income was the prerequisite for non-territorial networks, with which Genoa dominated European banking, and that allowed it to serve as a prototype for a cosmopolitan organization of capital accumulation.[27]

This became particularly apparent in one extraordinary type of business. Protagonists were the Spanish monarchy, the funding demands for their army stationed in the Netherlands, the Spanish silver imports from America and finally the Genoese merchant bankers, organizers of the financial fairs. The task was not only to secure regular and continuous funding to a Spanish dynasty that was faced with the irregularity of fiscal incomes and silver imports, but also to organize financial transactions stretching from Madrid to the sites of the far-off military undertakings of the Spanish. Starting point were contracts, *asientos*, by which the Spanish crown transferred great sums of money to their troops in the Netherlands, making use the Genoese trade connections, and offering American silver imports as compensation. This amounted to a complex financing system. When, for example, the Spanish finance authority entered into a contract with the Genoese bankers regarding ten million scudos to cover costs in the Netherlands, then the bankers vouched to deliver the sum via Antwerp and to pay advances for it; at the same time they had to ensure the receipt of the corresponding value in return from Spain. On the regular fairs – held four times a year – bills of exchange made out for Antwerp, as well as bills of exchange from Spain, were bought up in order to terminate the expected repayments. These transactions were made via various detours and intermediate purchases, whereby the bills of exchange themselves were paid for with exchanges of various origins. These operations could thus, in principle, be gone through without cash, even without expending equity capital. The end of the chain is marked by the redemption of payment commitments in the Netherlands (in gold) and their compensation by the Spanish Crown (via the shipment of sliver to Genoa).[28]

The Spanish imperialist politics thus initiated a private trade in bonds, which was dominated by the Genoese bankers and resulted in a European financial market. If Genoa thus becomes emblematic for the fifteenth- and sixteenth-century formation of a 'capitalist world system' in Wallerstein's sense, then this is not insignificantly due to a politics of public loans and the attendant 'divestiture of the state'.[29] Both the Genoese financial power, in the form of the Casa di San Giorgio, and the first international money markets come about thanks to the dynamic of state debt, and thus the interweaving of political action with private business activity.

Three settings – treasury [*fiskus*], minting politics, state debt – have shown how essential elements of modern politics and economy developed especially in their zones of indifference. Modernity has not only brought forth sovereign state apparatuses, internationally operating trading companies, influential financiers and decentralized markets. A particular type of power has taken shape, which can neither be adequately described via political structures nor via economic strategies; instead, it is constituted solely by the work of the two poles within each other. With a view to the monetization of the European economy since the Renaissance, and the enrichment effected by fiscal money politics, we might define this power as *seigniorial power* (from *seigniorage*). It is set apart from the various modes of state power by the fact that it coincides neither with the politico-juridical institution of sovereign power nor with the technologies of government, but is instead based on the integration of private agents and entrepreneurial practice. It is a form of power linked to the settings of politico-economic zones of indifference that come about in equal measure in the development of modern political orders and economic systems. It maintains an equivocal relation to both sides, it is both furthered and limited by state authority, it strengthens or checks the exertion of political power and it can stimulate the mechanisms of the market as much as to obstruct them.

A theoretical approach finds difficulty in this area because political as well as economic theories of modernity are organized, even for consistency, via definitions of system, form and structure. Political theory, to this day, is oriented towards the study of the form of political sovereignty; economic theory looks for coherent functional systems. In contrast, the figures of seigniorial power cannot be defined by the solidity of forms, the coherence of systems or the stability of structures. Their make-up tends to be informal, unstable and untranslatable into a concise systematic format. One might call this the situational interaction of forces of varied origin, the effectiveness whereof emerges from 'diagrammatic' arrangements.[30]

Seigniorial power can perhaps be defined by four features. First, this power is marked by a heterogenous make-up, in which the formation of capital power cannot be separated from the activation of power capital. The antagonism between 'state' and 'capital' is weakened, lifted or simply not markedly evident. The dominant position of the Genoese bankers in the Renaissance did not rest in the accumulation of private property, but in the ability to transform the political potential for action into business assets – and vice versa. Second, *the conversion of state power into capital*, and therefore the capitalization of power itself, is tied up with fiscal operations; it takes place via the divestiture of the state at the scenes of its emergence. A privileged example of the process is manifest in the cultivation and management of state debt begun in the North Italian city-states. Administrative pressure is fused with the development of new platforms for business. The commitments of the public loans are balanced by permanent taxation, by means of which the state appropriates individuals.[31] By securing future fiscal income, seigniorial power aligns itself with the *organization of the social field.*

Third, in this way, cycles of debt are initiated which justify their description as arch-scenes of capital. If 'capital' is understood as an expendable value amount that carries the promise of future profit, then the private management of public credit gives steady form to a speculative, 'capitalist' financing. Together with public debt, 'modern fiscality', which, as Marx notes, is founded on the taxation of 'the most necessary means of life', takes a decisive part in the 'capitalization of wealth'; in them, the 'most energetic lever of originary accumulation' is manifest.[32] With this *regime of accumulation*, the extraordinary has become the norm and the exception the rule. Fourth, this has led to a movement that is as effective as it is doubled. The extent to which the modern state is built on the making permanent of state debt and taxation is also the extent to which it has gained a quasi-sovereign fiscal power, which in its permanent state of emergency withdraws from the sovereign grasp (and which will take on its institutional format in the later central, national or note-issuing banks). This is how the precarious position of seignioral power is constituted. Here, divestiture, that is, privatization of state resources, meets with a political occupation of private finance. It is just this reciprocal, private-public incorporation that gives seignioral power its special position. With its fiscal side, it claims sovereign dignity; as an embodiment of private capital, it resists the political will. The formation of sovereign state apparatuses, in concert with business enterprise, has put into motion a dynamic that manifests itself in the eccentric becoming sovereign of seignioral power. With the object of finance – next to and set apart from state authority – a *domain of sovereignty* of its own kind has established itself.

NOTES

1. André Félibien, *Entretiens sur les vies et sur les ouvrages des plus excellens peintres anciens et modernes* (1685), new rev. ed., vol. 4 (London: D. Mortier, 1705), 28–31; *Journal des Sçavans pour l'Année 1685*, vol. 13 (Amsterdam: s.n., 1686), 12. [Translations of quotations are mine unless in English in the original source. – Trans.]

2. Cf. Richard Ehrenberg, *Das Zeitalter der Fugger: Geldkapital und Kreditverkehr im 16. Jahrhundert*, vol. 1: *Die Geldmächte des 16. Jahrhundert* (Jena: Gustav Fischer, 1896), 168–71.

3. Helmut Quaritsch, *Souveränität: Entstehung und Entwicklung des Begriffs in Frankreich und Deutschland vom 13. Jahrhundert bis 1806* (Berlin: Duncker & Humblot, 1986), 54–58; Georges Bataille, 'La souveraineté' [1950s], in *Bataille, Œuvres complètes*, vol. 8 (Paris: Gallimard, 1976).

4. Cardin Le Bret, *De la souveraineté du Roy* (Paris: J. Qiesnel, 1632), 428.

5. Jean Bodin, *Les six livres de la républiqu*e (Paris: Fayard, 1986) [Lyon: s.n., 1593], vol. 1, 179. See also Julian H. Franklin, *Jean Bodin and the Rise of Absolutist Theory* (Cambridge: Cambridge University Press, 1973), 41–42; Dieter Grimm, *Souveränität: Herkunft und Zukunft eines Schlüsselbegriffs* (Berlin: Berlin University Press, 2009), 16–18; Werner Mäder, *Vom Wesen der Souveränität: Ein deutsches und europäisches Problem* (Berlin: Dunker & Humblot, 2007), 19; Claudia Opitz-Belakhal, 'Ambivalenzen und Widersprüche: Jean Bodins Souveränitätskonzept im historischen Kontext', in *Souveränität: Theoretische und ideengeschichtliche Reflexionen*, ed. Samuel Salzborn and Rüdiger Voigt (Stuttgart: Franz Steiner, 2010), 44.

6. See Le Bret, *De la souveraineté du Roy*, 168 (also cf. 244–45, 396–98); Charles Loyseau, *Traicté des seigneuries* (Paris: Vve A. L'Angelier, 1609), 50–59; Bodin, *Six livres*, vol. 1, 331–34.

7. Bodin, *Six livres*, vol. 6, 62.

8. Bodin, *Six livres*, vol. 1, 334–38; vol. 6, 47, 67–68; Loyseau, *Traicté des seigneuries*, 61. For the 'paradox of taxation' in Bodin, see Franklin, *Jean Bodin and the Rise of Absolutist Theory*, 86–90; Quaritsch, *Souveränität*, 60–62.

9. Bodin, *Six livres*, vol. 6, 44, 88–92.

10. The German word *Fiskus* retains the Latin root of the term also retained in the adjectival use 'fiscal' in English. *Fiskus* denotes a treasury in reference to modern statecraft, but also the idea in political theory of the state as an economic subject. It also retains the memory of the 'fisc' as the contentious term for the prince's purse in medieval political theory, which is defined alternately as his private property or as public property. I translate the term as 'treasury' throughout but add [*Fiskus*] where relevant. – Trans.

11. Otto Giercke, *Das deutsche Genossenschaftsrecht*, vol. 3: *Die Staats- und Korporationslehre des Alterthums und des Mittelalters und ihre Aufnahme in Deutschland* (Berlin: Weidemannsche Buchhandlung, 1881), 59–61. For further discussion of these unanswered questions in the context of the Middle Ages, see Ernst Kantorowicz, *The King's Two Bodies: A Study in Political Theology* (Princeton, NJ: Princeton University Press, 1997), 178–79; Joseph Canning, *The Political Thought of Baldus de Ubaldis* (Cambridge: Cambridge University Press, 1987), 86–89, 120–21, 221–27.

12. Otto Giercke, *Das deutsche Genossenschaftsrecht*, vol. 4: *Staats- und Korporationslehre der Neuzeit* (Berlin: Weidemannsche Buchhandlung, 1913), 249–50. For similar ideas, for example regarding the Donation of Constantine, see Canning, *The Political Thought of Baldus de Ubaldis*, 86–87.

13. Giercke, *Das deutsche Genossenschaftsrecht*, vol. 4, 251–52.

14. Bodin, *Six livres*, vol. 1, 337–38; vol. 6, 39; and 42, regarding the problematic distinction between *aerarium* and *fiscus*.

15. Le Bret, *De la souveraineté du Roy*, 425, 621–26.

16. See also, and especially regarding the equation *christus/fiscus*, Kantorowizc, 164–92. The phrase about the treasury [*Fiskus*] as 'soul of the state' derives from Baldus. Observers ranging from contemporary commentators on Justinian law to those of modernity also associate the sacredness of the treasury [*Fiskus*] with treasures held in temples and churches. Accordingly, it was referred to as *sacratissimus fiscus* or *fiscus sanctissimus*. This sacral upgrade includes the claim made for fiscal ubiquity, an essential prerequisite for the modern interrelation of treasury and state. It is again Baldus who notes that 'the fisc is omnipresent and in that, therefore, the fisc resembles God'. Kantorowicz, *The King's Two Bodies*, 184; see also Bodin, *Six livres*, vol. 6, 42.

17. Loyseau, *Traicté des seigneuries*, 59. See also Marie-Thérèse Boyer-Xambeu, Ghislain Deleplace and Lucien Gillard, *Monnaie privée et pouvoir des Princes* (Paris: CNRS/Les Presses de Sciences Po, 1986), 16, 82–83, 113; Friedrich von Schrötter (ed.), *Wörterbuch der Münzkunde* (Berlin: Walter

de Gruyter, 1930), 419–21, 430–35, 603–4; *Von Aktie bis Zoll. Ein historisches Lexikon des Geldes*, ed. Michael North (Munich: C.H. Beck, 1995), 263, 267–68, 357.

18. In English in the original. – Trans.

19. See Boyer-Xambeu et al., *Monnaie privée et pouvoir des Princes*, 179–89, 240–69, whose focus is especially on French history; my own discussion follows their analysis in essence.

20. Boyer-Xambeu et al., *Monnaie privée et pouvoir des Princes*, 268, 354.

21. Boyer-Xambeu et al., *Monnaie privée et pouvoir des Princes*, 245, 260–61.

22. See Ehrenberg, *Zeitalter der Fugger*, vol. 1, 18–31; Jonathan Nitzan and Shimshon Bichler, *Capital as Power: A Study of Order and Creorder* (London: Routledge, 2009), 291–94; Hans Pohl (ed.), *Europäische Bankengeschichte* (Frankfurt am Main: Fritz Knapp, 1993), 114–20; Alain Guéry, 'Fondements historiques des finances de l'État', in *L'État, la finance et le social. Souveraineté nationale et construction européenne*, ed. Bruno Théret (Paris: La Découverte, 1995), 395–96. For a discussion of the repayability of princely debt in the seventeenth century, see Le Bret, *De la souveraineté du Roy*, 621–27.

23. As put by Kantorowicz, who discusses *necessitas in actu* versus *necessitas in habitus* in the commentary of high- and late-medieval legal commentaries on permanent taxation. Kantorowicz, *The King's Two Bodies*, 286–88. Also see Bodin, *Six livres*, vol. 6, 88–93; Ehrenberg, *Zeitalter der Fugger*, vol. 1, 28; vol. 2: *Die Weltbörsen und Finanzkrisen des 16. Jahrhunderts* (Hildesheim: Georg Olms, 1990) [Jena: G. Fischer, 1896], 82–84; Guéry, in Théret, *L'État, la finance et le social*, 398–402; Earl J. Hamilton, 'Origin and Growth of the National Debt in Western Europe', *The American Economic Review* 37.2 (1947): 118–30; David Stasavage, *Public Debt and the Birth of the Democratic State: France and Great Britain, 1688–1798* (Cambridge: Cambridge University Press, 2003), 65–66. For the relation of taxation and sovereignty, see Ralph G. Hawtrey, *Economic Aspects of Sovereignty* (London: Longmans, Green, 1952), 4 ff.

24. Ehrenberg, *Zeitalter der Fugger*, vol. 1, 29.

25. Werner Sombart, *Der moderne Kapitalismus*, vol. 1: *Die vorkapitalistische Wirtschaft* (1902) (Berlin: Duncker & Humblot, 1969), 661.

26. Fernand Braudel, *Civilisation matérielle, économie et capitalisme, XVe-XVIIIe siècle*, vol. 3: *Le temps du monde* (Paris: Armand Colin, 1979), 130; Ehrenberg, *Zeitalter der Fugger*, vol. 1, 353. See also Andreas M. Andréadès, *History of Bank of England, 1640–1903*, 4th ed. (London: Frank Cass, 1966), 78–79; Giovanni Arrighi, *The Long Twentieth Century: Money, Power and the Origins of Our Times* (London: Verso, 2010), 111–29; Boyer-Xambeau et al., 25–26; Braudel, *Civilisation matérielle*, vol. 3, 130–43; Ehrenberg, *Zeitalter der Fugger*, vol. 1, 324–55; Otto Giercke, *Das deutsche Genossenschaftsrecht*, vol. 1: *Rechtsgeschichte der deutschen Genossenschaft* (Berlin: Weidmannsche Buchhandlung, 1868), 991–92; Jacques Heers, *Gênes au XVe siècle: Activité économique et problèmes sociaux* (Paris: S.E.V.P.E.N., 1961), 97–190.

27. Arrighi, *The Long Twentieth Century*, 151–53.

28. For the Genoese fairs and related business practices, see Boyer-Xambeau et al., *Monnaie privée et pouvoir des Princes*, 283–309; Braudel, *Civilisation*

matérielle, vol. 2: *Les jeux de l'échange* (Paris: Armand Colin, 1979), 72–73, 346–47; Fernand Braudel, *Das Mittelmeer und die mediterrane Welt in der Epoche Philipps II*, vol. 2 (Frankfurt am Main: Suhrkamp, 1992), 222–36; Ehrenberg, *Zeitalter der Fugger*, vol. 2, 222–42.

29. Karl Marx and Friedrich Engels, *Das Kapital*, vol. 1, in *Marx-Engels-Werke*, vol. 23 (Berlin: Dietz, 1969), 782.

30. For a discussion of the diagram as a representation of relations of force, see Gilles Deleuze, *Foucault* (Paris: Les Éditions du Minuit, 1986).

31. For the rendering immediate of individuals in the tax state see Karlheinz Blaschke, 'Finanzwesen und Staatsräson in Kursachsen zu Beginn der Neuzeit', *Der Staat: Zeitschrift für Staatslehre, öffentliches Recht und Verfassungsgeschichte* 25.3 (1986): 380–81; for the mutual conversion of power and capital, see Nitzan and Bichler, 294–300, and throughout.

32. Marx and Engels, *Kapital*, vol. 1, 782–84; see Manuel Gottlieb, 'Political Economy of the Public Debt', *Public Finance* 11.3 (1956): 265–79; for a discussion of the term 'originary accumulation' in Marx's work, see Andre Gunder Frank, *The World Accumulation 1492–1789* (New York: Monthly Review Press, 1978), 238 ff.

BIBLIOGRAPHY

ANDRÉADÈS, A. *History of Bank of England, 1640–1903*. Fourth Edition. London: Frank Cass, 1966.

ARRIGHI, Giovanni. *The Long Twentieth Century: Money, Power and the Origins of Our Times*. London: Verso, 2010.

BATAILLE, Georges. 'La souveraineté' [1950s]. In *Bataille, Œuvres complètes*, vol. 8. Paris: Gallimard, 1976.

BLASCHKE, Karlheinz. 'Finanzwesen und Staatsräson in Kursachsen zu Beginn der Neuzeit'. *Der Staat: Zeitschrift für Staatslehre, öffentliches Recht und Verfassungsgeschichte* 25.3 (1986): 373–406.

BODIN, Jean. *Les six livres de la républiqu*e (1593). Paris: Fayard, 1986.

BODIN, Jean. *On Sovereignty*. Translated by Julian H. Franklin. Cambridge: Cambridge University Press, 1992.

BOYER-XAMBEU, Marie-Thérèse, Ghislain DELEPLACE and Lucien GILLARD. *Monnaie privée et pouvoir des Princes*. Paris: CNRS/Les Presses de Sciences Po, 1986.

BRAUDEL, Fernand. *Civilisation matérielle, économie et capitalisme, XVe-XVIIIe siècle*. Volume 2: *Les jeux de l'échange*. Paris: Armand Colin, 1979.

BRAUDEL, Fernand. *Civilisation matérielle, économie et capitalisme, XVe-XVIIIe siècle*. Volume 3: *Le temps du monde*. Paris: Armand Colin, 1979.

BRAUDEL, Fernand. *Das Mittelmeer und die mediterrane Welt in der Epoche Philipps II*. Volume 2. Frankfurt am Main: Suhrkamp, 1992.

CANNING, Joseph. *The Political Thought of Baldus de Ubaldi*s. Cambridge: Cambridge University Press, 1987.

DELEUZE, Gilles. *Foucault*. Paris: Minuit, 1986.

EHRENBERG, Richard. *Das Zeitalter der Fugger: Geldkapital und Kreditverkehr im 16. Jahrhundert*. Volume 1: *Die Geldmächte des 16. Jahrhundert*. Jena: Gustav Fischer, 1896.

EHRENBERG, Richard. *Das Zeitalter der Fugger: Geldkapital und Kreditverkehr im 16. Jahrhundert* (1896). Volume 2: *Die Weltbörsen und Finanzkrisen des 16. Jahrhunderts*. Hildesheim: Georg Olms, 1990.

FÉLIBIEN, André. *Entretiens sur les vies et sur les ouvrages des plus excellens peintres anciens et modernes* (1685). Nouvelle édition revue, corrigée et augmentée des Conférences de l'Académie royale de peinture et de sculpture. Volume 4. London: D. Mortier, 1705.

FRANKLIN, Julian H. *Jean Bodin and the Rise of Absolutist Theory*. Cambridge: Cambridge University Press, 1973.

GIERCKE, Otto. *Das deutsche Genossenschaftsrecht*. Volume 1: *Rechtsgeschichte der deutschen Genossenschaft*. Berlin: Weidmannsche Buchhandlung, 1868.

GIERCKE, Otto. *Das deutsche Genossenschaftsrecht*. Volume 3: *Die Staats- und Korporationslehre des Alterthums und des Mittelalters und ihre Aufnahme in Deutschland*. Berlin: Weidemannsche Buchhandlung, 1881.

GIERCKE, Otto. *Das deutsche Genossenschaftsrecht*. Volume 4: *Staats- und Korporationslehre der Neuzeit*. Berlin: Weidemannsche Buchhandlung, 1913.

GOTTLIEB, Manuel. 'Political Economy of the Public Debt'. *Public Finance* 11.3 (1956): 265–79.

GRIMM, Dieter. *Souveränität: Herkunft und Zukunft eines Schlüsselbegriffs*. Berlin: Berlin University Press, 2009.

GUÉRY, Alain. 'Fondements historiques des finances de l'État'. In *L'État, la finance et le social. Souveraineté nationale et construction européenne*. Edited by Bruno Théret. Paris: La Découverte, 1995, 390–431.

GUNDER FRANK, Andre. *The World Accumulation 1492–1789*. New York: Monthly Review Press, 1978.

HAMILTON, Earl J. 'Origin and Growth of the National Debt in Western Europe'. *The American Economic Review* 37.2 (1947): 118–30.

HAWTREY, Ralph G. *Economic Aspects of Sovereignty*. London: Longmans, Green, 1952.

HEERS, Jacques. *Gênes au XVe siècle: Activité économique et problèmes sociaux*. Paris: S.E.V.P.E.N., 1961.

Journal des Sçavans pour l'Année 1685. Volume 13. Amsterdam: s.n., 1686.

KANTOROWICZ, Ernst. *The King's Two Bodies: A Study in Political Theology*. Princeton, NJ: Princeton University Press, 1997.

LE BRET, Cardin. *De la souveraineté du Roy*. Paris: J. Quesnel, 1632.

LOYSEAU, Charles. *Traicté des seigneuries*. Paris: Vve A. L'Angelier, 1609.

MÄDER, Werner. *Vom Wesen der Souveränität: Ein deutsches und europäisches Problem*. Berlin: Dunker & Humblot, 2007.

MARX, Karl and Friedrich ENGELS. *Das Kapital*. Volume 1. In *Marx-Engels-Werke*. Volume 23. Berlin: Dietz, 1969.

NITZAN, Jonathan and Shimshon BICHLER. *Capital as Power: A Study of Order and Creorder*. London: Routledge, 2009.

NORTH, Michael (ed.). *Von Aktie bis Zoll. Ein historisches Lexikon des Geldes.* Munich: C.H. Beck, 1995.

OPITZ-BELAKHAL, Claudia. 'Ambivalenzen und Widersprüche: Jean Bodins Souveränitätskonzept im historischen Kontext'. In *Souveränität: Theoretische und ideengeschichtliche Reflexionen.* Edited by Samuel Salzborn and Rüdiger Voigt. Stuttgart: Franz Steiner, 2010.

POHL, Hans (ed.). *Europäische Bankengeschichte.* Frankfurt a.m.: Fritz Knapp, 1993.

QUARITSCH, Helmut. *Souveränität: Entstehung und Entwicklung des Begriffs in Frankreich und Deutschland vom 13. Jahrhundert bis 1806.* Berlin: Duncker & Humblot, 1986.

SOMBART, Werner. *Der moderne Kapitalismus.* Volume 1: *Die vorkapitalistische Wirtschaft* (1902). Berlin: Duncker & Humblot, 1969.

STASAVAGE, David. *Public Debt and the Birth of the Democratic State: France and Great Britain, 1688–1798.* Cambridge: Cambridge University Press, 2003.

VON SCHRÖTTER, Friedrich (ed.). *Wörterbuch der Münzkunde.* Berlin: Walter de Gruyter, 1930.

POSTAGE
R
ONE PENNY.
L

Chapter 2

Hobbes, sovereign power and money

Peter R. Sedgwick

It is a commonplace to assert that the era of globalization is upon us. This era is most obviously characterized by the increasingly rapid circulation of money on a worldwide scale, by the destabilization of once-apparently stable sets of norms and beliefs, and by growing movements of shifting population (populations who are all too often suffering refugees). Against this backdrop, it is ever more unclear what talk about 'sovereignty' might mean.[1] In spite of this, however, the concept of sovereignty appears today to be as powerful a component in political discussion as ever.[2] In the contemporary world, no less than over three and a half centuries ago when it was given its first explicitly modern theorization by Thomas Hobbes (1588–1679), sovereignty remains an abiding component of political discourse whose stubborn persistence resonates with implications of an enigmatic, near-religious (and therefore distinctly un-secular) source of power. The discussion offered here seeks to address this enigma by turning to Hobbes's *Leviathan* (1651). *Leviathan* is a text permeated by a religious ethos. Yet, at the same time, Hobbes's treatment of sovereign power marks a key theoretical moment in the emergence of a decisively secular understanding of sovereignty. This entwinement of religious and secular elements, as will become clear, has important implications for understanding the modern articulation of the concept of sovereignty, specifically in relation to the way notions of state power, civic life and citizenship are rendered amenable to being presented in the garb of a purportedly 'scientific' political discourse. What follows presents an exploration of Hobbes's account of sovereign power that seeks to make explicit the conjoining within it not only of secular and religious elements but also the role that notions of the body and money play in the text in tandem with them. This connection, it will be argued, reveals Hobbes's conception of sovereignty to prefigure the emerging governmental forms that will follow him in the eighteenth and nineteenth centuries in that his thinking, no less than that of these later forms, exhibits a powerful tendency to conceive of sovereignty in biopolitical terms.

Following Michel Foucault, one can characterize biopolitics as the exercise of political power by way of a turn to the management of the body and its biological propensities.[3] Biopolitics thereby marks a significant shift away from the classical notion of the citizen as an entity endowed with the spiritual characteristic of a free mind or soul over which sovereign power must exert discipline in order to rule. In place of this, the citizen is increasingly conceptualized as a body consisting of desires, propensities and drives that government aims to calculate, predict and direct. According to Foucault, the emergence of biopolitics marks a shift towards the kind of conception of government associated with the advent of scientific-economic liberalism and the demise of the classical approach epitomized by Hobbes. However, as an analysis of the role money and economics play in *Leviathan* reveals, Hobbes's account of sovereignty offers a significant 'pre-liberal' example of a biopolitical articulation of the concept of sovereignty. This articulation shares far more with the ethos of economic liberalism than either Foucault's or Carl Schmitt's contrasting but intersecting accounts of Hobbes suggest. It also implies a need to rethink the nature of the relationship between secular biopolitical discourse, religious faith, money and capital in terms that challenge the idea of a purely secular liberalism.

Hobbes, it will be shown, no less than the eighteenth-century exponents of what Foucault calls the 'art of government', constructs a theory of sovereignty which rests upon biopolitical themes. These are articulated in Hobbes's case in terms that relate to the management of population, consumption and the administrative regulation of money. At the heart of this is the Hobbesian presentation of the 'Leviathan', the 'Artificiall Man' created by an act of covenant to overcome the miserable condition of the war of all against all which, according to Hobbes, typifies life outside the civic realm. Hobbes's *Leviathan*, it will become clear, is an entity etched with biological features. These features (most notably revealed in Hobbes's use of blood as a metaphor for the circulation of money through the body politic) afford a point of entry for making explicit the biopolitical logic at work in *Leviathan*. An analysis of Hobbes's presentation of the 'Bloud of the Common-wealth' reveals the sovereign 'Soule' of the Leviathan (a 'Soule' which has the essential function of constituting the state itself as 'the people') to be a consumer and regulator of the economic conditions necessary for its own continued 'nourishment'. This feature is no less essential to the Leviathan's identity than its status as a sovereign legislator endowed with absolute authority over its citizens. The citizenry, which Hobbes sees as the dissolved 'multitude' of population, are the corpuscular elements whose economic behaviour constitutes the 'flow' of this 'Bloud'. Faith in money, coupled with that other secular faith, the faith in scientific method, constitutes the profane condition upon which Hobbes's biopolitical articulation of sovereignty rests. This secular faith is, however, at the same time conjoined with an eschatological proclamation of a theological faith in the coming of the 'Kingdome of Heaven' on Earth and the passing of profane government. The permanent deferral of the coming of this Kingdom of Heaven, it turns out, functions to warrant the continuance of secular sovereign power, replete with its faith in money. This religiously sanctioned secular faith is nothing less than faith in the unlimited power of sovereignty over the biological body. Understood from the standpoint of this form of secular power, all that remains of the citizen is its biology. The intersection of money, science and religiously sanctioned secular faith thus makes possible the expression of a mode of control that renders the citizen a biopolitical entity.

The discussion concludes with some reflections on the religious idolatry that lies concealed within the biopolitical notion of sovereignty outlined earlier in relation to its persistence in the modern era. It approaches this matter by way of Zygmunt Bauman's conception of 'liquid modernity'. The condition of liquidity initiated by globalization initiates a situation that finds its parallel in Hobbes's conception of the war of all against all which typifies the receding of sovereign power. The faith in money which drives globalization is the same faith that Hobbes identifies as nourishing sovereign power. Yet, in its globalized dimension, this faith undermines sovereignty. The discussion concludes by wondering if a resolution of the quandaries posed by late modernity might be found in cultivating a new and uncompromising scepticism with regard to the relation that exists between sovereign power, faith, science and money.

Looked at from a contemporary standpoint, Thomas Hobbes's *Leviathan* seems to broach two disparate worlds. On the one hand, the text concerns itself with 'profane' and profoundly 'modern' matters, namely, the mechanisms of sovereign power and the organization of the civic polity. At the same time, *Leviathan* possesses a distinctively religious aspect. The 'Kingdome of God', Hobbes tells us, will eventually come to displace temporal political power. This notion, he tells us, does not signify 'a metaphoricall Kingdome', since it springs from the 'force of our Covenant' with God rather than 'by the Right of Gods power'.[4] Just as the validity of sovereignty, on the Hobbesian view, rests on the contract forged between subject and ruler rather than a merely brute imposition of power (even if the origins of this contract may in some instances reside in subjugation by colonial imposition), so God's Kingdom as promised by Christian faith in the Resurrection rests on a covenant that conjoins the divine and the religious believer in a relationship of mutuality. As Giorgio Agamben notes, 'Eschatology in Hobbes has a concrete political significance'.[5] The powerful (and in many ways sinisterly authoritarian) secular political paradigm which Hobbes so brilliantly constructs in *Leviathan*, wherein sovereign power is conjured out of the voluntary contract made by stateless beings desperate to escape the state of nature (i.e. the miserable condition of lawlessness and fear generated by civil war[6]), has its theological parallel. Secular ends are bounded by eschatology. In Agamben's words, 'What defines Hobbes's theory is the fact that while the Kingdom of God and the profane Kingdom (the Leviathan) are perfectly autonomous, from the eschatological perspective they are somehow coordinated, since both take place on earth and the Leviathan will necessarily disappear when the Kingdom of God is realised politically in the world'.[7]

We might take this as a confirmation of the notoriously Hobbes-influenced Carl Schmitt[8] and his famous thesis concerning 'political theology', namely, that all political concepts in the modern era, the threshold of which Hobbes stands firmly on,[9] are little more than secularized theological concepts.[10] Such a thesis is pertinent not least because of Hobbes's place as ambivalent precursor to the economic liberalism of John Locke's political thought and the emerging seventeenth-century bourgeois economic social order that Locke, rejecting Hobbesianism, simultaneously reflected, justified and helped to fashion. Locke, in his rejection of Hobbes's exceptionalism, seeks to ground the state in the application of rationally derived constitutional norms. He rejects the notion of the exception simply because, according to Schmitt, its unruly (and un-rule-like) nature cannot be comprehended within the rationalist, constitutionalist paradigm.[11] At the same time, the rise of secularism that liberal rationalism promotes drives an emerging crisis in the grounding concepts of politics that the liberal state in fact depends upon. Denied recourse to divine sanction of the kind that Hobbes fences his politics within, the modern state begins to lose its justification and increasingly comes to appear arbitrary and incoherent. The dilemma this presents is strikingly outlined by Friedrich Nietzsche in *Human, All too Human*. The state, Nietzsche argues, has traditionally promoted religion as a tool to quieten the hearts of the masses. Religious belief helps secure civic peace and stability and shores up the 'power that lies in unity of popular sentiment'.[12] This strategy, however, assumes that government *is not popular government*. Modern liberal democracies change everything. For one thing, if a nation is religiously diverse, then a liberal state can no longer endorse one religion in favour of another without marginalizing and thereby imperilling itself. In response, the state is inclined to turn ever more secular. With this, the connection between the traditional religious notions upon which state power rests and the modern state itself is sundered. The demise of faith in religious institutions and holy authority threatens the demise of faith in earthly authority. This, Nietzsche suggests, has the additional consequence of inclining the relationship between individual and government to exist on increasingly pragmatic and instrumental terms. Pragmatic instrumentalism, in its turn, ushers in the privatization of the state and the withering of its power. Ultimately, the state will be got rid of: 'Private companies will step by step absorb the business of the state: even the most resistant remainder of what was formerly the work of government (for example, its activities to protect private person from private person) will in the long run be taken care of by private contractors'.[13] Secularization means that government ceases to be a matter of sovereign authority, and with that the concept of sovereignty is supplanted by the notion of service provision. The relationship between the ruler and the ruled is slowly transformed into a variant of the one that exists already between the buyer and the seller. Faith in the divine is thereby substituted in the political arena by the mundane primacy of the financially determined contractual relationship.

In Schmitt's terms, this tendency amounts to a 'negation of the political. . . . There exists a liberal policy of trade, church, and education, but absolutely no liberal politics, only a liberal critique of politics'.[14] For the liberal, the state becomes identified with the dominant social order, which is nothing more than 'an economic-technical system of production and traffic'.[15] The concept of sovereignty recedes in the face of the advance of mass culture. This is borne witness to by the citizen's being replaced by the 'mass of consumers' whose lives are orientated around 'a series of demilitarized and depoliticized concepts'[16] that promote the hegemony of economic forces in an attempt to rationalize and thereby negate the threat of the extreme situations which characterize the political realm.[17] Such a social order, which threatens to impose a unified world 'based exclusively on economics and on technically regulating traffic', would, Schmitt notes, 'be no more of a social entity' than would be a collection 'of tenants in a tenement house, customers purchasing gas from the same utility company, or passengers travelling on the same bus'.[18] What characterizes liberalism decisively is that it is inextricably bound up with economic discourse: that rational-instrumental calculation is, at the same time, financial calculation, a matter of means and ends that is based upon the relationships that inhere between the buyer and the seller. The liberal subject, in short, is articulated out of the nexus of financial exchange. Liberal secular culture is epitomized by its faith in the power of money.

Hobbes, writing amid the ethos of early modern seventeenth-century culture, in a context scarred by the horrors of the English Civil War, stressing, as we have seen, that the secular is bounded by the religious, could not appear to inhabit a world further removed from the one to which Schmitt's diagnosis of the managerialist faith in consumerist economy applies itself. It is no surprise, then, that Schmitt can turn on managerially inclined modernity by invoking the Hobbesian condition of extremity that is, for him, so alien to liberal political sensibilities, that is, the sovereign state of exception, to which no liberal invocation of constitutional rules can answer due to its being prey to an overwhelming desire to 'subjugate' politics to economic calculation.[19]

The desire which Schmitt castigates constitutes the kernel of what Michel Foucault has called the modern 'art of government'. This art, or rather technique, is characterized precisely by its move away from the consideration of governance as something which revolves around questions of sovereignty and the crisis of exception to the notion of government as the day-to-day management of population through the application of statistical methods.[20] Modern liberal governance does not merely recast the problems of authority and ruling in terms of economic trade and traffic; it at the same time reconceptualizes the relations of social order as flows of population to be managed. These flows, which are defined by statistically identifiable regularities (death rates, the threat posed by different diseases or varieties of risk from accidents, the prevalence of different forms of behaviour, the waxing and waning of customs, preferences of consumption etc.), are precisely what render social order susceptible to being conceptualized within the paradigm of economics. Politics, Foucault tells us, inexorably becomes political economy. Population becomes not merely the object of governmental concern but also the defining purpose of ruling. The fusion of economy and population defines the modern era, determining even its sense of purpose: 'What can the end of government be? Certainly, not just to govern, but to improve the condition of the population, to increase its wealth, its longevity, and its health'.[21] Sovereignty, therefore, is redefined by being allotted a role within a context dominated by techniques of calculation directed towards the manipulation and perfection of the population (the intention to make people longer-lived, more prosperous, etc.). The populous becomes a tool of government rather than the source of its sovereign legitimacy – even to the point where population may have to be taken into account when making governmental decisions (representative 'democracy'). Foucault believes that Hobbes resides on the other side of the historical divide that separates the modern government of population from sovereign rule. For Hobbes, Foucault comments, 'the sovereign is the person who can say no to any individual's desire, the problem being how to legitimize this "no" opposed to individuals' desire and found it on the will of the same individuals'. Modern governance, in contrast, is concerned with 'how to say yes to this desire' and in so doing cultivate it and reap the rewards of its beneficial effects.[22] Thus,

> the population is not . . . a collection of juridical subjects in an individual or collective relationship with a sovereign will [as the Hobbesian account would have it]. It is a set of elements in which one can note constants and regularities even in accidents, in which we can identify the universal desire regularly producing the benefit of all, and with regard to which we can identify a number of variables on which it depends.[23]

To oppose Hobbes to the modernist economic conceptualization of government, for better or worse, as Schmitt and Foucault in their related ways do, is however to ignore an important aspect of the Hobbesian articulation of sovereignty. This aspect can serve to enhance our understanding of the problem of modern governance by clarifying the complex question of the relationship that inheres in modern political sensibility between politics, population, faith and money. To approach these aspects, it is necessary to turn first to Hobbes's account of the Leviathan and the sovereignty which decisively characterizes it.

Hobbes famously conceives of social order and sovereignty as emanating from the 'the natural condition of Mankind' (*L* 86ff.).[24] He sketches this condition in stark terms: it is one of unremitting terror. In their 'natural condition' (which simply denotes a state of existence separated from the civil condition) humans are equal in so far as they each possess the quality of 'prudence', that is, every person has a degree of skill when it comes to identifying and pursing his or her own ends. It is this pursuit of particular ends, however, that ensures the natural condition of humanity to be one of conflict and misery, 'for if any two men desire the same thing, which nevertheless they cannot both enjoy, they become enemies' (*L* 87). People, as long as they 'live without a common power to keep them in awe', inexorably find themselves locked into 'that condition which is called Warre'. The essential point about war is not the mere fact of its violence but the mode of temporality that defines it. Like 'Foule weather', war is more than a series of terrible but short and unconnected events; its essence resides in the fact that it consists of 'a tract of time' (*L* 88). War is a kind of unity of sustained chaos, an ensemble of elements that coalesce into a disruptive form of corrosive unhistorical timelessness. Taken on these terms, war, like weather, constitutes something analogous to what Deleuze and Guattari designate as an haecceity. Haecceities are modes of 'individuation that are very different from a person, thing or substance. . . . Endowed with . . . a perfect individuality lacking nothing, even though this individuality is different from that of a thing, or a subject . . . concrete individuations that have a status of their own and direct the metamorphosis of things and subjects'.[25] War, in a similar manner, operates in Hobbes's thought as an individuated condition composed of discrete but continuous and related elements that descend like a pall on humanity to engulf it in hopelessness. War fashions and transforms subjectivity. What stands out with regard to war in this context is what it *subtracts* from the subject, as is revealed by what must be the most famous passage from *Leviathan*:

> Whatsoever [. . .] is consequent to a time of Warre, where every man is Enemy to every man; the same is consequent to the time, wherein men live without other security, than what their own strength, and their own invention shall furnish them withall. In such condition, there is no place for Industry; because the fruit thereof is uncertain; and consequently no Culture of the Earth; no Navigation, nor use of the commodities that may be imported by Sea; no commodious Building; no Instruments of moving, and removing such things as require much force; no Knowledge of the face of the Earth; no account of Time; no Arts; no Letters; no Society; and which is worst of all, continuall feare, and danger of violent death; And the life of man, solitary, poore, nasty, brutish, and short. (*L* 89)

War, as this passage reveals, is paradigmatic of a specific modality of time, the consequence of which is a radical de-historicization of human endeavour. War is, most strikingly, not merely the condition of existence lacking in security, memorably characterized by its solitude, violence and brevity, but it also possesses the power to mould subjects by denying them time. For the subject immersed in the condition of war, temporal possibilities are engulfed in a ceaseless cycle of the return of the violent present. This is a time without time, one in which neither past nor future can have concrete meaning. It denudes human life of its purposes. In such a situation, there can be no construction or maintenance of the things that make for a life endowed with sense. The world cannot be represented (mapped) or controlled and put to use (manipulated by 'instruments of moving'). Life cannot be expressed through aesthetic or other social means for there is nothing about it to be expressed beyond its brevity and terror. All that remains is the threat of violation and dissolution.

Hobbes's solution to the threat of dissolution is the construction of a 'Common-wealth' or Leviathan, a social order aimed towards the facilitation of commodious living which is established by leaving the natural condition through the act of making a covenant. In other words, humans caught in the state of nature withdraw from it by agreeing to submit to communal existence and the restrictive conditions which define it. In doing this, they project themselves and their desire to escape the bonds of fear onto a larger social canvas. The Leviathan 'is [thus] but an Artificiall Man; though of greater stature and strength than the Naturall, for whose protection and defence it was intended' (*L* 9).

The Leviathan, as the 'Artificiall' image implies, is best comprehended as a culturally generated *mechanism* for regulating and thereby gaining the time without which meaningful life is not possible. The features of this mechanism are akin to those of a human body that is itself composed, by way of a contract, of a coordinated multiplicity of individuated natural human bodies. Such a mechanism, fittingly, is envisaged in terms of *functions* which parallel the construction of the natural human form. These are 'Systemes, which resemble the similar parts, of Muscles of a body' (*L* 155).[26] The Leviathan is endowed with joints, tendons and nerves (*L* 167), a voice, hands, an eye and an ear (*L* 169).[27] It also possesses other bodily attributes, not least the possession of 'an Artificiall *Soul*' (*L* 9), that is a mind which animates and endows it with the artificial life without which it could not exist. This soul is sovereign power, for 'a Common-wealth, without Sovereign Power, is but a word' (*L* 245).

Sovereign power, for Hobbes, is a matter of *representation* in a strict and limited sense. Namely, sovereignty represents and thereby unites in one form the collective will (and therefore agreement) of suffering humanity to escape from the condition of war by seeking political life in the refuge of a civic body. Such power, whether it takes the form of an individual (a monarch) or a sovereign body (an assembly), exists only in virtue of the fact that it stands as a representation of a community of beings who have covenanted their allegiance to it. In so far as it stands for the Leviathan, the 'sovereign' is constituted as an entity that represents the will of the 'people'. As Agamben notes, on this view, the coming into being of sovereign power at one and the same time entails drawing a distinction between the 'people' of the commonwealth and the mere population of individuals (the 'multitude') out of which it coalesces and who subsequently compose it in the form of the 'dissolved multitude' of its population of subjects or citizens.[28] To be subject to sovereign power means to consent to be subjected to the will of the sovereign in so far as *the sovereign* (be it a monarch or a parliament) *is now the people*.[29] The 'people', therefore, through the body which stands as the representation of sovereign power, reigns over the multitude of its citizenry, in the form of a synthetic unity that orders and governs the multitude:

> A Multitude of men, are made One Person, when they are by one man, or one Person, Represented; so that it be done with the consent of every one of that Multitude in particular. For it is the Unity of the Representer, not the Unity of the Represented, that maketh the Person One. And it is the Representer that beareth the Person, and but one Person: And Unity, cannot otherwise be understood in Multitude. (*L* 114)

The multitude, it follows, is the body of the Leviathan, but the Leviathan itself, once sovereign power is instituted, becomes identified with the 'Soul' which denotes the presence of sovereign will, and what represents the commonwealth is not the population but the sovereignty of the 'Mortall God' to whom all citizens are indebted for their 'peace and defence' (*L* 121). Here is the paradox of sovereign power. For sovereignty, which is the soul of a commonwealth, to be generated a multitude must come together, but the essence which defines a commonwealth is not the multitude itself but the formation of the office of sovereign power which results from this coming together: 'The Essence of the Commonwealth . . . *is One Person, of whose Acts a great Multitude, by mutuall Covenants one with another, have made themselves every one the Author*. . . . And he that carryeth this Person is called SOVERAIGNE, and said to have *Soveraigne Power*; and every one besides, [is called] his SUBJECT' (*L* 121). Sovereignty is a representation in so far as it is an office, a formal role that is borne in the embodied personhood of the monarch or assembly that expresses the will of the commonwealth.

The Hobbesian commonwealth is, to use Michael Oakeshott's term, an 'artifact'.[30] It is something made in order to be put to use to satisfy the purpose of commodious living by way of gaining time. What happens as soon as a social covenant is instituted, however, is that those who acceded to it become, by virtue of the act of agreeing, entities whose civic meaning (i.e. their significance *qua* subjects or citizens) resides in their amenability to being put to use as instruments at the sole disposal of sovereign will. The artifact has become a *sovereign artifact*, a mechanism that now possess an authority that has the uncanny consequence of transforming those persons whose covenant gave rise to it into mere artifacts themselves (beings, one might add, who are thereby deprived of the ability to regulate their own time, since ultimately the conditions of commodious living are dictated by sovereign power alone).

Bearing this in mind, one can recall the concept of the dissolved multitude. This is the domain of individuated subject-bodies who make up the population of a commonwealth but are not, at the same time, to be confused with the 'people'. More specifically, one can relate the dissolved multitude of population to another aspect of the Leviathan that Hobbes emphasizes. The Leviathan, it should be recalled, is an 'Artificiall Body', but like any natural body, it needs to be nourished.[31] Nutrition, Hobbes tells his readers, consists 'in the *Plenty*, *Distribution of Materials* conducing to Life: In *Concoction* . . . and (when concocted) in the *Conveyance* of it, by convenient conduits, to the Publique use' (*L* 170). A commonwealth's nourishment involves the ingestion of animal, vegetable and mineral 'Matter' or, to put it only slightly differently, it necessitates the traffic of 'Commodities'. The Leviathan, that great artefact and producer of relief from the condition of perpetual war, is in short also a gigantic consumer. Consumption, be it by way of production through labour power, exchange or foreign war, is 'needfull for the maintenance and motion of the whole Body' since 'Common-wealths can endure no Diet' (*L* 171, 172). Sovereign power, in consequence, must be endowed with the right to oversee and regulate the flow of goods through the social order. The initial covenant which characterizes the narrative of the establishment of political community is in this way transposed into the ability to lay out and oversee the regulations which make up the world of commercial existence, of bargaining and 'mutuall contract', that is, the practices of 'buying, selling, exchanging, borrowing, lending, letting, and taking to hire' (*L* 174).

For sovereign power to endure, commercial transactions must be facilitated with a view to securing the future. This is achieved by an act of translation. Hobbes terms this translation 'reduction'. It is the process whereby all commodities that are not currently being consumed are 'reserved for Nourishment in time to come'. The temporal anxiety which captures the essence of Hobbes's description of humanity in its natural condition thus finds its parallel in the domain of the civic community. Civic life means having a tomorrow, as opposed to a mere existence in the perpetually threatened present which defines the state of the war of all against all. Tomorrow must be provided for in advance. Having a tomorrow requires foresight, calculation, the ability to translate tomorrow's needs into something that will hold value for the duration of the temporal gap which separates what is the case in the now from what will be the case in the future. The medium of translation must also be 'portable' so that the means of nourishment may go wherever 'men' are inclined to go:

> And this is nothing else but Gold, and Silver, and Mony. For Gold and Silver, being (as it happens) almost in all Countries of the world highly valued, is a commodious measure for the value of all things else between Nations; and Mony (of what matter soever coyned by the Soveraign of a Common-wealth,) is a sufficient measure of the value of all things else, between the Subjects of that Common-wealth. By the means of which measures, all commodities,

> Moveable, and Immoveable, are made to accompany a man, to all places of his resort, within and without the place of his ordinary residence; and the same passeth from Man to Man, within the Common-wealth; and goes round about, Nourishing (as it passeth) every part thereof; In so much as this Concoction, is as it were the Sanguification of the Common-wealth: For naturall Bloud is in like manner made of the fruits of the Earth; and circulating, nourisheth by the way, every Member of the Body of Man. (*L* 174)

Money is, for Hobbes, a universal standard of estimation. It is the measure of 'all things else'. It is that 'concoction' in virtue of which the subjects of a commonwealth relate to one another. Money ensures the passage of all things valued from person to person and, in passing between the members of the multitude, creates political life itself. Money is 'Sanguification', the making of living blood cells in the marrow of the civic body that, in circulating, animates every organ and brings about the movements of the body. Putting matters more bluntly, 'Mony [is] the Bloud of a Common-wealth'. It is that which makes 'Common-wealths move, and stretch out their armes, when need is, into foreign Countries' (*L* 174, 175). Money is what drives the limbs that facilitate colonial expansion (the resonance here of 'armies' and 'arms', weaponry and limbs, in the word 'armes' could hardly escape the notice of even the most casual of readers). Economic management, in other words, is what lies at the heart of the ruling of a commonwealth. For the management of economy ensures the security of the future. With this affirmation of 'blood' comes the need to control. Blood must be channelled so that healthy circulation can be ensured. This is done, Hobbes tells us, by an entire bureaucracy of 'Collectors, Receivers, and Treasurers': 'And in this also, the Artificial Man maintains his resemblance with the Naturall' (*L* 175) in that this blood, taken to the 'Heart', is injected with vitality and sent out again to be pumped through and around the circuit of the body politic.

The Leviathan, it is now possible to conclude, is no less an articulation of the government of population, of the emergence of the paradigm of biopolitics in the modern era, than the form of governmental 'science' that Foucault outlines as emerging in tandem with the perfection of statistical methods in the century following Hobbes. The Leviathan stands as a powerful symbol of the body and its management and of the emerging power that the sciences of the body promise to exert over the body. Hobbes himself is an eloquent exponent of these sciences.[32] The body is revealed in *Leviathan* as a central component in the self-consciously 'modern' political discourse that Hobbes fashions, a discourse that claims the right to trump all political discourse that has preceded it. It is telling in this regard that Hobbes is scathing of the past of the Western tradition of thought, not least of the 'erroneous Philosophy of the Greeks, especially of Aristotle' (*L* 418), belief in the authority of which is 'the mony of fooles' (*L* 29). Ancient wisdom is bad coin. Modern knowledge, for him, is paradoxically 'older' than ancient wisdom[33] since it rests upon a rejection of its accumulation of error; the new is more worthy of belief since it has time on its side.

The text of *Leviathan* lays out before us a giant, dissected body in the form of 'an Artificiall Animal' (*L* 9). The political is in this way rendered amenable to being explored function by function. Yet, at the same time, the language of divinity that Hobbes borrows to lay out his scientific account of the body politic cannot be erased. Indeed, as was noted at the beginning of this chapter, it looms large in the work. *Leviathan* sketches out its faith in the mortal divinity of sovereign power precisely because a theological faith in the immortality of divine power constitutes its possibility. About half of *Leviathan*'s 491 pages are devoted not to an elaboration of the profane commonwealth but to its divine counterpart, the 'Kingdome of God'. Tellingly, this kingdom, no less than any profane commonwealth, is 'a Civill Kingdome', the existence of which rests on a 'literall interpretation' of its meaning (*L* 284). 'The Kingdome therefore of God, is a real, not a metaphorical Kingdome', Hobbes informs his readers. It will exist 'by force of our Covenant, not by the Right of Gods Power' (*L* 283). This covenant constitutes the domain in which the faithful, those who make a covenant with God, will come to enjoy 'Eternall Life on Earth' (*L* 308). The Kingdom of God, which takes the form of a re-articulation of the 'Political government of the Jews on Earth' instituted by Moses, stands in Hobbes's text as the future promise of the demise of the politically profane and its supplanting with a divine but still profoundly *earthly* politics. The New Jerusalem will descend from the heavens to 'Gods people . . . and not they go up to it from earth' (*L* 308). Here is the promise of a new temporality in which the secular need to ensure the management of time with a view to securing the future will have passed away as the contingencies of history give way to the domain of divine eternal regulation.

It is only in so far as this New Jerusalem, the 'second coming' of Christ, has not yet happened that we are obliged to exist in a civil condition in order to ward off the threatened terror of life without government. The natural condition which threatens to engulf humanity necessitates government by 'Civill Sovereigns' (*L* 419) as a means to its temporary solution. With the second coming, however, comes the promise of an ultimate solution. With the arrival of the Kingdom of God the constitutional conception of the 'people' will vanish; there will be no mortal sovereign-gods, and the multitude and multiplicity of subjects which makes up the population will be transformed. The subjects in a divine commonwealth, Hobbes asserts, will be those 'that believe that there is a God that governeth the world . . . all the rest are to be understood as Enemies' (*L* 246). There is an obvious resonance in this with Carl Schmitt's well-known articulation of the political as residing in the 'friend-enemy' distinction.[34] Especially telling in this regard is the suggestion that the Kingdom of God will turn on those who 'understand no Precepts as his' and cast them out, which in effect means condemning them to eternal death. With the coming of the rule of divinity comes the purging of population. The earthly Kingdom of God is a theocracy through and through.

In practical (i.e. profane) terms, what matters, of course, is the deferral of this theocratic moment of exclusion. Hobbes's text cannot, any more than any other, claim access to more than a dimly intimated utopian future devoid of Leviathan, even as it is caught in the gesture of invoking faith in the inevitability of this future. It is, however, precisely this deferral that serves to warrant the continued existence of sovereign power and the administration of its functions, namely, the harmonization of elements and the regulation of flows which ensure the 'lawful' behaviour of a commonwealth's population of subjects. The 'Mortall God' abides precisely because the immortal God refuses, for now, to show itself. Faith in money endures and is justified in its enduring because the divine sacrament which ought to be the case is not yet the case. The subjection of population at the hands of the 'people' (which is the sovereign) is justified through this deferral and with that the multitude's reduction to the status of an element that obediently accedes to its role as part of the corpuscular flow which courses around the Leviathan's artificial body is also assured as it is legitimized.

As Michael Hardt and Antonio Negri note, the division between the people and the multitude is an act of exclusion which operates through, and at the same time warrants, the fact of the unequal ownership of property.[35] The multitude, reduced to one of the administrative tasks of sovereign power in the form of the latter's right to dictate and regulate economic behaviour and the flow of money, is repaid for its acceptance of this reduction by the promise of peace and security in the civic realm. The subjected citizen is obliged to rest content with the fact that he or she is prey to ending up living in a condition of peace that is as denuded of property as the condition of the war of all against all from which escape was sought. Seen from this perspective, the protection which the Leviathan promises is an illusion and faith in it deluded. The poor are, in reality, offered no more security in the civic community than they would find in the condition of being excluded from it. The regulation of time which justifies the establishment of a commonwealth is, it turns out, not a time that is to be held in common. Even as subjects situated within a commonwealth, the poor ultimately remain timeless beings, passively unhistorical entities dwelling in a narrative of the 'people' which excludes them even as it draws them into itself as subjects of sovereign power. The 'Artificiall Man' can offer the multitude no more than the bitter pill of an artificial peace accompanied by the compensatory emollient of a reserved place in the forthcoming Kingdom of God so long as they maintain their covenant with it – which means, naturally, so long as they submit to the 'Mortall God' who reigns in the present.

Hobbes's approach, it should now be clear, is even closer to the spirit of an economically inclined liberalism than Schmitt might suspect,[36] even as he uses Hobbesian concepts to attack it. The war of all against all which typifies the state of exception results in the justification of a form of sovereign power that does not merely harmonize with the liberal notion of a political order orientated around the mundane world of production, consumption and exchange, that is, the world of money that Schmitt rejects. Rather, it comes to embody it in the form of sovereign power itself. The sovereign, as has been shown, must take on the role of managing the flows of economic activity since it is itself above all else a consumer of the economic behaviour of those who are rendered subject to it. The sovereign feeds off the world of production, nourishing itself and thereby taking on the form of a consumer. Sovereign power is hence always already sovereign consumption, in so far as it is typified by the ability to regulate the biological and logistical flows of producing and consuming within a population and to arrange the means of storage and transfer that ensure a continuous feeding off the surplus nutrition carried by the 'blood' (in the shape of taxation, the granting of licenses etc.) that such activity generates.

Politics, science and money, those key elements which coalesce in modernist political consciousness to form the managerial liberal governmental culture which provokes Schmitt's fury and Foucault's critical historical discourse, come together already in *Leviathan*. Sovereignty, which is limited to the domain of profane things, is revealed as resting upon a profane faith in the unity of this trinity. Money is the universal political condition of reduction necessary for the continued animation of the body politic and the regulation which ensures its future. The maintenance of the 'Mortall God'[37] of sovereign power stands justified by 'scientific' knowledge. At the same time, profane sovereign power, which ought to be confined to the domain of the secular, becomes rendered divine by Hobbes's language, its body sanctified by 'Bloud' which is, after all, a symbol of Christian sacrament. Under the dominion of this sovereign power, this profane sacrament, the dissolved multitude is reduced to a corpuscular flow bound in servitude to an artifact, whose unassailability is legitimized and made palatable for modern sensibilities by scientific ratiocination. Political science – and among Hobbes's ambitions is the articulation a full-blown science of politics that takes its place alongside natural science[38] – stands revealed in its servitude to money and the sovereign power of exclusion.

Is Agamben, therefore, correct in suggesting that the history of European political discourse is biopolitical through and through? Ought we to follow the general thesis of his *Homo Sacer* and find a concern with the management of the body and its functions, its inclusion and exclusion from the realm of sovereign power, to be a defining feature of Western political thinking since the Greeks?[39] Certainly, Foucault's thesis concerning the emergence of modern government and the science of the body might, this reading of *Leviathan* suggests, be traced further back than the eighteenth century. But, at the same time, Hobbes in his rejection of the Greeks finds justification for this mode of exclusion in the Bible, in the Divine. Questions of origins aside, however, we might want to defer consideration of such issues in order to pose them in the context of another related question which will take us back to the question of the enigmatic nature of sovereignty alluded to at the beginning of this discussion. We might ponder whether faith in the constituent elements of secular government, faith in the commodity, money, the body as an object of the political gaze, and its peculiarly modern entwinement with rationalist scientific discourse entails, and even *facilitates*, a kind of regressive idol worship. In so far as it is affirmed in these terms, does the persistence of the notion of 'sovereignty' today perhaps also indicate the persistence of an archaic but paradoxically 'modern' tendency to the mythological and idolatry?[40]

It is possible to engage in a preliminary way with such a question by way of Zygmunt Bauman's notion of 'liquidity'. Liquidity, for Bauman, is the central feature of life in late modernity. Modernity in its most recent iteration is driven by globalization, that is, 'by capitalism's global triumph'.[41] Herein unresolved tensions lie, for the flow of global capital outstrips the power of the still extant but increasingly redundant-looking nation state to regulate and control it. This flow, signalled by the all-pervasive and largely unregulated dissemination of information through the World Wide Web, initiates the evaporation of traditional social boundaries. We live, Bauman notes, in the midst of 'the passage from the "solid" to a "liquid" phase of modernity: that is, into a condition in which social forms . . . can no longer . . . keep their shape for long, because they decompose and melt faster than the time it takes to caste them'.[42] Traditional distinctions collapse in the face of this rapid and continuous decomposition. Most notably, the distinction between 'inside' and 'outside', which has traditionally served to endow sovereign states with a sense of internal coherence through its power to differentiate and so separate one nation from another, begins to lose its meaningfulness. In the light of this, the openness of the liberal 'open society', once celebrated polemically by Karl Popper,[43] takes on a new and threatening guise. Being 'open', Bauman notes, comes to imply not merely the internal openness of so-called liberal principles of toleration but also a vulnerability to external threats. The forces of globalization render open societies 'impotent as never before' to 'the blows of fate'.[44] Primary among the threats is instability of conditions of employment. Some forms of work now shift away from liberal democracies to be taken by the lower-paid members of the global economy while, at the same time, the global movement of population in search of work (the 'foreign' worker driven away from home by poverty or war who will do the same job for less than the domestic worker) encroaches on traditional niches of employment at home. This is the phenomenon of '*negative* globalization', a situation typified by the ever greater permeability of the borders of the sovereign state, which is increasingly unable to resist the arrival of a new shifting multitude into its once more or less homogeneous internal political space. The inability of contemporary capitalism to absorb the new nomadic multitude of population which it has generated presents the prospect of it '*choking on its own waste products*'.[45] The creation of a vast ' "redundant" population'[46] living in close proximity to those who are deemed 'useful' brings a politics of fear, a condition in which insecurity is the norm and where modernity's ever more multicultural social orders become increasingly fragmented and conflict-ridden as the search for a now-lost sense of security reaches fever pitch.

Bauman conjures the image of modern global social order entering a condition of liquefaction. Indeed, the prospect is offered of fast-approaching putrefaction. This condition is not merely one of mere permeability to an unprecedented degree. It is rotten through and through: a corrupted, over-individuated, conflicted, a-social space that threatens in every direction to implode into a war of all against all. In effect, the condition of liquid modernity amounts to a situation that parallels the Hobbesian threat of civil war. It is the situation in which the markers of sovereign power that stake out the limits of civic life and police these limits are withdrawn so that all that remains is the prospect of the peculiar timelessness and loss of identity associated with unregulated and undirected human activity. The latter, in recognizing no bounds, brings with it the menacing possibility of unending conflict. Civil war signifies the ascendency of the chaotic multitude as it flows into the domain of the dissolved multitude. The multitude, one might recall, is for Hobbes one aspect of the corpuscular flow of 'blood' – that is of capital, of money – through the living body politic. Its condition, he notes in *Behemoth*, is inherently unstable. This is because the multitude is a plurality which consists not merely of those subjected to sovereign power but also of those subjected to the power of money. The merchant citizen's may be 'of all callings the most beneficial to the Common Wealth, by setting the poorer sort of people on work',[47] Hobbes comments, but the unregulated mercantile pursuit of wealth also drives social instability. The mercantile classes' pursuit of 'their onely glory', which is 'to grow excessively rich by the wisdom of buying and selling', drives them to dictate the conditions of existence of the poor, who are forced 'to sell their labour to them at their own prices'. Thus exploited, the working poor are hardly any better off than the inmates of a workhouse. There is little wonder that Hobbes comments that the conflict between the wealthy and the dispossessed fosters a dangerous tendency to rebellion. Civil war, the dissolution of sovereignty as a consequence of social liquefaction, is an ever-present condition of civic existence because it is ever present within it. It is the condition of rebellion which the flow of capital feeds even as it nourishes the state's power to resist it. In this sense, sovereignty is fed and nourished by the very thing that, at the same time, assures the possibility of its sickening and demise.[48]

Profane authority presupposes faith in money. But this faith continually undoes sovereign authority by threatening to dissolve it in the conflicts of the multitude that the existence of money and the possessiveness that go with it foster. The state needs its poison. The liquefaction that Bauman identifies in late capitalist modernity is revealed by an examination of Hobbes's complex entwinement of biological-political metaphors as being internal to sovereign power itself since the flows which characterize it are an essential constituent of its 'body'. The desire for sovereignty is, in this regard, contradictory, since it is the craving for a 'Mortall God', stable and enduring; yet the autonomy that is proclaimed on behalf of this god is necessarily an illusion since it is from the beginning in thrall to something from which it cannot escape and which promises to bring about its death. Stasis (civil war) is, as Agamben's work on Hobbes leads him to propose, the dominant political paradigm of the West. But, as Hobbes's text suggests, this paradigm is always already inherently unstable because it is also intrinsically economic. Speaking like, but also against, Schmitt, one might say that the problem of the exception is therefore an economic problem from the outset: no amount of craving for the security promised by the image of the sovereign will negate that problem. Speaking in a manner parallel to Foucault, one can say that the problem of sovereignty has not receded with biopolitics but, rather, reaches its crisis-ridden zenith with the contemporary era of liquefaction. The faith in money that epitomizes modern globalized liberal culture is the same faith that Hobbes articulates when he resorts to the metaphor of blood coursing through the Artificiall Man's circulatory system in order to endorse the unifying power of sovereign will. Such a faith in money rests on the faith in a sovereign autonomy that may be promised but cannot be fulfilled, since the money that is the necessary condition of the sovereign body through which it flows at the same time initiates its impending dissolution and likely death. The unhistorical time of the condition of the war of all against all is always already at play within the flow of monetary time that the condition of sovereign power seeks to coordinate and regulate with a view to securing the future.

The idea of sovereignty, like the Hobbesian 'Kingdome of Heaven', is in reality the illusory hope of autonomy that the dissolved multitude of population, living under conditions of an exploitation that mimic the state of civil war, can never hope to attain even as it is offered up to them as a path to the amelioration of their suffering. The 'Kingdome of Heaven' on Earth that marks out the eschatological limit of Hobbes's secular politics invades it precisely by way of its deferral, by way of its promise of a future that can never be. Faith in divine intervention in the long run ensures the continuing and unshakeable faith in the necessity of the profane sovereign order of the here and now, with its coordinated trinity of politics, science and money. It is this faith which characterizes most essentially modernity as the era of biopolitics. In so far as the desire for sovereignty might endure in the dissolved multitude it does so as an illusion of escape into the very conditions of subjection at the hands of money that sovereignty itself fosters. It is, in this regard, not sovereignty that is enigmatic. What is an enigma is the persistence of the faith in authority that provokes the desire for sovereignty. This desire, on suspects, is rooted in mythological fear. In this regard, the modern era is, in spite of its investment in science, essentially superstitious when it comes to the realm of the political.

To overcome this superstitious faith would require a lot more than merely invoking 'reason', as if reason existed as the pure opposite of mythological inclinations. It would mean no less than challenging the perceived reality of late modernity and its web of monetary-administrative interconnections; to reconceptualize the meaning of shifting homeless populations and 'sovereign' crises; to challenge the illusory metaphysical comfort of an economically attained future kingdom of heaven on Earth and the hegemony of the scientific-technological mode of imagining by which it is often held to be attainable given the appropriate administrative and sovereign apparatus. One would need to think the relation that inheres between administrative power, the multitude, sovereign power and ideas of economic advancement (so-called progress achieved through science) in a new way. That, for one thing, would mean stepping beyond dominant neoliberal conceptualizations of the economy and the sovereign state. It might also, perhaps, necessitate a reassessment and re-interpretation of the various counter-narratives offered by prominent critics of liberalism and capitalism (Marx among them). The utopianism of the 'Kingdome of God', as has been noted, can always serve the 'profane' world of economic existence as its justification, no matter what its form. The overcoming of this faith would thus have to resist recoiling into that variant of faith which opposes itself to the present by claiming theological access to the transcendent or the divine. Such overcoming would necessitate the birth of a new condition of unbelief, one that spurned simplistic faith in the universalist pretensions of science and 'method' as much as the temptations of theological epiphany; a scepticism of the future, no less. One can say, tentatively, that this would require the cultivation of an attitude that begins with questioning the theological-economic-scientific trinity that reveals itself in *Leviathan*'s outlining of sovereign power, a trinity that, as a problematic and inescapable biopolitical past and present, has an inexorable tendency to shape the ways in which we moderns are accustomed to think the future at all. This would mean working through the problems posed not within but *by* the very domains of theology, science, economy and political power by seeking what intimately relates them to one another, by thinking them *together* so as to develop a standpoint capable of resisting their common dubious tone of future promise. Then it might be possible to contemplate a new breaking of contracts, or, as Nietzsche might have put it, a smashing of tablets and a pushing over of boundary stones. And which of us is, as yet, sufficiently imaginative and daring for that?

NOTES

1. To take two reasons why this might be the case: (i) if the flow of money and population across national borders are increasingly at the behest of international capital rather than national governments, then the porous nature of such borders compromises the integrity of the nation state; (ii) if dominant forms of economic and other behaviour within the jurisdiction of nation states have consequences of a global magnitude, as is suggested by evidence of climate change, then the claimed autonomy of the nation state with regard to the management of its internal affairs is compromised, since the implications of such behaviour cannot be confined within the limits of national borders. See later for some additional discussion of this in relation to the work of Zygmunt Bauman.

2. Consider, for example, American president Donald Trump's 'America First' inauguration speech of 20th January 2017, shot through with what the

Guardian newspaper's editorial of 21st January 2017 describes as a 'crude and shameless' nationalism. The speech's advocacy a protectionist political agenda amounts to a rejection of the forces of globalization and a reassertion of national sovereignty, replete with non-porous borders. The United Kingdom's so-called Brexit vote in the European Union membership referendum of 23rd June 2016, which amounts to a resolution to sever established trade, legislative and cultural ties with European Union member states, is another obvious instance of the (some might say questionable) appeal that the notion of sovereign status has in the era of the global marketplace.

3. See, Michel Foucault, *The Birth of Biopolitics Lectures at the Collège de France, 1978–1979*, trans. Graham Burchell (Basingstoke: Palgrave Macmillan, 2008), lectures 2 and 3, 29–50, 51–73.

4. Thomas Hobbes, *Leviathan*, ed. Richard Tuck (Cambridge: Cambridge University Press, 1994), 283. Hereafter cited as *L* with page references in the text.

5. Giorgio Agamben, *Stasis: Civil War as a Political Paradigm*, trans. Nicholas Heron (Edinburgh: Edinburgh University Press, 2015), 47.

6. In Carl Schmitt's terms, this is the state of exception. See Carl Schmitt, *Political Theology. Four Chapters on the Concept of Sovereignty* (1922), ed. and trans. George Schwab, With a Foreword by Tracy B. Strong (Chicago: University of Chicago Press, 2005), 5ff.

7. Agamben, *Stasis*, 49–50.

8. 'The dreadful Carl Schmitt', as Avital Ronell calls him (see *Loser Sons: Politics and Authority* (Champaign, IL: University of Illinois Press, 2012), 5), clearly deserves his notoriety and our distaste in equal measure, but I do not intend to pursue those issues here.

9. Hobbes, Michael Oakeshott notes, is writing in 'the emerging conditions of a modern State where governing is recognized as a sovereign activity'. See Michael Oakeshott, *Hobbes on Civil Association* (Indianapolis: Liberty Fund, 1975), 125.

10. Schmitt, *Political Theology*, 36ff.

11. Schmitt, *Political Theology*, 9.

12. Friedrich Nietzsche, *Human, All too Human*, trans. R. J. Hollingdale (Cambridge: Cambridge University Press, 1986), section 472.

13. Nietzsche, *Human, All too Human*, section 472.

14. Carl Schmitt, *The Concept of the Political*, trans. George Schwab (Chicago: University of Chicago Press, 1996), 70.

15. Schmitt, *The Concept of the Political*, 72.

16. Schmitt, *The Concept of the Political*, 71.

17. 'That production and consumption, price formation and market have their own sphere and can be directed neither by ethics nor aesthetics, nor by religion, nor, least of all, by politics was considered one of the few truly unquestionable dogmas of this liberal age'. Schmitt, *The Concept of the Political*, 72.

18. Schmitt, *The Concept of the Political*, 57.

19. Schmitt, *The Concept of the Political*, 61.

20. Michel Foucault, *Security, Territory, Population: Lectures at the Collège de France, 1977–1978*, trans. Graham Burchell (Basingstoke: Palgrave Macmillan, 2009), 102–3.

21. Foucault, *Security, Territory, Population*, 105.

22. Foucault, *Security, Territory, Population*, 73.

23. Foucault, *Security, Territory, Population*, 74.

24. For an insightful discussion of this condition, see Oakeshott, *Hobbes on Civil Association*, 134.

25. Gilles Deleuze and Félix Guattari, *A Thousand Plateaus: Capitalism and Schizophrenia*, trans. Brian Massumi (London: Athlone Press, 1988), 261.

26. Of these 'systemes', the muscles correspond to what is lawful; 'Wens, Biles, and Apostemes engendered by the unnatural conflux of evil humours' to what is unlawful (*L* 165).

27. There is, in fact, more than one form of eye, for 'Forts, Garrisons, Guns . . . and continuall Spyes' are also a state's eyes (90). Others parts correspond to judges in courts of law (voices), those charged with receiving public petitions (ears), or ministers sent abroad charged with surveying another country (eyes).

28. See Agamben, *Stasis*, 33–34.

29. See Thomas Hobbes, *On the Citizen*, ed. R. Tuck and M. Silverthorne (Cambridge: Cambridge University Press, 1998), Chapter XII, section VIII.

30. Oakeshott, *Hobbes on Civil Association*, 43.

31. It also needs to have the means of its 'procreation' attended to, a need which is facilitated by '*Plantations*, or *Colonies*', but I leave that matter to one side.

32. Hobbes ends *Leviathan* by noting that after its conclusion 'I return to my interrupted Speculation of Bodies Naturall' (491).

33. *Leviathan*, 490: 'For if we will reverence the Age, the Present is the Oldest'.

34. See Schmitt, *The Concept of the Political*, 26ff.

35. Michael Hardt and Antonio Negri, *Commonwealth* (Cambridge, MA: Harvard University Press, 2011), 51: 'The lack of property, which excludes the poor [i.e. the multitude] from the people, is not a contingent fact for Hobbes but a necessary and constantly reproduced condition that allows those with property to maintain and increase it'.

36. Schmitt regards Hobbes's thought as containing within it the kernel of liberal tendencies. Thus, for example, Hobbes's inclusion of 'the right of private freedom of thought and belief into the political system', Schmitt comments, 'contained the seed of death that destroyed the mighty Leviathan from within and brought about the end of the mortal god'. Schmitt goes on to claim that shortly after Hobbes's time 'a liberal Jew [Spinoza] noticed the barely visible crack in the theoretical justification of the sovereign state. In it he immediately recognized the telling inroad of modern liberalism, which would allow Hobbes's postulation of the relation between external and internal, public and private, to be inverted into its converse'. See Carl Schmitt, *The Leviathan in the State Theory of Thomas Hobbes: Meaning and Failure of a Political Symbol*, trans. George Schwab (London: Greenwood Press, 1996), 57.

37. To recall *Leviathan*, 121, cited earlier.

38. See *Leviathan*, 61, for Hobbes's schematic representation of political science within the overall structure of science, defined as 'knowledge of Consequences; which is also called PHILOSOPHY'.

39. See Giorgio Agamben, *Homo Sacer: Sovereign Power and Bare Life*, trans. Daniel Heller-Roazen (Stanford, CA: Stanford University Press, 1998). According to Agamben, biopolitics is the defining characteristic of the political as such in the Western tradition since its inception. If one examines this tradition's origins in Greek thought, Agamben argues, it becomes plain that two key notions are articulated within it which exist in close but uneasy proximity to one another. These are *zoe*, which denotes the simple fact that an entity is a living organism, and *bios*, which denotes the way of life lived by a person or group of persons such that these persons can be deemed properly 'human'. *Bios* therefore relates to the kind of existence persons can lead in a political community or state, rather than to their merely biological existence (*zoe*). The division between *zoe* and *bios* is fateful. The withdrawal of a person's *bios* signals the withdrawal of his or her personhood in relation to his or her community or state. Someone denuded of *bios* thus becomes a being who is obliged to live beyond the law as a form of 'naked life', that is, as a merely biological entity who has had his or her socio-political biography and identity stripped away from him or her. Sovereign power, Agamben argues, is characterized by the ability to accomplish this stripping away. It is most obvious in the case of war. In war the 'enemy' is ultimately deemed as *zoe* and treated as such; that is, the enemy is a piece of mere biology whose living or dying is a matter that is beyond the law and who can consequently be exterminated with impunity (or, indeed, 'heroically' in so far as the combatant who kills in these circumstances can, under certain conditions, be rewarded for doing so through the giving of medals and other honours). Another obvious instance of the exercise of the power is the exclusion from the law which makes for the stateless person: the victim of the concentration camp or the refugee. See Agamben, *Homo Sacer*, 1–9ff.

40. The charge of idolatry is, of course, Nietzsche's. See Friedrich Nietzsche, *Thus Spoke Zarathustra*, trans. R. J. Hollingdale (London: Penguin, 2003), 75, 'On the New Idol'.

41. Zygmunt Bauman, *Liquid Times: Living in an Age of Uncertainty* (Cambridge: Polity, 2007), 28.

42. Bauman, *Liquid Times*, 1.

43. See Karl Popper's *The Open Society and Its Enemies* (1945) (London: Routledge, 2011). It is hard to escape noticing a Schmittian logic at work even in the title: that 'openness' requires the invocation of its enemies, of what is 'closed'.

44. Bauman, *Liquid Times*, 6.

45. Bauman, *Liquid Times*, 29.

46. Bauman, *Liquid Times*, 32.

47. Thomas Hobbes, *Behemoth, or the Long Parliament*, ed. Paul Seaward (Oxford: Oxford University Press, 2010), 276.

48. Like any living entity that needs nourishing, the 'Artificiall Man' is susceptible to disease. Hobbes's text reflects this in being replete with images of

illness. There is, for example, talk of the 'Venime' which afflicts the blood following the infectious bites of 'Democraticall writers' (*L* 226), or the dangers posed when a commonwealth becomes schizoid and develops multiple personalities (i.e. a division of powers) which undermine its ability to conjoin the nutritional levying of money, executive command and the rational ability to make laws, that is the condition of having 'more than one Soule': 'To what Disease in the Naturall Body of man, I may exactly compare this irregularity of a Common-wealth, I know not. But I have seen a man, that had another man growing out of his side, with an head, armes, breast, and stomach, of his own: If he had had another man growing out of his other side, the comparison might then have been exact' (*L* 228). Likewise, Leviathan is prey to distemper, pleurisy, epilepsy and convulsions. Of the diseases Hobbes points to, one that stands out concerns the relation of capital to the city. A town filled with many 'Corporations' of merchants organized in pursuit of profit takes on the guise of an infection of 'many lesser Common-wealths in the bowels of a greater, like wormes in the entrayles of a natural man' (*L* 230). The blood of money fosters parasites; yet, as we have seen, these parasites are themselves constituents of that 'Bloud'.

BIBLIOGRAPHY

AGAMBEN, Giorgio. *Homo Sacer: Sovereign Power and Bare Life*. Translated by Daniel Heller-Roazen. Stanford, CA: Stanford University Press, 1998.

AGAMBEN, Giorgio. *Stasis: Civil War as a Political Paradigm*. Translated by Nicholas Heron. Edinburgh: Edinburgh University Press, 2015.

BAUMAN, Zygmunt. *Liquid Times: Living in an Age of Uncertainty*. Cambridge: Polity, 2007.

DELEUZE, Gilles and Félix GUATTARI. *A Thousand Plateaus: Capitalism and Schizophrenia*. Translated by Brian Massumi. London: Athlone Press, 1988.

FOUCAULT, Michel. *The Birth of Biopolitics: Lectures at the Collège de France, 1978–1979*. Translated by Graham Burchell. Basingstoke: Palgrave Macmillan, 2008.

FOUCAULT, Michel. *Security, Territory, Population: Lectures at the Collège de France, 1977–1978*. Translated by Graham Burchell. Basingstoke: Palgrave Macmillan, 2009.

HARDT, Michael and Antonio NEGRI. *Commonwealth*. Cambridge, MA: Harvard University Press, 2011.

HOBBES, Thomas. *Behemoth, or the Long Parliament*. Edited by Paul Seaward. Oxford: Oxford University Press, 2010.

HOBBES, Thomas. *Leviathan*. Edited by Richard Tuck. Cambridge: Cambridge University Press, 1994.

HOBBES, Thomas. *On the Citizen*. Edited by R. Tuck and M. Silverthorne. Cambridge: Cambridge University Press, 1998.

NIETZSCHE, Friedrich. *Human, All too Human*. Translated by R. J. Hollingdale. Cambridge: Cambridge University Press, 1986.

NIETZSCHE, Friedrich. *Thus Spoke Zarathustra*. Translated by R. J. Hollingdale. London: Penguin, 2003.

OAKESHOTT, Michael. *Hobbes on Civil Association*. Indianapolis: Liberty Fund, 1975.

POPPER, Karl. *The Open Society and Its Enemies* (1945). London: Routledge, 2011.

RONELL, Avital. *Loser Sons: Politics and Authority*. Champaign: University of Illinois Press, 2012.

SCHMITT, Carl. *The Concept of the Political*. Translated by George Schwab. Chicago: University of Chicago Press, 1996.

SCHMITT, Carl. *The Leviathan in the State Theory of Thomas Hobbes: Meaning and Failure of a Political Symbol*. Translated by George Schwab. London: Greenwood Press, 1996.

SCHMITT, Carl. *Political Theology. Four Chapters on the Concept of Sovereignty* (1922). Translated and Edited by George Schwab. With a Foreword by Tracy B. Strong. Chicago: University of Chicago Press, 2005.

Chapter 3

'Accelerator despite Itself'

Credo, crisis, Katechon

Arthur Bradley

> The darkness drops again but now I know
> That twenty centuries of stony sleep
> Were vexed to nightmare by a rocking cradle,
> And what rough beast, its hour come round at last,
> Slouches towards Bethlehem to be born?[1]

In recent decades, Carl Schmitt's *Katechon* – the mysterious Pauline 'restrainer' who holds back the appearance of the lawless one or anti-Christ until the appointed hour – has come to be recognized as one of the most important concepts in his political thought.[2] It first explicitly emerges in his work during the decisive winter of 1941/42 in a little-known essay called 'Beschleuniger wider Willen, oder: Problematik der westlichen Hemisphare [Accelerator despite Itself: The Problem with the Western Hemisphere]' (1942).[3] As the failure of the Russian invasion and the entry of America into the war threw the Wehrmacht onto the defensive for the first time, the German legal theorist recalled that people in antiquity believed that 'a mysterious delaying power' existed called 'kat-*echon* (from the Greek for "to hold down")' which 'prevented the long-overdue apocalyptic end of times from happening now' ('ADI' 436). For Schmitt, this 'mysterious delaying force' assumed many different forms throughout world history: the Roman Empire, the Germanic Empire, the British Empire, the USA and even the Third Reich. In each case, the state acted as a theological 'restrainer and delayer [*Aufhalter und Verzögerer*]' ('ADI' 436) of some imminent historical state of chaos or lawlessness.

To put it in the words of Schmitt's own private notebooks, which were posthumously published as the *Glossarium*, the *Katechon* is not simply a normative concept or historical fact in his thought but something close to a personal article of faith: 'I believe in the *Katechon*', he writes, 'for me, it is the only possibility for understanding history and considering it meaningfully as Christian'.[4] It goes without saying, however, that Schmitt's notorious reputation within modern political theory – supposed 'crown jurist' of the Third Reich, political and religious anti-Semite, apologist for a quasi-divine sovereign decisionism, master theorist of the *polemos* of friend and enemy as the condition of the political – has inevitably led many influential critics to view this appeal to the *Katechon* with suspicion. If Schmitt often seems to appeal to the *Katechon* as the only genuine theological ground for political action, Jacob Taubes and other commentators have interpreted this gesture as a crude *politicization* of theology in the interests of preserving state power in perpetuity as a bulwark against an alleged anarchy. In Taubes' well-known account, this Christian political theology of order reaches its nadir in the German legal theorist's alliance with National Socialism as the Weimar Republic disintegrated into chaos in the early 1930s.[5]

This chapter seeks to offer a new reading of Schmitt's political theology of the *Katechon* – his own credo in a time of crisis – from its first appearance in 'Accelerator despite Itself' to its paradoxical re-emergence in the discourse of neoliberal biopolitics. To quickly outline my argument in what follows, I want to propose that Schmitt's *Katechon* turns out to be not simply a restrainer but an *accelerator* of historical change. For the German political theorist, what unites all historical *katechons* from the Roman Empire to the Third Reich is a mysterious power to neither simply preserve nor destroy the status quo so much as to preserve order *by* accelerating the forces of world history. If Schmitt's logic of sovereign acceleration has its origin in the political, financial and military crises of the 1930s, I want to conclude by tracing this logic – in which *nomos* and *anomia*, law and lawlessness increasingly coincide – into contemporary biopolitics of security. What then is the place of the *Katechon* within Schmitt's political theology? How does it change from its first appearance in 'Accelerator despite Itself' to classic later works like *The* Nomos *of the Earth* (1950)? To what extent might the real horror of Schmitt's 'restrainer' be that it is actually a (conscious or unconscious) *accelerator* of history?

In his first letter to the Christian community at Thessalonica, the Apostle Paul – or whoever signs the letter in that name[6] – compares the time that remains to the process of giving birth.[7] It seems that our time is pregnant with another time – or rather our time is *already* in the process of giving birth to that messianic time if we could but realize it. To anyone who does not want to heed this message – anyone tempted to believe that the current world will endure indefinitely – Paul issues a dire warning: 'When they say "There is peace and security" then sudden destruction will come upon them, as labour pains come upon a pregnant woman, and there will be no escape'! (1 Thessalonians 5:2–4). However, in his Second Letter to the Thessalonians, Paul gives an intriguingly different account of the relation between the time that remains and the time of the Messiah. If the purpose of the earlier letter seems to be to warn his readers that they must prepare themselves for the imminent end, Paul's second letter to the Thessalonian community (whose apocalyptic enthusiasm had apparently led them to abandon worldly authority altogether and embrace hedonistic excess) not only seems to suggest that the existing order might endure a little longer than he earlier implied but offers a (qualified) defence of this order. For Paul, it now seems that historical forms of power – the very demand for 'peace and security' that he scorned in his earlier letter as futile – possess eschatological value in their own right. What has changed in the balance of power between history and eschatology?

To answer this question, the Paul of the Second Letter to the Thessalonians speaks of a mysterious new figure who stands between historical and eschatological time – the time that remains and the time of the end – and this figure is the *Katechon*. It seems that a complex sequence of events – a kind of eschatological domino theory – must now unfold before the return of the Messiah which was confidently declared to be imminent in the first Letter. Firstly, Paul asserts that a 'lawless one [*anomos*]' (who the early church identified to be the anti-Christ mentioned in John's letters) will be revealed who will go on to oppose himself to God and declare himself to be God. Yet the letter next asserts that, in fact, 'the mystery of lawlessness is already at work' and the only reason why the lawless one has not fully revealed himself is because someone or something is temporarily restraining him. For Paul, this mysterious figure holding back the appearance of the lawless one until the appointed time is the *Katechon*:

> Do you not remember that I told you these things when I was still with you? And you know what is now restraining [*to katechon*] him, so that he may be revealed when his time comes. For the mystery of the lawlessness is already at work [*energeitai*], but only [*monon*] until the one who now restrains [*ho katechon*] it is removed. And then the lawless one will be revealed, whom the lord Jesus will destroy with the breath of his mouth, annihilating him by the manifestation of his coming. (2 Thessalonians 2:6–7)

If the sudden appearance of the *Katechon* remains one of the most opaque moments within Pauline theology – and even as eminent an authority as Augustine of Hippo confesses that he has no idea what Paul is talking about at this moment in the Second Letter – it does provide some kind of answer to one of the most persistent aporias in the former's thought, namely, the competing claims of historical and eschatological sovereignty upon the Christian community in the time that remains. Why should a Christian obey a worldly sovereign like the Roman emperor when (as the first letter to the Thessalonians reminds us) destruction will be visited upon that authority at any moment, like labour pains upon a pregnant woman? In his appeal to the figure of the *Katechon*, Paul seems to give a response: a form of worldly power or sovereignty is necessary to hold back, if only temporarily, what we might call the birth before the birth, that chaos before the chaos, which will be the full revelation of the lawless one.

In the early centuries of the Christian church, the mysterious figure of the *Katechon* evidently grew in significance as the time between the first and second comings of the Messiah became more and more protracted.[8] To begin with, Hippolytus and Tertullian began to appeal to the figure of the Pauline restrainer in the second century to legitimize the post-Eusebian Church's political accommodation with its erstwhile enemy the Roman Empire. It was Tertullian's audacious claim, for example, that Christians should pray for the safety of the emperor because he is the *Katechon* who is holding back the rising tide of anarchy which would sweep Christians and pagans alike away. After the fall of the Roman Empire in the Middle Ages, we find similar katechontic claims being made for the Byzantine, Carolingian and Holy Roman Empires: they are all, in their different ways, politico-eschatological restrainers of the end of the world. However, as many scholars have observed, the essentially finite status of the original Pauline figure of the *Katechon* becomes obscured as the time that remains begins to extend indefinitely into the future. If Paul's Second Letter clearly depicts the restrainer as a temporary stopgap in a larger eschatological story which will conclude with the return of the Messiah, Christian political theology subtly transforms it into a permanent fixture in an interregnum that now seemingly stretches outwards towards infinity. For Augustine of Hippo – whose own political theology decisively breaks with the post-Eusebian rapprochement between Jerusalem and Rome – the Pauline *Katechon* is, revealingly, inexplicable: 'I must admit that the meaning of this [2 Thessalonians 2:6–7] completely escapes me'.[9] In the coruscating view of Taubes, as we will see later on, Christianity's katechontic complicity with state power ends up betraying its Jewish messianic origins and becoming something close to an eschatologized Caesarism.[10]

What can we add to the wealth of exegesis on the relationship between the *Katechon* and the anti-Christ in Paul's Second Letter to the Thessalonians? It is 2 Thessalonians 7 that unpacks the precise chronological sequence of events that leads to the return of the Messiah: 'The mystery of the lawlessness is already at work, but only [*monon*] until the one who now restrains it is removed'. As we have seen, the orthodox reading of this verse is that the *Katechon* is simply holding back the full revelation of the anti-Christ. Yet, arguably, this account condenses the complex temporal logic ('already. . . but only until') at work here. Not only has the state of lawlessness already arrived in spite of the attempt to restrain it, but the gesture of restraint itself takes the form of a qualified *liberation* of that lawlessness. To turn the orthodox reading upside down, the *Katechon* does not just restrain the mystery of lawlessness but rather *enables* it to operate under its own jurisdiction: 'Only until the one who now restrains it is removed'. For Roberto Esposito, who offers a compelling reading of this eschatological dynamic in *Immunitas* (2002), the Pauline restrainer becomes a kind of theological precursor to the biopolitics of immunization in which a political body seeks to protect itself against external threats by incorporating its own negation with it:

> [T]he *katechon* restrains evil by containing it, by keeping it, by holding it within itself. It confronts evil, but from within, by hosting it and welcoming it, to the point of building its own necessity to the presence of evil. It limits evil, defers it, but does not eradicate it, because if it did, it would also eliminate itself. We could go so far as to say that the *katechon* – its constitutive juridical principle – opposes the absence of law by taking it up inside itself, and thereby, in some way, giving it form, rule, and norm. The *katechon* antinomically assigns a *nomos* to anomie, thus restraining its catastrophic unfolding.[11]

If Esposito is correct that Paul's *Katechon* can only uphold the law by immunologically incorporating something of this chaos within itself – transforming it into a kind of restricted or contained chaos which prevents a total or absolute chaos from unfolding – then we move beyond any simple political theological opposition between *nomos* and anomia, the restrainer and the restrained, the *Katechon* and the anti-Christ into a kind of zone of indistinction or undecidability. Perhaps we might go so far as to speak of the *Katechon* less as an eschatologized Caesarism than as a kind of juridico-political, concrete messianism or sovereign anomia. In order to prevent Yeats's 'rough beast' from reaching its gates, it seems that the city of Bethlehem must paradoxically permit it entry – or even *become* the beast itself.

In many ways, Carl Schmitt's reflections on the *Katechon* are themselves somewhat katechontic: a burst of writings that occupy a kind of interregnum between the major works of the 1920s and 1930s on political theology, sovereignty and decisionism and the great texts of the 1940s, 1950s and 1960s on *nomos*, space and political theology again. It seems he became interested in the Pauline figure as early as 1932, but it first explicitly appears in 'Accelerator despite Itself' (1942), recurs through his magnum opus *The* Nomos *of the Earth* (1950), only to disappear completely after '*Die andere Hegel-Linie* [The Other Hegel Tradition]' (1957). As Felix Grossheutschi has shown, Schmitt's reading of the restrainer also seems to evolve over his career: what begins as a negative term – which is used to signify the futile attempts of ageing imperial powers like Britain or the USA to arrest the march of world history – increasingly becomes a positive conceptual descriptor. To recall Schmitt's words in *The* Nomos *of the Earth*, the *Katechon* seems to play what we have seen to be its classic political theological role from Paul to Tertullian and beyond of squaring the circle between worldly power (*potestas*) and sacred power (*auctoritas*), Rome and Jerusalem, Empire and Kingdom:

> I do not believe that any historical concept other than *katechon* would have been possible for the original Christian faith. The belief that a restrainer holds back the end of the world provides the only bridge between the notion of an eschatological paralysis of all human events and a tremendous historical monolith [*Geschichtsmächtigkeit*] that of the Christian empire of the Germanic Kings.[12]

If Schmitt read the *Katechon* as a 'bridge' between history and eschatology, though, many of his subsequent critics suspected that the German jurist really saw the Pauline restrainer as a way of burning that bridge down once and for all. For Taubes, of course, Schmitt's reading of the *Katechon* effectively replaces the 'eschatological paralysis' that afflicts all human events in the time that remains with a *political* paralysis which extends this interregnum infinitely:

> This is what [Schmitt] later calls the *Katechon*: The restrainer [*der Aufhalter*] that holds down the chaos that pushes up from below. That isn't my worldview, that isn't my experience. I can imagine as an apocalyptic: let it go down. I have no spiritual investment in the world as it is. But I understand that someone is invested in this world and sees in the apocalypse, whatever its form, the adversary and does everything to keep it subjugated and suppressed, because from there forces can be unleashed that we are in no position to control.[13]

In this *contretemps* with Schmitt, Taubes pinpoints a classic paradox at the heart of the theology of the *Katechon:* any attempt to delay the anti-Christ also delays the advent of the Messiah himself (because the latter's return is, of course, whose own return is contingent upon the reign of anarchy instituted by the anti-Christ) and thus ends up upholding the prevailing historical order more or less permanently.[14] To what extent, then, is the Schmittean *Katechon* a harbinger of the immanent return of the Messiah or an anti-messianic signifier of the indefinite *postponement* of the end of the world?[15]

To try to resolve the ambiguity at the heart of the Schmittean *Katechon*, I want to focus on the little-read 1942 text in which he appeals to the figure of the Pauline restrainer for the very first time: 'Accelerator despite Itself: The Problem with the Western Hemisphere'. It is Schmitt's ambition in this article, which was published in the best-selling Nazi Party weekly newspaper *Das Reich*, to offer a historical and political assessment of Germany's new Anglo-Saxon enemy following the attack on Pearl Harbor in December 1941: the USA.[16] As we have already suggested, Schmitt's first reference to the *Katechon* takes the form of an attack on imperial decadence: people in antiquity believed that 'a mysterious delaying power' existed called 'kat-*echon* (from the Greek for "to hold down")', he recalls, which 'prevented the long-overdue apocalyptic end of times from happening now' ('ADI' 436). For Schmitt, the USA has succumbed to the political fate of all great empires from Rome to the British Empire: they all become 'restrainers and delayers [*Aufhalter und Verzogerer*]' of history. If American is a delayer of history, then there is little doubt who or what it is delaying: the Third Reich, naturally enough, is the new 'great mover [*grosse Beweger*]' on the world stage which the old imperial powers like Britain and the USA are vainly seeking to hold back. In this essay, then, Schmitt begins by emphatically placing himself on the side of the 'great mover' rather than the 'restrainers and delayers' – even at the expense of casting the Third Reich in the role of secular anti-Christ – but, intriguingly, he then goes on to complicate this simple opposition between the delayers and the accelerators of history. Why has the American *Katechon* turned from a restrainer and a delayer into an 'accelerator despite itself' ('ADI' 436)?

For Schmitt, as he makes clear in this and other contemporaneous political reflections on the geopolitical stage,[17] the United States at this critical juncture in its history finds itself caught in a contradiction between two incompatible roles. It must now choose between the great Schmittean polarities of land and sea, between being a territorial power and an oceanic power, or, more widely, between remaining just one continental actor (alongside, say, Germany) in an essentially multipolar world or seeking to become a transcontinental, universal actor in a unipolar world. At the level of both base political calculation and larger political philosophy, Schmitt's own preference is very clear: the USA should embrace a limited territorial identity – and by implication come to some kind of political accommodation with the Third Reich – instead of pursuing a spurious liberal depoliticization and neutralization which would merely unleash a new and unpredictable set of conflicts.[18] Yet, in fact, the biggest danger of all in Schmitt's account is not that the USA will take the right or wrong decision but that it will not take a decision at all: rather, it will be overcome 'by a lack of decision [*Entscheidunglosigkeit*]' which leaves it adrift in the maelstrom of history (*Mahlstrom der Geschichte*) ('ADI' 436). If the USA seeks to restrain the forces of history by not taking a decision – by avoiding decisionism at all – then Schmitt argues that it will become 'neither a great mover [*grosse Beweger*], nor a great restrainer [*grosse Verzogerer*], but can only end up, against its will, as an accelerator' (*Beschleuniger wider Willen*) ('ADI' 436). In order to live up to its historical role as a *Katechon*, and arrest the dangerous process of acceleration it has inadvertently set in motion, the USA must paradoxically *stop* delaying – and act.

In re-evaluating the essay today, 'Accelerator despite Itself' seems less interesting as a reflection upon contemporary geopolitics than as an insight into Schmitt's own political theological imaginary. It had already been overtaken by events by the time it was written and its bellicosity towards the USA now reads more like anxious bravado: America had, of course, already taken its world historical 'decision' – and ended any chance of a negotiated peace – when it entered the war months earlier. As a matter of fact, it was the Third Reich – whose armies were floundering on the eastern front and now faced a formidable new western enemy as well – that ironically now found itself in the position of an imperial *Katechon*, vainly holding back the 'great movers' of history. However, what is remarkable about Schmitt's early essay is how it pre-emptively challenges the binary terms – order and chaos, delay and acceleration, holding back the end of the world and letting all go down – in which the debate on the *Katechon* has since been conducted. To recall the aporia we located in Paul's original discussion, Schmitt's ideal *Katechon* is by no means a simple restrainer: it maintains order *through* chaos, paralyses by catalysing, preserves by accelerating change. By taking a world-transforming decision – land or sea – the USA can live up to its destiny and become a genuine *Katechon* rather than a mere 'involuntary' accelerator of history. If Schmitt seeks to secure an eschatological mission for other imperial projects like the Holy Roman Empire in other inter-war works like *Land and Sea* (1942) it is not simply to preserve the past but to determine the future on its own terms: the

German emperor Rudolf II and other historical 'delayers' are not merely reactive figures who seek to preserve the status quo but dynamic actors who plunge into the becoming of world history.[19] In Schmitt's 'Accelerator despite Itself', we re-encounter the very sovereign *beastliness* we first found in Paul's Letter: Schmitt's *Katechon* does not merely restrain lawlessness but seeks to incorporate or internalize a kind of anomia into itself as its own sovereign principle.

What if the real scandal of the Pauline *Katechon*, then, is that it may only be possible to delay the apocalypse *by* accelerating, to preserve the world *by* destroying it, by letting it all go down (Taubes), but from *above* (Schmitt)? It is going to be my hypothesis that the figure of the restrainer is not the site of a simple opposition between order and chaos – nor of a choice or decision one way or the other depending upon one's particular orientation – but of a more complex and variegated field of political theological force. As we will see, Schmitt's belated diagnosis of the USA's historical fate in essays like 'Accelerator despite Itself' is (albeit radically divested of its Christo-Hegelian teleology) also uncannily prescient of what we might call the constitutive aporia of contemporary neoliberal politics of 'security'. To briefly foreshadow the conclusion of this essay, I want to propose that the Schmittean figure of the restrainer arguably finds something close to its late modern or postmodern successor in the familiar figure of the (political, military or financial) *securer* of the present political dispensation who today finds himself equally caught in the position of being a – voluntary or involuntary – accelerator. If the Pauline *Katechon* is not a simple delayer or restrainer of the end of history, if something like 'acceleration' is ultimately unavoidable, then the modern katechontic question thus becomes *what* to accelerate, how and why, and this is the question to which we will now turn. For contemporary politics of security, the *Katechon* is less the name of an attempt to impose *nomos* on *anomia* – order upon chaos, law upon lawlessness – than to make *anomia* itself into a new kind of *nomos*, to unleash a kind of state anarchy or lawlessness. In Schmitt's later work, we will see that the essential political question posed by the *Katechon* is whether it is possible to transform the necessary contingency of state power into a principle of enduring political formation – whether, to borrow Samuel Beckett's famous phrase, it is possible for a failed state to 'Fail again. Fail better'.[20]

In order to understand Schmitt's appeal to the *Katechon*, we not only need to see it in its original theological context but in the much more contemporary political context of the conservative revolution in (post-) Weimar Republic Germany. It is now becoming clear, for example, that the attempt to defend state power by appealing to a mysterious 'restrainer' was no mere personal theological eccentricity of Schmitt's but a wider intellectual phenomenon in Germany in the 1920s and 1930s. As Marc de Wilde has argued in a recent essay exploring the political and theological genesis of the concept, Schmitt's reading of the *Katechon* overlaps significantly with that of his friend and contemporary Hans Freyer (1887–1969).[21] To remember Freyer's monumental *World History of Europe* (1949), for instance, European history is depicted as the history of a series of very familiar 'restraining forces [*haltende Mächte*]' holding back social and historical acceleration: Rome, Byzantium, the Church and the German Reich. Yet, as Freyer goes on to make clear in the essay entitled 'Progress and Restraining Forces' (1952), the *Katechon* is not merely designed to hold back the forces of change: 'What merely delays and prevents change no longer plays a role in history; brakes will wear out and then the wagon will really thunder on'. If the restraining forces do not simply hold back progress, it is because their real task is 'to take progress up in the right way'. For Freyer, they do not seek 'to slow down the progressive course' but 'to appropriate it and to communicate to it osmotically that which can never emerge autogenously in secondary systems: vitality, human sense, human fullness and fruitfulness'. This theory of the *Katechon* as a creative and revolutionary as much as a conservative force is cited approvingly by Schmitt in his last major text on the Pauline restrainer 'The Other Hegel Tradition' (1957).[22] What does it mean to reconcile enduring state power with historical change so that the state can become a kind of accelerator 'in the right way'?

To catch a glimpse of how future *Katechon*s might avoid the fate of their predecessors – how they might fail better – I want to turn to the text that offers Schmitt's definitive account of the figure: *The* Nomos *of the Earth*. It seems that he wrote much of this text between 1942 and 1945 – as it became clear that Germany would lose the war – and it is often read today as an exercise in self-exculpation. As Zarmanian observes, the book is remarkable for the absence of any discussion of contemporary events: a text on the new world order never mentions the Nazi occupation of Europe.[23] Yet this work remains deeply invested in the question of why political empires fail and, more crucially, of how imperial projects can survive their own finitude. For Schmitt, it is again the *Katechon* that holds the key to understanding the life and death – the life *after* death – of the Christian empire of the Middle Ages:

> This Christian empire was not eternal. It always had its own end and that of the present eon in view. Nevertheless, it was capable of being a historical power. The decisive historical concept of this continuity was that of the

> restrainer: *katechon*. 'Empire' in this sense meant the historical power to restrain the appearance of the Antichrist and the end of the present eon; it was a power that withholds (*qui tenet*) as the Apostle Paul said in his Second Letter to the Thessalonians.[24]

In a curious sense, then, the Christian Empire's power lies in its capacity to occupy a simultaneously historical and eschatological sovereign position at the same time: it is both (eschatologically) weak and (historically) strong, both (eschatologically) finite and (historically) enduring, both (eschatologically) able to keep its own end in view and, nevertheless, (historically) able to thrive as an imperial project.

If Schmitt self-consciously places his own thinking within a specifically Christian tradition, Julia Hell had recently sought to situate the Schmittean *Katechon* within an older and distinctly pagan genealogy of end-time thinking that stretches from Spengler, Volney and Gibbon back to the Greco-Roman historian Polybius: ruin-gazing. It is this classic trope of imperial decline and fall – in which historians imagine themselves gazing melancholically upon the future ruins of a seemingly invincible empire like Rome – that is re-mobilized in Schmitt's own reflections on the finitude of every imperial project. At the same time, imperial ruin-gazing also offers an intriguingly pagan equivalent to the Christian historico-eschatological perspective of the *Katechon*. To quickly unpack Hell's argument, imperial ruin-gazing is paradoxically a means, not of mourning the demise of, but of *perpetuating* the imperial project: a ruin-gazer is not merely a passive or impotent observer but a political actor who subtly serves to recapitulate the power of colonizer over colonized even at the moment of his defeat. For Hell, what is significant is that this imperial subject consistently remains in a position of '(scopic) mastery' throughout the ruin-gazing scenario: the European subject is always the one who is 'doing the looking', in other words, even when what they are looking at is the ruins of Europe itself.[25] By giving the imperial subject *himself* the power to bear witness to the ruins of empire – rather than conferring that privilege on some notional post-imperial observer like the Goths or the Turks – the classical trope of the ruin-gazer ironically perpetuates and aesthetically reintegrates empire. In the end, empire survives – in order to serenely contemplate empire's own end.

For Schmitt, I want to argue that the figure of the *Katechon* embodies precisely this power to aesthetically transform the *end* of the empire into *empire's* very own end. It's time is not messianic time, the time that remains or even what Giorgio Agamben calls '*the time that time takes to come to an end*',[26] but something closer to Jean-François Lyotard's time of the future perfect (*futur antérieur*): the time of the *will have been.*[27] As Hell observes, the imperial ruin-gazer keeps empire's end in view by granting itself the imperial privilege of bearing future witness to its own demise through the eyes of its own conquerors: the Goths, the Turks and so on. To keep its own power, Schmitt's imperial *Katechon* similarly adopts the victorious perspective, not of the Goth, the Turk or the Muslim in this case, but of its own ultimate nemesis: the rough beast slouching towards Bethlehem to be born that is the anti-Christ. If the aesthetic perspective of the ruin-gazer thus enables Schmitt to square the historico-eschatological circle of power – to transform the end of empire into empire's own end – we must always remember that the Schmittean restrainer is not *just* a kind of conservative, anti-messianic equivalent to what Taubes scathingly calls the 'aesthetic messianisms' of utopian thinkers like Ernst Bloch.[28] In Schmitt's *Katechon*, we do not confront a kind of aesthetico-political thought experiment – which merely seeks to imagine what a future in which it no longer existed would look like – but a real political actor that seeks to capture that future and put it to work, here and now, in the interests of its own continuing survival.

To what extent, then, can we pursue this new theory of the *Katechon* as the protagonist of a kind of sovereign anarchy into the wider field of Schmitt's political theology? It goes without saying, of course, that Schmittean political theology is a vast and complex field whose perimeters far exceed the scope of this chapter, but I want to argue that not only does the *Katechon* make possible a counter-reading of some of the familiar conceptual markers of this field – sovereign decisionism, the state of emergency and so on – but may also help to explain its (tragic or culpable) historical fate. To recall Walter Benjamin's famous claim in the 'Theses on the Philosophy of History' (1940), which Giorgio Agamben not implausibly claims was written in secret dialogue with Schmitt's *Political Theology*, the political state of exception [*Ausnahmezustand*] undergoes something close to the same extension as the *Katechon* in Christian theology: the '"state of emergency" is which we live is not the exception but the rule'.[29] Yet the Pauline figure of the restrainer – whose constitutive juridical principle, as Esposito puts it, is to give form, rule and law to the very absence of law – arguably clarifies why this state of permanent exceptionality is no accident. If Schmitt argues that sovereignty and anarchy exist in a 'clear antithesis' in the conclusion to *Political Theology*, he also recognizes that they share an uncanny symmetry which renders them mirror images of each other: 'Bakunin, the greatest anarchist of the nineteenth century, had to become in theory the antitheologian of theology and in practice the dictator of an antidictatorship'.[30] For me, the

Pauline *Katechon* occupies precisely this permanent state of sovereign anarchy where above and below, *nomos* and antinomianism, dictatorship and antidictatorship, Schmitt and Bakunin coincide. What if the state of emergency is not the restraint but the *liberation* or *acceleration* of anomia within its own limited jurisdiction? What if the becoming-rule of the state of exception famously imagined by Benjamin is the katechontic taking up of anomia as its own enduring sovereign principle? What if the real tragedy of Schmitt's *Katechon* is that *Katechon* and anti-Christ, sovereignty and anarchy, Bethlehem and the beast become impossible to tell apart from one another?

In 'Security Unleashed', a 2006 marketing campaign designed to promote its security products to both national governments and multinational corporations, the American information technology company Unisys Corporation posed a series of intriguing questions: 'What if security wasn't a cage? What if, instead of keeping things out, it let amazing things in? What if, it made you bolder, more ambitious, and enabled you to accomplish more than you ever thought possible? What if security unleashed your full potential?'[31] It is now surely impossible to deny that something called 'security' – whether cyber, civil, financial or military – has become the dominant political ontology of our epoch, to which all other ends or goods must be subordinated. As the Unisys Corporation's self-promotion eloquently testifies, though, the philosophy of security in the contemporary epoch has undergone something of a paradigm shift. For the political theorist Michael Dillon, security today is less in the business of securing persons, property and states prophylactically against a set of contingencies which may befall them from without, than by exposing them to, participating in and seeking to master, a radical contingency which is now revealed to be the basic ontological condition of life itself: the securitization of the living is accomplished via the 'regulation of life's exposure to, and its productive and profitable exploitation of, contingent happenings and effects, including not only those occurring in nature but also those that follow from the independent actions and interventions of biological being itself'.[32] If Dillon largely dates this transformation in the field of security to the modern epoch – or more precisely to the complex aesthetic, political and philosophical field of formation he names the Baroque – I want to conclude by hypothesizing that it can also be seen as the outworking of an ancient aporetic logic that can be traced all the way back to that proto-politics of security: Paul's Second Letter to the Thessalonians. What is the *Katechon* we have been describing here, after all, if not the embodiment of 'security unleashed'?

To reiterate my thesis one final time, the Pauline figure of the restrainer is an accelerator despite (or today perhaps even *because* of) itself: it does not seek to simply hold back the end of the world so much as to *accelerate* it, pre-emptively, and on its own terms.[33] It is this messianic vocation – bodily lifted out of its original Judeo-Christian eschatological context and newly transplanted into an ontology of radical anti-teleological contingency – that paradoxically survives unscathed in our contemporary biopolitics of security. As the radical messianic voluntarism of the Unisys manifesto makes abundantly clear, risk is no longer conceived as an external threat to a stable or self-identical body, but an opportunity for unlocking a seemingly infinite potential within that very body: 'Security is no longer a defensive measure. It's an enabling catalyst for achievement'.[34] If contemporary politics of security often seems to be presiding over the destruction of everything it seeks to secure – civil rights, national, international and military law, sovereignty – this is not a performative self-contradiction, but the realization of its own project of maximizing life's own inherently productive (and destructive) properties. For our modern security *Katechons*, any political solution to the 'chaos' of market crashes, cyber-crime and terrorist attacks and so on necessarily entails *more* chaos, security unleashed, the apocalypse from above: 'resilience', 'disaster preparedness', 'stress-testing', 'future-proofing', the creative destruction that is neoliberal capitalism itself. In this contemporary Bethlehem, the rough beast reigns supreme.

In all these ways, then, we are perhaps still living in the time of the *Katechon*. It is not so much that we are living in the time that remains – that the end of the world prophesized by Paul is still to come – but that holding back the end of the world has become our sole messianic task – for there is no other world but this world, no other time than katechontic time. As this chapter has sought to argue, though, we are also living in the time of the *Katechon* because the end of the world has *already* happened – is happening infinitely and endlessly – in the sense that modern sovereignty has itself assumed the eschatological vocation of creator and destroyer of worlds. However, there is one more *Katechon* I want to consider – one more rough beast at the heart of the city – before closing, and this is the figure of the modern neoliberal sovereign himself. To be sure, our contemporary sovereign immediately grasps the defining eschatological challenge of the modern epoch: 'how do we secure the future for our party and for our country' in a 'world fast forwarding to the future at unprecedented speed'? If we are to secure this future, it cannot be by seeking to preserve the way things are, but rather by embracing the ever-accelerating force of change itself: 'The pace of change can either overwhelm us, or make our lives better and our country stronger. What we can't do is pretend it is not happening. It is replete with opportunities, but they only go to those swift to adapt, slow to complain, open, willing and able to change'. For British prime minister Tony Blair, speaking at the apogee of his own power and arguably of the neoliberal order itself in September 2005, such a messianic politics can be accomplished only through what he intriguingly calls the 'patient courage of the change-maker': 'Unless we "own" the future, unless our values are matched by a completely honest understanding of the reality now upon us and the next about to hit us, we will fail'.[35] In the figure of the modern sovereign – who seeks to secure the future by becoming the change-maker – the Pauline *Katechon* completes its transformation from a restrainer into an accelerator of history.

NOTES

1. W. B. Yeats, 'The Second Coming', in *Selected Poems*, ed. Timothy Webb (London: Penguin, 1991), 124.

2. It has, of course, been the subject of significant readings by such diverse thinkers as Alain Badiou, Giorgio Agamben, Paolo Virno, Roberto Esposito and Massimo Cacciari in the past years alone. See Alain Badiou, *Saint Paul: The Foundation of Universalism*, trans. Ray Brassier (Stanford, CA: Stanford University Press, 2003); Giorgio Agamben, *The Time That Remains: A Commentary on the Letter to the Romans*, trans. Patricia Dailey (Stanford, CA: Stanford University Press, 2005); Paolo Virno, *Multitude: Between Innovation and Negation* (New York: Semiotext(e), 2008); Roberto Esposito, 'The Katechon', in *Immunitas: The Protection and Negation of Life*, trans. Zakiya Hanafi (London: Polity, 2011), 52–79, and 'The Katechon', in *Two: The Machine of Political Theology and the Place of Thought*, trans. Zakiya Hanafi (New York: Fordham University Press, 2015), 76–82; and Massimo Cacciari, *The Withholding Power: An Essay on Political Theology*, trans. Edi Pucci, intr. Howard Caygill (London: Bloomsbury, 2017).

3. Carl Schmitt, 'Beschleuniger wider Willen, oder: Problematik der westlichen Hemisphare', in *Staat, Grossraum, Nomos: Arbeiten aus den Jahren 1916–1969*, ed. Günter Maschke (Berlin: Duncker and Humblot, 1995), 436. In calling this essay 'Accelerator despite Itself', I am following Julia Hell's elegant translation (hereafter cited as 'ADI' with page references in the text), but the title has been equally translated as 'Accelerator against its will' or 'Involuntary accelerator'.

4. Carl Schmitt, *Glossarium: Aufzeichnungen aus den Jahren 1957–51*, ed. Eberhard Freiherr von Medem (Berlin: Duncker & Humblot, 1991), 63.

5. Jacob Taubes, *The Political Theology of Paul*, trans. Dana Hollander (Stanford, CA: Stanford University Press, 2004), 103.

6. As any biblical scholar will be only too aware, the authorship of 2 Thessalonians is widely disputed. For many Paul scholars today, the letter was most likely written by a disciple of Paul after the latter's death in imitation of the style

of 1 Thessalonians. In what follows, though, I continue to attribute the text to Paul for clarity and economy's sake.

7. See *Paul and the Philosophers*, ed. Ward Blanton and Hent de Vries (New York: Fordham University Press, 2013); Theodore Jennings, Jr., *Outlaw Justice: The Messianic Politics and Paul* (Stanford, CA: Stanford University Press, 2013), and Ward Blanton, *A Materialism for the Masses: Saint Paul and the Philosophy of Undying Life* (New York: Columbia University Press, 2014) for recent cutting-edge readings of Paul which have influenced my own.

8. See Heinrich Meier, *Die Lehre Carl Schmitts* (Stuttgart: J. B. Metzler, 1994); Günter Meuter, *Der Katechon: Carl Schmitts fundamentalistischer Kritik der Zeit* (Berlin: Duncker & Humblot, 1994); Felix Grossheutschi, *Carl Schmitt und die Lehre vom Katechon* (Berlin: Duncker & Humblot, 1996); and Ruth Groh, *Arbeit an der Heillosigkeit der Welt: Zur politisch-theologischen Mythologie und Anthropologie Carl Schmitts* (Frankfurt: Suhrkamp Verlag, 1998) for important assessments of Schmitt's account of the *Katechon*.

9. Augustine of Hippo, *City of God*, trans. Henry Bettenson (Harmondsworth: Penguin, 1972), Book 20, chap. 19, 935; insertion mine.

10. Taubes, *The Political Theology of Paul*, 103.

11. Esposito, 'The Katechon', 63.

12. Carl Schmitt, *The* Nomos *of the Earth in the International Law of the Jus Publicum Europaeum*, trans. G. L. Ulmen (New York: Telos, 2003), 60.

13. Taubes, *The Political Theology of Paul*, 103.

14. To be sure, we cannot do any justice here to the complexities of the Schmitt-Taubes debate. In lieu of a more detailed examination, let me simply say here that Taubes's own rejection of Schmittean political theology should not be interpreted as a rejection of the possibility of a political theology per se *à la* Eric Petersen: I prefer to follow Marin Terpstra and Theo de Wit's description of Taubes's philosophy as a 'negative political theology', where political power is theologically delegitimized, in contrast to Schmitt's 'positive political theology', which seeks theological sanction for politics. See Marin Terpstra and Theo de Wit, '*No Spiritual Investment in the World as It Is:* On the Negative Political Theology of Taubes', in *Flight of the Gods: Philosophical Perspective on Negative Theology*, ed. I. N. Bulhof and L. ten Kate (New York: Fordham University Press, 2000), 320–53.

15. See Julia Hell, '*Katechon*: Carl Schmitt's Imperial Theology and the Ruins of the Future', *The Germanic Review* 84.4 (2009): 283–326; Michael Hoelzl, 'Before the Anti-Christ Is Revealed: On the Katechontic Structure of Messianic Time', in *The Politics to Come: Power, Modernity and the Messianic*, ed. Arthur Bradley and Paul Fletcher (London: Continuum, 2010), 98–110; Michael Dillon, 'Spectres of Biopolitics: Eschatology, *Katechon* and Resistance', *South Atlantic Quarterly* 110.3 (Summer 2011): 780–92; and Marc de Wilde, 'Politics between Times: Theologico-Political Interpretations of the Restraining Force (*katechon*) in Paul's Second Letter to the Thessalonians', in *Paul and the Philosophers*, ed. Ward Blanton and Hent de Vries, 105–26 for excellent recent discussions of Schmitt and the *Katechon* that have influenced my own.

16. See William Hooker, *Carl Schmitt's International Thought: Order and Orientation* (Cambridge: Cambridge University Press, 2009), 118–22 for one of the only Anglophone discussions of Schmitt's essay. In what follows, I am indebted to Hooker's commentary, notwithstanding any differences of interpretation or emphasis.

17. See, for example, Carl Schmitt, 'The Changing Structure of International Law', trans. Antonio Cerella and Andrea Salvatore, *Journal for Cultural Research* 20.3: special issue on Carl Schmitt, Political Theology and Modernity, ed. Antonio Cerella and Arthur Bradley (2016): 310–28. In this 1942 lecture, which was delivered in Madrid, Schmitt again documents what he sees as the USA's 'oscillations between self-isolationist neutrality and pan-interventionism'.

18. Carl Schmitt, 'The Age of Neutralizations and Depoliticizations', in *The Concept of the Political*, trans. George Schwab (Chicago: University of Chicago Press, 2007), 80–96.

19. Carl Schmitt, *Land and Sea*, trans. Simona Draghica (Washington, DC; Plutarch Press, 1997). In this 1942 text, Schmitt explicitly identifies the *Katechon* with a number of historical figures and institutions. To begin with, the Eastern or Byzantine Roman Empire prevented the spread of Islam to Italy following the Arab conquest of Carthage in 698. If the Easter Roman Empire has been absent, Schmitt argues, 'Italy would have become part of the Muslim world, like North Africa, and all of the Ancient and Christian Civilization would have been destroyed' (*Land and Sea*, 8). Finally, Schmitt also argues that the German emperor Rudolf II (1552–1612) succeeded in keeping Europe's early modern religious wars outside of Germany's borders and held off the chaos of the Thirty Years' War.

20. Samuel Beckett, *Worstward Ho* (London: John Calder, 1999), 7.

21. See de Wilde, 'Politics between Times'. In this paragraph, I am relying on de Wilde's account of Hans Freyer on pp. 117–19.

22. De Wilde, 'Politics between Times', 119.

23. Thalin Zarmanian, 'Carl Schmitt and the Problem of Legal Order: From Domestic to International', *Leiden Journal of International Law* 19.1 (2006): 55.

24. Zarmanian, 'Carl Schmitt and the Problem of Legal Order', 59–60.

25. Hell, '*Katechon*', 292.

26. Agamben, *The Times That Remains*, 67.

27. Jean-François Lyotard, 'Answer to the Question: What Is Postmodernism?', in *The Postmodern Explained to Children: Correspondence 1982*–85, trans. Thomas M. Pefanis (London: Power Institute of Fine Arts, 1992), 24.

28. Taubes, *The Political Theology of Paul*, 70–76.

29. Walter Benjamin, 'Theses on the Philosophy of History, in *Illuminations*, ed. and intr. Hannah Arendt, trans. Harry Zohn (New York: Schocken, 1968), 257.

30. Carl Schmitt, *Political Theology: Four Chapters on the Concept of Sovereignty*, trans. George Schwab (Chicago: University of Chicago Press, 2006), 66.

31. See Michael Dillon, 'Underwriting Security', in *The Biopolitics of Security: A Political Analytic of Finitude* (London: Taylor and Francis, 2015), 99–122 for an indispensable discussion of the contemporary theory and praxis of security to which I owe this reference to Unisys Corporation. In writing this chapter, I have

benefited hugely from many conversations with Mick about the politics of security over the years.

32. Dillon, *The Biopolitics of Security*, 104.

33. In recent Marxist and post-Marxist political discourse, of course, the concept of accelerationism refers to the speeding-up of technological processes to reveal and exacerbate the structural tensions within capitalism, but my own claim here is that a discourse of 'accelerationism' – whatever its merits – is by no means simply the province of the left. See Robin Mackay and Armen Avanessian, *The Accelerationist Reader* (Berlin: Merve, 2014) for a range of responses to the accelerationist movement.

34. Dillon, *The Biopolitics of Security*, 99.

35. Tony Blair, keynote speech to the Labour Party Conference, 27 September 2005, http://news.bbc.co.uk/1/hi/uk_politics/4287370.stm (last accessed 26 February 2017).

BIBLIOGRAPHY

AGAMBEN, Giorgio. *The Time That Remains: A Commentary on the Letter to the Romans*. Translated by Patricia Dailey. Stanford, CA: Stanford University Press, 2005.

AUGUSTINE OF HIPPO. *City of God*. Translated by Henry Bettenson. Harmondsworth: Penguin, 1972.

BADIOU, Alain. *Saint Paul: The Foundation of Universalism*. Translated by Ray Brassier. Stanford, CA: Stanford University Press, 2003.

BECKETT, Samuel. *Worstward Ho*. London: John Calder, 1999.

BENJAMIN, Walter. 'Theses on the Philosophy of History'. In *Illuminations*. Edited and with an Introduction by Hannah Arendt. Translated by Harry Zohn. New York: Schocken, 1968. 253–64.

BLAIR, Tony. Keynote speech to the Labour Party Conference, 27 September 2005; http://news.bbc.co.uk/1/hi/uk_politics/4287370.stm. Last accessed 26 February 2017.

BLANTON, Ward. *A Materialism for the Masses: Saint Paul and the Philosophy of Undying Life*. New York: Columbia University Press, 2014.

BLANTON, Ward and Hent DE VRIES (eds.). *Paul and the Philosophers*. New York: Fordham University Press, 2013.

CACCIARI, Massimo. *The Withholding Power: An Essay on Political Theology*. Translated by Edi Pucci. Introduction by Howard Caygill. London: Bloomsbury, 2017.

DE WILDE, Marc. 'Politics between Times: Theologico-Political Interpretations of the Restraining Force (*katechon*) in Paul's Second Letter to the Thessalonians'. In *Paul and the Philosophers*. Edited by Ward Blanton and Hent de Vries. New York: Fordham University Press, 2013. 105–26.

DILLON, Michael. *The Biopolitics of Security: A Political Analytic of Finitude*. London: Taylor and Francis, 2015.

DILLON, Michael. 'Spectres of Biopolitics: Eschatology, *Katechon* and Resistance'. *South Atlantic Quarterly* 110.3 (Summer 2011): 780–92.

ESPOSITO, Roberto. 'The Katechon'. In *Immunitas: The Protection and Negation of Life*. Translated by Zakiya Hanafi. London: Polity, 2011. 52–79.

ESPOSITO, Roberto. 'The Katechon'. In *Two: The Machine of Political Theology and the Place of Thought*. Translated by Zakiya Hanafi. New York: Fordham University Press, 2015. 76–82.

GROSSHEUTSCHI, Felix. *Carl Schmitt und die Lehre vom Katechon*. Berlin: Duncker & Humblot, 1996.

GROH, Ruth. *Arbeit an der Heillosigkeit der Welt: Zur politisch-theologischen Mythologie und Anthropologie Carl Schmitts*. Frankfurt a.M.: Suhrkamp, 1998

HELL, Julia. '*Katechon*: Carl Schmitt's Imperial Theology and the Ruins of the Future'. *The Germanic Review* 84.4 (2009): 283–326.

HOELZL, Michael. 'Before the Anti-Christ Is Revealed: On the Katechontic Structure of Messianic Time'. In *The Politics to Come: Power, Modernity and the Messianic*. Edited by Arthur Bradley and Paul Fletcher. London: Continuum, 2010. 98–110.

HOOKER, William. *Carl Schmitt's International Thought: Order and Orientation*. Cambridge: Cambridge University Press, 2009.

JENNINGS, Jr., Theodore. *Outlaw Justice: The Messianic Politics and Paul*. Stanford, CA: Stanford University Press, 2013.

LYOTARD Jean-François. *The Postmodern Explained to Children: Correspondence 1982–85*. Translated by Thomas M. Pefanis. London: Power Institute of Fine Arts, 1992.

MACKAY, Robin and Armen AVANESSIAN. *The Accelerationist Reader*. Berlin: Merve, 2014.

MEIER, Heinrich. *Die Lehre Carl Schmitts*. Stuttgart: J. B. Metzler, 1994.

MEUTER, Günter. *Der Katechon: Carl Schmitts fundamentalistischer Kritik der Zeit*. Berlin: Duncker & Humblot, 1994.

SCHMITT, Carl. 'The Age of Neutralizations and Depoliticizations'. In *The Concept of the Political*. Translated by George Schwab. Chicago: University of Chicago Press, 2007. 80–96.

SCHMITT, Carl. 'Beschleuniger wider Willen, oder: Problematik der westlichen Hemisphare'. In *Staat, Grossraum, Nomos: Arbeiten aus den Jahren 1916–1969*. Edited by Günter Maschke. Berlin: Duncker & Humblot, 1995. 431–36.

SCHMITT, Carl. 'The Changing Structure of International Law'. Translated by Antonio Cerella and Andrea Salvatore. *Journal for Cultural Research* 20.3: special issue on Carl Schmitt, Political Theology and Modernity. Edited by Antonio Cerella and Arthur Bradley (2016): 310–28.

SCHMITT, Carl. *Glossarium: Aufzeichnungen aus den Jahren 1957–51*. Edited by Eberhard Freiherr von Medem. Berlin: Duncker & Humblot, 1991.

SCHMITT, Carl. *Land and Sea*. Translated by Simona Draghica. Washington, DC: Plutarch Press, 1997.

SCHMITT, Carl. *The* Nomos *of the Earth in the International Law of the Jus Publicum Europaeum*. Translated by G. L. Ulmen. New York: Telos, 2003.

SCHMITT, Carl. *Political Theology: Four Chapters on the Concept of Sovereignty*. Translated by George Schwab. Chicago: University of Chicago Press, 2006.

TAUBES, Jacob. *The Political Theology of Paul*. Translated by Dana Hollander. Stanford, CA: Stanford University Press, 2004.

TERPSTRA, Marin and Theo DE WIT. '*No Spiritual Investment in the World as It Is:* On the Negative Political Theology of Taubes'. In *Flight of the Gods: Philosophical Perspective on Negative Theology*. Edited by I. N. Bulhof and L. ten Kate. New York: Fordham University Press, 2000. 320–53.

VIRNO, Paolo. *Multitude: Between Innovation and Negation*. New York: Semiotext(e), 2008.

YEATS, William Butler. 'The Second Coming'. In *Selected Poems*. Edited by Timothy Webb. London: Penguin, 1991.

ZARMANIAN, Thalin. 'Carl Schmitt and the Problem of Legal Order: From Domestic to International'. *Leiden Journal of International Law* 19.1 (2006): 41–67.

Section two

THE LIVING SOUL OF MONEY

Chapter 4

The Bank of England in ruins

Photography, money and the law of equivalence

Christopher John Müller and Ian Wiblin*

> ... O MONEY, Money! ... Well art thou called the God of this world; for in thy presence and absence consists all the heaven or hell of human affairs.[1]

The establishment of the Bank of England in 1694 played a subtle but decisive role in the rise of today's financial system. It was founded as an issuing bank that could sell government bonds, and in 1709 it was granted a near-monopoly on printing bank notes secured against the future tax income of the state. This move invented national debt, a revolutionary new form of credit. In the wake of its own success, the Bank also pioneered a less well-known architectural revolution. As Eva Schuman-Bacia explains, since their emergence in the twelfth century, 'European banking institutions had always been housed in temporary, rented accommodation in palaces, hotels or town halls', a custom upheld in continental Europe until the mid-nineteenth century. In the Bank of England, as Schuman-Bacia elaborates, 'we have the first building to be conceived to serve the specific functions of a banking institution'.[2] The very act of constructing a designated building to house the Bank in the 1730s signalled an exploratory move away from the transience of borrowed space towards a new kind of permanence. By occupying a building of its own, the Bank, and with it the banking system it helped inaugurate, finds a new place in the world. From this moment on it begins to enclose a space that is entirely its own, a space sculpted by an architecture that gradually assumes a monumental gravity that helps underwrite the very credit it makes available.

Yet the Bank's architectural solidity is haunted by the performative contradiction it represents: as a structure built to issue notes and advance credit, it is the solid shell of something that is necessarily intangible, abstract, and insecure. While grappling with the novel idea of 'Publick Credit' (national debt) in 1710, Daniel Defoe captures this paradox in a manner that inadvertently also offers an intimate portrayal that breaches the Bank's walls. He exposes a flaw that the monumental nature of today's building automatically counteracts:

> *Like the Soul* in the Body, it [credit] acts all Substance, yet is it Self Immaterial; it gives Motion, yet it Self cannot be Said to Exist; it creates *Forms*, yet has it Self no *Form*; it is neither Quantity or Quality; it has no *Whereness*, or *Whenness*, *Scite*, or *Habit*. If I should say it is the essential Shadow of something that is Not [.][3]

While standing on Threadneedle Street opposite the Bank of England, or when looking at the cover of this book, which depicts part of the Bank's façade, one can witness credit acting 'all Substance'. In 1732, roughly twenty years after Defoe's words were published, the foundation stone of the first purpose-built bank was placed, a structure which was successively extended and remodelled until in 1828 it eventually filled its present 'island site', 3.5 acres in size and fully encircled by roads.[4] The massive windowless perimeter wall designed by Sir John Soane, the Bank's most famous architect, adds to the sense that the building stands apart from the rest of London, giving it an air of seemingly unmovable permanence. Soane's wall seems designed to appear as if it is sinking into the ground, pulled down by the weight of the gold reserves in its subterranean vaults. The solidity of the wall also fulfilled the practical function of providing a buttress to shield the Bank from a riotous populace, which at times saw the building garrisoned with a protective force of fifty soldiers.[5] Yet, in light of Defoe's words, the Bank of England also seems at a remove from its own tangible nature, which is quite literally the petrified 'shadow' of something that is 'Not': a building that was erected on the promise of the very form of credit the establishment of the Bank helped institute and guarantee. The building's imposing presence gives a first indication that the dematerialization and resulting 'spiritualization'[6] of monetary value through the institution of national debt is entirely contingent on the gradual solidification and technologization of banking infrastructures. This is a solidity of a very particular kind, as it rests on a necessarily borrowed, immaterial foundation with a temporal horizon, for credit (and money in general) is a matter of trust and belief. As such, Georg Simmel observes in *The Philosophy of Money*, it must on some level remain absolutely unknowable, speculative and insecure: loans might be defaulted, a given currency might collapse, notes or coins might not be accepted.[7]

It is this discrepancy between money as an empirically knowable object and its inherently speculative nature that we discuss in this chapter. The

Bank of England (and the financial system and model of monetary usage it helped inaugurate) does not merely stand on a foundation that is necessarily unstable; it was incorporated in the first place to conjure up and channel this mysterious 'Not', this otherworldly force without 'Quantity or Quality . . . *Whereness*, or *Whenness*, *Scite*, or *Habit*'. How can we conceive of the inalienable 'otherness' of money, 'the fundamental distance between money and the things whose circulation it mediates',[8] a distance, we suggest, that quite literally brings things into contact by holding them apart, by effecting and enshrining *krisis*, that is, a 'dispute', 'separating', 'decision', 'choice', 'election' and 'judgment'?[9] How has this *krisis*, this incision, this opening of a destabilizing void of negotiation and indecision between things (and at the heart of things), evolved since it was released into the world on a grand scale when the Bank of England began to print state-backed notes?

To answer these questions, we revert to an approach that Siegfried Kracauer calls 'reportage'. At the outset of *The Salaried Masses*, a 1928 study on the rise of waged employment in Berlin, Kracauer explains that 'reportage is counterpoised to the abstractness of idealist thought'; its focus lies on 'concrete existence', but it must also guard itself against 'losing its way in the life that idealism cannot find' and turn into mere description. 'A hundred reports from a factory remain for all eternity a hundred views of the factory', and as such they fail to transcend the specific empirical record they represent. Kracauer's solution is to adopt an approach that retains a focus on a concrete object – in our case the tangible architectural structure of the Bank of England – while responding to this object through the assembly of a *mosaic* combining multiple points of view. 'Life must be observed for it to appear', Kracauer explains, but it is by no means contained within observational results', it is 'found solely in the mosaic that is assembled from single observations'. If reportage were able to 'photograph life', Kracauer concludes, then 'such a mosaic would be its image'.[10]

The 'life' at issue in this chapter is entirely artificial, 'inanimate' to use David Wills's term.[11] It is the life that money gives to trade, innovation, salaried labour, the life it gives to the forces of progress by opening a distance between things that facilitates exchange and negotiation. The establishment of the Bank of England, and the monetization of the economy in the wake of the model of monetary usage it pioneered, led to the exponential amplification of money's animating force, its ability to add momentum and motivation, to accelerate, intensify and quicken progress, fund research, buy objects that do not yet even exist. As such, this secularizing force, for all its benevolence, is also beginning to openly portray ruinous tendencies and a potentially terminal velocity. To capture and conceptualize the peculiar life of money, our mosaic combines material focused on the Bank of England as an institution with broader reflections on the nature of money as such. The latter are mainly sourced from German media theory and approaches inspired by Georg Simmel's *The Philosophy of Money*. Rather than seeing in photography a mere analogy as Kracauer does, we seek to mobilize the photographic image as a revelatory force in its own right. Ian Wiblin's photographic engagement with the architecture of the Bank of England, shot on expired film of unreliable and unpredictable quality, records 'shadow[s] of something that is Not' in ways that we will discuss as the argument advances, for the 'dematerialization' of money, which coincides with the materialization and increasing technologization of a banking infrastructure has an uncanny double in the evolution of the photographic image, and its seemingly direct connection to its subject. The moment 'digital' photography breaks its bond to precious metals – silver-based photographic film be it in colour or black and white – it begins to effect 'the ruin of any pretence at photographic veracity'.[12]

Montage, manipulation and falsification may have always been part of the fabric of photography, but a profound shift occurs the moment photographs are no longer processed from a negative but from a data file containing 1s and 0s. As we will discuss at length, the digital image has been liberated from its constraining bond to the referent and has openly become an object of speculation. 'Although a digital image may look just like a photograph when it is published in a newspaper', as William Mitchell already noted in 1992, 'it actually differs as profoundly from a traditional photograph as does a photograph from a painting'.[13] The constancy of the reality effect that images generate thus covers over momentous ruptures beneath their signifying surface. In section two, 'Romantic Idealism Ruined', we align the technologization of pictorial representation – from painting to photograph to digital image – with the development of money – from gold or silver coin to bank note to number in a database – to think through the 'tragic arch' along which money as an accelerant of trade and innovation is propelling us to (future) ruin at an ever faster rate. Before doing so, we discuss the crucial act of speculation that the establishment of the Bank of England constituted in its own right, for this is the decisive step in the technologization of money at issue here. By inaugurating the 'mechanical reproduction of money' in the form of state-backed notes, the Bank speculated (and managed to corroborate) that 'the value of money', in the words of Sybille Krämer, 'actually consists in its legally determined institutionalization as a state-approved symbol of economic value', and not, as was widely (and falsely) believed, in the scarce precious metals from which money was made.[14] As such, the dematerialization and virtualization of money pioneered by the Bank of England amounted to an epistemological discovery no less momentous than the discovery of gravity.

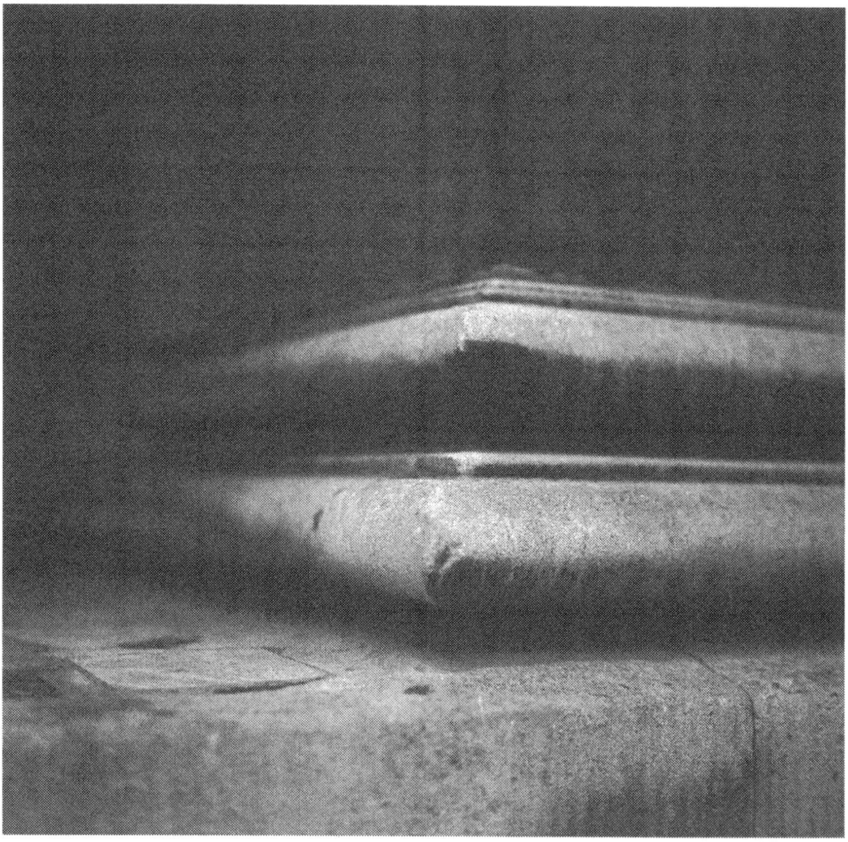

By severing its bond to precious metals, that is, by invoking a *krisis* with regard to its own source of value, money as 'a state approved symbol of value' begins to reveal, harness and formalize an invisible force that was already always at work in every act of exchange: the law of equivalence. In order to set the ground for the photographic and philosophical speculation this chapter engages in, it is necessary to begin by spelling out the manner in which this law is mediated by money.

Money 'relates things to one another and makes them equivalent'.[15] A valid, accredited £20 note can be converted into anything that has a price, regardless of what this might be. Money's true source of value, its usefulness, lies in this capacity to act as a mediator between even the most incongruent things. As such, money presents itself as the 'homogenous in the heterogeneous', to use Krämer's succinct wording;[16] it serves as a common denominator that mediates *exchange* (and not just ownership or value).[17] This means that the value of money is in permanent flux, because its purchasing power is only ever borrowed from what it can buy. Its effective value is contingent on a whole set of other variables that may affect prices. The law of equivalence thus boils down to a tautology that is as obvious and impenetrably solid as Sir John Soane's curtain wall: £20 is only ever worth what it buys. This tautology, however, reveals the unique property that makes money what it is. Because money is merely a placeholder for value that can be exchanged for anything purchasable, 'the "quality" of money', as Krämer sums up Simmel, 'consists only in its quantity'.[18] In the final instance, the quantification (the fact that there is a number) and not the national currency (£), material substance or even the actually printed number 20 'defines' the £20 note. The mere presence of a numerical value suffices to translate the law of equivalence from an intangible sentiment into a quantified relationship, not just between everything that has a price and monetary value, but also between all other currencies. Here we can begin to identify more clearly the 'Something that is Not' which Defoe contemplates in his mediation on credit. As even £0 or a negative amount (–£20) are quantifications of monetary value (and hence also qualities), the dematerialization of money that the Bank of England began to pioneer unlocks the inalienably abstract, exclusively symbolic existence of monetary value, which allows money to do what no other object can: even when it is 0, it can still 'be'; it even increases its pragmatic grip when it becomes a negative number in a register, for it liberates hope at the risk of chaining those in debt to the reality this '–' represents.

It is here that the tragic flaw of this now most ubiquitous and mundane 'thing' called money begins to be exposed: money has a value because it values things against one another. As a mediator of equivalence, it has no fixed value itself, for £20 might buy thirty apples today, but this will transmute into forty apples after a bumper crop. Because there is no final price set before trade happens, money's only constant is its serpentine inconsistency, which tempts us with the prospect of getting more for 'it'. Although it is no secret that the value of money is a matter of fluctuation, inflation and deflation, our carefree reliance on money in daily life is secured by our pragmatic inability to comprehend that the abstract purity of the 20 on a £20 note symbolizes a value that is speculative, never fully known or at peace with itself. In spelling out the tension that the empirical reality of money resolves for us, Krämer beautifully captures the discrepancy between money as a thing (number, coin, note) and money as a mediator of exchange: 'In money the abstract form of value not only prevails over the concrete natural form, but rather this abstraction also manifests itself: something invisible is literally and materially objectified and becomes empirically real'.[19] In this chapter we suggest that the discrepancy between our immediate sense-certainty that money *is* and the inalienably abstract law of equivalence that by its very essence decrees that money *is never what it is* arrests the history of monetization in a tragic arch. Classical temples not only acted as the architectural foil for Soane's extension of the Bank of England, but the building itself is also the site from which the kind of self-fulfilling prophecy emanates that we know from Greek tragedy. By issuing notes and floating a currency, the Bank began to furnish the law of equivalence with a universal *numerical* calculus, which exposes existence to the annihilating force of speculation, a law which could only become operative as a mathematical equation *after* money was dematerialized, printed, in wide use and a ubiquitous object in the world. This law operates like a natural force, reliably, all by itself, without history, immutably like a universal constant. It is this ability to numerically quantify and equate, to cite Defoe, which makes money 'the vehicle of providence, the great medium of conveyance, in which all the physic of the secret dispensation in human Affairs is administered'.[20] Yet the tragic fact we wish to contemplate is that despite its abstract, timeless purity the quasi-natural law of equivalence is also 'a physic' that is entirely man-made. It is artificial through and through, and as such, it is bound to technological infrastructures needed to support and animate it. Even though a gold coin serves to establish equivalence just as a printed note does, this pragmatic continuity also masks most profound and ruinous ruptures.

This brings us to the painting from which this chapter borrows its title: Joseph Michael Gandy's *An Imagined View of Soane's Bank of England in Ruins*. The painting was commissioned by Sir John Soane himself and was exhibited at the Royal Academy in 1830. It marked the completion of the extension and remodelling of the Bank under Soane's stewardship, a tenure that had begun forty-two years earlier in 1788. Gandy's painting presents the Bank as an idealized ruin that opens a cut-away perspective on the building's interior. The style echoes Giovanni Piranesi's depictions

Joseph Michael Gandy, *An Imagined View of Soane's Bank of England in Ruins*, 1830.

of the ruins of Rome, which were highly popular in Georgian Britain and served as a source of inspiration for the neo-classical architecture typical of this era. 'Gandy', as Gillian Darley reflects on the painting's deployment of a popular style, 'worked for Soane very much as a modern architect might employ a trusted photographer to convey the idealized image of his building, perfectly lit'.[21] This analogy to photography, we suggest, opens a perspective onto the Bank and the 'spiritualized' monetary system it began to inaugurate that far exceeds Darley's comparison of Gandy's painting to a promotional photograph. For the painting also acts like an intimate portrayal of the space, the Bank begins to enshrine; it begins to visually expose the annihilating force of speculation, the very insecurity of value that opens a chasm at the edge of which the Bank is precariously poised in the painting. If it is to bring things into contact with one another, money needs this insecurity. In fact, embodying this 'Not', this 'void', 'otherness', 'distance', *krisis* is money's sole *raison d'être*. The establishment of the Bank in 1694 began to release it into the world on a grand scale.

Ian Wiblin's turn to ruined and expired film was inspired by Gandy's painting. The images included in this chapter were not produced to illustrate this piece. While preparing a collaborative exhibition of this work in 2015, we began to recognize the images' potential to act as a screen for the various vectors and registers of thought assembled here.[22] As such, this chapter is a first hyperbolic reportage emerging from an ongoing project with an emphatically speculative remit. Wiblin's very gesture of using ruined film amplifies the inherently speculative nature of photography and can serve to conceptualize the technological corruption at the heart of our relationship to money in all its enigmatic obscurity. The spiritualization of money, as we wish to think it here, truly is both 'miracle and machine', to borrow Michael Naas's phrase.[23] Before turning directly to the deep, uncanny connection between the machine-mediated art of photography and the machinistic nature of monetary value, we will look at the history of the Bank of England itself, and the crucial role the Bank played in establishing what we are accustomed to call 'the secular world', with its faith in demystifying sciences, quantification and progress – what Jacques Derrida calls 'the temptation of knowledge'.[24]

In section one, 'Nietzsche's Lantern', we respond to Philip Goodchild's suggestion that the incorporation of the Bank of England was the 'actual deed which caused the murder of God' (*Capitalism and Religion*, 30) by discussing Defoe's essay on 'Publick Credit'.[25] The emergence of the Bank, as Goodchild and Defoe will help us see, truly is the apotheosis of the money-machine, of a 'god' scattered across and alive in uncounted shrines that we can carry along and spend. These shrines take the form of coins, notes and credit cards but can also assume a more monumental guise. In the second section, 'Romantic Idealism Ruined', we return to the highly creative but ultimately ruinous force this god, who is no longer in need of any believers, begins to extol: a force that is amplified the moment worship is automated and outsourced, to happen all by itself wherever money is put to use.

NIETZSCHE'S LANTERN: THE BANK OF ENGLAND AND 'THE MURDER OF GOD'

In the 'The Murder of God', the first chapter of *Capitalism and Religion*, Philip Goodchild turns to Friedrich Nietzsche's famous parable of the madman to reflect on how the rise of the secular world is connected to the institution of the Bank of England. In Goodchild's reading, Nietzsche's words imply that the transition to the secular world happens in the marketplace. It is worth repeating Nietzsche's parable here:

> Haven't you heard of that madman who in the bright morning lit a lantern and ran around the marketplace crying incessantly, 'I'm looking for God! I'm looking for God!' Since many of those who did not believe in God were standing around together just then, he caused great laughter. Has he been lost then? Asked one. Did he lose his way like a child? Asked another. Or is he hiding? Or is he afraid of us? . . . The madman jumped into their midst and pierced them with his eyes. 'Where is God?' He cried; 'I'll tell you! *We have killed him* – you and I! We are all his murderers. But how did we do this? How were we able to drink up the sea? Who gave us the sponge to wipe away the entire horizon? What were we doing when we unchained this earth from its sun?'[26]

The question 'how did we do this?' introduces an array of additional questions that map out the magnitude of the deed. Before we turn to these, we will elaborate on what Goodchild presents as the decisive aspect of the passage: the marketplace setting. The marketplace implies that 'the murder of God' is effected by what Goodchild calls 'a progressive reorganization of daily life' (*Capitalism and Religion*, 27), an increasing reliance on money as an 'impersonal calculus' and mediator of value 'introjected' into 'human thought' (*Capitalism and Religion*, 28) to give everything a price. For Goodchild, the madman observes that God is 'no longer the organizing idea behind all aspects of daily life, endowing all dimensions of existence with a ritual meaning' (*Capitalism and Religion*, 27). God has been replaced by an activity that has become utterly mundane: the interaction with coins, notes and bank accounts. It is easy to neglect and overlook the radical shift in the monetary infrastructure that the introduction of the state-backed bank note represented. Up to the eighteenth century, the rise of monetary economies was constrained by 'the finite total of coinage in circulation' (*Capitalism and Religion*, 29). Because it breaks loose from this constraint, Goodchild presents the incorporation of the Bank of England as the 'final' but 'subtle move' that 'enabled a credible, durable and secure value to be attributed to bank notes for the first time'. The production of money, once limited by scarce raw materials (gold and silver), has theoretically become unlimited. With this schism a new form of transcendence found its way into the world, an infinitely extendable amount of money, a debt that can extend into the trillions and beyond. As such, Goodchild presents the establishment and gradual state takeover of the Bank of England as the 'actual deed which caused the murder of God' (*Capitalism and Religion*, 30). By beginning to cut the ties to precious metals, a dead weight in money's apotheosis, the Bank liberated money into its openly spiritualized form.

While there is 'no consensus' among historians about how the various aspects of the interrelationship of the British State and the Bank of England (which was not state owned until 1946) played out in detail during the eighteenth century, H. V. Bowen does conclude that 'a strong case can be made for the Bank's contribution being indispensable to the development of the state' and for 'the growth of the eighteenth-century economy'. Beside the vast expansion of the British Empire, the Bank also helped finance the Industrial Revolution.[27] To underline the central role of the Bank, Bowen cites an address by Lord North to the House of Commons in 1781, which celebrates the Bank's achievements: 'By prudent management, by judicious conduct, wise plans, and exact punctuality, in establishing its own credit, [The Bank of England] had contributed very essentially to establish the national credit'.[28] North's retrospective account, as Bowen elaborates, 'risks implying' an idea of 'steady advance and progression', which conceals that the Bank's emergence was punctuated by crises and most severe doubt in the entire model of monetary usage and printed notes it helped establish.[29] Nevertheless, North's words also indicate that by the 1780s the Bank's miraculous ability to raise money was recognized and even deemed indispensable.[30]

The financial infrastructures the Bank pioneered and its gradual takeover by the state had a very concrete outcome: the proliferation of paper money and coins made of base metals, the rise of a 'spiritualized', reliable national currency that we use without doubt or hesitation. This mechanism of self-validation is at stake in Defoe's essay on 'Publick Credit', a mechanism, which Lord North inadvertently gestures towards when surmising how the Bank had managed to 'establish its own credit'. At first sight, Defoe's text might strike one as being the template for Lord North's celebration of the Bank's success, for North matches Defoe almost verbatim: 'Credit is produc'd, and grows insensibly, from fair and upright Dealing, punctual Compliance, honourable Performance of Contracts and Covenance'.[31] This similarity, however, is highly deceptive. Unlike North, Defoe is not speaking about an institution but about the 'Credit' that might grow between individual trading partners, who might be willing to advance goods on promise of future payment *when insufficient coinage is available* to complete a transaction. Credit is here presented as an exclusively 'spiritual' entity, which is animated by honourable comportment in past transactions. As such, 'Credit', Defoe insists, is not 'chain'd to Mens Names, but to their Actions; not to Families, Clans, or Collections of Men; no, not to Nations chained' for it attains its life from the way its owner lives his or hers.[32] This exclusively performative quality makes credit 'the essential Shadow of something that is Not', for it is 'insensibly produced' and appears as if out of nowhere as a divine reward when traders prove through the very act of granting credit that they trust each other enough to let go of goods on a secured promise of future payment. For Defoe, there is no shortcut to this form of interpersonal credit as it can be raised only through fair dealings.[33]

Defoe illustrates the spiritual and intangible nature of credit in a beautiful passage that brings us a step closer to the tragic trajectory the law of equivalence begins to chart when being furnished with a reliable currency. In doing so, he also introduces us to credit as a force that animates and accelerates trade:

> CREDIT is a Consequence, not a Cause; the Effect of a Substance, not a Substance; 'tis the *Sun-shine*, not the Sun; the quickning SOMETHING, *Call it what you will*, that gives Life to *Trade*, gives Being to the Branches, and Moisture to the Root; 'tis the *Oil* of the Wheel, the *Marrow* in the Bones, the Blood in the Veins, and the *Spirits* in the Heart of all the Negoce, Trade, Cash, and Commerce in the World.[34]

Although sunshine is here quite literally 'unchained' from the sun, to recall Nietzsche's question, Defoe's image leaves the Earth very much in place. As credit is 'insensible', as it radiates not from a sun but from honourable actions, it is presented as a great force for good. Contained by the self-interest of the trader, who needs to be fair if he or she is not to risk losing access to this priceless resource, credit accelerates us towards a better world.

The tone markedly shifts, however, when Defoe begins to contemplate the form of 'Credit' that gives his essay its title, the credit that is a 'Public Thing', 'rightly call'd by some of our Writers, NATIONAL CREDIT', a new, mysterious kind of spirit that 'has for some Years been the Nations happy Guest, by whose Aid such mighty Things have been done'.[35] In stark contrast to the scene he has just described, national credit, as Defoe recognizes, is radically impersonal. It is not maintained by honest dealings, but by a well-oiled government machine, which Defoe compares to a '*National Clockwork*'.[36] Defoe's reflection on 'Publick Credit' dates from almost the precise moment the Bank of England began to issue notes under state license, thus inaugurating the decisive moment in the evolution of money that Krämer alerts us to when reiterating that 'the value of money actually consists in its legally determined institutionalization as a state-approved symbol of economic value'. This means that by the time Lord North declares that the Bank has managed to 'establish its own credit', he is no longer referring to people, but to the success and growing power of an institution. In the course of seventy years, Defoe's idealized description of credit as a thing that can be maintained only by direct personal interaction has been re-valued and radically inverted, for the value of the credit notes the Bank of England begins to issue is absolutely 'chained to nations'; they are issued in the name of the 'Public' and thus have no identifiable source but are tied to an abstract entity called 'the State'.

The no doubt idealistic account of interpersonal credit Defoe offers shows us the effective 'deed' that according to Goodchild constitutes 'the murder of God'. The establishment of the Bank begins to transform the *metaphysical* definition of credit that Defoe provides – 'CREDIT is a Consequence, not a Cause; the Effect of a Substance, not a Substance' – into the simple description of an empirical object in the world. Credit is a consequence of holding money; it is effected by the note I hold in my hand. My fair treatment of others has become optional; it will not impact on the worth of my cash (even if it is merely borrowed). It is this objectification of credit which begins to give rise to a national currency, this act of magically printing sunshine onto notes, so they can begin to shine an entirely artificial, impersonal light that unchains 'this earth from its sun'. Free from its connection to people, the accredited note assumes a life of its own. It has liberated itself from the constraints of substance and personal affiliation. It allows strangers to trade, regardless of their character, background or integrity. Money, as Defoe puts it in 1707, is a 'Mighty Neuter', a 'great jack-a-both sides of the world', a 'charm that . . . unscrews nature' to stand between all humans and make 'the friend turn traitor, the brother a stranger and Mankind devils'.[37] But it is only with the proliferation of the note that this force of indifference is properly released to accelerate trade and innovation, concentrate power and propel us ever faster into the bright new dawn into which Nietzsche's madman shines his unperceived light. Nietzsche's lantern illuminates how the dematerialization of money leads not to a consciously changed belief system, but to a progressive reorganization of life around the law of the marketplace that is facilitated by the gradual monetization of the economy itself.

The murder of God, as we read it here, is nothing other than the silent, gradual and ongoing apotheosis of the universal law of equivalence, a law that can only become operative *as* money becomes a ubiquitous object in the world. This law allows God to be killed without leading to his disappearance, for murder here signifies the animation of a new form of transcendence: money that can be multiplied without limit or end. Pragmatically speaking, the question 'how did we do it?' can be given a simple answer: printed money, national currencies and mass-produced coins were beginning to be trusted. It is only now, under these conditions, as state power has entered into its reciprocal and accumulative relationship to the currency it issues, that the annihilating law of equivalence can become fully operative, for this law is contingent on the existence of an impersonal mediator that acts as a universal numerical calculus. In view of Goodchild's reading and Nietzsche's concluding question 'what then are these churches now if not the tombs and sepulchres of God?', it is no small irony that in 1781, the very year when Lord North was celebrating the Bank's success in parliament, the parish church of St. Christopher le Stocks was demolished to make way for the massive expansion of the buildings housing the Bank of England, the completion of which was marked by Gandy's painting some forty-nine years later.

The ruin the painting depicts stands precariously on what looks like a widening chasm that threatens to make the building crash into an abyss. It is this chasm, we suggest, that Nietzsche's madman illuminates with all the clairvoyance of a seer, for the light of his lantern shows us something that cannot be seen. The questions which radiate from the madman's 'how did we do it?' diagnose a fundamental disorientation that sets in as the law of equivalence becomes a numerical equation and begins to replace God as the 'organizing idea behind all aspects of daily life'. They decree that the future direction of the Earth is unknown ('where is it moving now?'). They suggest that we are no longer moving through an identifiable space ('aren't we straying as though through an infinite nothing?'; 'is there still an up and a down?'). They describe a world grown dark and inhospitable ('hasn't it gotten colder? Isn't night and more night coming again and again?'). For all their enigmatic pathos, these words can be given an immediate referent. In fact, we routinely hold this radically empty space without '*Whereness* or *Whenness*' in our hand or carry it in our pocket, for what Nietzsche's lantern shines into is the inalienably abstract, indifferent, non-dimensional space that turns money into an infinite, bottomless placeholder of value.

The madman's questions thus name the 'void' the law of equivalence needs in order to become operative, a law with the sole indestructible axiom: £1 is worth exactly what it buys. In each singular moment of transaction, it cannot be worth more and cannot be worth less.

To see what makes this axiom tragic, we need to remind ourselves of the curious indeterminacy of the numbers that adorn coins, notes or bank balances, for it is inevitable that we on some level miss the fact that each of these numbers merely acts as a quantified void that can transmute into the things it can buy. Money works because it is impossible to see, disenchant or ever fully understand this void that is opened only because we trust our senses when they apprehend money as something that *is* rather than seeing in it a speculative entity with a radically contingent value that is never what it is. Money 'contains' and swallows this void to ensure that it can remain empty and function properly, unburdened by sentiment and concern. When holding a £1 coin that was issued in, say, 1997, we remain to some extent oblivious to the fact that this coin will have had a higher value at the time of issue; we might know, but we cannot see or even feel, that its function as a pure placeholder means that money stands apart from its identity as a material object and even from its specific numerical value. For neither the '£' nor the '1' embodied by the coin has a definite existence; every time the coin is exchanged, its value is renegotiated, meaning that with each use, it is a brand-new £1, despite also being a worn-out object with an identifiable age.

This inherent newness is confirmed by the peculiar way in which we treat money as an empirical object. Although the creases in a given bank note and the numerous signs of wear and tear which affect money like other material objects disclose that a given note or coin has a past life, possibly even a criminal one, although the object itself may have been implicated in hundreds of transactions, might have been used to buy sex or buy and snort drugs, it remains entirely unaffected by this past.[38] A second-hand coin is usually not perceived as such. Its past life is wiped out with every transaction for it was only ever a promise of value, never *primarily* a thing. The ruined object here merely affirms the atemporal, *non-ruinable*, abstract permanence of the note's function, which is maintained by the issuing bank itself. 'Because the natural form of money wears itself out', as Krämer elaborates, 'the continuity of its value can only be guaranteed *in practice* through the financial institution's promise to replace worn-out money for free'.[39] Even though our treatment of money as an *object* gestures towards its eternal newness, singularity and abstractness, money can only succeed and proliferate as a *mediator of value and exchange* because we cannot fully escape the immediate, empirical reality of holding a comfortingly heavy dark-golden coin that has been stubbornly, serenely and entirely truthfully making us believe that it has been worth exactly £1 since the very day it was minted. Ultimately, then, the material representation of monetary value (the note, bank balance, coin) protects us from the knowledge that the '1' the coin embodies is not a number in the traditional sense, for it is quantified only so it can stay 'indeterminate'. The coin's innocent truth is deceit. For although the bold claim 'ONE POUND' embossed onto its face automatically makes us believe otherwise, we cannot know what it is worth until it is spent on the marketplace.

The reality of the marketplace is indeed cold and godless. The credit that Defoe still saw growing 'insensibly' out of fair dealings to bless probity and offer itself as a reward that all can try to claim has long since been replaced by a vast computational infrastructure that can itself be instrumentalized to accrue money. Where probity and justice were the (idealized) law of credit, the latter's transmutation into a number in a register has liberated the law of equivalence in its purely abstract numerical form, which relates quantified values to one another by making certain prices rise and others fall. In the course of such transactions, the law of equivalence, by its very nature, does not know a right price, let alone a fair price for things, because equivalence is automatically achieved as soon as money changes hands. In pure terms of equivalence, it is inconsequential if I generously overpay or stick to a suggested price. I can aggressively use my market share and buying power to make a price fall to an insufferably low level and use advertising to raise it; I can even enforce a price by law or violence. Yet the moment money changes hands, equivalence (a perfect '=') is achieved, ownership has changed and money is again free to be spent (exactly *one time*) by its new owner. Even if this equivalence were later to be renegotiated, for instance in view of a court ruling, equivalence would have always been preserved, for merely the quantitative and not the qualitative relationship between money and what it buys is at issue. Fluctuations in the price, as Simmel reiterates, merely 'signify a change' in the relation of things or of one currency to one another; '[m]oney, viewed in terms of its pure function, has not changed its value'.[40] Walter Benjamin's suggestion that capitalism has a 'religious structure', that it is a 'pure religious cult, perhaps the most extreme there ever was' because it knows no 'special dogma, no theology', finds pragmatic confirmation here.[41] For it is a religion that limits itself to binding its believers through one thing alone: the circulation of money, the use of money in everyday life so it can act as an impersonal calculus that quantifies how one thing can be changed into another: 'An inferno rages in the soul of the commodity, for all the seeming tranquillity lent it by the price'.[42]

ROMANTIC IDEALISM RUINED: PHOTOGRAPHY AND THE TRAGIC INVERSION OF EQUIVALENCE

As already noted, Joseph Michael Gandy's painting of the Bank of England in ruins marked the completion of the monumental building designed by Sir John Soane, the surviving remnant of which still houses the institution that pioneered the dematerialization of money.[43] The motive behind the commission of this 'extraordinary vision' of 'the master work of Britain's premier architect rendered as a ruin' is usually seen as a desire to convey a sense of 'architectural integrity' and achievement.[44] As Christopher Woodward explains, 'in an age when ruin was regarded as inevitable this painting asserted survival, not oblivion: viewed in centuries to come the ruins of the Bank will be as impressive as those of ancient Rome'.[45] These readings foreground the contradictory relationship to time idealized ruins embody in Romanticism: although their crumbling stone makes the passage of time visible, the result of this corrosion looks 'timeless'. This tension between time and timelessness is the subject of a canonical reflection on the Romantic trope of ruins, written in 1907 by none other than Georg Simmel, seven years after the publication of *The Philosophy of Money*. 'It is the fascination of the ruin', as Simmel puts it, 'that here the work of man appears to us entirely as a product of nature. The same forces which give a mountain its shape through weathering, erosion, faulting, growth of vegetation, here do their work on old walls'.[46] The ruin, like a mountain, seems to have always been there.

> If now nature becomes once more completely mistress over it [the material the building is made of], she is merely exercising a right which until now has remained latent but which she never, so to speak, has renounced. For this reason, the ruin strikes us so often as tragic – but not as sad – because destruction here is not something senselessly coming from the outside but rather the realization of a tendency inherent in the deepest layer of existence of the destroyed.[47]

The ruin, as Simmel suggests here, confronts us with something that cannot be ruined itself: the laws of nature shaping matter. These decree that whatever is erected will eventually be pulled down and rearranged by nature's gravitating force. As such, the ruin visualizes temporality, a condition that is itself timeless and that affects any material reality, be it a building, a mountain, a coin or a living being. The ruin stages its own tragic inevitability. It makes us witness a self-fulfilling prophecy, which can be deferred only temporarily by the effort of preservation and reconstruction, or be usurped and accelerated by wanton destruction. Either way, nature humbles all that assumes a form from within the heart of

matter itself. This makes the Romantic ruin as much a symbol of defiance as of submission; 'it is tragic, but not sad'.

Although Gandy's painting of the Bank draws on these Romantic registers of meaning, we have began to foreground how the painting also acts as a portrayal of the non-dimensional, purely abstract space the Bank began to enshrine by issuing notes. This space without '*Whereness* or *Whenness*' is the un-ruinable 'void' that allows money to mediate exchange and act as the 'homogeneous in the heterogeneous'. When read as a depiction of money's speculative nature, the painting does not merely reveal the inherent, ruinous potential of money's indeterminate value; it also signals that this potential ruin is given a new form of existence in the world with the *construction* of the Bank. Ruin is here no longer the effect of erosion and decay, quite the opposite; as argued at length, money's 'deepest layer of existence' (in Simmel's terms) is the 'quasi'-cosmic, timeless law of equivalence, which money provides with a numerical calculus that allows things to be valued against one another. The timeless mathematical purity (x = x) of this law can *only* become operative as *a mathematical law* as money becomes a ubiquitous object in the world. We compared the Bank's discovery that money is valuable because it is 'a state approved mediator of value' to the discovery of gravity above, but Simmel's 'the Ruin' also alerts us to a crucial difference. The successive monetization of the marketplace and the ongoing technologization of money does not simply discover this law; it *establishes* a numerical calculus that automatically translates intangible and radically personal and sentimental attributions of value into numerically quantifiable interrelations.

Unlike gravity, equivalence as a mathematical operation does not happen 'by itself'. It is absolutely contingent on the existence of a numerical calculus that allows the x in a given equation (£x = 1 apple) to be the subject of ongoing speculation and renegotiation. Put otherwise, the '=' sign is the product of a machine that allows us to harness energy in the form of motivation from a quantified 'void' that can be exchanged for anything with a price. Advances in monetary technology harness this void as if it were a natural force, but rather than manipulating gravity's *constant* downward pull with artificial wings, this form of technological mastery amplifies and mobilizes the essential *inconsistency* of monetary value, the only constant of which is its speculative nature, as this value can only be established on the marketplace. It is a law that can only make us soar by enshrining ruin. As such, the painting of the Bank in ruins shows us how the supposedly timeless struggle between man and nature that Simmel's 'The Ruin' stages is tragically inverted as modernity unfolds. The forces that are leading to the proliferation of ruins today, whether because of foreclosed mortgages, globalization and automated production, environmental destruction, mechanized war or advances in medical technology, are not effected by nature itself, but by our own mastery over it.[48] Such man-made ruins act as tragic mementos that we have fallen into the abyss of speculation and impersonal calculation that Nietzsche's light shines into when illuminating the marketplace, with its appetite for growth, ever better products, which, mathematically speaking, cannot have a 'fair', 'just' or 'sustainable' price as they are worth always exactly what people are willing to pay. This circumstance, however, makes Gandy's painting all the more tragic. It confronts us not with our powerlessness before nature but with a powerlessness before the hyper-complexity of technological and corporate infrastructures and globalized markets that have grown since the onset of the Industrial Revolution (which the Bank helped finance).

The sense of paralysis in view of the hyper-complexity of financial and economic processes and the unprecedented concentrations of wealth and power that we are witnessing today brings us back to Kracauer's definition of reportage, for he assembles his mosaic from a number of incongruous perspectives to disclose and counteract the discrepancy that is opening between the mundane, same old world our perception presents us with and the changing reality this veneer of lived normality conceals. Viewed through the lens of Kracauer (as well as Benjamin's and Anders') engagements with the rise of consumer culture, our inability to imagine credible alternatives to capitalism – widely diagnosed as a 'crisis of imagination' – attains a very specific nuance, for this crisis is itself rooted in a crisis of perception that the limitations of photography can expose. Whereas a photograph 'can endow any soup can with cosmic significance', as Benjamin puts it, it 'cannot grasp a single one of the human connections in which it exists'. The enchanted, detached nature of the soup can in the advert distracts us from the hidden costs the existence of this commodity accrues. These remain hidden, as Benjamin continues by citing Brecht, because 'less than ever does the mere reflection of reality reveal anything about reality. A photograph of the Krupp works or the A.E.G. tells us next to nothing about these institutions. Actual reality has slipped into the functional. The reification of human relations – the factory say – means that they are no longer explicit. So something must in fact be *built up*, something artificial, posed'.[49] A photograph of a factory – or of the soup can it produces – imparts little about the complex realities we energize and tacitly approve of the moment we open a tin of soup. The photograph of the factory does not show us the corrosive effects of wage labour, global commodity markets and chains of supply, and does not show us the desires that need to be fabricated alongside products. These unsettling forces are concealed and placated by the tangible and concrete existence of the factory we can behold and the soothing goods we can buy. The growing discrepancy between perception and reality that Benjamin, Brecht and Kracauer begin to gesture towards is powerfully summed up by Günther

Anders: 'As nonsensical as this may sound, our perception has become a variety of phantasy'. It is 'too short sighted to show us the enormous', 'supra-liminal' dimensions and consequences of our way of life.[50]

Put more concretely, instead of seeing the chains of violence that the commodities on the marketplace are implicated in, instead of seeing the costs and ruinous effects of permanent growth, we see appealing products and enjoy warming soup. 'It is not in the wide land of imagination that escapists of today like to hide', Anders concludes, 'but in the ivory tower of perception'.[51] What is true of the factory seems to apply doubly to the Bank of England. Looking at the Bank or at a photograph of its façade tells us little about the contagious 'life' of money, the 'quickening' of trade and acceleration of progress that the dematerialization of monetary value effects, because such an image automatically shows us a false equation. It acts as the mirror of a deceptive normality that suggests that there is 'nothing' to see, or at least 'nothing worth thinking about'.[52] Like the coin in our hand or the credit card in our pocket, the photograph can conceal itself in the perfect visibility that makes it blend into the banality of the everyday.

Yet the very limitations of photography, its shallowness and tendency to meander along the surface of things, can also serve to 'unmask' and subvert the false sense certainty of our perception. The mosaic of perspectives that Kracauer envisages serves as an act of imagination that attempts to pierce the deceptive veneer of normality that the photographic image is so adept at consolidating. Wiblin's response to Gandy's painting, his use of ruined film that is prone to blurring, discoloration and other corruptions that translate into the exposed image, opens such a view. Like Gandy's painting itself, his photographs can offer visual cues that allow us to contemplate the untouchable and immaculate void the Bank protects. They do so not on the level of symbolism, but by amplifying the inherent artificiality of the photographic image itself. They forground the camera's role as a mediator between subject and image. They expose us to something that we usually miss and look straight through: the photographic film itself, which is part of a machine that does not just 'capture' an image but creates and fabricates it in the first place. At the risk of intellectualizing these photographs, their ghostly presence can help us conceptualize the hyper-complex technological infrastructures that mediate monetary value today. By showing us a shadow of the mediated nature of the photographic image (film, camera, darkroom, digital processing suite) the photographs display the link between the photograph and the wall; they disclose a process of equation, a machinic '=' sign which is subject to ongoing technological change. These images shot on the obsolete medium of analogue film point us in direction of a future that can be anticipated as little as Wiblin can predict what kind or quality of image his degraded films will actually produce (if they are not too ruined to actually support an image). By enshrining indeterminacy through a corrupted technological medium, Wiblin's photographic gesture exposes an uncanny parallel between the evolution of photographic and monetary technology to confront us with the absolute ruin that acts as the horizon of all speculation.

A famous passage from Roland Barthes's *Camera Lucida* can serve to reiterate the specificity of analogue film which we need to bear in mind to understand the stakes, namely, the direct link to the referent that the photographic negative represents, regardless of how manipulated, distorted and fake the image becomes while being processed: 'The photograph is literally an emanation of the referent. From a real body, which was there, proceed radiations which ultimately touch me, who am here; the duration of the transmission is insignificant; the photograph of the missing being, as Sontag says, will touch me like the delayed rays of a star'.[53] For Barthes and Sontag, the potentially awe-inspiring aura of photography is its ability to act as a material bridge to a sun that was shining in the past. Light reflecting off a weathered wall ruins the purity of a pristine photosensitive surface to leave an imprint that comes alight again when developed, even if the building has gone or has been altered or its walls repaired. The resulting image is automatically credible: it leaves us under the immediate impression that the wall was there. In a very literal sense, then, the photograph fulfils Defoe's idealized definition of credit, which we discussed in detail earlier. The photograph 'is a Consequence' of pointing a camera at an existing wall; it is 'not a Cause', it is 'the Effect of a Substance, not a Substance', it truly is 'the *Sun-shine*, not the Sun'.

Yet here we also come face to face with our man-made tragedy. For although we see the sun shining in the photograph, and although we believe, as the *phos* (light) in photography underlines, that photographic images are 'imprints' left by the sun or another source of light, the evolution of photographic technology begins to reveal that this sacred link to the referent is curiously contingent on the technological medium. The photograph's link to the actual wall is a mere product of the silver-based film that creates the image – it is not an inherent trait of photography. In a perfect parallel to the history of monetization, the photographic image begins to dematerialize and break with the precious silver that makes the photographic film a surface that physically records light. This leads both to the proliferation of the photographic image and to a multiplication of its uses, but it also heralds entirely new modes of photographic manipulation and image technology. With the advent of the digital photograph, as Mitchell elaborates on this break with the referent, 'the currency of

the great bank of nature has left the gold standard: images are no longer guaranteed as visual truth – or even as signifiers with stable meaning and value – and we endlessly print more of them'.[54] Today, the photograph is no longer the placeholder of something that necessarily exists. In fact, it has become a pixelated mosaic that can be altered at will or built up from scratch.

We do not mention Mitchell's analogy to the gold standard because of nostalgia for a lost past, in which money was still made of gold and photography still shot on film, or even better, a painting or a line on a cave wall. We seek to draw attention to the processes that happen beyond the photographic image we can see, for it is here that we can begin to understand why Mitchell insists that 'a digital image may look just like a photograph when it is published in a newspaper', but 'it actually differs as profoundly from a traditional photograph as does a photograph from a painting':

> Unlike silver-based photographic film the digital image does not consume scarce, non-renewable resources. It does not require a time-consuming and expensive chemical development process. It can be stored compactly, accessed by computer, manipulated freely, and transmitted to remote locations within seconds of creation. And, by virtue of its inherent manipulability, it always presents a temptation to duplicity.[55]

While describing the new possibilities digital image technology creates, Mitchell allows us to contemplate why the continuity of the placeholder function that both the photograph and money fulfil conceals the radical discontinuity of the actual technological registers involved in establishing an equation, for the digital image and digital number can do what none of their material equivalents ever could. If money and the camera both act as miraculous '=' signs, as machines that relate things to one another, then Mitchell's assessment of the digital image alerts us to the fact that the technological processes and interventions that are operative in establishing this equivalence can open possibilities that in actual fact fundamentally transform the nature of money and photograph. Even though digital money is in some sense identical to the primitive coin, the materialization of complex technological infrastructures that support the proliferation of money also begins to expose us to constellations of power and possibilities of manipulation and control that could never be supported by a gold coin or a primitive paper note. Jaron Lanier's polemical verdict on the world that has configured itself around computational finance, trading algorithms and hyper-complex investment and tax avoidance schemes acts as a reminder of just how far we have come since the Bank began to print

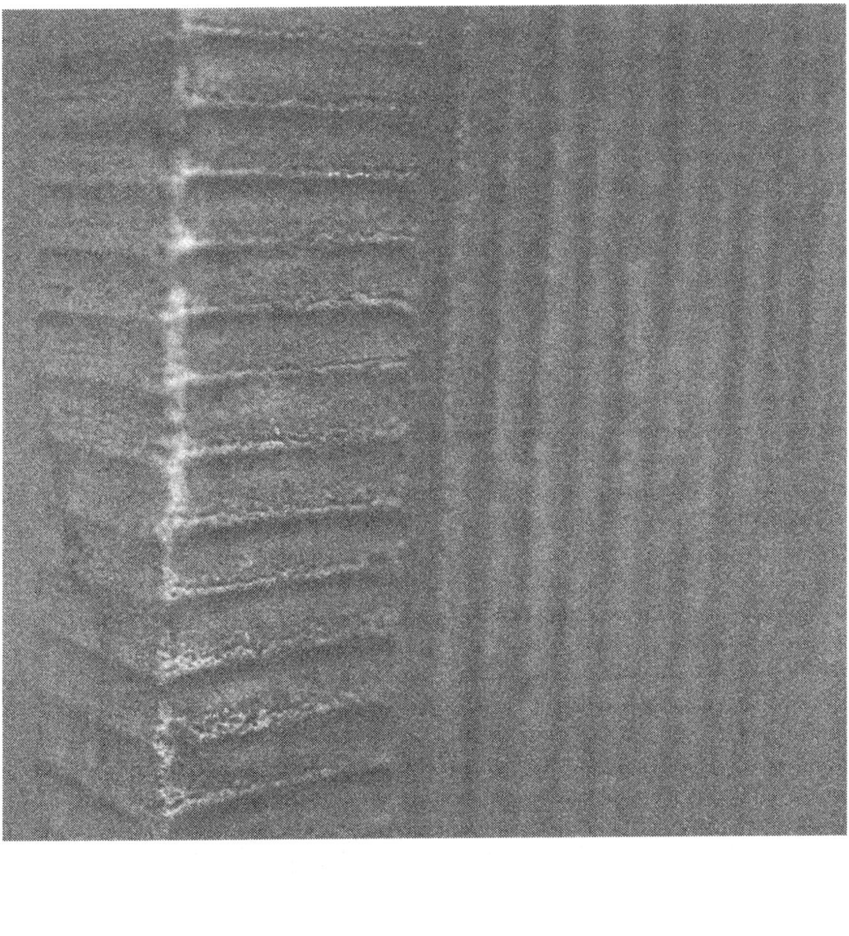

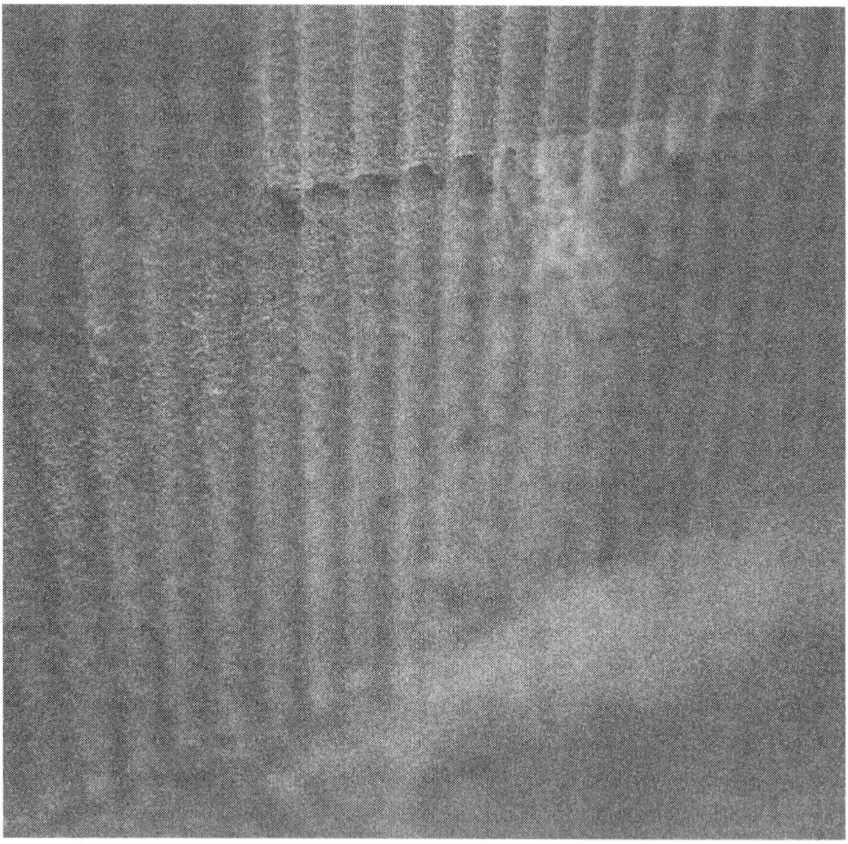

'dematerialized' notes. 'If you own the fastest computers with the most access to everyone's information, you can just search for money and it will appear'.[56] With this miraculous apparition of money out of a machine, we return to Georg Simmel's reflections on the infernal discrepancy between the power unleashed by the abstract mathematical purity of the law of equivalence and the concrete realm of human need, necessity and valuation that makes money so desirable and indispensably useful because it can mediate and organize the exchange of goods and labour.

The 'Analytical Part' of *The Philosophy of Money* opens with an alternative way of staging the opposition between nature and human artifice than the one we are offered in 'The Ruin'. Simmel introduces the law of equivalence by evoking 'the uniform law of existence' that everything is subject to: There is absolute 'equality before the law of nature': 'the constant sum of matter and energy, the convertibility of the most diverse phenomena into one another, transform the differences that are apparent at first sight into a general affinity, a universal equality' (*Philosophy of Money*, 61). The idealized Romantic ruin perfectly stages this timeless law. Although it is being reduced to rubble, this decay is merely a reflection of how energy rearranges matter into forms that will themselves be rearranged, interminably, until the end of all things. Our sentiment is moved because we find ourselves included in this 'universal equality', the 'constant sum of matter and energy' that all that is adds up to, despite being permanently rearranged. The very fact that we might be awed, feel sorrow or a sense of waste at the sight of a ruin, see in it a premonition of our own fate and bodily decay, also gives us an immediate explanation of why Simmel goes on to suggest that this law of universal equality is forever abstract and 'psychologically subordinate' to the law of equivalence from which money derives its value, for our emotive attachment is contingent on the fact that we see in the ruin more than just matter. The law of equivalence that regulates exchange, a law, which as Simmel insists is always a law that measures a *sacrifice* (*Philosophy of Money*, 87) – if I am not prepared to give something up, there cannot be exchange – can be operative only because we are 'not satisfied with this indifferent necessity that natural science assigns to objects'. Instead, Simmel continues, 'We arrange them in another order – an order of value – in which equality is completely eliminated'. In value relationships the 'fundamental quality is not uniformity, but difference' (*Philosophy of Money*, 61).

Without looking too deeply into the abyss of ontology Simmel opens up here, we can hold that the law of equivalence, and money as the objectification of this law, only works because we want and need things, and can be made to want and need some things more than others. Money has a use only because we negotiate and articulate, look for a common denominator not just when thinking about a price, but also when negotiating meaning, define what something 'is' (x = x). Without our incessant compulsion to seek equivalence (x = ?), without the experience of value and difference that animates such measurement, there would be no exchange, no fluctuation in our sensibility, no sensibility for the value of things, no awe at beauty, no sense. This makes the law of equivalence the universal constant of affection. However, as we have tried to show in this piece, it is only with the invention of money and its successive dematerialization that this law arrives at a numerical calculus. With this, we are no longer merely subject to the idealized law of nature, which Simmel presents us with in 'The Ruin', but also to an autonomous 'physik' (Defoe), a timeless, indifferent, quasi-cosmic law that is operative wherever money acts as a mediator that brings things into contact only by holding them apart. By putting the value of things into *krisis*, that is, into *something to be decided* through numerical calculation, by acting as an abhorrent mirror reflecting the possibility that nothing is 'sacred', that is, beyond sacrifice, untouchable by quantification and without a price, a new tragedy begins. The Romantic opposition between art and nature's indifference now lies in ruins itself, for we find ourselves confronted by our own technological mastery and money's artificial 'indifference', released, channelled and built up solely by human art.

What Goodchild calls 'the murder of God', the growing cultural significance of money, its dematerialization through 'mechanical reproduction', leads to the intensification of trade and the incessant acceleration of innovation. The more things there are to buy, and the better these things become, the more *perfect*, useful and valuable money is also, for its value is only ever borrowed against the marketplace. The value of a given amount of money, as Simmel puts it, is 'equal to the value of any object for which it might be exchanged plus the value of *free choice* between innumerable other objects' that might be bought (*Philosophy of Money*, 228–29; emphasis added). This equation is at the heart of the secular world, the credo of which is the delusional fantasy that *we can choose what to buy*, and buy whatever we can afford, research, fund, imagine and ultimately create. Photography, which can already today present us with credible photorealist images of techno-scientific utopias, merely serves to accentuate how the absent referent of such images is rapidly playing catch-up to put itself in the frame. The *krisis* – 'separation', power of 'choice' and 'judgement' – that money installs between the things it values against one another has long since wandered into the heart of things themselves. Stoked by the logic of the marketplace, which demands new and better goods every day and which needs to be kept alive through consumption, things are being re-arranged, perpetually altered, enhanced and reproduced in the quest for new markets. Viewed with the 'indifferent necessity that natural science assigns to objects', every bond – be it human or atomic – exists only because it can be split.

Ray Brassier, in a recent defence of accelerationist politics, mobilizes nature's 'indifference' to call for a world in which nothing is sacred, as 'there is no reason to assume a predetermined limit to what we can achieve or to the ways in which we can transform ourselves and our world. But of course, this is precisely what theological propriety and empiricist good sense jointly denounce as dangerous hubris'.[57] Perhaps the image of ruin evoked in this piece can serve to illustrate that such scientism and unbridled faith in progress merely serves to reiterate that what matters is not merely the target condition, a techno-utopian existence in which all needs are instantaneously met, but the social and environmental realities that we are creating in its pursuit. Our crisis today, as we might echo Anders, does not affect utopian thought in the ordinary sense; it is not 'that [we] are unable to actually produce' the better world we 'are able to visualize'. Our problem, rather, is that 'we are unable to visualize what we are actually producing'.[58] With this inversion of utopia we borrow the eyes of Walter Benjamin's angel of history to cast one last glance at Joseph Michael Gandy's *Vision of the Bank of England in Ruins* and the void the incorporation of the Bank of England so inadvertently began to enshrine. Not bound by earthly perception, it confronts us with the invisible 'Not', the secret life of money and the all-prevailing, creative force of ruin that modernity is so ingeniously summoning forth:

> There is a picture by Klee called Angelus Novus. It shows an angel who seems about to move away from something he stares at. His eyes are wide, his mouth is open, his wings are spread. This is how the angel of history must look. His face is turned toward the past. Where a chain of events appears before us, he sees one single catastrophe, which keeps piling wreckage upon wreckage and hurls it at its feet. The angel would like to stay, awaken the dead, and make whole what has been smashed. But a storm is blowing from Paradise and has caught in his wings; it is so strong that the angel can no longer close them. This storm drives him irresistibly into the future, to which his back is turned, while the pile of debris before him grows towards the sky. What we call progress is *this* storm.[59]

NOTES

* All uncaptioned images are by Ian Wiblin from the series *BANK*, 2010–2016 (colour photographs, 89; 92-3; 113-118, and Polaroids, 107-8).

1. Daniel Defoe, *Review of the State of the British Nation* 106, 16 October 1707 (London: s. n.).

2. Eva Schumann-Bacia, *John Soane and the Bank of England* (London: Lingman, 1991), 21.

3. Daniel Defoe, *An Essay upon Publick Credit: Being an Inquiry How the Publick Credit Comes to Depend upon the Change of the Ministry, or the Dissolutions of Parliaments; and Whether It Does so or No* (London: Printed, and Sold by the Book-sellers, 1710), 7. We would not have discovered Defoe's essay without Valerie Hamilton and Martin Parker's brilliant book *Daniel Defoe and the Bank of England* (Winchester: Zero, 2016). Hamilton and Parker briefly discusses this essay (55), and we are here also indebted to their reflections 'on the projected', that is, spectral nature of the Bank (esp. 155–59) and their suggestive opening contemplation that 'the Bank of England, nowadays materialized as timeless rusticated stone, was originally no more than some conversations in a coffeehouse concerning a speculative merchant bank' (5).

4. Schumann-Bacia, *John Soane*, 32; 77.

5. Schumann-Bacia, *John Soane*, 42.

6. See Georg Simmel, *The Philosophy of Money*, trans. David Frisby (London: Routledge, 2011), 198.

7. '[I]t is the essence of credit that the probability of realising it is never one hundred percent, no matter how closely it may approach it'. For Simmel, this uncertainty at the heart of credit 'is' not just the essence of credit, but of money itself: 'The possibility that the claim that money represents will not be satisfied confirms the character of money as mere credit'. Simmel, *Money*, 192.

8. Sybille Krämer, *Medium, Messenger, Transmission: An Approach to Media Philosophy*, trans. Anthony Enns (Amsterdam: Amsterdam University Press, 2015), 111. We wish to thank Jernej Markelj for drawing our attention to the work of Sybille Krämer, which was instrumental to the reading offered here.

9. Liddell and Scott's *Greek-English Lexicon*, s. v. *κρίσις*.

10. Siegfried Kracauer, *The Salaried Masses: Duty and Distraction in Weimar Germany*, trans. Quintin Hoare (London: Verso, 1998), 32.

11. See David Wills, *Inanimation: Theories of Inorganic Life* (Minneapolis: University of Minnesota Press, 2016), ix. Wills's notion of 'inanimation' mobilizes the obsolete verb 'to inanimate', 'to enliven, quicken' to sublate the modern adjective that means lifeless.

12. Ian Wiblin, 'Photography, Performance, Ruin: Performing Photography in Site of Architecture', *Performance Research* 20.3 (2015): 128.

13. William Mitchell, *The Reconfigured Eye: Visual Truth in the Post-Photographic Era* (Cambridge, MA: MIT Press, 1992), 4.

14. Krämer, *Messenger*, 114. 'There is only money', as Krämer elaborates, 'if something is accepted as money', which means that the value of money needs to be guaranteed: 'An object only becomes money when it is enthroned as money by a central institution' (113).

15. Krämer, *Messenger*, 114.

16. Krämer, *Messenger*, 114.

17. 'Money is totally indifferent to the objects [it can acquire], because it is separated from them by the fact of exchange. What money mediates is not the possession of an object but the exchange of objects' (See Simmel, *Money*, 226).

18. Krämer, *Messenger*, 113.

19. Krämer, *Messenger*, 113.

20. Defoe, *Review*, 16 October 1707.

21. Gillian Darley, *John Soane: An Accidental Romantic* (New Haven, CT: Yale University Press, 1999), 146.

22. For information about the exhibition *BANK*, October–November 2015, and 'Speculation in Ruins – a Conversation between Ian Wiblin and Christopher John Müller' see http://www.schwarzwaldallee.ch/index.php/bank/ (last accessed 27 February 2017). The present text is by Christopher Müller and was written in a dialogue with Ian Wiblin. See also Wiblin, 'Photography, Performance, Ruin'.

23. See Michael Naas, *Miracle and Machine: Jacques Derrida and the Two Sources of Religion, Science, and the Media* (New York: Fordham University Press, 2012).

24. See Jacques Derrida, 'Faith and Knowledge: The Two Sources of "Religion" at the Limits of Reason Alone', trans. Samuel Weber, in *Acts of Religion*, ed. and intr. Gil Anidjar (London: Routledge, 2010): 'The temptation of knowing, the temptation of knowledge, is to believe not only that one knows what one knows (which wouldn't be too serious), but also to believe that one knows what knowledge is, that is, free, structurally, of belief or of **faith** – of the fiduciary or of trustworthiness' (68; bold in the original).

25. See Philip Goodchild, *Capitalism and Religion: The Price of Piety* (London: Routledge, 2002). All references are provided in the text.

26. Friedrich Nietzsche, *The Gay Science*, trans. Josefine Nauckhoff, ed. Bernard Williams (Cambridge: Cambridge University Press, 2001), 119–20.

27. See H. V. Bowen, 'The Bank of England during the Long Eighteenth Century, 1694–1820', in *The Bank of England 1694*–1994, ed. Richard Roberts and David Kynaston (Oxford: Oxford University Press, 1995), 1.

28. As cited by Bowen, 'The Bank of England', 3.

29. For an excellent account of the turbulent early history of the Bank, see Sandra Sherman, *Finance and Fictionality in the Early Eighteenth Century: Accounting for Defoe* (Cambridge: Cambridge University Press, 1996).

30. As Bowen goes on to discuss, in 1776, Adam Smith had already famously stated in the *Wealth of Nations* that the Bank 'acts not as an ordinary bank, but as a great engine of state', so much so that Smith deems that 'the stability of the Bank of England is equal to that of the British Government' ('The Bank of England', 9–13). A comprehensive overview of the evolution of the Bank and its relationship to the British State can be accessed on the website of the Bank of England: http://www.bankofengland.co.uk/about/Pages/history/default.aspx (last accessed 30 December 2016).

31. Defoe, *publick credit*, 9.

32. Defoe, *publick credit*, 10.

33. Defoe's account of the usefulness of money in the form of credit provides a vivid illustration of Goodchild's suggestion that trade was restricted by the limited amount of coins: 'The Course of Trade being thus turned, from exchanging of Goods for Goods, or *Delivering* and *Taking*, to *Selling* and *Paying*, all the Bargains in the World are now stated upon the Foot of *a Price* in Money; and tho' it be at

any Time an Exchange of *Goods* for *Goods*, yet even those Goods are on either side rated at a *Price* in Money. Tho' this was a great Assistant to Trade, and gave a liberty to the increase of Commerce more than ever it had before, *yet* such was the great increase of Trade, *that it even over-run the Money itself* [emphasis added], and a all the Specie in the World could not answer the Demand, or be ready just at Time, Trade called for it. *This occasioned*, That when *A* Bought more Goods of *B* than *A* had Money to pay for; and *B* having no Need of any Goods that *A* had to Sell; it behoved, that *A* should leave his Goods with *B* for a certain Time, in which *A* was to provide the Money for the said Goods: And this was done, both from the Occasion *B* had to sell his Goods, the Occasion *A* had to buy them, and the Opinion *B* had of *A*'s Integrity and Ability for Payment' (Defoe, *publick credit*, 8–9).

34. Defoe, *publick credit*, 9.

35. Defoe, *publick credit*, 15.

36. See Defoe, *publick credit*, 16–17: 'The *Honour*, the *Probity*, the *exact*, punctual *Management*, which has raised our *Credit* to the pitch it is now arriv'd at, has not been merely the Great Wheel in *the Nations Clockwork*, that turn'd about the Treasure, but the Great Spring that turn'd about that Wheel, and this is the QUEEN and PARLIAMENT. *The one*, the Spring (*still keeping to the Allegory*) that gives Motion or Life to the whole; *the other*, the Balance or Pendulum, that regulates that Motion, keeps it true to, and exact in the performance of the General Work, (*viz.*) the equal and punctual dividing the smallest measures of Time'.

37. Defoe, *Review*.

38. As Hartmut Winkler elaborates, 'chemical analysis has actually shown that micro-traces of heroin and cocaine can be found on 90% of European bank notes. A great proportion of money is thus undoubtedly corrupted, but this only seems to have a small impact on the way money changes hands every day'. See Hartmut Winkler, *Diskursökonomie: Versuch über die innere Ökonomie der Medien* (Frankfurt: Suhrkamp, 2004), 46; my translation. The curious discrepancy between money as a material object and its economic value is the subject of Edgar Allen Poe's witty poem 'Epigram for Wall Street', which is worth reproducing here:

> I'll tell you a plan for gaining wealth,
> Better than banking, trade or leases –
> Take a bank note and fold it up,
> And then you will find your money in *creases*!
> This wonderful plan, without danger or loss,
> Keeps your cash in your hands, where nothing can trouble it;
> And every time that you fold it across,
> 'Tis as plain as the light of the day that you *double* it.
> See *The Great Western Advertiser,* Bristol, 13 April 1844, 1.

39. Krämer, *Messenger*, 115.

40. Simmel, *Money*, 130.

41. Walter Benjamin, 'Capitalism as Religion', trans. Chad Kautzer, in *The Frankfurt School on Religion*, ed. Eduardo Mendieta (New York: Routledge, 2005), 259.

42. Walter Benjamin, *The Arcades Project*, as cited by David Michael Kleinberg Levi in *Gestures of Ethical Life: Reading Hölderlin's Question of Measure after Heidegger* (Stanford, CA: Stanford University Press, 2005), 151.

43. In the 1920s, the ruin the painting depicts was actualised to make room for a further expansion of the Bank. The screen wall was left intact, but the interior of Soane's building was demolished: 'The great white hulk that now telescopes up above the height of the wall', as Wiblin elaborates, 'arose unsentimentally out of Soane's architecture that was laid waste in the name of progress'. See Wiblin, 'Photography, Performance, Ruin', 129.

44. Christopher Evans, 'Megalithic Follies: Soane's "Druidic Remains" and the Display of Monuments', *Journal for Material Culture* 5.3 (2000): 348.

45. Christopher Woodward, 'Catalogue', in *Visions of Ruin: Architectural Fantasies & Designs* (London: Sir John Soane's Museum, 1999), 49. The cataclysmic void that we are projecting onto the painting can be softened by a redeeming anecdote. According to a guard in the Sir John Soane's Museum, Soane may have commissioned the painting to save his friend Gandy from bankruptcy, which gives the ruin a very particular significance.

46. Georg Simmel, 'The Ruin', trans. David Kettler, *The Hudson Review* 11.3 (1958): 381.

47. Simmel, 'Ruin', 382.

48. We take our cue from Günther Anders here, who wrote the following response to Simmel's 'the Ruin' into his diary upon returning to the ruins of Berlin after the Second World War: 'Like a sunset glow, the ruin was seen as opening a perspective on the fundamentally futile struggle of freedom against nature's gravity. It may be melancholic, but like the evening sun, the ruin is "beautiful", yes, even doubly so, because it belongs both into the realm of artistic beauty and natural beauty. How naïve, how worth of envy this pre-war philosophy is today! This relegation of dialectic into the opposition of freedom and necessity, humanity and nature! . . . No, these walls have not decayed. . . . These ruins were produced, they are works of man. If they too have fallen to "nature", then only because we have conjured up its elemental forces to ruin our own creations with nature's aid'. Günther Anders, 'Ruinen heute', in *Tagebücher und Gedichte* (Munich: C.H. Beck, 1985), 214–60 (246–47); my translation.

49. See Walter Benjamin, 'A Small History of Photography', in *One-Way Street*, trans. Edmund Jephcott and Kingsley Shorter (London: Verso, 1997), 255.

50. See Günther Anders, *Besuch im Hades* (Munich: C.H. Beck, 1996), 39–40; my translation.

51. Günther Anders, 'Theses for the Atomic Age', *The Massachusetts Review* 3.3 (Spring 1962): 497. For a detailed discussion of Kracauer and Anders's perspectives on unregistered violence and the limits of perception see Christopher Müller, 'Part III: Anaesthetic Lives', in *Prometheanism: Technology, Digital Culture and Human Obsolescence* (London: Rowman & Littlefield International, 2016), 121–64.

52. See Günther Anders, 'Die Antiquiertheit des Aussehens', in *Die Antiquiertheit des Menschen 2* (Munich: C.H. Beck, 2002), 34–37.

53. Roland Barthes, *Camera Lucida: Reflections on Photography*, trans. Richard Howard (New York: Farrar, Straus and Giroux, 1981), 80–81.

54. Mitchell, *Eye*, 57.

55. Mitchell, *Eye*, 19.

56. See Jaron Lanier, 'Money as Seen through One Computer Scientist's Eyes', in *Who Owns the Future?* (London: Penguin, 2013), 27.

57. Ray Brassier, 'Prometheanism and its Critics', in *The Accelerationist Reader*, ed. Robin Mackay and Armen Avanessian (Berlin: Merve, 2014), 471–72.

58. Anders, 'Theses', 496.

59. Walter Benjamin, as cited in Michael Löwy, *Fire Alarm: Reading Walter Benjamin's 'On the Concept of History'*, trans. Chris Turner (London: Verso, 2016), 60 ff. See also Chapter 5 'Naming that Mechanical Angel' of Wills's *Inanimation*.

BIBLIOGRAPHY

ANDERS, Günther. *Besuch im Hades: Auschwitz und Breslau 1966; Nach 'Holocaust' 1979*. Munich: C.H. Beck, 1996.

ANDERS, Günther. 'Die Antiquiertheit des Aussehens'. In *Die Antiquiertheit des Menschen 2: Über die Zerstörung des Lebens im Zeitalter der dritten industriellen Revolution*. Munich: C.H. Beck, 2002 [1980]. 34–37.

ANDERS, Günther. 'Ruinen heute'. In *Tagebücher und Gedichte*. Munich: C.H. Beck, 1985, 214–60.

ANDERS, Günther. 'Theses for the Atomic Age'. *The Massachusetts Review* 3.3 (Spring 1962): 493–505.

BARTHES, Roland. *Camera Lucida: Reflections on Photography*. Translated by Richard Howard. New York: Farrar, Straus and Giroux, 1981.

BENJAMIN, Walter. 'A Small History of Photography'. Translated by Edmund Jephcott and Kingsley Shorter. *One-Way Street*. London: Verso, 1997. 240–58.

BENJAMIN, Walter. 'Capitalism as Religion'. Translated by Chad Kautzer. In *The Frankfurt School on Religion*. Edited by Eduardo Mendieta. New York: Routledge, 2005. 259–62.

BOWEN, H. V. 'The Bank of England during the Long Eighteenth Century, 1694–1820'. In *The Bank of England 1694–1994*. Edited by Richard Roberts and David Kynaston. Oxford: Oxford University Press, 1995. 1–19.

BRASSIER, Ray. 'Prometheanism and Its Critics'. In *The Accelerationist Reader*. Edited by Robin Mackay and Armen Avanessian. Berlin: Merve, 2014. 467–87.

DARLEY, Gillian. *John Soane: An Accidental Romantic*. New Haven, CT: Yale University Press, 1999.

DEFOE, Daniel. *An Essay upon publick credit: Being an Inquiry How the publick credit Comes to Depend upon the Change of the Ministry, or the Dissolutions of Parliaments; and Whether It Does so or No*. London: Printed, and Sold by the Book-sellers, 1710.

DEFOE, Daniel. *Review of the State of the British Nation 106* (16 October 1707). London: s. n.

DERRIDA, Jacques. 'Faith and Knowledge: The Two Sources of "Religion" at the Limits of Reason Alone'. Translated by Samuel Weber. In *Acts of Religion*. Edited and with an Introduction by Gil Anidjar. New York and London: Routledge, 2002. 42–101.

EVANS, Christopher. 'Megalithic Follies: Soane's "Druidic Remains" and the Display of Monuments'. *Journal for Material Culture* 5.3 (2000): 347–66.

GOODCHILD, Philip. *Capitalism and Religion: The Price of Piety*. London: Routledge, 2002.

HAMILTON, Valerie and Martin PARKER. *Daniel Defoe and the Bank of England: The Dark Arts of Projectors*. Winchester: Zero, 2016.

KLEINBERG LEVI, David Michael. *Gestures of Ethical Life: Reading Hölderlin's Question of Measure after Heidegger*. Stanford, CA: Stanford University Press, 2005.

KRACAUER, Siegfried. *The Salaried Masses: Duty and Distraction in Weimar Germany*. Translated by Quintin Hoare. London: Verso, 1998.

KRÄMER, Sybille. *Medium, Messenger, Transmission: An Approach to Media Philosophy*. Translated by Anthony Enns. Amsterdam: Amsterdam University Press, 2015.

LANIER, Jaron. *Who Owns the Future?* London: Penguin, 2013. 25–31.

LÖWY, Michael. *Fire Alarm: Reading Walter Benjamin's 'On the Concept of History'*. Translated by Chris Turner. London: Verso, 2016.

MITCHELL, William. *The Reconfigured Eye: Visual Truth in the Post-Photographic Era*. Cambridge, MA: MIT Press, 1992.

MÜLLER, Christopher John. *Prometheanism: Technology, Digital Culture and Human Obsolescence*. London: Rowman & Littlefield International, 2016.

MÜLLER, Christopher John and Ian WIBLIN. 'BANK: Speculation in Ruins'. http://www.schwarzwaldallee.ch/files/Interview_BANK.pdf. Last accessed 27 February 2017.

NAAS, Michael. *Miracle and Machine: Jacques Derrida and the Two Sources of Religion, Science, and the Media*. New York: Fordham University Press, 2012.

NIETZSCHE, Friedrich. *The Gay Science*. Translated by Josefine Nauckhoff. Edited by Bernard Williams. Cambridge: Cambridge University Press, 2001. 119–20.

POE, Edgar Allen. 'Epigram for Wall Street'. *The Great Western Advertiser, Bristol* (13 April 1844): 1.

SCHUMANN-BACIA, Eva. *John Soane and the Bank of England*. London: Lingman, 1991.

SHERMAN, Sandra. *Finance and Fictionality in the Early Eighteenth Century: Accounting for Defoe*. Cambridge: Cambridge University Press, 1996.

SIMMEL, Georg. *The Philosophy of Money*. Translated by David Frisby. London: Routledge, 2011.

SIMMEL, Georg. 'The Ruin'. Translated by David Kettler. *The Hudson Review* 11.3 (1958): 380–85.

WIBLIN, Ian. 'Photography, Performance, Ruin: Performing Photography in Site of Architecture'. *Performance Research* 20.3 (2015): 126–34.

WILLS, David. *Inanimation: Theories of Inorganic Life*. Minneapolis: University of Minnesota Press, 2016.

WINKLER, Hartmut. *Diskursökonomie: Versuch über die innere Ökonomie der Medien*. Frankfurt a.M.: Suhrkamp, 2004.

WOODWARD, Christopher. 'Catalogue'. In *Visions of Ruin: Architectural Fantasies & Designs*. Compiled by The Soane Gallery. London: Sir John Soane's Museum, 1999. 18–51.

Chapter 5

Seeing is believing

Looking at the gold standard

Nicky Marsh

It is surprising that we have no sustained cultural history of the ending of the Bretton Woods agreement, the moment in which Nixon disconnected money from gold and ushered in a new economic moment in America in the early 1970s.[1] It is surprising because the event is routinely named as a foundational moment in post-war histories of America, and it is surprising because visual representations of it can be found in the most iconic and visible of public places – in satirical political cartoons, in graphic and fine art – even popular children's cartoons of the period feature anxieties about the substitution of real gold with a counterfeit, with mere paper. These visual representations of such an over-determined event are important, I want to suggest, for indicating both what is missing from our historical understanding of the moment and for what enlarged methodologies we need to best respond to it.

I want to explore the visual representations of this moment because of the ways in which they complicate the prevalent cultural narrative for this moment in which it serves as a shorthand for a truncated version of the post-modern that involves a loss of meaning, an intensification of money's alienation and a debilitating ascendancy of abstraction. My argument, most simply put, is that it was not merely a crisis in meaning but also the emergence of a new kind of real, a market fundamentalism, that culture was responding to in this moment and that we can best understand this through combining a visual archive with a methodology specifically attuned to *seeing* what it suggests.

The argument relies on three stages. The first reviews the theoretical understanding of money prevalent in literary and cultural studies through the approaches that other disciplines, particularly economic history and anthropology, have developed. The second draws on these approaches in order to explore the ways in which the political cartoons and art of this period suggest a vocabulary for understanding how the political debates of this period were concerned not with the epistemological efficacy of the dollar but with its political negotiation of the radically changing relationship between state and market. The third, by way of a conclusion, examines the way in which these relations were explored in fine art, concluding with a new reading of the work of Andy Warhol, who, I argue, was not simply acquiescent to the post-modern logic of the commodity that emerged in the early 1970s: he was ironically destructive of its assumptions.

The simplest of examples serves well as an introductory example here: an episode of *The Scooby-Doo Show* from 1976 features the gang locked into Capitol Hill's 'Splitsonian' museum during a dramatically rainy night in which they discover that the mannequins dressed as the traitors of the American Revolution – Benedict Arnold, William Dumont and Major John Andrew – are actually counterfeiters, who have tunneled under the museum and are using its dollar plates to print new money.[2] The plan is unravelled, the traitors unmasked, the gang self-congratulatory. Yet the federal agents who appear for the arrest that inevitably attends the moment of unmasking reveal that the threat that the traitorous figures had represented had itself been a false one: the dollar bills about to be smuggled from the museum lacked the signature that would turn them into real money and the gang had been attempting to make away with only worthless paper.

The cartoon neatly encompasses a familiar history for American money. It represents counterfeiting as monumentally unpatriotic, as nothing less than the betrayal of the American independence which was both fought over and gained via the printing of paper money.[3] The predictable Manichaeism of this plot dissolves in the moment of its resolution when it is recognised that the dollar bill is not actually real money, its value is derived only from a signature. It is thus easy to read the conclusion through the 'Nixon Shock', the moment in which money lost its material value and contributed to what David Harvey influentially described as 'a more general crisis of representation. The central value system, to which capitalism has always appealed to validate and gauge its actions, is dematerialised and shifting, time horizons are collapsing, and it is hard to tell exactly what space we are in when it comes to assessing causes and effects, meanings or values'.[4]

The episode was perhaps more knowledgeable about the contemporary debates about money than its form would suggest: by locating itself in the 'Splitsonian' Museum the show appears to nod to the 'Smithsonian Agreement' of December 1971 that had allowed for the devaluation of the dollar and had attempted to realign currencies and preserve a set of fixed exchange rates outside of the gold standard. If so, the show was not the first to note the irony of the fact that the Bretton Woods agreement was finally relegated to history from within the nation's monument to its own heritage. Citibank's ever-loquacious Walt Wriston, for example, had noted four years earlier in a speech given to bankers, 'The Global Attic', that 'irreverent souls have dubbed the Smithsonian Institution America's attic, for into it we have poured all the assorted memorabilia of this country. After the recent meeting of the Group of Ten Finance Ministers in the Romanesque common room of the Smithsonian to design a new international financial package, the ministers left behind monetary memorabilia'.[5] Yet, whereas the makers of *Scooby-Doo* use the museum setting to imply that the creation of paper money was a kind of betrayal of America, Wriston does the opposite; he uses the coincidence to celebrate the progress that floating exchange rates bring, suggesting that museums are 'treasure houses of the past; they are places where people go to see beautiful or valuable objects or to see things which were once important, but no longer have a useful function in our society'. For Wriston, the gold-standard and fixed-exchange rates are now relics, and it is entirely fitting that they should 'take their place beside Eli Whitney's cotton gin, the Spirit of St. Louis and rocks from the moon' because they are not only irrelevant but, in a key and recurring neoliberal gesture, they are not even real: 'Perhaps we should be hanging up a suit of the Emperor's clothes in the costume gallery at the Smithsonian because the world perceived that those twin vestments of our monetary system existed for a period long after they had ceased to have any reality'.[6]

Although the two accounts of this moment turn on the same irony, their views of money could not be more different. The use of paper money causes an odd disruption to the narrative resolution of *Scooby-Doo*, a resolution in which order must be restored and any attempt at duplicity – evident in the recurring stories featuring disguises, forgeries, concealments and counterfeiting – successfully routed. In this episode this moment is deferred, the return to the real is problematised, as the ghost at the centre of the plot is not the disguised janitor but the dollar itself, which was, as Marc Shell has noted in a very different context, already a kind of 'phantom' in America, as 'understanding the relationship between substance and sign was complicated by the known existence and practical monetary validity of counterfeit notes (i.e. illegal copies of legitimate ghost moneys)'.[7]

For Wriston, conversely, the reality of this paper dollar lies in the fundamentalist truth of the market and the gold-dollar standard against which it can be compared is not only anachronistic but, actually, fantastic. Wriston elsewhere described the 'outworn doctrine of the controlled economy' as 'a manifestation of the persistence of illusion over reality'[8] and the assumption that fixed exchange rates were connected to post-war prosperity as 'no more than a polite fiction' because, actually, such fixed exchange rates had never actually existed and were but 'a myth' that we 'have long paid lip service to'.[9] For Wriston, as for Milton Friedman, the gold standard was a fig leaf for the state intervention that fixed exchange rates represented and thus both are a kind of autocratic delusion. The moment of unmasking, the moment in which the real is announced, ironically *requires* paper money: it alone carries the disciplined reality of the market and is closer to the laissez-faire logic of the nineteenth-century gold standard than the post-war Bretton Woods order of fixed exchange rates. It is hard to overestimate how influential Wriston's version of reality was at this moment. He had been dubbed the most important man in American finance, more powerful than even the chairman of the Federal Reserve,[10] and his hyperbolic rhetoric is clear that he is forming 'a new world, and the fact is, the information standard is more draconian that any gold standard. . . . For the first time in history the politicians can't stop it'.[11]

What politicians couldn't 'stop' was, of course, the dominance of American capitalist imperialism which was, as Leo Panitch and Sam Gindin have argued, secured rather than abandoned or weakened by the ending of the Bretton Woods agreement as national self-interest was subsequently defined 'in terms of acting not only on behalf of its own capitalist class but also on behalf of the extension and reproduction of global capitalism'.[12] This was the moment, Christine Marazzi has also suggested, that tied 'the fate of American workers to the *risks* of American capital' and relaunched 'the *material* expansion of *American* capital in the world economy, eliminating all of the spaces in which the money created by the Federal Reserve was *no longer* transforming itself into capital'.[13]

Yet the analysis of what was occurring in money in the mid-1970s emerging from literary and cultural studies was much more attuned to the anxiety represented by *Scooby-Doo*, to the loss of the real, than to the ebullient assertion of the new imperial real being declared by Walt Wriston. Marc Shell's description of paper money as both legitimate and ghostly, for example, is commensurate with his elucidation of a philosophical tradition in which money is analogous to language, is a 'system of tropes' and also an ' "internal" participant in the logical or semiological organization of language, which itself refers to a system of tropes'.[14] This conception of money as a token of exchange comparable to language depends upon the ancient Greek division between barter, in which 'a property was a property whose transfer was seen by others' and money, which is 'a property whose transfer is not seen'.[15]

The theoretical assumptions of literary studies have broadly followed in this tradition for the past two decades, accepting the necessary invisibility of the universal equivalent. The impossibility of re-materialising that which has been abstracted and rendered anonymous was apparent not only in 'New Economic' criticism but also in subsequent historical and theoretical work. It was exemplified by Slavoj Žižek's exploration of the shared qualities of money and the unconscious, as both are constituted by concealment. For Žižek this means that the deconstructive moment of critique, the moment when we look at money and realize what it is (either the embodiment of human labour or a mere piece of paper), is impossible. We 'know very well', he suggests, that money 'suffers the effects of use, that its material body changes through time, but in the social *effectivity* of the market we none the less *treat* coins as if they consist 'of an immutable substance, a substance over which time has no power, and which stands in antithetic contrast to any substance found in nature'.[16] Mary Poovey's account of the development of the credit economy in eighteenth- and nineteenth-century Britain uses a very different and much more historically precise register but also contends that the effective functioning of money depends upon its naturalisation, the fact that we can no longer *read* it as a text, 'money has become so familiar that its writing has seemed to disappear and it has seemed to lose its history as (various forms of) writing'. It is only in moments of 'fiscal crisis', Poovey suggests, that it 'becomes visible', and this very visibility is destructive to the functioning of the text as money, and it 'can jeopardize the prevailing model of value, the conventions that facilitate trust, and the signs that convey creditworthiness'.[17]

The alternative tradition emerging from anthropology and recent economic history suggests that the post-Saussurian structuralist approaches to money, that understand 'language' to be 'interior to the money form, and vice versa', fail to comprehend the significance of both its social and material meanings.[18] Bill Maurer's overview of the field suggests two alternative methodologies that are particularly useful in exploring how looking at representations of money allows us to re-imagine the cultural and economic politics of this moment. The first explores the role money plays as a creature of both the market and the state. Keith Hart's seminal anthropological analysis foregrounds the 'two sides' of money's 'coin':

> on one side is 'heads' – the symbol of the political authority which minted the coin; on the other side is 'tails' – the precise specification of the amount the coin is worth as payment in exchange. One side reminds us that states underwrite currencies and that money is originally a relation between persons in society, a token perhaps. The other reveals the coin as a thing, capable of entering into definite relations with other things, as a quantitative ratio independent of the persons engaged in any particular transaction.[19]

Accepting this tension between money as a symbol of our relationship with the state and money as a token of exchangeability, a 'quantitative ratio', allows us to explore the ways in which the dissonance between these two sides of money was expressed in its aesthetic reproduction. Maurer's second approach points to Webb Keane, who has drawn upon the work of pragmatist Charles Sanders Peirce, in order to offer a reading of money's signs more motivated than the negative, arbitrary connections assumed in the Saussurian tradition. Keane draws on Peirce's model of the sign to emphasise the additional properties of the sign, specifically the iconic and indexical, in which the former functions through resemblance (e.g. smoke for fire) and the latter through 'causal or proximal linkages' in which a sign is 'determined by its dynamic object by virtue of being in a real relation to it' (e.g. a number for a value).[20]

A methodology that interrogates the limitations of Saussure's insistence on the arbitrary nature of the visual sign is, of course, hardly unknown in literary studies. Scholars of modernist typography, such as Johanna Drucker and Jerome McGann, have both placed great weight on the semantic importance of the material properties of the text. Drucker has made the useful distinction between an 'unmarked' largely private text which aims to appear 'as uniform, as neutral, as accessible and seamless as possible' and the public marked text, which she associates especially with advertising, which 'aggressively situates the reader in relation to the various levels of enunciation in the text – reader, speaker, subject, author – though with manipulative utilisation of the strategies of graphic design'.[21] The dollar can, of course, be read against both definitions. On the one hand, it is clearly unmarked, its meaning residing in the authority of the signature that it bears and, as Mary Poovey would argue, it doesn't avail itself to being read. Yet, on the other, as cultural historians of the dollar have demonstrated, it is also a piece of exuberant graphic design whose meanings are intended to interpolate its possessor in very specific ways, which its cultural reproductions can make evident.[22]

The dollar's marked properties often correspond to a Peircean definition of the iconographic: they are figurative depictions of key national monuments and emblematic faces. Indeed, in popular culture, it often seems as if this rich history of dollar iconography has been condensed into a single portrait of George Washington, and that he has become a familiar synecdoche for relationship between the dollar and the state. The dollar's unmarked properties, alternatively, correspond to its role as the universal mechanism of exchange, to the abstractions of social relations that are simultaneously embodied and concealed in the numerical face value – the quantitative ratio – that each note also bears. Visual representations of the unmarked properties of the dollar, those which do not avail themselves to being 'read', thus correspond to a Peircean definition of the indexical; they are represented not by a resemblance but by the dollar sign that has an obvious link to the value that it represents in exchange. Drucker offers us a strategy for reading the dialectic between these two codes; she suggests that the 'challenge is take into account the physical, substantial aspects of production as well as the abstract and system-defined elements. By proposing that materiality combine the two, a dialectical relation is assumed in which neither presence as substance or absence as difference can ever be left fully alone: each continues to irrupt into the domain of the other . . . the historical inflection present in the visual, material form is largely significant (that is, capable of signifying) only to the extent that the form is part of a cultural code'.[23]

These tensions between the marked and the unmarked text, between the public address of the state and the occluded relations of the market, can be discerned in the visual re-representation of the dollar that surrounded the dollar crisis of the late 1960s and early 1970s. I want to firstly examine the ways in which these differences were negotiated in the political cartoons about the dollar, which revealed an active contestation between the market and the state as a source of authority, before examining the way in which fine art's critique of this division also points to its collapse. What we can see in the visual representations of the dollar is a cultural contestation over the meaning of what one anthropologist described as America's 'savage dime', that makes not the power of the state symbolised by the 'heads' but the power of the 'tails', the 'market that converts money into a *commodity* with a price' the 'best bet' and suggests that this is a coin that is being spun not only 'at Wall Street and other major financial centres but also towns and villages around the world'.[24]

One of the first cartoons to speak specifically to the ending of the gold-dollar standard appeared in *The New Yorker* in June 1971, three months prior to the event itself. The image, according to its own descriptive tag, featured a 'group of island natives discussing [the] monetary situation' and comprises four male figures, coded by their dress and by the ornate head statues and masks arranged behind them as a popular notion of Polynesian, in some kind of formal conference. At the bottom of the cartoon the punch-line reads: 'Then it's agreed. Until the dollar firms up, we let the clamshells float'.[25] The cartoon seems to compare the move from fixed to floating exchange rates to the 'great transformation' of monetary theory (itself understood by anthropologists Bloch and Parry as a kind of 'Western folk theory' according to Bill Maurer), to suggest that the change which is about to occur is comparable to the shift from a barter to a monetary economy. Yet the cartoon isn't suggesting that this shift will fundamentally alter, or even threaten, what we know money to be. Rather its reversal of this most orthodox of narratives, its representation of the 'primitive' islanders as currency traders acting to exploit US uncertainty, suggests a sophisticated level of knowingness about the event. Indeed, it was a political attitude towards the dollar's relationship to either market or state, rather than an existential crisis about the collapse of it as a reference point for value, that characterised its visual representations in this period.

Articles in *The New York Times,* for example, illustrated their cautious optimism about Nixon's economic policies with cartoons that position the heady play of new market freedoms against the containing stability of the state. Illustrations by Robert Pryor accompanied articles such as 'Economic Analysis: Currencies Afloat' and 'Learning to Love Floating Exchange Rates'. The image accompanying the former depicts the dollar sign as a warship bouncing on rugged seas and the latter places the dollar sign on a kite.[26] The image of the boat supports an upbeat article which draws on the ubiquitous and bombastically optimistic words of Walter Wriston but is tempered by the pitching of America's boat, the fear that it will be unable to quite catch the waves the other currencies ride high-on. The same ambivalence is apparent in the second article as it excoriates Central Bankers who do 'not trouble to understand' the needs of businessmen but the image of the $ on a kite being flown by George Washington positions the iconic Washington as a force that tethers the indexical floating dollar. The real threat, the cartoon suggests, comes from the bunched European kites, with sterling just drifting free of them, that corresponds to the fear of a common European floating rate (a forerunner of the euro) that would lead the United States to worry about a 'possible international monetary war' and, from there, 'its own irresponsibility in domestic economic policy'.[27]

The writings of those journalists and academics who were explicitly critical of the political implications of the Nixon shock were, conversely, accompanied by images which showed the tensions in the divided dollar as threatening, as undermining of the unity suggested by its national iconography. For some writers the division between market and state suggested a decline in American power itself. An article from 1970 by the Keynesian economist Robert Lekachman in *Harper's Magazine*, for example, lamented the failure of three successive American presidents to properly heed Keynesian principles of deficit spending and was accompanied by two images of the silver dollar.[28] The Roman elegance of John F. Kennedy's literally iconic profile on a coin minted in 1970 but never released for circulation, seems to be a nostalgic lament for a past moment of national unity and promise. That this is followed several pages later by an image of a reversed coin presented as a setting sun, sinking below a cloudy horizon, both reinforces this lament and adds a sly reference to the land of the 'rising sun' that was perceived as the primary threat to America's economic dominance.[29] The work of writers who were more critical of America's capitalist imperialism, and who explicitly warned of 'the steady erosion of the ability of national governments to exercise rational [economic] control' in the face of it, was accompanied by images of paralysed contradiction: an image of a tandem rendered static by the furious pedalling of men in suits headed in opposing directions.[30]

This interest in making visible the increasingly paradoxical but mutually constitutive tensions between the iconic (state) and indexical (market) meanings of money is one that can be traced through a longer history of twentieth century-American art and in an edition of *Art in America* from the very start of the 1970s; for example, art critic Jean Lipman provides a comprehensive overview of this work in contemporary American art, establishing a division between artists concerned to interrogate the implications of the material iconicity of the dollar form and those concerned with exploring arts role in increasingly financialised networks, with its indexical value, in other words.[31]

The former tradition is particularly evident through Lipman's inclusion of two collections of work from the mid-1960s in which artists were invited to re-imagine the national money. The first collection, created in response to a call issued by the director of the Guggenheim in 1963 for *Art in America's* 'Art for Everyday Living' feature, included a set of coins which were made from an impressive array of materials (plastic, gold, nickel, steel, silver, aluminium, bronze) but were uniformly characterised by a confident re-assertion of the solidity of the coin as a symbol of the republic. The design of each coin is classically clean and, if they bear any words at all, it is the idealistic *'E pluribus unum'* (one from many) rather than the more imperious and passive 'In God we trust' which had actually replaced it as the official motto of the United States some years earlier. The coins feature no obviously iconic or presidential imagery; rather they are dominated by linear abstractions which seem to only partially evoke eagles or suns: they are serious, authoritative, 'unmarked' in Drucker's definition. Lipman sets this collection against one that appeared in the graphic art journal *Avant-Garde* some five years later. This collection, entitled *Revaluation of the Dollar: 19 Artists Design a New Dollar Bill*, suggested something quite different about the authority of the coin in America.[32] In this piece the classical austerity of the coins from the early 1960s are replaced by gaudy mockeries of state seignorage. The difference can, of course, be attributed to the different organisations and artists involved – the comparison places the Guggenheim against graphic design. Yet it is also tempting to imagine that both the headiness of 1968 and the invitation to reproduce a paper text rather than a solid coin were partly responsible for the radical differences between the interpretations of this identical task. The dollar bill by Gerry Gersten that takes centre place on the front cover of *Avant-Garde* replaces *'E Pluribus unum'* with the crude 'in gawd we rusk' alongside two caricatured and reversed mirrored profiles: a monochrome image of a large-nosed and well-lived Washington is reflected back as a large-nosed, well-lived Nixon, but coloured in purple and wearing a crown and ermine. The sense is clearly of Nixon as a fraudulent carnivalesque king, and it is his position as an illegitimate and undemocratic president, rather than the gaudy reproduction itself, that makes this reproduced dollar a mockery. Nixon's involvement in Vietnam, as a symbol of American imperialism, is explicit on many of these notes as well as in the journal's introduction: 'all in all, these dollars won't pay the rent, but then they won't buy an M-16 rifle, either. And in these days, that's something'.[33] Another dollar by Etienne Delessert changes the arrows held by the bald Eagle from 'Jonathan's arrows' (signifying unity and peace in the original design) for explicit symbols of the contemporary war and one by Ernie Smith features a balance sheet, with an itemised list of the sources of income for Federal America, that reveals that the amount received from individual income tax is equivalent to that spent on national defence.[34]

Lipman contrasts this tradition to the conceptual work, including work by artists such as Robert Morris, Les Levine, Edward Kienholz and Larry Rivers, who were all concerned with exploring art's interrogation of the processes of financialisation, its own role as a market within other financial markets. Lipman specifically references the 'Anti-Illusion' show held in the Whitney in 1969 in which Robert Morris exhibited 'a three-way exchange of letters between the artist, the staff of the Whitney Museum and a stockbroker-collector, an agreement was reached (and carried out as a routine financial transaction through the Morgan Guaranty Trust Company): to loan the Whitney $50,000 at an interest rate of 5% per annum for the duration of the Anti-Illusion exhibition. . . . The concept, the actual profit to the artist, and the collector's-item documentation of the transaction are all aspects of the work of art'.[35] The interest in tracing the similarities, and differences, between the financial and artistic worlds became, of course, increasingly significant throughout the 1980s and 1990s as art itself proved such a peculiarly resistant but lucrative asset class.[36]

The work of Andy Warhol can be read against both traditions: he was clearly interested in the materiality of the dollar as a sign, and yet he was also the artist for whom 'business art is the step that comes after art . . . being good in business is the most fascinating kind of art'.[37] Indeed, for many critics it is this apparent collapsing of art and money that leads Warhol to fulfil Marx's account of a commodity form that is intent on absorbing everything within it, a process that reaches its climax in the aesthetic fetishisation of money itself. Charles Taylor, for example, reads Warhol as the direct cultural corollary of the failure of the Bretton Woods agreement, suggesting that the 'paper currency' of this moment allowed for the 'aestheticisation of the commodity in which the token of exchange becomes a work of art. Money and art meet in the sacred cow whose fictive value is established by the "act of the artist."' For Taylor, a fiat money begets a fiat art and the loss of the real that follows is near-apocalyptic; there are 'disastrous consequences' when it becomes possible to mistake 'illusions for reality'.[38] Thierry de Duve and Rosalind Krauss also read Warhol through the fetishising logic of the commodity, suggesting that this 'is the cynicism of capital interiorized even by those it causes to suffer; this is the pleasure of the prostitute'.[39]

Jennifer Doyle has explored the way in which the rhetoric of prostitution is invoked by Warhol's critics to render perverse his interest in the financial value of his work and, additionally, to figure this lack through a 'perverse, unnatural or destructive relationship to sex'.[40] For Doyle, Warhol utilises a 'queer' logic not in order to act as a passive conduit for the processes of exchange but, rather, to realise in a more optimistic manner 'what art, as mediated exchange, can do'. For Doyle, Warhol's critique is aimed at the disingenuity of the art world, the 'refusal of art to acknowledge its status as a commodity. Thus, the homology between pornography and art – where porn makes an industry out of selling representations of something that is not supposed to have a market (but clearly does), what we might call Warhol's money shots obscenely undress the extent to which the art world (and often art criticism) is invested in its disavowal of its relationship to the art market'.[41]

I want to extend the frames of Doyle's critique to suggest that Warhol's queered dollar doesn't only make explicit the art world's complicity with the processes of commodification that it critiques but that its excesses also disrupt the futurist logic that it relies upon, the processes of accumulation which 'rest', as Andrew Parker has drawn on Hannah Arendt to suggest, 'on the equation of productivity with fertility'.[42] Although images of Warhol's dollar signs have become a ubiquitous signifier for late modernity, these changed significantly over his career and I want to contrast his dollars from the early 1960s with those from the early 1980s to better understand the recurring ambivalence, the simultaneous production and destruction of the value of the dollar, that is at the centre of these images.

Warhol's photographs of the silkscreened dollar note were first shown in 1962 as part of a series that explored the implications of reproducing iconography and their juxtaposition alongside *Campbell's Soup* foregrounded the significance of these texts as commercial graphic designs. The comparison allowed Warhol to draw attention to money not only as the universal equivalent, as the object of exchange and site of accumulation which was at the centre of Robert Morris and Les Levine's conceptual concerns with the dollar at this point in time, but rather as a graphic object, 'marked' in Drucker's sense, an object capable of being given material meanings outside of the abstracted relations of exchange.

His account of the production of these notes is suggestive in terms of his sense of their materiality. Warhol recalls that 'you weren't allowed to do dollar bills that looked like dollar bills, so you couldn't do a silkscreen. Then I thought, well how do you do these things? The dollar bill I did was like a silkscreen, you know; it was commercial – I did it myself. And then somebody said that you can do it photographically – you know they can just do it, put a photograph on a screen-so that's when I did my first photograph'.[43] The process of reproducing a reproduction calls attention to the materiality of both the object and the mode of its replication. Critics such as Sebastian Egenhofer suggest that what emerges from Warhol's paintings of this time is not the iconic referent that is their ostensible subject but rather the instruments of their reproduction. 'Despite their iconic force and recognizability', as Egenhofer elaborates, 'these pictorial motifs must be conceived not as the subjects of a representation, but as the traces of the transformed process of reproduction that he uses'.[44] In reminding us of the 'instrument' that created money, of course, Warhol was reminding us of the act of state seignorage.

Yet the apocryphal origins of these notes also complicate this potential critique. The origins of the inspiration for these dollars are somewhat obscured by the anecdotes that surround Warhol but Emilio de Antonio has suggested that the idea was art gallery owner Eleanor Ward's, who told Warhol that ' "I'll give you a show, but you've got to paint me a two dollar bill". She said, "I always carry my lucky two dollar bill with me". And, so, she whipped out a two dollar bill, and Andy made a painting out of it, and that was the first *Two-Dollar Bill*. He then had a show'.[45] Warhol's first silkscreened dollars were thus created as an act of social exchange – the dollar in return for the exhibition – and celebrated a bill that was most frequently associated not with monetary exchange but with social relations (this was a 'lucky two-dollar bill' – not scarce enough to be collectible but often given and retained as gifts). Hence Warhol's dollar wasn't an attempt to emulate real money or monetary exchange (in the way of J. S. Boggs's, a decade later, for example) but spoke of money as a symbol of social exchange that existed paradoxically outside of the financial system.

The dollars that Warhol created in the early 1980s, which were shown in a solo exhibition in Leo Castelli's gallery in January 1982, suggested something quite different in terms of both production and circulation yet they repeated the destructive ambivalence of these earlier notes. These later dollars were single dollar signs rather than contact-like sheets of entire multiple notes. They were richly coloured and individually differentiated and were clearly exuberant parodies of the dollar sign rather than the faithful reproductions. The introduction to Warhol's *Making Money* contextualises these pieces in terms of the economic excesses of the 1980s and Warhol as a figure who 'worked hard to make money and enjoyed spending it . . . he was a workaholic and a shopaholic. During the years I worked with him, Andy was always afraid that his money would disappear'.[46] de Duve and Krauss represent Warhol's creation of these dollars in cynical ways, suggesting that it was done 'to satisfy demand [. . .], and while it was mere Monopoly money on the currency markets [. . .] it was gold on the art market' yet this is a reading that doesn't capture the self-destructive ironies of the act. These particular dollar signs were *not* simply 'gold on the art market', but they were critically panned when first exhibited by Castelli and were not fully rehabilitated as a part of Warhol's oeuvre until an exhibition in the late 1990s. Arthur C. Danto's account of this exhibition, for example, ruefully recollects that its negative critical reception led to an exhibition of the dollar signs that was a dismal 'financial failure: not one painting sold. . . . Somehow everything about the show seemed to reflect the fact that it was a corporate endeavour'.[47] Even *Artforum,* that had included the 'Forged Images' Centrefold alongside an advert for the exhibition, carried a review damning the exhibition only two months later (a review that surprised Warhol as he had donated his Centrefold piece to *Artforum* for free as a way of supporting Castelli's advert). The review notes that although 'there once was a time when Andy Warhol was producing what was undoubtedly some of the most important art in New York. . . . In recent years his shows have been increasingly disappointing and this is the most disappointing yet. It is beginning to look as if Warhol has hit the bottom'. It describes the dollar signs as an 'overlarge reprieve of what was essentially a one-line joke anyway' and offers 'no food for eye or brain' but rather only a 'gentle ribbing for those wonderful people who commission portraits, the wonderful people who think that supply-side economics and an increased military budget is wonderful too'.[48]

Yet the failure of the exhibition can also be seen as a paradoxical enactment of Warhol's desire to destroy money, to witness its disappearance. Critics have since noted that the badly reviewed exhibition was actually only a partial one, and that Warhol's decision to show only dollar notes was a last minute one, that he had originally planned to include the *Guns and Knives* series alongside the dollar images because he had wanted to combine 'issues of money, power and violence during a time that witnessed the dawning of the neo-conservative Ronald Reagan era and sectarian conflicts around the globe'.[49]

The irony of Warhol's failure to produce a show critical of this American imperialism is made complete by the fact that he then gave away, rather than sold, many of these pieces which subsequently made their 'way into private homes and apartments'. As Vincent Fremont elaborates further on this gesture, 'Andy with this symbol that he even had his versions of the dollar sign screened on white cotton pocket squares and large-sized Calvin Klein men's briefs that would be given away as presents'.[50] The point at which Warhol's dollar reach its fetished zenith, when he printed dollar signs to feed his anxiety about their imminent disappearance and withheld his own critical awareness of their relationship to a militarised economy, was also the point at which their value in the financial economy radically declined. What emerged in its place, according to those close to him, were the complex and harder to trace values of the gift economy, in the image of the printed Calvin Klein's, at least, these are suggestively rendered queer. The gift, of course, can have both an opposing and an equivalent relationship to money; as Kojin Karatani has recently noted, it is an effective alternative to money because it is subject to exchange but cannot be extracted from circulation and hoarded, and it 'does not possess the right to own other things: to the contrary, it brings with it the obligation to give things away . . . whereas money promotes stockpiling and expanding possession', the gift 'functions as a force that rejects ownership'.[51]

Warhol's desire to destroy money can also be found, in way of a conclusion, through the epigrammatic statements he makes about it in *The Philosophy of Andy Warhol*. He begins with a literal definition of money worthy of Milton Friedman, suggesting that only 'GREEN BILLS' are actually money and that the bonds and checks of the credit industry are defiantly not.[52] And yet, only a page later, he reverses this to the point of absurdity by widening his definition of money to include all aspects of financial transactions: till receipts, evidence of money's absence, become money as the squanderous Warhol describes how the 'more receipts I get, the bigger the thrill. They're even getting to be like money to me now'.[53] The denial of the 'reproductive futurism' that Lee Edelman has identified with a heteronormativity is evident in Warhol's celebration of the evidence of its absence.[54] Warhol, for example, mocks the 'Rothschild manner' of folding 'each bill separately, lengthwise, and then folded it again lengthwise. All new money' that makes it 'last longer', and he contrasts the clean precision of the rentier class whose money extends into future generations against his own lack of reverence, suggesting that 'the best way I like to carry money, actually, is messily. Crumpled wads. A paper bag is good' and that 'Money is money. It doesn't matter if I've worked hard or easy for it. I spend it the same. . . . I don't look at dates'.[55]

NOTES

1. Although we lack a comprehensive cultural history of this moment, we certainly do not lack economic histories: Fred L. Block, *The Origins of International Economic Disorder: A Study of United States International Monetary Policy from World War II to the Present* (Berkeley: University of California Press, 1977), John S. Odell, *U.S International Monetary Policy* (Princeton, NJ: Princeton University Press, 1982), Diane B. Kunz, *Butter and Guns: America's Cold War Economic Diplomacy* (New York: Free Press, 1997), Allen J. Matusow, *Nixon's Economy: Booms, Busts, Dollars and Votes* (Kansas: University of Kansas Press, 1998).
2. *The Scooby-Doo Show,* 'The Traitors of '76', first aired on 18 December 1976, ABC.
3. As Jason Goodwin argued, 'There is a niggling list of grievances right at the beginning of the Declaration of Independence which seemed, at the time, crucially important, though few people nowadays read or remember them, what they actually mean is: we agreed to have paper money, and you simply shut us down. *Greenback: The Almighty Dollar and the Invention of America* (London: Penguin, 2003).
4. David Harvey, *The Condition of Postmodernity* (Oxford: Blackwell, 1989), 298.
5. Walter B. Wriston, 'The Global Attic: An Address before the Bankers' Association for Foreign Trade on 9 May 1972 in Colorado Springs, Colorado', Tufts Digital Library, http://dl.tufts.edu/catalog/tei/tufts:UA069.005.DO.00283/chapter/c1 (last accessed 26 February 2017).
6. Wriston, 'The Global Attic'.
7. Marc Shell, *Money, Language and Thought* (Baltimore: Johns Hopkins University Press, 1982), 7.
8. Walter B. Wriston, *Risk & Other Four-Letter Words* (New York: Harper & Row, 1986), 200.
9. Walter B. Wriston, *New York Times*, 3 March 1973.
10. 'The Most Influential People in 12 Fields – as Ranked by their Peers', Who Runs America? Annual Survey, *U.S. News & World Report,* 21 April 1975, 30.
11. Cited in Richard Roberts and David Kynaston, *City State: A Contemporary History of the City of London and How Money Triumphed* (London: Profile Books, 2001), 119–20.

12. Leo Panitch and Sam Gindin, 'Global Capitalism and American Empire', *Socialist Register* 40: 'The New Imperial Challenge' (2004): 36.
13. Christian Marazzi, *Capital and Language: From the New Economy to the War Economy*, trans. Gregory Conti (Los Angeles: Semiotext(e), 2008), 36.
14. Shell, *Money, Language and Thought*, 3.
15. Marc Shell, *The Economy of Literature* (Baltimore: Johns Hopkins University Press, 1978), 32.
16. Slavoj Žižek, *The Sublime Object of Ideology* (London: Verso 1989), 20.
17. Mary Poovey, *Genres of the Credit Economy: Mediating Value in Eighteenth and Nineteenth Century Britain* (Chicago: University of Chicago Press, 2008), 4.
18. Bill Maurer, 'The Anthropology of Money', *Annual Review of Anthropology* 35 (2006): 15–36.
19. Keith Hart, 'Heads or Tails? Two Sides of the Coin', *Man* 21.4 (1986): 637–56.
20. T. L. Short, *Peirce's Theory of Signs* (Cambridge: Cambridge University Press, 2007).
21. Johanna Drucker, *The Visible Word: Experimental Typography and Modern Art, 1909–1923* (Chicago: University of Chicago Press, 1994), 97.
22. David Ovason, *The Secret History of the Dollar Bill* (New York: Barnes and Noble, 2008).
23. Drucker, *The Visible Word*, 43.
24. C. A. Gregory, *Savage Money: The Anthropology and Politics of Commodity Exchange* (Amsterdam: Harwood Academic Press, 1997), 14.
25. Ed Fisher, *The New Yorker*, 19 June 1971.
26. H. Erich Heineman, 'Economic Analysis: Currencies Afloat', *New York Times,* 3 March 1978, and Harry G. Johnson, 'Learning to Love Floating Exchange Rates', *New York Times*, 18 March 1978.
27. Johnson, 'Learning to Love Floating Exchange Rates'.
28. Robert Lekachman, 'Money in America: The End of the Economists' Dream', *Harper's Magazine* (August 1970): 31, 34.
29. Lekachman, 'Money in America', 34.
30. David P. Calleleo, 'The Shaky Dollar', *New York Times*, 6 March 1973.
31. Jean Lipman, 'Money for Money's Sake', *Art in America* 58.1 (January–February 1970): 76–83.
32. Ralph Ginzburg, *Revaluation of the Dollar: 19 Artists Design a New Dollar Bill*', ed. Ralph Ginzburg, *Avant-Garde* 3 (May 1968).
33. *Revaluation of the Dollar*, ed. Ginzburg, 4.
34. *Revaluation of the Dollar*, ed. Ginzburg, 7.
35. Lipman, 'Money for Money's Sake', 77.
36. Collections such as Katy Siegel and Paul Mattick's *Art Works: Money* (London; Thames and Hudson, 2004) and, indeed, Paul Crosthwaite, Peter Knight and Nicky Marsh's *Show Me the Money: The Image of Finance, 1700 to the Present* (Manchester: Manchester University Press, 2014) explore both traditions at some length.
37. Cited in Mark C. Taylor, *Disfiguring: Art, Architecture, Religion* (Chicago: University of Chicago Press, 1994), 145.

38. Taylor, *Disfiguring: Art*, 152.
39. Thierry de Duve and Rosalind Krauss, 'Andy Warhol, or the Machine Perfected', *October* 48 (Spring 1989): 6.
40. Jennifer Doyle, *Sex Objects: Art and the Dialectics of Desire* (Minneapolis: University of Minnesota Press, 2006), 70.
41. Doyle, *Sex Objects*, 70.
42. Hannah Arendt, cited in Andrew Parker, 'Unthinking Sex: Marx and Engels and the Scene of Writing', in *Fear of a Queer Planet: Queer Politics and Social Theory*, ed. Michael Warner (Minneapolis: University of Minnesota Press, 1993), 35.
43. Benjamin H. D. Buchloh, 'An Interview with Andy Warhol', in *I'll Be Your Mirror: The Selected Andy Warhol Interviews, 1962–1987*, ed. Kenneth Goldsmith, intr. Reva Wolf (New York: Carroll and Graf, 2004), 323.
44. Sebastian Egenhofer, 'Subjectivity and the Production of Meaning in Warhol's Early Work', in *Andy Warhol: The Early Sixties: Paintings and Drawings 1961–1964*, ed. Bernhard Mendes Bürgi and Nina Zimmer (Basel: Kunstmuseum Basel, 2011), 36.
45. Sterling McIlhenny and Peter Ray, 'Inside Andy Warhol', 2, at http://www.warholstars.org/andy_warhol_2.html (last accessed 26 February 2017).
46. Vincent Fremont, 'Andy and the Dollar Sign', in *Andy Warhol: Making Money*, ed. Andy Warhol and Berkeley Reinhold (New York: Skira Rizzoli Publications, 2010), 11.
47. Arthur C. Danto, *Andy Warhol* (New Haven, CT: Yale University Press, 2009), 131.
48. Thomas Lawson, 'Andy Warhol', *Art Forum* 20 (April 1982), 75.
49. Joseph D. Ketner, 'Warhol's Last Decade: Reinventing Painting', in *Andy Warhol: The Last Decade*, ed. Joseph D. Ketner, II (Milwaukee: Milwaukee Art Museum; Munich and New York: DelMonico Books/Prestel, 2010), 26.
50. Andy Warhol's *Making Money* originated as a present to the daughter of a close friend; Fremont; 'Andy and the Dollar Sign', 13.
51. Kojin Karatani, *The Structure of World History* (New York: Duke University Press, 2014), 51.
52. Andy Warhol, *The Philosophy of Andy Warhol* (London: Harcourt and Brace, 1975), 129.
53. Warhol, *The Philosophy of Andy Warhol*, 130.
54. Lee Edelman, *No Future: Queer Theory and the Death Drive* (Durham, NC: Duke University Press, 2004).
55. Warhol, *The Philosophy of Andy Warhol*, 130, 134 and 136.

BIBLIOGRAPHY

BUCHLOH, Benjamin H. D. 'An Interview with Andy Warhol' (1985). In *I'll Be Your Mirror: The Selected Andy Warhol Interviews, 1962–1987*. Edited by Kenneth Goldsmith. Introduction by Reva Wolf. New York: Carroll and Graf, 2004. 321–32.

BLOCK, Fred L. *The Origins of International Economic Disorder: A Study of United States International Monetary Policy from World War II to the Present*. Berkeley: University of California Press, 1977.

CALLELEO, David P. 'The Shaky Dollar'. *New York Times*, 6 March 1973.

CROSTHWAITE, Paul, Peter KNIGHT and Nicky MARSH (eds.). *Show Me the Money: The Image of Finance, 1700 to the Present*. Manchester: Manchester University Press, 2014.

DANTO, Arthur C. *Andy Warho*l. New Haven, CT: Yale University Press, 2009.

DE DUVE, Thierry and Rosalind KRAUSS. 'Andy Warhol, or the Machine Perfected'. *October* 48 (Spring 1989): 3–14.

DOYLE, Jennifer. *Sex Objects: Art and the Dialectics of Desire*. Minneapolis: University of Minnesota Press, 2006.

DRUCKER, Johanna. *The Visible Word: Experimental Typography and Modern Art, 1909–1923*. Chicago: University of Chicago Press, 1994.

EDELMAN, Lee. *No Future: Queer Theory and the Death Drive*. Durham, NC: Duke University Press, 2004.

EGENHOFER, Sebastian. 'Subjectivity and the Production of Meaning in Warhol's Early Work'. In *Andy Warhol: The Early Sixties: Paintings and Drawings 1961–1964*. Edited by Bernhard Mendes Bürgi and Nina Zimmer. Basel: The Kunstmuseum Basel, 2011. 32–45.

FISHER, Ed. *The New Yorker*, 19 June 1971.

FREMONT, Vincent. 'Andy and the Dollar Sign'. In *Andy Warhol: Making Money*. Edited by Andy Warhol and Berkeley Reinhold. New York: Skira Rizzoli Publications, 2010. 11–14.

GINZBURG, Ralph (ed.) *Revaluation of the Dollar: 19 Artists Design a New Dollar Bill*. *Avant-Garde* 3 (May 1968).

GOODWIN, Jason. *Greenback: The Almighty Dollar and the Invention of America*. London: Penguin, 2003.

GREGORY, C. A. *Savage Money: The Anthropology and Politics of Commodity Exchange*. Amsterdam: Harwood Academic Press, 1997.

HART, Keith. 'Heads or Tails? Two Sides of the Coin'. *Man* 21.4 (1986): 637–56.

HARVEY, David. *The Condition of Postmodernity*. Oxford: Blackwell, 1989.

HEINEMAN, H. Erich. 'Economic Analysis: Currencies Afloat'. *New York Times*, 3 March 1978.

JOHNSON, Harry G. 'Learning to Love Floating Exchange Rates'. *New York Times*, 18 March 1978.

KARATANI, Kojin. *The Structure of World History*. New York: Duke University Press, 2014.

KETNER, Joseph D., II. 'Warhol's Last Decade: Reinventing Painting'. In *Andy Warhol: The Last Decade*. Edited by Joseph D. Ketner. Milwaukee: Milwaukee Art Museum; Munich and New York: DelMonico Books/Prestel, 2010. 14–27.

KUNZ, Diane B. *Butter and Guns: America's Cold War Economic Diplomacy*. New York: Free Press, 1997.

LAWSON, Thomas. 'Andy Warhol'. *Art Forum* 20 (April 1982), 75–76.

LEKACHMAN, Robert. 'Money in America: The End of the Economists' Dream'. *Harper's Magazine* (August 1970): 29–34.

LIPMAN, Jean. 'Money for Money's Sake'. *Art in America* 58.1 (January–February 1970): 76–83.

MARAZZI, Christian. *Capital and Language: From the New Economy to the War Economy*. Translated by Gregory Conti. Los Angeles: Semiotext(e), 2008.
MATUSOW, Allen J. *Nixon's Economy: Booms, Busts, Dollars and Votes*. Kansas: University of Kansas Press, 1998.
MAURER, Bill. 'The Anthropology of Money'. *Annual Review of Anthropology* 35 (2006): 15–36.
McILHENNY, Sterling and Peter RAY. 'Inside Andy Warhol'. 1–4, http://www.warholstars.org/andy_warhol_2.html. Last accessed 26 February 2017.
'The Most Influential People in 12 Fields – as Ranked by Their Peers'. Who Runs America? Annual Survey. *U.S. News & World Report,* 21 April 1975.
ODELL, John S. *U.S. International Monetary Policy*. Princeton, NJ: Princeton University Press, 1982.
OVASON, David. *The Secret History of the Dollar Bill*. New York: Barnes and Noble, 2008.
PANITCH, Leo and Sam GINDIN. 'Global Capitalism and American Empire'. *Socialist Register* 40: 'The New Imperial Challenge' (2004): 1–42.
PARKER, Andrew. 'Unthinking Sex: Marx and Engels and the Scene of Writing'. In *Fear of a Queer Planet: Queer Politics and Social Theory*. Edited by Michael Warner. Minneapolis: University of Minnesota Press, 1993. 19–41.
POOVEY, Mary. *Genres of the Credit Economy: Mediating Value in Eighteenth and Nineteenth Century Britain*. Chicago: University of Chicago Press, 2008.
ROBERTS, Richard and David KYNASTON. *City State: A Contemporary History of the City of London and How Money Triumphed*. London: Profile Books, 2001.
SHELL, Marc. *The Economy of Literature*. Baltimore: Johns Hopkins University Press, 1978.
SHELL, Marc. *Money, Language and Thought*. Baltimore: Johns Hopkins University Press, 1982.
SHORT, T. L. *Peirce's Theory of Signs*. Cambridge: Cambridge University Press, 2007.
SIEGEL, Katy and Paul MATTICK (eds.). *Art Works: Money*. London; Thames and Hudson, 2004.
The Scooby-Doo Show, 'The Traitors of '76', first aired on 18 December 1976. ABC.
TAYLOR, Mark C. *Disfiguring: Art, Architecture, Religion*. Chicago: University of Chicago Press, 1994.
WARHOL, Andy. *The Philosophy of Andy Warhol*. London: Harcourt and Brace, 1975.
WRISTON, Walter B. 'The Global Attic: An Address before the Bankers'. Association for Foreign Trade on 9 May 1972 in Colorado Springs, Colorado'. Tufts Digital Library, http://dl.tufts.edu/catalog/tei/tufts:UA069.005.DO.00283/chapter/c1. Last accessed 26 February 2017.
WRISTON, Walter B. *Risk & Other Four-Letter Words*. New York: Harper & Row, 1986.
ŽIŽEK, Slavoj. *The Sublime Object of Ideology*. London: Verso, 1989.

Chapter 6

Universal Shylockery

Money and morality in The Merchant of Venice

Simon Critchley and Tom McCarthy

What if Nietzsche were a Jew, and a mean-minded Venetian Jew at that? We'd like to begin with the thought experiment of imagining *The Merchant of Venice* as a genealogy of morality and imagining Shylock as Nietzsche. What is *The Merchant of Venice* about? What is at stake in this oddly inside-out drama, where a piece of good-old Elizabethan comic Jew-baiting rotates 180 degrees into a devastating study of Christian anti-Semitism only to flip back into what it seemed to deny? Our initial hypothesis is that it is nothing less than an inquiry into the origin of our moral concepts of justice, good and bad, and more particularly guilt, law, mercy and love. It is here that a link with Nietzsche suggests itself, particularly with the Second Essay of *On the Genealogy of Morals*.

How do we breed an animal with the right to make promises? For Nietzsche, the human being is an originally forgetful creature, like a young child. To make this originally forgetful creature remember requires physical discipline; it behoves punishment. The teaching of morality was never gentle, it never droppeth from heaven like gentle rain. On the contrary, if something is to be retained in memory, it must be burned in. The origin of memory lies in pain and cruelty: 'Man could never do without blood, torture and sacrifices when he felt the need to create a memory for himself'.[1] Nietzsche's first, astonishing hypothesis in the Second Essay is that the origin of concepts like responsibility and conscience lies in cruelty – cruelty administered and maintained through a corporal and corporeal regime. Further, as religions are systems of cruelty, all forms of asceticism originate in the same painful place. 'Consider the German punishments', Nietzsche proposes – and we all know that there's nothing quite like the German punishments: stoning, breaking on the wheel, piercing with stakes, tearing apart or trampling with horses, boiling in oil, flaying alive, cutting straps from the flesh, smearing the wrongdoer with honey and leaving him or her to the flies in the blazing sun. As Nietzsche quips, with magnificent understatement, 'With the aid of such images and procedures one finally remembers five or six "I will not's" '(*GM* 62). It is on the basis of this burned-in memory of cruelty that good, decent, upright burghers such as ourselves acquired the habit of moral reasoning:

> Ah, reason, seriousness, mastery over the affects, the whole sombre thing called reflection, all these prerogatives and showpieces of man: how dearly they have been bought! how much blood and cruelty lie at the bottom of all 'good things'! (*GM* 62)

'Dearly bought': let's hold onto that trope of purchasing. In another extraordinary passage of the Second Essay, Nietzsche explains the origin of thinking itself in terms of economic activity:

> Setting prices, determining values, contriving equivalences, exchanging – these preoccupied the earliest thinking of man to so great an extent that in a certain sense *they* constitute thinking *as such* [*das Denken* ist]. (*GM* 70)

In the beginning was trade. Human activity begins with exchange, with the to and fro of buying and selling, which are forms of life older than all other social alliances and organization. It is from here, Nietzsche insists, that human beings arrive at the first moral canon of justice:

> 'everything has its price; *all* things can be paid for' – the oldest and naïvest moral canon of *justice*, the beginning of all 'good-naturedness', all 'fairness', all 'good will', all 'objectivity' on earth. (*GM* 70)

Which brings us to the origin of *das Bewusstsein der Schuld* and *schlechtes Gewissen,* the consciousness of guilt and bad conscience. Nietzsche's hypothesis here, and our theme is beginning to come into focus, is that the origin of guilty conscience lies in the relation between a creditor and debtor, *Gläubiger und Schuldner*. The spiritual concept of guilt, *Schuld*, originates in the very material concept of *Schulden*, debts. Guilt in, say, Saint Paul's sense of the essential self-division of the Christian subject, a subject constituted by the guilt that divides it – 'for the good that I would, I do not, but the evil that I would not, that I do', *Romans* VII – lies in a fundamentally *contractual* relationship, *Vertragsverhältnis*. The spirituality of Christian guilt is but the airy halo that floats over the materiality of a contract. In other words, morality begins with what Shylock would call a *bond*.

With that in mind, consider the meaning of punishment. The apparently self-evident, universal and even natural idea that punishment is imposed because the criminal knew how to act virtuously, but acted viciously, and is therefore *responsible* for his crime, is a lie. On the contrary, for Nietzsche, punishment is necessary because the victim of the crime believed that the culprit could pay back their crime through their pain. That is, punishment is a corporeal payment for a criminal act and has nothing to do with something as ethereal as responsibility. The point is that the punishment of the criminal gives *pleasure* to the punisher. This, it would seem, is precisely what is in Shylock's mind in Act 4 of *The Merchant of Venice*.

We'll come back to this – but for the moment let's take stock of where we've got thus far: morality points back to contractual relations, and these contractual relations point back in turn to merchandise, to mercantile relations of 'buying, selling, barter, trade and traffic' (*'Kauf, Verkauf, Tausch, Handel und Wandel'* – *GM* 63). The thought here is etymologically contained in the central and essentially contested Christian concept in *The Merchant of Venice*, namely *mercy*. The mercy that cannot be strained, that should season justice, that the Jew should show, and which is even, according to Portia, cross-dressed as the young lawyer Balthazar, an attribute of God himself, is derived from *mercēs*. That is, from the same root as merchant, meaning payment, recompense and revenue. What is *revenu* in talk of mercy is mercantile revenue. Christianity is the spiritualization of the originally material. *The Merchant of Venice* might be viewed as an essay in the genealogy of morals.

Let's look more closely at the play. To describe it as a play about economics is stating the obvious – the bleeding obvious, as Portia might add – but the extent to which its rhetoric is drenched in the diction of the market simply cannot be overstated. Flip through the text to almost any passage and you will find variants on owing, exchanging, bequeathing, expending, accounting and converting applied as the default vocabulary for all manner of subjects and phenomena one would not normally consider to be 'economic': gender, mood, reason and so on. Again and again, the two grand ontological axes, that of spirit – the airy and ethereal, the index of all that's elevated and sublime – and that of matter – the objective, quantifiable and bodied – are hinged together around economic signs, economic mechanisms, economic practises. Take the very first scene: right at the beginning we are told that Antonio's mood, the state of his soul, is index-linked to his merchandise: his mind lies in his bottoms. This is the thesis Salerio advances to explain the enigma of Antonio's melancholia with which the drama begins in Act, line 1: 'In sooth, I know not why I am so sad'. Were

I in your position, Salerio conjectures, even the font of the divine spirit, 'the holy edifice of stone', would make me think of all-too solid rocks,

> Which touching but my gentle vessel's side
> Would scatter all her spices on the stream,
> Enrobe the roaring waters with my silks,
> And in a word, but even now worth this,
> And now worth nothing. (1.1.32–36)[2]

The scenario he alarmingly, if well-meaningly, paints binds that most abstract of concepts, value, to a material, even visceral event whose imagery of 'ribs', torn sides and spilt innards anticipates the violence Shylock will threaten to wreak on Antonio. And it does so by evoking both ends of the economic scale: that is, by envisaging a dual-movement of surfeit or surplus – abundance, overflowing, splendour – and of loss, of surfeit which *is* loss. The motif is almost immediately reprised by Gratiano, who warns Antonio:

> You have too much respect upon the world;
> They lose it that do buy it with much care. (1.1.74–75)

When excessive expenditure occurs, too much runs into too little. Anyone with basic economic sense could tell you this – but Shakespeare has this economic figure underpin a whole subjective state, a state of being-in-the-world and contemplating it; and here, incidentally, Gratiano's use of the word 'care' anticipates the quasi-economic terminology Heidegger will use to describe the way we mortals gather and store the world in thought and language.

Bassanio, the luxurious young man who projects such splendour out into the world (the clothes, the entourage), has also moved to both ends of the economic scale, done deficit and surplus at the same time: he has surpassed himself, expanded his persona beyond its natural bounds,

> By something showing a more swelling port
> Than my faint means would grant continuance. (1.1.124–25)

In so doing, Bassanio has 'disabled [his] estate'. In short, Bassanio is both leading a lavish lifestyle *and* skint. This bad economic practise is what lies behind his self-projections; it both constitutes and ruins him. The sliding gap that opens up within what we could call his subjectivity, a schism or chasm founded on an economic gap between expense and means, anticipates the many faults that will open up within the play's tectonics: between inside and outside, appearance and reality, word and deed and so on.

Bassanio's solution is not to close the gap down again but rather to open up another one, an interval of credit and of credence. And he does this by quite brilliantly invoking the logic of venture capital itself, of speculation, the logic on which Antonio's whole life and livelihood is founded, by invoking the parable of the lost and found arrow. Bassanio says:

> In my school days, when I had lost one shaft,
> I shot his fellow of the self-same flight
> The self-same way, with more advised watch
> To find the other forth, and by adventuring both,
> I oft found both: I urge this childhood proof
> Because what follows is pure innocence.
> I owe you much, and (like wilful youth)
> That which I owe is lost, but if you please
> To shoot another arrow that self way
> Which you did shoot the first, I do not doubt,
> (As I will watch the aim) or to find both,
> Or bring your latter hazard back again,
> And thankfully rest debtor for the first. (1.1.140–52)

The real profit, his logic seems to go, lies not in having possession of a commodity in the here-and-now, but rather in buying into a deferred return, investing in an imaginary future. This Freudian *Fort-Da* credo underpins stock markets to this day. The commodity upon which Bassanio and Antonio are speculating in this case is a lady in Belmont, Portia, who is 'richly left', and in order to woo her Bassanio needs dough, and he needs ducats. Therefore, if Antonio extends his good name – that is, his credit rating – to Bassanio, and if he shoots a second arrow to follow the first, then he might get double the return on his investment. Here, too, in Bassanio's ad-hoc loan pitch, the language of Heidegger is foreshadowed: the kinetic *Geworfenheit* or flungness of the flighted arrow, the belief vested in 'adventuring' and 'hazard'. For Heidegger, being flung into the world involves a *Wagnis*, venture, and venture involves danger, *Gefahr*. 'If that which has been flung remained out of danger', he tells us in *Wozu Dichter?*, 'it would not have been ventured'.[3] No pain, no gain.

Antonio, overextended himself, allows for his own credit – the measure of his sovereignty and status – to be, as he says, 'rack'd': widened, extended, but an image which also suggests those old Germanic tortures. Thus begins a set of ventures, of deferrals and suspensions, of withdrawals and disappearances, as joined up and mutually dependent as the giant networks of global capital itself: Bassanio's trip to Belmont, Shylock's plot, Jessica's elopement and so on – you know the story, or at least we will credit you with knowing the story. But what we, here, want to emphasize about the economic system that is *The Merchant of Venice* is what we also want to underline about post-gold-standard economy itself: its tendency, on the one hand, towards immateriality (money, in a sense, *is* not; it is not a substantial commodity as Marx sometimes thought; it has disappeared within the fibre-optic relays of the world's far-flung banking systems; even on paper it represents no more than a promise, 'I promise to pay the bearer on demand the sum of. . .' or a deferred act of trust underwritten by the metaphysical authority of God, as in the dollar bill) and, on the other hand, the very opposite. Let's ask: what is at stake within *The Merchant of Venice*'s ventures, what steps into the intervals, delays and gaps that speculation opens up? The answer, which takes us back to Nietzsche, is the body. When the soul, the sovereign soul, the good soul of the merchant of Venice is ventured, that venture will be held accountable in pounds and ounces, and that holding to account – measure for measure – will be called justice.

If *The Merchant of Venice* is one large economic system, then its central drama is the conflict between two co-existing yet contradictory conceptions of economy itself. We might call these the *Antonian* and the *Shylockean*, and we would like these two meanings of economy to overlay, for reasons that will soon become obvious, a distinction inherited from Aristotle between *oikonomia* and *techne chrematisike*, between natural economy and the art of money-making. Crudely stated, this is the distinction between the good, Antonian natural economy of the *oikos* and the bad, Shylockean artificial economy that arises when money *(to khrema)* appears on the scene. Derrida, in a fascinating passage from *Given Time: I. Counterfeit Money*, summarizes Aristotle's distinction between economics and chrematistics thus:

> For Aristotle, it is a matter of an ideal and desirable limit, a limit between the limit and the unlimited, between the true and finite good (the economic) and the illusory and indefinite good (the chrematistic).[4]

'Economics' comes from *oikos* – home, hearth, seat of the family, the household, indeed of all those things that Derrida lists under 'the proper' – and 'chrematistics' from *to khrema*, money, the unlimited exchangeability of goods that occurs when money appears on the scene. As Bacon writes in his essay 'Of Usury', which is roughly contemporary with *The Merchant of Venice,* 'They say. . . it is against nature for *Money* to beget *Money*'.[5] Money begetting money is bastard begetting. The distinction between economy and chrematistics is reflected not only in that between the limited and the unlimited but also in that between, continuing the preceding quote, 'the supposed finiteness of need and the presumed infinity of desire'. Once money, *to khrema*, has appeared on the scene, the infinity of desire will always transcend the finitude of need. Money is the desire of desire itself, *apriori* unsatisfied by any object one might actually need – behold, the logic of shopping! The fact that Derrida's language recalls that of Levinas (need/desire, finitude/infinity) is perhaps not accidental, for in opposition to an anti-monetary tradition in philosophy that begins with Aristotle and culminates with Marx (communism is the name of a society without the alienating spectrality of money), Levinas is one of the rare thinkers, like Locke indeed, who reserve a privileged place for money in his work. He writes in 'The Ego and Totality':

> Money then does not purely and simply mark the reification of man. It is an element in which the personal is maintained while being quantified – this is what is proper to money and constitutes, as it were, its dignity as a philosophical category.[6]

Connecting this line of thought with Derrida, he continues the passage from *Given Time* with a gesture that will be familiar to readers of his work: 'As soon as there is the monetary sign – and first of all the sign – that is, *différance* and credit, the *oikos* is opened and cannot operate its limit'. Money, in effect, is deconstruction; *différance* is credit, opening the closure of the *oikos*, what Levinas calls totality, to the unrestricted 'economy' of desire where money circulates and where wealth is accumulated or squandered.

It is crystal clear from the first scene of the play that the meaning of Antonio's being, as it were, is determined economically in terms of *oikonomia*. When Shylock says that Antonio is a good man, and Bassanio asks if he has heard otherwise, Shylock replies:

> Ho no, no, no, no: my meaning in saying he is a good man, is to have you understand me that he is sufficient. (1.3.12–15)

This, a line that we will return to when we look at Marx later, is simply the echo of Antonio's own elision, when speaking to Bassanio, of his 'purse' and 'person':

> My purse, my person, my extremest means
> Lie all unlock'd to your occasions. (1.1.138–39)

Personality is pursonality. But Antonio's purse is empty, for his argosies with portly sail are also far-flung, all abroad in Tripoli, Mexico, the Indies, England and the whole imagined geography of the commercial orb of which the *urbs* of Venice is both the mirror and the marketplace.[7] The *urbs* of Venice is the orb of the emergent world market and a prospect of what Elizabethan London might turn into in the ensuing centuries. So Bassanio uses Antonio's name, his good, clean, proper name, to gain credit from the usurer. It is with the issue of credit that we pass from Antonian *oikonomia* to Shylockean chrematistics.

Shylock hates Antonio because Antonio abused him and spat upon him at the marketplace of the Rialto and called him a dog. 'Hath a dog money?' Shylock quips in one of his unnerving mimic voices (note how his speeches are constantly interspersed with acts of ventriloquy – Shylock do the police in different voices). But, more fundamentally still, Shylock hates Antonio because he is bad for business. He lends money without interest and thus threatens the livelihood of Shylock and the shadowy Tubal, who is the real power player in the play. As everyone knows, Christians were forbidden to lend money for profit, and Antonio ceaselessly attempts to cancel out the chrematistic logic of credit by restoring the natural economy of interest-free exchange. Shylock explains the beneficial effects of interest with the slightly baroque biblical story of Laban's sheep tended by Jacob, where these 'wooly breeders' illustrate the way in which money can breed. To Antonio's sly question, 'Or is your gold and silver ewes and rams', Shylock wittily replies, 'I cannot tell, I make it breed as fast' (1.3.90–91). As Marc Shell points out, there is a delightful word play at work in this passage between Jews or Iewes, Ewes and Use.[8] *Iewes use like Ewes*. That is, Jews are usurers that make money breed as fast as Jacob's sheep. If we were feeling a little reckless, then we might even speculate on the link between *'iewes'* and *'iusticia'*, between original justice and Jewishness.

Oikonomeia runs over into chrematistics once desire appears on the scene: desire is another name for this excessive tendency that ruptures the limit of the *oikos*. This is exactly what happens in *The Merchant of Venice*, not just once but multiply. Antonio's self-sufficiency is opened up into a larger *chrematon* by Bassanio's desire for Portia. Conversely, Bassanio's possession of what has become his *oikos* – home, hearth and wife – is suspended and ruptured by the demands of Antonio, who makes it pretty clear in act 4, scene 1 that he desires Bassanio (he describes him as his 'love'). We could go as far as to say that Shylock desires Antonio, in as much as he wants his body; in this respect, Shylock uses his chrematistic trading zone as his wooing bower, his pick-up pad. Antonio may be able to reject Salerio's opening thesis about his melancholia, the commerce theory, and to reject also Solanio's, the love theory – 'Why then you are in love', 'Fie, Fie' says Antonio – but taken together, overlaid, the two theses between them hit the nail on the head. In and around Shakespeare's Venice, desire *is* an economy, to be both experienced and expressed in purely economic terms. More precisely, what is going on in the drama of

The Merchant of Venice is the transformation of the language of courtly love into commerce, where the supposedly natural economy of eros is broken open by the chrematistic logic of money-making. Bassanio's quest for Portia is largely a fiscal one: underwritten by a loan, semi-secured against her fortune. Her remarkable declaration of love to him in act 3, scene 2 is couched in the language of accountancy, appreciation and conversion: 'only to stand high in your account', she says, 'I would exceed account' and 'be trebled twenty times myself. . . a thousand times more fair, ten thousand times more rich'. 'Myself and what is mine to you and yours/Is now converted' (3.2.149–67).

Portia is a body and an estate, that which exceeded the body of her father. From her first entry into Shakespeare's text this dualism, this double-act of the body and its surplus which is at once spectral and material, makes itself felt: 'By my troth', she tells Nerissa, 'my little body is aweary of this great world' – whereupon Nerissa immediately talks of 'abundance', 'surfeit' and 'superfluity' (1.2.1–9). The several physical descriptions we get of her are steeped in the rhetoric of surplus, of exceeding: she is 'fair, and (fairer than that word)/ Of wondrous virtues' (1.1.161–63); her physical form outruns her portrait to the same measure as the portrait exceeds Bassanio's description of it in act 3, scene 2. In winning Portia, Bassanio acquires what he calls 'new int'rest' (3.2.220). Before that interest can be converted or cashed in for Portia's body, though, two things must take place. Firstly, a ring must be exchanged: a ring whose loss, Portia explains in exemplary fiscal diction, would 'presage the ruin of your love/And be my vantage to exclaim on you' (3.2.173–74). Secondly, there is that other matter of interest being cashed in for a body: I promise to pay the bearer on demand the sum of one pound – of my flesh. And yet has not Shylock's extremism been played out already, in the casket lottery? Saturday night game shows and reality TV have never gone this far, even in Japan. The set-up that Portia's father, brilliantly depraved producer, has created demands that contestants stake their body parts against the prize. And not just any body part: they have to stake their penis – or let us rather say its 'natural', productive use in women.

This moneying of love, this economization of eros in whose chrematistic machinations vital body parts get caught, is not restricted to *The Merchant of Venice*. It is everywhere in Shakespeare – not least in the sonnets, from whose outset we are treated to a litany of economic terms and conditions: increase, contract, abundance, waste, 'niggarding' or miserliness. Sonnet 4 is typical in this respect:

> Unthrifty loveliness, why dost thou spend
> Upon thyself thy beauty's legacy?
> Nature's bequest gives nothing, but doth lend,

And being frank, she lends to those are free:
Then, beauteous niggard, why dost thou abuse
The bounteous largesse given thee to give?
Profitless usurer, why dost thou use
So great a sum of sums, yet canst not live?[9]

If you don't reproduce you can leave no 'acceptable audit':

Thy unused beauty must be tombed with thee,
Which usèd, lives th'executor to be.

In the context of *The Merchant of Venice*, the interplay of 'use', 'abuse' and 'usurer' cannot have escaped your attention. Shakespeare returns to this grouping in Sonnet 6, arguing again for natural reproduction:

That use is not forbidden usury
Which happies those that pay the willing loan

– a 'willing loan' that is the opposite of being 'self-willed': the latter option will make you 'death's conquest and make worms thine heir'.

This is the image presented Morocco, Portia's first suitor: his casket contains a death's head and a poem about tombs and worms, contents which condemn him to a life of self-willing (onanism) or homosexuality – both 'unnatural', forbidden forms of expenditure, abuses rather than good usages of seminal (and here we use the word in all its senses) credit. The pun on 'willing' and 'willed' also recalls Portia's complaint that 'the will of a living daughter' is 'curb'd by the will of a dead father'. In Sonnet 135 this word 'will' appears thirteen times:

Whoever hath her wish, thou hast thy Will,
And Will to boot, and Will in overplus;
More than enough am I, that vex thee still,
To thy sweet will making addition thus.

– and so on. Will is desire, testament, proper name and sexual organ – both male and female: the poet at one point saucily requests to 'hide my will in thine', 'whose will is large and spacious'. This hermaphroditic ambiguity also appears in Sonnet 20, whose effeminate male addressee, 'the master mistress of my passion', was 'for a woman. . . first created'.

Till nature as she wrought thee fell a-doting,
And by addition thee of me defeated,
By adding one thing to my purpose nothing. . .

That is, 'she pricked thee out for women's pleasure'. Will, prick, is surplus: adding one to nothing. Portia uses exactly the same trope when proposing her and Nerissa's transvestitism: men 'will think we are accomplished with what we lack' (3.4.61–62). (Jessica, echoing Portia in more directly fiscal terms, calls her own gender-switch 'my exchange' (2.6.35) – and this as she drops a weighty casket of her father's money down on Lorenzo). With this new surplus, this hermaphroditic excess, begins a further set of projections and investments and self-flingings (Bassanio will fling both himself and his ring at Balthazar, Gratiano ditto at the clerk) – ventures that, again, threaten the finite order of the *oikos*. Not only the economy of desire but also that of the body itself, its use and status, has been opened up to chrematistic excess and can no longer operate its good and natural limit.

This situation, this dreadful, unnatural condition, almost proves fatal for Antonio in act 4. But right from the beginning he was sensing its first rumblings, in the way that animals first sense approaching earthquakes or neurotics the returning rumblings of the repressed. Antonio, title character and model citizen of the Venetian state, is sad: melancholy, anxious, as though manifesting the symptoms of a trauma brought on by a disaster that has not yet happened, or has not yet (as Beckett would say) taken its course. The disaster, we say, is none other than *to khrema*, at once the excessive tendency that carries desire beyond the limits of the proper *and* a global credit system or finance capitalism. Its avatar is Shylock. Shylock's logic threatens so much more than just the good, Christian economic order: spilling beyond this, it threatens all the world's natural regimes, all its good usages. The Antonian melancholy that frames *The Merchant of Venice* is the anticipation of a system of universal Shylockery: the world as a market regulated by a credit system where one's being is determined by a credit rating, by the nature and extent of one's debt.

Shylock is *to khrema*'s avatar – and yet in the central exchange of the drama he appears to break with the chrematistic logic of usury. He says that he wants to be friends with Antonio and Bassanio and decides to give not for interest, but in kind, out of kindness. He offers, in a merry sport, the bond of the pound of Antonio's flesh, to which the latter retorts:

> Content in faith, I'll seal to such a bond
> And say there is much kindness in the Jew. (1.3.48–49)

It is here that the parallel between *The Merchant of Venice* and Nietzsche's Second Essay is most striking, where it is difficult to imagine that

Nietzsche didn't have a copy of the text, or at least the Schlegel-Tieck translation, open as he penned these lines:

> To inspire trust in his promise to repay, to provide a guarantee of the seriousness and sanctity of his promise, to impress repayment as a duty, an obligation upon his own conscience, the debtor [*Schuldner*] made a contract with the creditor [*Gläubiger*] and pledged that if he should fail to repay he would substitute something else that he 'possessed', something he had control over; for example, his body, his wife, his freedom or even his life. [. . .] (*GM* 64; insertions ours)

But Nietzsche continues a few lines later, even more strikingly:

> Above all, however, the creditor could inflict every kind of indignity and torture upon the body of the debtor; for example, cut from it as much as seemed commensurate with the size of the debt. (*GM* 64)

Of course, what we are perhaps confronting here is the Roman source for both Nietzsche's genealogy of morals and Shylock's flesh-bond. According to the first-century legal historian, Aulus Gellius, the Roman law on debt stipulated that, should the debt be unpaid, the debtor would be confined for a period of sixty days after which time he could be condemned to death and 'the laws allowed (the creditor) to cut the man to pieces if they wished, and share his body'.[10]

Another parallel suggests itself here. It is tempting to imagine that Freud was thinking of *The Merchant of Venice* when he mapped the complex neural relays and deferrals of his patient the Rat Man. This neurotic is obsessed with two things: debt and torture. A chance anecdote by an officer on some military manoeuvres has planted in his mind the image of Chinese rat-torture, in which a bucket containing a hungry rat is attached to the victim's buttocks and the rat eats its way up the victim's rectal passage. It doesn't take Freud long to forge a link between the large debts (*Schulden*) of the patient's *Spielratte* (compulsive gambling) father, the guilt or *Schuld* felt by the patient, his accompanying obsession with paying off a sum of money that in reality he doesn't actually owe (a debt that he experiences as inextricably linked to systems of transit and transportation, like Antonio's) and his fear of rats that, anally concentrated and covering up for its opposite, desire, opens up a homosexual dimension within his sexual constitution. Money itself, the paper currency, is dirty, and so are children, *Ratten*, little rug-rats. 'In his delirium', writes Freud, 'he had coined himself a regular rat-currency, and converted into this all the accumulation of interests around his father's legacy'. Will and will again, in overplus.

Good genealogist and maybe even proto-Freudian that he is (and how could any major Shakespeare character not be a proto-Freudian, given that so many of Freud's insights are based on Shakespeare's works?) Shylock is seeking compensation from his debtor by torturing his body. But, as Nietzsche emphasizes, Shylock desires this torture not because he holds Antonio *responsible* but because he will find recompense in the *pleasure* he feels in enacting his bond,

> the pleasure of being allowed to vent his power freely upon one who is powerless, the voluptuous pleasure *'de faire le mal pour le plasir de le faire'*. (*GM* 65)

This is why Shylock refuses to be paid twice or thrice over in money for his bond: he desires the *pleasure* of torturing Antonio's body. Shylock stands for Venetian law, and he will have his bond, but the desired outcome is pleasure through the other's pain. With characteristically hyperbolic gusto, Nietzsche goes on to imagine festivals of pain at the service of intense pleasure and one imagines gladiatorial contests, public executions and the sort of sadistic glee seen on the faces of the torturers at Abu Ghraib prison in Baghdad. The point here, again, is that the origin of our moral concepts like guilt, conscience and duty is soaked in blood and reared in cruelty. Even the categorical imperative smells of cruelty, Nietzsche insists, which is confirmed by Kant's claim in the *Critique of Practical Reason* that the feeling induced by moral law might be described as *Schmerz,* pain. And the example of Kant illustrates Nietzsche's point: namely, that the history of morality is its increasing spiritualization, where moral 'progress' means less and less physical pain and more and more psychological torture. The materiality of the creditor-debtor relation becomes the spirituality of bad conscience, where I experience my being-indebted, my *Schuldigsein* as the basic expression of my subjectivity. The history of morality is, thus, the inwardization or internalization *(Verinnerlichung)* of pain, where it becomes at once more intense and more subtle. Rather than punishing others, we learn to punish ourselves, inhibiting our desires, despising our instincts and loathing our bodies and their disgusting functions. Nietzsche cites Pope Innocent the Third, who innocently catalogues the horrors of the body,

> impure begetting, disgusting means of nutrition in his mother's womb, baseness of the matter out of which man evolves, hideous stink, secretion of saliva, urine, and filth. (*GM* 67)

Christian morality culminates in a paroxysm of self-laceration, a guilty rage against the self, that is not articulated as rage or laceration, but – and this is the nadir of Christian hypocrisy – as *love* or *mercy*. Nietzsche concludes:

> Here is *sickness*, beyond any doubt, the most terrible sickness that ever raged in man; and whoever can still bear to hear (but today one no longer has ears for this!) how in this night of torment and absurdity there has resounded the cry of *love*, the cry of the most nostalgic rapture, of redemption through *love*, will turn away, seized by invincible horror. (*GM* 93)

With this is mind, we would like to consider the central dramatic *agon* of *The Merchant of Venice*, the trial scene from act 4. At stake is the conflict between mercy and justice. It is assumed by the Doge who presides at the trial, by Portia, Antonio and his retinue that mercy is the truth of justice, just as the New Law is the fulfilment of the Old Law and Christianity is the truth of Judaism.[11] Shylock, the Jew, is therefore asked to show mercy. But – cunning genealogist that he is – he refuses and says 'I stand here for law' (4.1.142). That is, he stands for a more original conception of justice based on the bond between creditor and debtor. From the Nietzschean/Shylockean perspective, Portia's transvestite eloquence about the quality of mercy, 'It droppeth as the gentle rain from heaven upon the place beneath' (4.1.181–82) is a travesty that serves to disguise the basic hypocrisy of the Christian-Moral interpretation of the world. But it's a fascinating travesty, in that it invokes the very principle of surplus and abundance, of prodigality, what Mauss and Bataille call 'expenditure without return' – in short, those tendencies that have so rattled the whole order of the play. Mercy is *mercēs* without measure that, doubly blessed and blessing, tends to infinity. Portia invokes excess, infinity – *to khrema*, one could almost say – then, in a perfectly executed U-turn, does exactly the opposite: she bans it. If one iota of Antonio's flowing silks enrobes the water, if blood that's surplus to the bond be shed, then Shylock will be held accountable for this excess, even to the point of death. By carrying this logic to its end, she recuperates not just Antonio's body from the chrematistic mechanism it has been caught up in, but also all of Shylock's own estate, and, beyond that, his Judaism – that is, in the context of the trading zone of Shakespeare's Venice, his right to practise chrematology itself. Humiliated by the Christians, betrayed by his daughter, bankrupt and compelled to convert, Shylock exits with a whimper, whispering, 'I am not well' (4.1.392).

This brutal reversal, this act of casuistry that, barbaric and elaborate at the same time, Christianizes the Judaic and recuperates the chrematistic into the closed economy of *oikos*, wraps up the central agon. Yet, incredibly, Portia does another U-turn and induces another act of excess, of a giving that breaks the boundary of the proper, of the marriage hearth: still in drag, she persuades Bassanio to let go of his ring. It's as though she wanted to kick-start the cycle of anxiety all over again, in order to recuperate and close it down once more: classic *Fort-Da.* As soon as the men's guilty secret breaks out, the text erupts with images of physical castration ('Would that he were gelt' (5.1.144)), transsexualism ('if a woman live to be a man' (5.1.160)) and sexual infidelity (I slept with Balthazar, Portia tells Bassanio; and I slept with his clerk, Nerissa adds to Gratiano). This new eruption is quickly reined in by the production of a letter – and with this comes, in a lame but necessary plot-twist, the larger recuperation of the ships and merchandise whose venturing enabled the main cycle to take place. Another wrap-up – although Shakespeare cannot resist signing off with a final open gesture that at least registers the spectre of chrematology's possible return. A ring, symbol of value tightly wrapped around the body, limiting its affections by embodying a bond, can still be removed; virtue can still be ventured through the body. Sexual ambiguity even creeps back in through Gratiano's bawdy bottom diction of sore rings. The play's final lines are:

> Well, while I live, I'll fear no other thing
> So sore, as keeping safe Nerissa's ring. (5.1.306–307)

A ring is a cycle, too, of course, a symbol of repetition: nothing ever *really* ends. . .

Which brings us, in a coda, to another student of Shylock and sometime Shakespearean: Karl Marx. Considering the monumental scale of Marx's research into political economy and the capitalist economic system, analyses which, whatever failings they may have, nonetheless merit revisiting in light of the spread of what we all too easily call globalization, he says relatively little about the central issue of *The Merchant of Venice*, namely credit. One finds a few fascinating remarks on credit scattered in *Capital* Volume 3, where Marx identifies a structural ambiguity in the late nineteenth-century credit system: on the one hand, it develops exploitation to its most pure form through what Marx calls 'gambling and swindling'; on the other hand, in its development of a world market the credit system raises the capitalist mode of production to 'a certain degree of perfection' and anticipates the advent of the rule of associated labour:

> The credit system will serve as a powerful lever during the transition from the capitalist mode of production to the mode of production of associated labour.[12]

The modern credit system is, thus, a strange mixture of 'swindler and prophet'. More than a century after Marx's remarks, it would appear that the swindlers have won out over the prophets.

More interesting and more Shakespearean is a much earlier text from 1844, written during the same extraordinary creative burst as the Paris Manuscripts: 'Excerpts from James Mill's *Elements of Political Economy*'.[13] It is here that Marx begins to analyse money and extends the theoretical tools honed in his critiques of Hegel, Feuerbach and Bauer into the analysis of political economy. Marx asks, in an oddly Heideggerian-sounding formulation, after the *Wesen* of credit:

> What constitutes the essence of credit? We disregard here the *content* of credit which is once again money. We disregard then the content of this trust according to which a man accords *recognition* to another man by advancing money to him and . . . expresses his confidence that his fellow human being is a 'good' man and not a scoundrel. By a good man the creditor, like Shylock, means a 'sufficient' man. (*EW* 263)

Money functions as the mediator by means of which the products of human labour become *entfremdet*, estranged or alienated. *Money is essentially alienating*. For Marx, it is alienated species-being, our estrangement from the being of being human, from our common humanity and from the community itself. As long as the human being does not recognize himself and others as human but as a credit rating, community or *Gemeinwesen* will only appear in the form of self-estrangement, becoming what Marx calls a commercial society, where 'each of its members is a *merchant*' (*EW* 266). The idea of money as mediator leads Marx to the statement that money is the veritable God, or rather it is Christ-like. Just as in Christianity, the person of Christ is the mediating instance in the relation of God to the human being, so too with money. As Marx insists in so many of his early texts, there is a peculiar and powerful mirroring between religious self-alienation and secular self-alienation where money is the medium of alienation in capitalist society. Money, as Marx will later claim in *Capital,* is the universal equivalent for commodities in the process of exchange. Things lose their meaning insofar as they are transformed into commodities and 'natural' Antonian economic relations become dehumanized.

The banking and credit system does not, as Saint-Simon and even Proudhon thought, humanize monetary activity. On the contrary, it deepens estrangement and alienation into the heart of man, literally into his flesh. This is the truth of Shylock's identification of goodness with good credit. Under conditions of finance capitalism, good credit is a sufficient condition of goodness. Continuing the preceding quote from the text on James Mill, Marx writes:

> Credit is the *economic* judgement on the *morality* of man. In the credit system *man* replaces metal or paper as the mediator of exchange. However, he does this not as man but as the *existence (Dasein) of capital and interest.* (*EW* 264)

In the credit system, man becomes transformed into money, and money has literally been incorporated into him. Like some financial parody of the Eucharist, credit infuses the heart with the alienating divinity of money. Shylock, in his determination to have Antonio's flesh, is therefore enacting the essence of credit insofar as goodness equals economic sufficiency and this becomes flesh. By contrast, the person without credit is 'a social pariah and a bad man' (*EW* 265). Marx goes on:

> The substance, the body clothing, the *spirit of money* is not money, paper, but instead it is my personal existence *(Dasein)*, my flesh and blood, my social worth and status. Credit no longer actualises money-values in actual money but in human flesh and human hearts. (*EW* 264)

In Heideggerese, we could say that the essence of alienated human *Dasein* is monetary – one could imagine here an entire rewriting of Heidegger's analysis of inauthenticity and authenticity in economic terms, where the human being is literally being-indebted, *Schuldigsein* and where human beings are flung into the facticity of financial flows.

We can link the above, particularly the identification of money with divinity, to another triangulation of Shakespeare, Marx and money from 1844. On this occasion, the allusion is not to *The Merchant of Venice* but to *Timon of Athens*, where the idea of the divinity of money is coupled with its whore-like character. Money, Marx writes, is the pimp between need and object, making available all objects and objectifying all beings, especially human beings, into prostitutes for my imagined needs. In a quotation repeated in *Capital* Volume 1, Marx cites Shakespeare speaking of money as 'Thou common whore of mankind' and,

> Thou *visible god,*
> That solder'st *close impossibilities,*
> And mak'st them kiss.[14]

Money is the visible God and common whore of mankind. That is, there is nothing that money cannot solder together, no two commodities for which money will not be the pimp that permits the exchange. In a mercantile society, everything is for sale and everyone is a prostitute insofar as their value is ultimately determinable in monetary terms. Playing on the connotations of the German *Vermögen*, the availability of money determines my capacity and my ability in terms of my wealth. As such, Marx goes on, money is the alienated *Vermögen* of humankind, that is, wealth is alienated human capacity and ability. Money is an extraordinary power of inversion, transforming wishes from imagination to reality and making reality illusory, into what Marx will describe in *Capital* as the vast phantasmagoria of commodity fetishism, more plainly stated, the world market. Money transforms imagined need (say the need for plastic surgery) into real objects and real need into imagined objects (making, say, poverty either invisible or the fault of the poor). As such, money is the bond that binds together capitalist society, it is what Marx calls in an arresting phrase 'the bond of all bonds':

> If *money* is the bond which ties me to *human* life and society to me, which links me to nature and to man, is money not the bond of all *bonds*? Can it not bind and loose all bonds? Is it therefore not the universal *means of separation*? It is the true *agent of separation* and the true *cementing agent*, it is the *chemical* power of society. (*EW* 377)

Yet most interesting in this regard are the final pages of the slightly earlier text, 'On the Jewish Question' from 1843, where Marx engages in a set of reversals and double-reversals no less extraordinary than those undertaken by Shakespeare. Marx offers an essentially anti-Semitic, Antonian argument. That is, if Nietzsche can be thought of as Shylock, then Marx sounds like Antonio or some portly cross-dressed Portia. What is strange about Marx is the utterly Christian logic of his argument: credit is bad and immoral, money dehumanizes. Marx's utterly provocative thesis is that the bourgeois world, the Antonian world of Christian capitalism, has become Shylockean. That is, Christendom has become dominated by *Judentum,* by what Marx calls 'practical Jewishness', and by its secular God, money. Christians have become practical Jews, not what Marx calls *Sabbatsjuden*, Sabbath Jews, but *Alltagsjuden*, everyday Jews. In one of his choicest dialectical inversions, Marx writes:

> Christianity derives from Judaism. It has once again been dissolved into Judaism. From the very beginning the Christian was the theorising Jew, the Jew therefore is the practical Christian, and the practical Christian has again become a Jew.[15]

In other words, capitalism is a system of universal Shylockery, where all Antonian limits of the *oikos,* the hearth, the home, the *Heimat,* the homeland and the human, have been burst apart by the energy of chrematistic exchange and excess. The giving of credit has shifted from a marginal practice allotted to Jews in a handful of mediaeval and renaissance cities to the increasingly global manner in which identity is constituted. I am, you are, we all are a credit history, a record of debt, against which our goodness, our sufficiency is measured. I owe, therefore I am. And if I do not owe, I am not. Being is being in debt, goodness is good credit. Ontology and ethics flow from the same money pot.

Postscriptum: one of the authors of this chapter recently moved to a job in New York – contemporary Venice – and has been unable to get a credit card. Why? Because he does not have a credit history, a history of debt. How, he asked, after the third company had turned him down, might he get in debt? Well, of course, the answer was by getting a credit card. A beautiful economic ring, if still slightly sore.

NOTES

1. Friedrich Nietzsche, *On the Genealogy of Morals: A Polemic*, trans. Walter Kaufmann and R. J. Hollingdale, in *On the Genealogy of Morals and Ecce Homo*, ed. Walter Kaufmann (New York: Vintage, 1967), 61; hereafter cited as *GM* with page references in the text.
2. All references to William Shakespeare's *The Merchant of Venice*, ed. J. R. Brown (London: Methuen, 1955), are given parenthetically in the text with act, scene and line numbers.
3. Martin Heidegger, *Holzwege* (Frankfurt a.M.: Klostermann, 1950), 273 and *passim*.
4. Jacques Derrida, *Given Time: I. Counterfeit Money*, trans. Peggy Kamuf (Chicago and London: University of Chicago Press, 1992), 158.
5. Quoted in Shakespeare, *The Merchant of Venice: Texts and Contexts*, ed. M. Lindsay Kaplan (Boston and New York: Bedford/St. Martin's, 2002), 207.
6. Emmanuel Levinas, 'The Ego and Totality', in *Collected Philosophical Papers*, trans. Alphonso Lingis (Dordrecht: Kluwer, 1987), 45.
7. See the extracts from *Coryats Crudities* in *The Merchant of Venice: Texts and Contexts*, 139.
8. See 'The Wether and the Ewe: Verbal Usury in *The Merchant of Venice*', in *Money, Language and Thought*, ed. Marc Shell (Baltimore and London: Johns Hopkins University Press, 1993), 47–83.
9. Quotations are from *William Shakespeare's Sonnets*, ed. Katherine Duncan-Jones (London: Thomson Publishing, 1997).
10. Quoted in John Gillies, *Shakespeare and the Geography of Difference* (Cambridge: Cambridge University Press, 1994), 127.
11. Derrida places the question of the relation of mercy and justice, and in particular the question of mercy as the overcoming or *relève* of justice, at the centre of his reading of the play in 'What Is a "Relevant" Translation?', trans. Lawrence Venuti, *Critical Inquiry* 27.2 (Winter 2001): 174–201.

12. See the chapter on 'Pre-Capitalist Relationships', in *Capital, Volume 3,* trans. David Fernbach (London: Penguin, 1981), 728–48 (743).

13. In Karl Marx, *Early Writings*, trans. R. Livingstone and G. Benton (London: Penguin, 1975), 259–78; hereafter cited as *EW* with page references in the text. We would like to thank Daniel Morris for drawing this text to our attention and also for his stimulating conversations about Marx.

14. Marx, 'Economic and Philosophical Manuscripts', in *Early Writings*, 376. See also Karl Marx, *Capital, Volume 1*, trans. Ben Fowkes (London: Penguin, 1976), 230.

15. In Karl Marx, *Early Political Writings*, ed. Joseph O'Malley (Cambridge: Cambridge University Press, 1994), 55.

BIBLIOGRAPHY

DERRIDA, Jacques. *Given Time: I. Counterfeit Money*. Translated by Peggy Kamuf. Chicago and London: University of Chicago Press, 1992.

DERRIDA, Jacques. 'What Is a "Relevant" Translation?' Translated by Lawrence Venuti. *Critical Inquiry* 27.2 (Winter 2001): 174–201.

GILLIES, John. *Shakespeare and the Geography of Difference*. Cambridge: Cambridge University Press, 1994.

HEIDEGGER, Martin. *Holzwege*. Frankfurt a.M.: Klostermann, 1950.

LEVINAS, Emmanuel. *Collected Philosophical Papers*. Translated by Alphonso Lingis. Dordrecht: Kluwer, 1987.

MARX, Karl. *Capital, Volume 1*. Translated by Ben Fowkes. London: Penguin, 1976.

MARX, Karl. *Capital, Volume 3*. Translated by David Fernbach. London: Penguin, 1981.

MARX, Karl. *Early Political Writings*. Edited by Joseph O'Malley. Cambridge: Cambridge University Press, 1994.

MARX, Karl. *Early Writings*. Translated by R. Livingstone and G. Benton. London: Penguin, 1975.

NIETZSCHE, Friedrich. *On the Genealogy of Morals: A Polemic*. Translated by Walter Kaufmann and R. J. Hollingdale. In *On the Genealogy of Morals and Ecce Homo*. Edited, with commentary, by Walter Kaufmann. New York: Vintage, 1967.

NIETZSCHE, Friedrich. *Zur Genealogie der Moral*. Edited by G. Colli and M. Montinari. Berlin and New York: De Gruyter, 1988.

SHAKESPEARE, William. *The Merchant of Venice*. Edited by J. R. Brown. London: Methuen, 1955.

SHAKESPEARE, William. *The Merchant of Venice: Texts and Contexts*. Edited by M. Lindsay Kaplan. Boston and New York: Bedford/St. Martin's, 2002.

SHAKESPEARE, William. *Shakespeare's Sonnets*. Edited by Katherine Duncan-Jones. London: Thomson Publishing, 1997.

SHELL, Marc. *Money, Language and Thought*. Baltimore and London: Johns Hopkins University Press, 1993.

Chapter 7

'We are all prostitutes'

Crisis and libidinal economy

Benjamin Noys

That capitalism is a libidinal economy is something that Marx noted in his *Economic and Philosophical Manuscripts* of 1844 when he stated prostitution 'is only a *particular* expression of the *universal* prostitution of the *worker*' (1975: 350, n.4; italics in original).[1] Here that experience is presented negatively, as one of use and abuse and, as Carole Pateman noted,[2] problematically: the choice of prostitution as a symbol of wage labour relies on its degraded and feminized status to make the critical point, thereby revealing that prostitution is *not* the same as wage labour. I want to explore a brief and spaced-out sequence of theoretical interventions that take seriously, and even literally, the notion of capitalism as an experience of 'universal prostitution'. These are Pierre Klossowski's *La monnaie vivante* (orig., 1970), which traces the libidinal experience of capitalism as a site of suffering and subversion; Jean-François Lyotard's *Libidinal Economy* (1973), which makes the radical identification of capitalism with libidinal economy, suggesting the libidinal enjoyment that capitalism provides; and, finally, the activist-collective Tiqqun's *Preliminary Materials for a Theory of the Young-Girl* (1999), which returns to Klossowski to argue for resistance against capitalist nihilism in which we are all tradeable bodies.

These turns to the notion of capitalism as libidinal economy are also theological or, more precisely, instances of Christian theology. While the relationship between sexuality and Christian theology and religious practice has often, rightly, been regarded as highly conflictual, the work of Pierre Klossowski explicitly engages theology, in a highly heterodox manner, to explore living currency as a form of universal prostitution. This theological thread remains in Lyotard's work, although often obliterated by his more strident attempt at a purely intensive libidinal discourse. For

Tiqqun theological discourse is a more dispersed resource which echoes in their discourse as they aim to traverse the nihilism of capital. In each case a theological structure penetrates in terms of a belief in the powers of the body qua 'living currency'. Poised uneasily in relation to capitalism's exploitation and extraction of value from the body, these libidinal discourses aim to explode the support of capitalism in the identity imposed on the body as a source of value. At the same time, they also engage with the tension of capitalism's exploitation of the libidinal body as a source of value. These structurally uneasy sets of works, while a seemingly 'minor' sequence of theoretical reflection, offer a striking attempt to come to terms with capitalism's capacity to subsume the most seemingly outré elements of human behaviour to the value-form.

These discourses all pre-date the moment of global capitalist crisis, beginning in 2008, but also echo, uncannily, in that moment. Each, in their different ways, tries to engage with capitalism as a totalizing system, one which reaches right down into the body and so into the libidinal and even into the 'soul'. In this way they engage with the contemporary experience of capitalism as global – the crisis has affected everyone, although in remarkably uneven fashion. They also engage with our attachment to capitalism, with the ways in which we are libidinally galvanized to produce and consume the world rendered as a world of value. Finally, they also engage with the theological dimension of this attachment as one of desire and belief. While I will consider these discourses as problematic, often as much mirrors of capitalism's own libidinal structure as critiques of it, they pose to us the difficulty of a detachment from capitalism that would liberate us from the tyranny of value.

MARX AVEC SADE

In 1970 Pierre Klossowski published *La monnaie courante* (*Living Currency*),[3] which Eleanor Kaufman describes as 'a genre-defying book that is part economic analysis and part pseudo-pornographic photography and illustration'.[4] The original version of the work paired text with photographs and illustrations of 'Roberte' (Klossowski's wife Denise Morin-Sinclaire) in erotic *tableaux vivants*, although here I will be concerned only with the text. Klossowski's fundamental argument is that there is a libidinal economy of pulsations, intensities and desires, on which the industrial system depends and which it tries to neutralize and contain.[5] If Marx suggested that capitalism was always vampiric on 'living labour',[6] Klossowski suggests it is parasitic on 'living currency': 'all modern industry is based on a barter that is mediated by the sign of inert currency, neutralising the nature of the objects exchanged' and this 'inert currency' is reliant on pre-existing labour-power or living currency.[7] 'Beneath' living labour is living currency, a distribution of exchangeable bodies that found their initial formulation in the writing of Sade, with their 'orgies are arranged like mechanical ballets'.[8] Sade's 'sensuous polymorphy'[9] prefigures a social system of 'pure' exchange.

This prefiguration was, however, problematic. Klossowski, instead, turns to the 'long-buried' project of Charles Fourier: the nineteenth-century utopian communist who stressed that sociality is founded on the play of passions (*MV* 26). For Klossowski, Fourier's utopian vision of phalansteries – communities in which passions would be freely exchanged and shared – refuses the logic of punitive labour (*MV* 27). Unlike Sade's 'mechanical ballets', in which perversion is always bound to the norms it violates and incarnates the death drive, Fourier celebrates the 'malleability' and 'plasticity' of drives (*MV* 29). For Sade, we might say, eroticism tends to a zero-sum game and what Sade reveals is the economic role of libidinal exchanges. Fourier, in contrast, resists the industrial system of exchange and postulates an irreducible play of passions. Sade offers the anti-utopia of violation, and so Sade is the truth of the present, while Fourier offers a utopia of the harmony of the passions and so a possible vision of the future (*MV* 31).

Sade recognizes that 'free exchanges' are, in fact, a form of universal prostitution. His schemas of sexual exchange and exploitation reveal the importance of the object, of the victim, with repetition as the common factor of perversion and industrial production. The Sadean libertine desires the same victim again and again, either in the form of the indestructible victim, magically restored to wholeness after every violation, or in the form of a replica, to substitute in a series. Manufacturing does the same, by turning out durable objects of use that are the same but can be exploited to destruction. This is not to be decried as such, since the sterility of the industrial system reveals 'primordial perversion' – the sterility that Klossowski had previously identified in Sade's insistence on the 'the irreducible, primitive fact of sodomy' (*SMN* 6), which 'suppresses the specific borders between the sexes' (*SMN* 29) and refutes reproduction. This is why we have to read Marx avec Sade, in the same way Lacan reads Kant avec Sade.[10] Sade is the truth of Marx, revealing the perverse system of sterility on which the industrial system depends.

Klossowski's argument, therefore, is not limited to the claim made by Adorno and Horkheimer: that Sade is the truth of Kant and the Enlightenment, in terms of the reduction of humanity to manipulated material.[11] A similar thesis underlies Pasolini's film *Salo* (1975), which adapts Sade's *120 Days of Sodom* as an allegory of the fascist manipulation and exploitation of the vulnerable body. Klossowski is more (perversely) dialectical. Sade reveals the true economy of the exchange of bodies underlying capitalist exchange, but this can figure a new libidinal economy in common that ruptures the limits of exchange value. This is figured in relation to money. Money functions as a mediator, but as a mediator between the integral and unexchangeable desires of the pervert and the system of institutional norms. Money is, as Marx argued, the 'general equivalent',[12] but one that serves also a perverse purpose. Within the generalization of exchange, the pervert perverts this mediation to insinuate the true universal communication as '*the exchange of bodies through the secret language of bodily signs*' (*MV* 61; emphasis in original). If Marx had suggested the 'neutrality' of exchange value occluded exploitation through the extraction of surplus value, Klossowski deliberately corrupts this argument. While Marx treated 'universal prostitution' as the metaphoric truth of capitalist society, for Klossowski the pervert literalizes this metaphor, but to reveal the truth of another form of exchange.

Sade is not solely the figure of complete manipulation, because he maintains a link between passions and the living object. This link is severed by the industrial economy, which undertakes the production of simulacra – erotic images which can circulate on the market as they pervert that market. These simulacra are generated from the singular perverse phantasm but become exchangeable objects, in a transformation from a use value into an exchange value. This politics of transformation is a spiritual politics. Marx had noted the theological element of money and capital, in its function of mediation and transubstantiation of labour into value.[13] Sade turns this effect into a ludic transaction, a game that plays on the appropriative and exploitative function of money. The fact that accumulated money embodies accumulated exploitation and suffering is, precisely, a reason for the Sadean libertine to waste it on their own pleasure, to put it back into circulation. Their purchase of pleasure is increased by the knowledge that the medium of purchase is a medium of misery.

Klossowski's dream is the replacement of the system of capitalism or, as he prefers, modern industry, by the direct exchange of living bodies. This system is already in operation, but in the form that creates 'living slaves' – people treated as objects of exploitation, including sexual exploitation as simulacra. Klossowski's example is the film star Sharon Tate and the way in which her tragic fate, brutally murdered by the so-called Manson family in 1969, became an object of fascination (*MV* 74). To be valued as living currency would destroy this exploitation, because we would become a sign of value, integral value, constituted by perversion. The realization of Fourier's utopia is possible, due to industrial development, but only by the abolition of our sense of fictional unity. Klossowski's aim is not to restore the dignity of the libidinal body occluded by industrial culture, but rather to explode the very sense of economy in a system of exchanges and interchanges that 'abolish the ownership of the body'.[14] His aim is not a naturalist return to a 'true' instinctual libido but a profound de-naturalization of the libido into a play of exchanges.

The theological intervenes at this point as the explosion of identity in living currency constitutes a system of unstable exchanges that Klossowski formulates in his fiction as the circulation of bodies and souls, or 'breaths'. In his novel *The Baphomet* (1965), Klossowski rewrites the fate of the Knights Templar – persecuted for heresy and tortured into confessing to sodomy, the defiling of the host and worship of the pagan idol Baphomet – as a Nietzschean fable in which the knights commit the crimes they were accused of as a series of eternally recurring 'breaths' (*souffles*).[15] The result is a situation in which these 'breaths' circulate in an exchangeable form, without identity, repeating their transgressions now as states of intensity.[16] This is obviously a heretical conception, in which the unity of God is exploded and, as a result, so too the unity of the individual. Klossowski's explosion of identity also links to his earlier discussion of Sade. Sade, as we've seen, indicates an economy of bodies, but remains trapped within the system of perversion and a rationalist atheism. If Sade exceeded his desire to transgress and defile he would approach a new economy of circulation defined by a Nietzschean 'innocence of becoming' (*SMN* 34). This 'polytheism'[17] explodes the unity of one God but does not depart from the religious altogether. In fact, we enter a new mythical space of exchange at the end or edge of history.[18]

There is a notable equivocation in Klossowski's discourse of 'living currency'. On the one hand, living currency is revealed through the mechanisms of capital that impose a generalized regime of exchange and industrial development. This is in line with Marx's argument that capitalist society is the society in which the commodity, in the form of exchange value, dominates over all,[19] which means for Klossowski living currency can only be realized in capitalist society of exchange. On the other hand, the explosion of identity found in this generalized exchange goes beyond, Klossowski claims, capital's own tendency to dissolve identity: 'It has drowned the most heavenly ecstasies of religious fervor, of chivalrous enthusiasm, of philistine sentimentalism, in the icy water of egotistical calculation'.[20] The dominance of *egotistical* calculation suggests the persistence of the ego, which is exactly Klossowski's target. Again, this is in line with Marx's argument that capitalism is the necessary condition of a new society and that capitalism imposes fetters on the realization of this society. Capitalism makes living currency a possibility, while restricting and containing the circulation of all bodies as living currency. The temporal instability of this realized utopia – at once future state and, as in *The Baphomet*, archaic and out of time – suggests the difficulty Klossowski has in inscribing living currency as a possibility that could be actualized. It will be this tension that lies at the heart of Lyotard's redeployment of Klossowski's living currency.

THE EVIL BOOK

At the age of eleven or twelve, Lyotard reflected, 'I wanted either to become a monk (especially a Dominican), a painter, or historian'.[21] His first choice of vocation, one obviously abandoned, was religious. He also remarked of his work *Libidinal Economy* 'that it was my evil book, the book of evilness that everyone writing and thinking is tempted to do'. The book was sinful in its attempt to abolish mediation, to directly inscribe intensities, and its readers, according to Lyotard, 'gave no consideration to the upheaval it required of my soul'.[22] The theological resonances suggested by Lyotard, and explicit in the aggressive attempt to traverse what Lyotard regards as the religious nihilism of critique, pose the necessity of the 'detour' *through* theology as the means to grasp libidinal economy. Also, Lyotard explicitly rewrites Klossowski's libidinal economy, trying to shift it away from its 'critical' act of posing libidinal economy against industrial economy and towards an identification of libidinal economy with capitalism.

Lyotard's book is dedicated to the construction of a libidinal economy that resists the theatricality of representation. Klossowski's thought of the phantasm, fabricated out of pulsional force, is crucial for this project if it can be detached from perversion. This is because, for Lyotard, perversion is 'a theology of dissimilitude' which is only the reverse of an Augustinian theology of *similtudo*.[23] In Lyotard's libidinal language Augustine imposes a theatrical separation of intensity from signification, while also being suspicious of the intensities the theatrical can produce (*LE* 67). The difficulty Klossowski faces is not of simply generating another theatre based on an outside – this time not God or natural theology, but perversion and paganism. For Lyotard such a move drains the energy of the libidinal and erects it merely as another theology. To justify libidinal economy in terms of a 'great Signifier' (*LE* 73) is to rob it of its disruptive force.

Lyotard tries to intensify the disruptive aspect of Klossowski's living currency, while cutting it off from a reference to a perverse economy that somehow underlies the 'actual' economy. Such a discourse of perversion implies not only a norm but also a turning-away, a loss of energy, as we pervert something that is, supposedly, natural. This is also true of the distinction Klossowski makes between phantasm – as singular erotic intensity – and simulacrum – as exchangeable sign. Lyotard rejects what he regards as nihilist substitution or de-intensification from one economy to another. There is no underlying libidinal economy betrayed by its expression. These are all forms of 'dualism which we, libidinal economists, will terminate' (*LE* 91).

In relation to capitalism, this means there is one economy and it is libidinal. There is no use value and no erotic value that underlies it, no anterior site of force:

> We here perceive in outline what, for us, is the most important thing of all, the possibility of imagining syntax, the law of value, and finally trade, and hence this meta-trade which is capital, as *intensive* regions, not merely deintensifying. (*LE* 79; italics in original)

Lyotard 'corrects' Klossowski to suggest we do not have a choice of libidinal economy as past or future utopia, but it is already here, present in the intensities released by capitalism: '[Klossowski] sees in capitalism the return, but unaffirmed and unrecognized as such, of what it rejects, that is, libidinal intensity, in the very heart of the most apparently neutralized exchanges' (*LE* 91). The idea that we could achieve or recover the status of 'living currency' is, strictly speaking, impossible (*LE* 87) – it is a fantasy, because living currency cannot be detached from the system of capitalism as a system of exchange. What is only possible is an intensification of the system of exchange. What happens to the metaphor or reality of prostitution, if there is nothing to be prostituted? Prostitution and Klossowskian adultery become, for Lyotard, figures of indiscernibility, not separate realms but passages between order and intensity (*LE* 81). Prostitution mixes price and the exorbitant. In this way prostitution is not a separate realm or the 'truth' of capitalism as such, but another realization of capitalism that would not distinguish in what way the body is being used.

Lyotard affirms the singular libidinal economy, aligned with the pulsional forces of capitalism. There is no alternative, no betrayal or origin, 'only *prices without values*' (*LE* 93; italics in original). This is the scandal of what I have elsewhere called Lyotard's 'accelerationism': there is only capitalism, one libidinal economy, and only its intensification as the libidinal band.[24] With religion identified with critique (*LE* 6), then the abandonment of both leads into 'pure' affirmation. Of course, the abandonment of transcendence does not necessarily rule out a theological reference, as theology can also be correlated with a thinking of immanence.[25] The radical disenchantment that Lyotard aims at can result in a surreptitious re-enchantment of capitalism as the site of true intensities and their explosive force. This would be Lyotard's own conclusion, as he rejected this attempt to render intensities in their own voice, without meditation.

Despite this obvious difficulty, Lyotard's libidinal accelerationism offers a useful rendering of capitalism qua libidinal economy. Lyotard's attempt to dismantle discourses of alienation or recuperation, which suppose an original force somehow corrupted, registers the dominance and penetration of capitalism as it 'liquifies' its own grounds to further feed the acceleration of value. What Lyotard poses is the tension of any attempt to render libidinal economy as a counter-economy, whether that is by Klossowski, Bataille or Deleuze and Guattari. This is what Lyotard calls 'the phantasy of a non-alienated region' (*LE* 107). In this way Lyotard registers the closure of the global horizon of capitalism, if there is no subversive region, but only as the full realization of capitalism without contradiction or tension, which might be to say as God.

CALLIPYGIAN ECONOMY

Klossowski and Lyotard's accounts of libidinal economy have been taken up again by the grouping Tiqqun, a deliberately anonymous 'theory-collective' who have been persecuted by the French state as potential 'terrorists'.[26] Tiqqun are predominantly indebted to the theoretical work of Giorgio Agamben in their characterization of the present moment, although also to a nexus of related thinkers: Michel Foucault, Gilles Deleuze, Carl Schmitt and Walter Benjamin. The use of the concept of libidinal economy predominates in one of their most controversial works: *Preliminary Materials for a Theory of the Young-Girl*. While not wanting to force this work into a dialectical schema, we can note that it synthesizes elements of Klossowski, whom it directly references, and Lyotard. From Klossowski it retains a sense of the instability of the libidinal, while from Lyotard it retains the insistence that there is no 'outside' to contemporary capitalism.

Tiqqun therefore articulates a critical use of libidinal economy, but a critique that is internal to capitalism as a system that exploits and canalizes the libidinal. Capitalism is, for them, a global system that imposes itself in the neutralization of all differences and contradictions – as a desert. This neutralization is, however, violent, and the situation of global capitalism is one of perpetual civil war.[27] Civil war operates on the terrain of bodies and lives, transforming our 'form of life' into accessible and exploitable identities subject to accumulation. The signature example of such a transformation is the figure of the 'young-girl', as the neutralization of libidinal force in a mode of capture that at once incites sexual desire and constrains a neutral field of marketable differences.[28]

The 'young-girl' is a figure of abstraction and 'total nihilism' (*PM* 91): 'she' is the figure of every subject in the libidinal economy of contemporary capitalism. The obvious difficulty is that much as Marx risked minimizing the specificity of prostitution and its gendered form, so Tiqqun have been criticized for their figuration of capitalism in a female figure, which risks or courts misogyny.[29] This risk is evident in one of the most controversial statements in this controversial work is: 'It appears that all of the concreteness of the world has taken refuge in the ass of the Young-Girl' (*PM* 91). The young-girl is the realization of Klossowski's 'callipygian test' (*SMN* 29): sodomy as the suppression of differences. For Tiqqun, however, this 'concrete' is the reign of abstraction realized and specified in an identity that makes itself into 'living currency' as source of value. Klossowski's attempt to explode the function of identity is in turn absorbed by capitalism as the distribution of saleable intensities.

Jaleh Mansoor's sympathetic but critical reconstruction of Tiqqun's argument suggests the importance of the young-girl as 'stand[ing] for the universal prostitution of the human in the interest of objectified profit'. Like Klossowski and Lyotard, Tiqqun do not suppose a return back to a stability that could save this libidinal economy, but rather a traversal of the nihilism of capital to a disequilibrium or dissymmetry that would disrupt the 'geometry of rationalization'.[30] For Tiqqun the aim is fundamentally what they call ethical: the need to make possible a 'polarization' (*ICW* 20), which can combat the neutralization of capitalist empire. The tension lies in this act of polarization carried out across the virtual body of the young-girl: is polarization a traversal of this body or still, somehow, a rejection of it in the name of polarization? This tension is expressed in the fact that for Tiqqun 'she is a contradiction frozen in tomblike immobility' (PM 125) *and* a 'transitory form' (*PM* 131). The equivocation is restated when they suggest: 'The question is not of the emancipation of the Young-Girl, but of emancipation *in relation* to the Young-Girl' (*PM* 132; italics in original). It is left unclear whether anything remains on the ground of the realization of libidinal economy to be liberated, or exactly what 'relation' we have to form to depart or traverse this figure.

Tiqqun, again, confront the ambivalence of living currency and libidinal economy as a site of absorption and exit, enchantment and disenchantment, faith and atheism, which we have explored. The young-girl, at times, stands for a figure of almost pure negativity: 'The pure void of her form, her profane hostility to everything that is, will condense into explosive blocs of negativity' (*PM* 132). The young-girl becomes a figure of total domination, of abstraction without redeeming qualities, except in the fatal explosion of negativity, in a kind of active nihilism. At this point misogyny returns with a vengeance, as the 'symptom' or 'figure' of capital becomes a something that must be rejected. Here we can see a Gnostic or angelic orientation, in which sex becomes the figure of all attachments to the operation of capital.[31] The anorexic body of the young-girl described by Tiqqun inscribes escape as the turning against the self, a self-hatred or 'decreation', to use Simone Weil's term.[32] At this point the articulation of living currency founders between Klossowski and Lyotard, and between utopia and dystopia.

The artist collective Claire Fontaine, founded in 2004 and involving some members of Tiqqun, places a more militant spin on this tension. The problem of libidinal economy is to be resolved by the human strike, which involves 'the whole of life'.[33] The human strike poses life on and against the 'level' field of capital, which has posed all bodies as sources of value. Again, we have the problem of symmetry: 'The anonymous bodies portrayed [in pornography] were absolutely whatever and because of this very reason generically desirable. Images of real human beings had become for the first time in history objects of desire on a massive scale, and therefore objects'.[34] To inscribe dissymmetry in this libidinal economy is the role of the human strike, as a politics of refusal. In Claire Fontaine's words the 'human strike can be read as an extreme attempt to reappropriate the means of production of struggle-force, of love-force, of life-force'.[35] This is the return of the libidinal vitalism that haunted Klossowski's discourse, in which the 'strong movements of life'[36] are registered as a flux of intensities.

Libidinal economy as site of both 'danger' and 'saving' introduces a tension that has to be resolved. In the case of Tiqqun we can only resolve this tension on the site of the nihilism of capital through a rupture from within the figure of the young-girl traversed to a new 'form of life'. This ethical task requires a polarization and, even, weaponization of the young-girl; as we've noted the equivocation here appears to be how much faith Tiqqun actually have in this possibility. Claire Fontaine follows a similar logic, if tending to substantialize this rupture in the vitalist figure of the 'life force' that escapes all specification. This logic is, of course, vulnerable to Lyotard's objection that there is no external point of 'higher' intensity, no 'great signifier' that would underpin and guarantee an excessive act of resistance. The difficulty with accepting Lyotard's argument is that not only does it problematize an external point of resistance, but it seems to collapse any resistance at all into a stance of merely intensifying the liquefying forces of capitalism.

IN 'THE PROSTITUTIONAL ELEMENT' IMMERSE

In his seminars devoted to exploring the problem of the present as one of 'democratic materialism', a situation in which 'there are only bodies and languages',[37] Alain Badiou remarks that this democratic materialism involves 'the prostitutional element'.[38] In a discussion of the writer Pierre Guyotat who, for Badiou, is the writer of this 'prostituted universe',[39] Badiou indicates the contours of this universe:

> It means the reduction of every vital norm to the immediate mercantile potentialities of bodies; and, more generally, the transformation of the destitute, the weak, all those who compose the immutable bottom layer of the planet's popular human masses, into exchangeable bodies offered up to brute desire, cruelty, destruction, and consumption.[40]

Badiou draws attention to the fact, via Guyotat, of the uneven distribution of these forms of 'prostitution'. Badiou also notes, elsewhere, that in the contemporary West this experience of being 'living currency' is lived under the reign of 'the emblem of enjoyment'.[41] While Badiou rejects any 'angelic' solution of withdrawal from sexuality – he obviously has in mind Guy Lardreau and Christian Jambet, whose work he had criticized in the 1970s[42] – Badiou turns away from sexuality to argue for a contestation of 'democratic materialism' as such. While carefully not neglecting sexual enjoyment, or arguing for a new asceticism, Badiou nonetheless implies a certain turning-away from sexuality as a site of politics.

This is in broad agreement with the trend of the brief theoretical sequence we have traced. Klossowski tried for the difficult task of imagining an alternative sexual economy that was not a regression to a 'natural' state, but which would pass through and explode the limits of the libidinal economy of 'industrial society'. Lyotard realized this through the acceptance of capital but somehow transformed or intensified into a potential libidinal economy that could exceed its own 'naturalism'. In Tiqqun we return to critique in the denouncing of capitalist nihilism through the figure of the young-girl, which leaves us with the slim hope of forming a new relation out of the debris of capitalist relations. It would be easy enough to dismiss the impasses of libidinal economy as the result of theoretical excess and misplaced faith. It is easy enough to tell another story of failure and despair, which would suit the mood of our chastened moment, when even the smallest gestures of reform are treated as dangerous revolutionary acts.

This sequence also indicates a real impasse in the capacity to engage with sexuality as a political site, to have faith in sexuality, we could say. While this could be regarded as the fault of a badly posed problem, we could note the tension in contemporary queer theory between a radically negative vision of sexuality as extinction, articulated by Lee Edelman, in which sexuality is an anti-social act of delinking, and the response by José Estaban Munoz, which tries to reinstate a utopian element of hope and belief in the future of queer sexuality.[43] What this attests to is a difficulty in having faith in the present, especially a present which has now turned into a long drawn-out moment of crisis. Faith is, I think, part of the problem. Posing the issue in terms of faith or belief already indicates an inability to come to terms with the present moment.

It may be, instead, that we have to abandon the dialectic of nihilism and belief, despair and redemption, to come to terms with 'the prostitutional element'. While such a differentiation and analysis is crucial, the role of theories of 'living currency' is still useful in posing the tension of fungibility and exchange. It also allows us access to the theological effects generated out of a capitalist matrix of exchange, in which living bodies become the material which capital posits as its ground and while play an unstable role as a recalcitrant and problematic 'base'.[44] This theological 'transubstantiation' that capital performs to turn living bodies into sources of value is one which also operates upon the 'materiality' of sex. Our problem, then, is the difficult one of imagining liberation out of this shifting ground and a liberation that interrupts rather than replicates a capitalist logic that would transform the body from mere material into mere resource for exploitation. The scandal of living currency is that while, as The Pop Group once sang, 'we are all prostitutes/we all have our price', this is a situation we cannot simply escape by some claim to purity or desexualization. It is certain that the metaphor of universal prostitution is problematic, but at the same time it is a problem we have to confront and cannot merely wish away.

NOTES

1. The use of the figure of 'universal prostitution' persists into Marx's later work; in the *Grundrisse* Marx discusses how universal exchangeability is equivalent to universal venality, concluding: 'Universal prostitution appears as a necessary phase in the development of the social character of personal talents, capacities, abilities, activities' (1973b: 163). Here it is more sympathetically presented as a necessary condition to be traversed, an element of a future communism.

2. Carole Pateman, 'What's Wrong with Prostitution?' *Women's Studies Quarterly* 27.1–2 (1999): 58.

3. I am indebted to the translation by Jordan Levinson, available at: http://anticoncept.phpnet.us/Livingcurrency.htm?i=1 (last accessed 28 February 2017).

4. Eleanor Kaufman, *The Delirium of Praise: Bataille, Blanchot, Deleuze, Foucault, Klossowski* (Baltimore: Johns Hopkins University Press, 2003), 113.

5. Kaufman, *The Delirium of Praise*, 114.

6. Karl Marx, *Capital, Volume 1*, intr. Ernest Mandel, trans. Ben Fowkes (London: Penguin, 1990), 342.

7. Pierre Klossowski, *La monnaie vivante* (Paris: Rivages Poche, 1997), 70; hereafter *MV* with page references in the text.

8. Theodor W. Adorno, *Quasi una Fantasia: Essays on Modern Music*, trans. Rodney Livingstone (London and New York: Verso, 1992), 173.

9. Pierre Klossowski, *Sade My Neighbour*, trans. and intr. Alphonso Lingis (London: Quartet Books, 1992), 23; hereafter *SMN* with page references in the text.

10. Jacques Lacan, 'Kant with Sade', trans. James B. Swenson, Jr., *October* 51 (1989): 55–75.

11. Theodor W. Adorno and Max Horkheimer, *Dialectic of Enlightenment*, trans. John Cumming (London: Verso, 1979), 81–119.

12. Karl Marx, *Grundrisse*, trans. Martin Nicolaus (Harmondsworth: Penguin, 1973), 127.

13. Marx, *Grundrisse*, 308.

14. Kaufman, *The Delirium of Praise*, 114.

15. Pierre Klossowski, *The Baphomet*, trans. Sophie Hawkes and Stephen Sartarelli (New York: Marsilio Publishers. 1992).

16. Ian James, 'Evaluating Klossowski's *Le Baphomet*', *Diacritics* 35.1 (2005): 126.

17. Pierre Klossowski, *Such a Deathly Desire*, trans. Russell Ford (New York: SUNY Press, 2007), 99–122.

18. Vincent Descombes, *Modern French Philosophy*, trans. L. Scott-Fox and J. M. Harding (Cambridge: Cambridge University Press, 1988), 184.

19. Marx, *Capital, Volume 1*, 125.

20. Marx and Engels, in Karl Marx, *The Revolutions of 1848*, ed. and intr. David Fernbach (Harmondsworth: Penguin, 1973), 70.

21. Jean-François Lyotard, *Peregrinations: Law, Form, Event* (New York: Columbia University Press, 1988), 1.

22. Lyotard, *Peregrinations*, 13.

23. Jean-François Lyotard, *Libidinal Economy*, trans. Iain Hamilton Grant (London: Athlone, 1993), 72; hereafter cited as *LE* with page references in the text.

24. Benjamin Noys, *The Persistence of the Negative: A Critique of Contemporary Continental Theory* (Edinburgh: Edinburgh University Press, 2010), 5–6.

25. Jan Urpeth, 'Religious Immanence: A Critique of Meillassoux's "Virtual" God', *Angelaki: Journal of the Theoretical Humanities* 19.1 (2014): 49–64.

26. Alberto Toscano, 'The War against Pre-Terrorism', *Radical Philosophy* 154 (2009): 2–7.

27. Tiqqun, *Introduction to Civil War*, trans. Alexander R. Galloway and Jason Smith (Los Angeles: Semiotext(e), 2010); hereafter cited as *ICW* with page references in the text.

28. Tiqqun, *Preliminary Materials for a Theory of the Young-Girl* [1999], trans. Ariana Reines (Los Angeles: Semiotext(e), 2012), 89; hereafter cited as *PM* with page references in the text.

29. Nina Power, 'She's Just Not That into You', *Radical Philosophy* 177 (2013): 33–34.

30. Jaleh Mansoor, 'Notes on Militant Folds: Against Weigel and Ahern's "Further Materials toward a Theory of the Man-Child"', *Claudius App V* (2013),

15 October 2013, http://theclaudiusapp.com/5-mansoor.html (last accessed 28 February 2017).

31. This Gnostic 'angelism' was prefigured and given its most extreme expression in Guy Lardreau and Christian Jambet's *L'Ange: Pour une cynégétique du semblant* (Paris: Grasset, 1976); see Benjamin Noys, '"The End of the Monarchy of Sex": Sexuality and Contemporary Nihilism', *Theory, Culture & Society* 25.5 (September 2008): 104–22 for a reconstruction of this 'anti-sex' current in contemporary theory.

32. Simone Weil, *Gravity and Grace*, trans. Emma Crawford and Mario von der Ruhr (London and New York: Routledge, 2002), 32–39.

33. Claire Fontaine, *Human Strike Has Already Begun and Other Writings* (Lüneburg and London: PML Books, 2013), 39.

34. Fontaine, *Human Strike Has Already Begun and Other Writings*, 45.

35. Fontaine, *Human Strike Has Already Begun and Other Writings*, 48.

36. Alphonso Lingis, 'Impulsive Forces in and against Worlds', *Diacritics* 35.1 (2005): 62.

37. Alain Badiou, *Logics of Worlds*, trans. Alberto Toscano (London and New York: Continuum, 2009), 1.

38. Quoted in Frank Ruda, 'Idealism without Idealism: Badiou's Materialist Renaissance', *Angelaki: The Journal of the Theoretical Humanities* 19.1 (2014): 91.

39. Alain Badiou, 'Pierre Guyotat, Prince of Prose', in *The Age of the Poets*, intr. Emily Apter and Bruno Bosteels (London and New York: Verso, 2014), 198.

40. Badiou, 'Pierre Guyotat', 198.

41. Alain Badiou, *The Adventure of French Philosophy*, ed. and trans. Bruno Bosteels (London and New York: Verso, 2012), 54.

42. Badiou, *The Adventure of French Philosophy*, 203–22.

43. See Lee Edelman, *No Future: Queer Theory and the Death Drive* (Durham, NC: Duke University Press, 2004), and José Esteban Muñoz, *Cruising Utopia: The Then and There of Queer Futurity* (New York and London: New York University Press, 2009).

44. Gavin Walker, 'The Absent Body of Labour Power: Uno Kōzō's Logic of Capital', *Historical Materialism* 21.4 (2013): 201–34.

BIBLIOGRAPHY

ADORNO, Theodor W. *Quasi una Fantasia: Essays on Modern Music*. Translated by Rodney Livingstone. London and New York: Verso, 1992.

ADORNO, Theodor W. and Max HORKHEIMER. *Dialectic of Enlightenment*. Translated by John Cumming. London: Verso, 1979.

BADIOU, Alain. *The Adventure of French Philosophy*. Translated and Edited by Bruno Bosteels. London and New York: Verso, 2012.

BADIOU, Alain. *Logics of Worlds*. Translated by Alberto Toscano. London and New York: Continuum, 2009.

BADIOU, Alain. 'Pierre Guyotat, Prince of Prose'. In *The Age of the Poets*. Introduced by Emily Apter and Bruno Bosteels. London and New York: Verso, 2014. 194–205.

DESCOMBES, Vincent. *Modern French Philosophy*. Translated by L. Scott-Fox and J. M. Harding. Cambridge: Cambridge University Press, 1980.

EDELMAN, Lee. *No Future: Queer Theory and the Death Drive*. Durham, NC: Duke University Press, 2004.

FONTAINE, Claire. *Human Strike Has Already Begun and Other Writings*. Lüneburg and London: PML Books, 2013.

JAMES, Ian. 'Evaluating Klossowski's *Le Baphomet*'. *diacritics* 35.1 (2005): 119–35.

KAUFMAN, Eleanor. *The Delirium of Praise: Bataille, Blanchot, Deleuze, Foucault, Klossowski*. Baltimore: Johns Hopkins University Press, 2003.

KLOSSOWSKI, Pierre. *The Baphomet*. Translated by Sophie Hawkes and Stephen Sartarelli. New York: Marsilio Publishers, 1992.

KLOSSOWSKI, Pierre. *La monnaie vivante*. Paris: Rivages Poche, 1997.

KLOSSOWSKI, Pierre. *Living Currency* [1971]. Translated by Jordan Levinson. 2014; http://anticoncept.phpnet.us/Livingcurrency.htm?i=1. Last accessed 28 February 2017.

KLOSSOWSKI, Pierre. *Sade My Neighbour*. Translated and with an introduction by Alphonso Lingis. London: Quartet Books, 1992.

KLOSSOWSKI, Pierre. *Such a Deathly Desire*. Translated by Russell Ford. New York: SUNY Press, 2007.

LACAN, Jacques. 'Kant with Sade'. Translated by James B. Swenson, Jr. *October* 51 (1989): 55–75.

LARDREAU, Guy and Christian JAMBET. *L'Ange: Pour une cynégétique du semblant*. Paris: Grasset, 1976.

LINGIS, Alphonso. 'Impulsive Forces in and against Worlds'. *diacritics* 35.1 (2005): 60–70.

LYOTARD, Jean- François. *Libidinal Economy* [1974]. Translated by Iain Hamilton Grant. London: Athlone, 1993.

LYOTARD, Jean-François. *Peregrinations: Law, Form, Event*. New York: Columbia University Press, 1988.

MANSOOR, Jaleh. 'Notes on Militant Folds: Against Weigel and Ahern's "Further Materials toward a Theory of the Man-Child"'. *Claudius App* V (2013), 15 October 2013. http://theclaudiusapp.com/5-mansoor.html. Last accessed 28 February 2017.

MARX, Karl. *Capital, Volume 1*. Introduction by Ernest Mandel. Translated by Ben Fowkes, London: Penguin, 1990.

MARX, Karl. *Early Writings*. Introduction by Lucio Colletti. Translated by Rodney Livingstone and Gregory Benton. Harmondsworth: Penguin in association with *New Left Review*, 1975.

MARX, Karl. *Grundrisse*. Translated by Martin Nicolaus. Harmondsworth: Penguin, 1973.

MARX, Karl. *The Revolutions of 1848*. Edited and Introduced by David Fernbach. Harmondsworth: Penguin, 1973.
MUÑOZ, José Esteban. *Cruising Utopia: The Then and There of Queer Futurity*. New York and London: New York University Press, 2009.
NOYS, Benjamin. '"The End of the Monarchy of Sex": Sexuality and Contemporary Nihilism'. *Theory, Culture & Society* 25.5 (September 2008): 104–22.
NOYS, Benjamin. *The Persistence of the Negative: A Critique of Contemporary Continental Theory*. Edinburgh: Edinburgh University Press, 2000.
PATEMAN, Carole. 'What's Wrong with Prostitution?' *Women's Studies Quarterly* 27.1–2 (1999): 53–64.
POWER, Nina. 'She's Just Not That into You'. *Radical Philosophy* 177 (2013): 33–34.
RUDA, Frank. 'Idealism without Idealism: Badiou's Materialist Renaissance'. *Angelaki: The Journal of the Theoretical Humanities* 19.1 (2014): 83–98.
TIQQUN. *Introduction to Civil War*. Translated by Alexander R. Galloway and Jason Smith. Los Angeles: Semiotext(e), 2010.
TIQQUN. *Preliminary Materials for a Theory of the Young-Girl* [1999]. Translated by Ariana Reines, Los Angeles: Semiotext(e), 2012.
TOSCANO, Alberto. 'The War against Pre-Terrorism'. *Radical Philosophy* 154 (2009): 2–7.
URPETH, Jim. 'Religious Immanence: A Critique of Meillassoux's "Virtual" God'. *Angelaki: Journal of the Theoretical Humanities* 19.1 (2014): 49–64.
WALKER, Gavin. 'The Absent Body of Labour Power: Uno Kōzō's Logic of Capital'. *Historical Materialism* 21.4 (2013): 201–34.
WEIL, Simone. *Gravity and Grace*. Translated by Emma Crawford and Mario von der Ruhr. London and New York: Routledge, 2002.

Chapter 8

The materiality of belief

On the real death of Mammon

Hollis Phelps

A common narrative about the financial crisis of 2007–2008 is that it shook our collective faith in the principles that govern the global economy. In testimony to the US Congress in October 2008, former chairman of the Federal Reserve Alan Greenspan famously admitted as much when he conceded that the crisis had left him and numerous other economic players 'in a state of shocked disbelief'.[1] Philip Goodchild has suggested that what the financial crisis ultimately revealed is the end of the unrestrained quest for wealth as the principle of global cooperation. 'Mammon has been exposed and killed', he writes.[2] Although ten years out the economic conditions of people, institutions and states have changed, often for the worse, little has changed in terms of the functioning of the economy and in the normal, day-to-day activities that prop the latter up.[3] Faith in the economy may have been shaken, but the creation of wealth as a governing principle and means of social organization continues, it seems, unabated.

What follows is a provisional attempt to think through this seeming disconnect, via a discussion of how money, wealth and the various attitudes, practices and institutions that support them, which, following Goodchild and the Christian theological tradition, I collectively name Mammon, exert power over individuals. Although it is always possible to name bad actors, for most people allegiance to Mammon cannot be reduced to a moralizing discourse that ultimately rests on individual volition and desire. Faith in Mammon, which manifests itself in the material activities of individuals, is not so much a choice but, rather, essential to what Mammon is and what it does. Understanding how Mammon functions in this fashion, which I discuss in terms of Mammon's power to attract belief in itself as the value of values in terms of its structural, affective and sovereign dimensions via debt, is essential if we are to think and act beyond Mammon, if we are to speak of its death.

MAMMON'S MURDER OF GOD AND THE MATERIALITY OF BELIEF

Philip Goodchild has suggested that Nietzsche's famous declaration of God's death should be understood more in terms of a murder. It names, in other words, the dissolution of one form of life for another, the active destruction of a particular way of organizing life in favour of an alternative. God's murder, in this sense, does not result in a vacuum: the demise of Christianity and its God as the symbolic locus of individual and social organization does not leave human beings bereft of a locus of value. Nietzsche's rhetoric, at times, does lead in this direction, and there is no shortage of critiques of modernity that correlate God's death with a lack of value.[4] It is more accurate to say, as Goodchild does, that God's murder signifies 'a shift in pieties'.[5] Goodchild writes, 'God has stopped paying us our ordered existence; or rather, there is another god who pays us, who responds more immediately, directly and tangibly to our prayers: Mammon'.[6] God's murder, in this sense, is only feasible so long as something else has already replaced God, so long as God is no longer necessary. As Goodchild puts it, the murder of God implies that 'one already has an alternative source of meaning and value for practice'.[7]

For Goodchild, this alternative source is Mammon. Mammon, in the Christian theological tradition and the popular imagination, is usually understood in terms of money and wealth, and is considered a rival to God, in the sense that both demand absolute loyalty, or faith. Hence Jesus' famous claim, 'No one can serve two masters; for a slave will either hate the one and love the other, or be devoted to one and despise the other. You cannot serve God and wealth' (Matthew 6:24; cf. Luke 16:12). Mammon, however, can also be understood more broadly as signifying a total means of governance, one that shapes attitudes, desires, practices and institutions according to a particular logic.[8] Goodchild notes that, when speaking of Mammon's murder of God, Mammon signifies the reorganization of daily life according to the mandates of economic rationality. He writes:

> Where the activities of daily life had been ordered by the expectations of the community or obligations to a deity, economic rationality brings an abstract symbolization of space and time. Enclosure of the commons, the replacement of communal resources with private property, changes the function of work from producing for one's own community to producing for the market; similarly, market relations enact an 'enclosure' of time, whereby the quantity of labour takes on more significance than the lived experience of work. Once subjected to the abstract representation of private property, daily life can become regulated by economic rationality, which had formerly been limited by a consensus on the limitation of needs.[9]

The adoption of economic rationality as the organizing principle of life, which entails holding up money and its related institutions as the source or value of values, is, Goodchild emphasizes, an 'act of faith' applicable in its sovereignty.[10]

We should not understand this 'faith', however, primarily in ideational terms, or even in terms of volition. What Goodchild refers to as a 'shift in pieties'[11] cannot, in other words, be reduced to mere intellectual assent, to a decision to believe a certain way as opposed to another. One does not simply choose, in other words, to adopt an alternative source of meaning and value, even if it may appear so retroactively. Piety is better understood as a material phenomenon or, as Goodchild says in the preceding quotation, a practice. As he puts it in his more recent *Theology of Money*, what is at issue in determining the value of values is the way in which that value structures time, attention and devotion.[12] The murder of God, then, names the ascendancy of a *different* organization of time, attention and devotion; it indicates an alternative expression of life. One can, of course, still 'believe' in God, but such belief remains practically ineffectual – or 'dead', as Nietzsche put it – for the organization of life, if time, attention and devotion are directed elsewhere, that is, towards Mammon.

This is an important point, since few people would actually narrate their daily activities, their lives, in light of devotion to Mammon. Otherwise put, few would directly correlate their faith and belief with Mammon. They would instead likely appeal to other motivating factors, perhaps a belief in God, even if these often and ultimately remain secondary at best in practice. Nietzsche himself, of course, was aware of this phenomenon when he indicated the gap between God's death and its real recognition.[13] Faith, however, should not be reduced to stated beliefs or motivations; it is, rather, encapsulated and expressed materially, in what we actually do. This is what Goodchild means when he describes Mammon in terms of the organization of life and in terms of time, attention and devotion. But it is also helpful, here, to refer to Slavoj Žižek's discussion of how ideology functions cynically, especially in relation to the fetishistic illusion of money. Žižek notes that, when pressed, most people would acknowledge that money is a construction, a sign that expresses basic social relations. In their actions, however, they show otherwise. Žižek writes:

> The problem is that in their social activity itself, in what they are *doing*, they are *acting* as if money, in its material reality, is the immediate embodiment of wealth as such. They are fetishists in practice, not in theory. What they 'do not know', what they misrecognize, is the fact that in their social reality itself, in their social activity – in the act of commodity exchange – they are guided by the fetishistic illusion.[14]

Another way to put the matter is to say that belief is a phenomenon that is deeply embedded in our material activities and practices. The question, however, is how money as Mammon is able to exert this power over individuals and is able to fashion our normal, day-to-day activities as faith in Mammon, even if individuals do not necessarily understand – or, perhaps better said, want to understand – their activities in these terms.

MAMMON'S POWER AS DEBT: MONEY, AFFECT, POWER

One way to understand the power of Mammon as the value of values is to focus on debt. Focusing on debt as a means of understanding the ways in which Mammon requires what we could call religious devotion establishes an immediate link between it and the Christian theological tradition. Nietzsche, it is well known, traced morality and its component notions, such as freedom, responsibility and guilt, to the various relationships between creditors and debtors. Indeed, the contractual substrate of human relationality, which locates moral sensibility in the mundane activities of exchange and the violence that accompanies them, remains marked linguistically, in the lexical relationship between 'guilt' and 'debt'. 'Have these genealogists of morals had even the remotest suspicion that, for example, the major moral concept *Schuld* [guilt] has its origin in the very material concept *Schulden* [debts]', he asks rhetorically in the Second Essay of *On the Genealogy of Morals*.[15] Nietzsche did not attribute the material origin of 'bad conscience' as such to Christianity, but he does argue that Christianity capitalizes on it in a specific way. 'The advent of the Christian God, as the maximum god attained so far', he writes, 'was therefore accompanied by the feeling of guilty indebtedness on earth' (*GM* § 20). On the one hand, Christianity interprets normal human behaviour, which Nietzsche associates with animal instincts, in terms of self-denial and guilt. Christianity, that is, places human beings vis-à-vis the seemingly inescapable judgement of God. On the other hand, Christianity simultaneously offers salvation from this very condition, through God's sacrifice of Godself, as a means of redeeming the unredeemable. This is Christianity's 'stroke of genius', Nietzsche writes: 'God himself sacrifices himself for the guilt of mankind, God himself makes payment to himself, God as the only being who can redeem man from what has become unredeemable for man himself – the creditor sacrifices himself for his debtor, out of *love* (can one credit that?), out of love for his debtor! – ' (*GM* § 21).

The offer of redemption, however, does not necessarily erase the general sense of indebtedness on which Christianity capitalizes. Redemption is, of course, dialectically related to sin, meaning that both have to remain in place for Christianity to function. The actual release of sin qua debt would, ironically, also get rid of the *need* for salvation, which would erase the very conditions that create the possibility of Christianity in the first place. It is in this sense that Christianity creates what it redeems and, as Gilles Deleuze notes in his reading of Nietzsche on this point, represents a 'deepening of debt'.[16] For instance, this is why Anselm, who can be credited with systematizing the notion of sin as debt in the Western theological tradition, still conceives of the result of satisfaction in terms of debt. Although, on Anselm's reading, the God-man erases the indebtedness of sin through his satisfaction of God's violated honour, human beings still owe God a *post-hoc* 'debt of gratitude', on top of their original, prelapsarian debt of obedience, the violation of which had gotten them into trouble in the first place.[17]

Nevertheless, although, as Nietzsche argues, Christianity universalizes the sense of indebtedness, it still holds out the *promise* of redemption. That promise, again, presupposes the entire Christian *dispositif*, including the so-called original sin that necessitates Christ's incarnation, death and resurrection. But it still poses redemption to the individual as something desirable and possible, albeit according to a specific logic. Walter Benjamin argues that this is not so with capitalism, at least in its essential features. Benjamin suggests in his short fragment 'Capitalism as Religion' that capitalism has some of the salient features of religions, and specifically Christianity, in the sense that it 'serves to allay the same anxieties, torments, and disturbances to which the so-called religions offered answers'.[18] It does so, however, not through redemption, but through the sheer creation and multiplication of guilt. Benjamin writes, 'Capitalism is probably the first instance of a cult that creates guilt, not atonement. . . . Capitalism is entirely without precedent, in that it is a religion which offers not the reform of existence but its complete destruction'.[19] Like Nietzsche, whom he cites, Benjamin references the dual sense of *Schuld*, but whereas Nietzsche constructs a genealogy, Benjamin plays with what he refers to as the 'demonic ambiguity' of the term.[20] Thus, when we read that capitalism functions through the creation of 'guilt', we should simultaneously read 'debt', holding together the theological, moral and economic sense of that term.

Benjamin's articulation of capitalism as religion dovetails with the claim made in the previous section that the death of God coincides with the ascendency of Mammon, as the principle governing contemporary life. Benjamin's claim, in this sense, is not so much about secularization but replacement, a shift in the locus of piety or devotion. Benjamin, for instance, says that '[c]apitalism has developed as a parasite of Christianity in the West . . . until it reached the point where Christianity's history is essentially that of its parasite – that is to say, of capitalism'.[21] Nevertheless, what remains lacking in Benjamin's all-too-brief statement about the religious nature of capitalism is how it is able to maintain itself as religion. How, in other words, is capitalism, as an incarnation of Mammon, able to inculcate a proper sense of devotion among individuals, a devotion that is required if Mammon is to keep its place as the value of values?

This is no small matter, at least in the terms that Benjamin lays out. Despite his open disdain for Christianity, Nietzsche could at least understand its attraction, however twisted he thought it to be: redemption is, of course, an appealing solution to guilt, even if Nietzsche himself does not buy it. The problem, however, is that it is religion's most appealing aspect (i.e. redemption) that is lost in the rise of capitalism as religion, at least if Benjamin's analysis holds any weight. Capitalism is, for Benjamin, a religion without redemption, which is seemingly a contradiction in terms, at least if religion is understood along Christian lines. Benjamin, to be sure, suggests that capitalism still offers a semblance of redemption, insofar as it works to alleviate anxieties, torments and disturbances, but what attracts people to Mammon, especially when it takes the form of indebtedness?

The usual theological answer to such questions takes on a moral form, emphasizing the disordered desire, the sin, of the individual, which finds expression in the abandonment of so-called higher things for material existence. Augustine writes in his *Confessions*, for instance, 'All these [material] things and their like can be occasions for sin because, good though they are, they are of the lowest order of good, and if we are too much tempted by them we abandon those higher and better things, your truth, your law, and you yourself'.[22] Hence the reason that much of the theological literature concerned with critiquing capitalism tends to focus on the putative problem of overconsumption, as a symptom of unconstrained desire.[23] The remedy, from this perspective, is to consume rightly, which in theological jargon entails the reorientation of desire towards God. Commenting on Augustine, William T. Cavanaugh notes, for example, that the 'key to true freedom is no just following whatever desires we happen to have, but cultivating the right desires. This means that the internal movement of the will is not a sufficient condition for freedom; we must consider the end toward which the will is moved'.[24] For Augustine, Cavanaugh and many other theological commentators of an orthodox bent, this end is, of course, God, the source of being and of all good.[25] Such critiques do not necessarily result, at least practically speaking, in an anti-materialist or detached stance, of course.[26] Nevertheless, in reducing the power of Mammon to the realm of individual desire, they ultimately fail to grasp the manner in which Mammon wields power in and over social sphere as a whole.

To understand how Mammon works within the social sphere to produce allegiance to it as the value of values, it is helpful initially to look at the nature of money. Perhaps the most common understanding of money is that it arises naturally as a means of easily facilitating exchange. Such an understanding of money relies on what David Graeber has referred to as 'the myth of barter'.[27] We find this myth expressed for instance, in Aristotle, who argued that money arose out of the growth of complex exchange. Although barter, the direct trade of goods for goods, served in more simple forms of social organization as a relatively adequate means for gaining access to the 'necessaries of life', increasing interdependence among human beings and societies led to a more formal, translatable means of exchange. 'When the inhabitants of one country became more dependent on those of another, and they imported what they needed and exported what they have too much of, money necessarily came into use', he writes in *Politics*. 'For the various necessaries of life are not easily carried about, and hence men agreed to employ in their dealings with each other something which was intrinsically useful and easily applicable to the purposes of life, for example iron, silver, and the like'.[28]

For Aristotle, this leads to retail trade, which he criticizes for its penchant for turning money into an object of desire in its own right. Money certainly has a legitimate use for Aristotle, but it devolves, on his account, into the 'art of getting wealth', which has no concern for 'living well'.[29] This distinction between a 'natural' and 'unnatural' use of money greatly influenced medieval discussions of money, especially regarding certain forms of trade and the practice of usury.[30] But it is Adam Smith's articulation of the myth of barter that, perhaps, has had the most influence on contemporary economic discussions of the nature of money, although the basic outline is the same. For Smith, money essentially arises out of the division of labour, which in turn arises out of a 'certain propensity in human nature' to 'truck, barter, and exchange'.[31] Once a division of labour is established, however, the majority of our wants and needs will be met through exchange, since each individual only produces a small portion of these on her own. Smith thus notes that '[e]very man thus lives by exchanging, or becomes in some measure a merchant, and the society itself grows to be what is properly called a commercial society'.[32]

Smith speculates that at some point in its establishment, this division of labour becomes too unwieldy to operate efficiently, and for the good of all:

> But when the division of labour first began to take place, this power of exchanging must frequently have been very much clogged and embarrassed in its operations. One man, we shall suppose, has more of a certain commodity than he himself has occasion for, while another has less. The former consequently would be glad to dispose of, and the latter to purchase, a part of this superfluity. But if this latter should chance to have nothing that the former stands in need of, no exchange can be made between them. The butcher has more meat in his shop than he himself can consume, and the

> brewer and the baker would each of them be willing to purchase a part of it. But they have nothing to offer in exchange, except the different productions of their respective trades, and the butcher is already provided with all the bread and beer which he has immediate occasion for. No exchange can, in this case, be made between them. He cannot be their merchant, nor they his customers; and they are all of them thus mutually less serviceable to one another. In order to avoid the inconveniency of such situations, every prudent man in every period of society, after the first establishment of the division of labour, must naturally have endeavoured to manage his affairs in such a manner, as to have at all times by him, besides the peculiar produce of his own industry, a certain quantity of some one commodity or other, such as he imagined few people would be likely to refuse in exchange for the produce of their industry.[33]

A barter economy, Smith argues, depends on what economists call a double coincidence of wants: for trade to take place, person *x* has to have something that person *y* wants, but person *y* must also have what person *x* wants. In a relatively simple society, that may not pose much of a problem, but in more complex societies, it is incredibly cumbersome and inhibiting to the circulation of goods and services, for both individuals and the whole, hence the need for an agreed-upon, neutral medium, 'one commodity', as Smith refers to it. This is what we call money. It does not really matter what this medium is, materially speaking. Precious metals, such as gold and silver, have historically taken on the role, not so much for their intrinsic value as the ease with which they can be weighed, denominated and transported. What matters, rather, is the broad consent that allows the object in question to function as medium: there must be an agreement on a particular commodity to function as money.

Graeber, among others, has stressed that there is little physical evidence to support this myth of barter, historically speaking, though it remains a staple of much mainstream economic thinking, popular understandings of money and common wisdom. The problem, however, is conceptual as well. As Geoffrey Ingham points out, it is almost impossible to explain the emergence of money with reference solely to exchange, as commodity theories of money tend to do. More specifically, widespread, almost spontaneous, agreement among economic actors to recognize a specific commodity as money would be required, but how that occurs is difficult, if not impossible, to account for. For Ingham, the confusion that locates the origin of money in exchange rests on mistaking the specific commodity for money of account or 'moneyness', that quality that allows the commodity to function as money in exchange. That quality, for Ingham, is money proper, and it logically precedes its role in exchange. 'The very *idea* of money, which is to say, of abstract accounting for value, is *logically anterior and historically prior to market exchange*'.[34] Otherwise put, agreement is not an emergent property but comes first, and it is that prior agreement that allows something to function as money in exchange, and not the other way around.

What, then, is money? Money for Ingham is primarily a social relationship, but one that expresses relations of credit and debt.

> [M]oney *is* itself a social relation; that is to say, money is a 'claim' or 'credit' that is constituted by social relations that *exist independently of the production and exchange of commodities*. Regardless of any *form* it might take, money is essentially a provisional 'promise' to pay, whose 'moneyness', as an 'institutional fact', is assigned by a description conferred by an abstract money of account. In the most basic sense, the possessor of money is owed goods. But money also represents a claim or credit against the issuer – monarch, state, bank and so on. Money has to be 'issued'. And something can only be issued *as money* if it is capable of canceling *any* debt incurred by the issuer.[35]

Two things are important, here. First, in order for something to function as money, it has to be legitimated or issued by a recognized authority, which means that money, at least in the terms that we know it and currently use it, depends on sovereignty. 'Monetary societies are held together by networks of credit/debt relations that are underpinned and constituted by sovereignty', Ingham notes. 'Money *is* form of sovereignty, and as such it cannot be understood without reference to an authority'.[36] Second, money relies on social relations of credit and debt but also, simultaneously, makes them possible by substituting itself for the immediacy of face-to-face interactions. It does so by taking over from individuals the 'trust' normally required in transactions. Ingham writes, 'Money is *assignable* trust. In the face of real-world radical uncertainty, self-fulfilling long term trust is rooted in a social and political legitimacy whereby potentially personally untrustworthy strangers are able to participate in complex multilateral relationships'.[37] Money, then, is a sort of social 'lubricant', one that not only expresses certain relationships but also makes them possible.[38]

It is in this sense that, as Ingham argues, exchange with money is structurally different from barter, because the former operates on two levels simultaneously. On the one hand money is, of course, exchanged for goods or services, similar to what we might find in so-called barter. But money also functions abstractly, as the medium through which the value and price of the goods exchanged are determined, measured and stored.[39] This is the 'moneyness' of money, that which enables it to facilitate exchange. Without this notion of abstraction, monetary exchange is really just barter in another guise.

An actual exchange, however, is secondary to the social component at work in transactions, which have to do with relations of credit and debt. That is, money operates in exchange as the means to cancel the incurred debts of exchange. Referring to Alfred Mitchel-Innes's work on the credit theory of money, Ingham writes that, in exchange, 'goods and money "change hands", but the money is also cancelling the *debt* incurred for the goods priced in the money of account in abstract value. A sale does not involve an exchange for "some immediate commodity called the 'medium of exchange', as it would do if money were no more than 'efficient' barter. Rather, a sale is the exchange of a commodity for a 'credit' which, in accordance with the 'primitive law of commerce', represents the 'debt' in the next purchase"'.[40]

In most day-to-day exchange relationships, of course, we do not necessarily recognize our actions in terms of credit and debt. We mistake, in other words, the social mediation of credit and debt through money for the immediacy of exchange. Indeed, even the use of consumer credit for run-of-the-mill transactions often does not change this recognition, as it works in the same way as a so-called cash transaction, at least in the act of exchange itself.[41] So understood, money can function as a sign of individual freedom: money names, in other words, the ability to have an amount of control over one's relations and, to some extent, opt out of them. The point of exchange, that is, is that one does not have to enter into particular exchanges if one decides, for whatever reason, not to. That is certainly true to some extent, and there is no doubt that, at a certain level, money does provide a semblance of freedom when compared to other forms of relationship. It enables, in other words, consumption, which at least in the popular ideology correlates with a freedom to choose.

Nevertheless, large purchases almost invariably involve credit, the use of debt as a means to offset the sticker price through regular payments, at interest, of course. Such consumption is, in this sense, almost entirely debt driven, at least for most consumers. Since wage stagnation settled in since the 1970s, the purchase of day-to-day needs and necessities also often relies on credit.[42] Even if one can ostensibly steer clear of the use of credit for such purchases, it remains the case that it is virtually impossible to opt out of exchange as such and the use of money as its medium. There is, in this sense, an element of coercion at work in participation in the market and the social relations that subsist therein, even if we often experience matters otherwise, in terms of the so-called freedom that attends to consumer choice. 'Through consumption', Lazzarato writes,

> we maintain an unwitting relationship with the debt economy. We carry within us the creditor-debtor relation – in our pockets and wallets, encoded in the magnetic strip on our credit cards. Indeed, this little strip of plastic

> hides two seemingly harmless operations: the *automatic* institution of the credit relation, which thereby establishes *permanent* debt. The credit card is the simplest way to transform its owner into a permanent debtor, an 'indebted man' for life.[43]

To say that subjectivity is essentially an indebted subjectivity is, of course, to conjure Maurizio Lazzarato's recent argument made in *The Making of the Indebted Man*. For Lazzarato neoliberal capitalism is not so much founded on exchange, as its primary feature, as it is debt; otherwise put, it is debt – the interplay between credit-debt/creditors-debtors – that makes exchange possible and, ultimately, drives economic growth. Lazzarato's emphasis on debt dovetails with the understanding of money discussed earlier, but also more specifically draws out the implications of this relationship in terms of the government of individuals and populations. Under neoliberalism, he argues, debt at a macro-level constitutes subjects in its image, as essentially indebted.

The creation of indebted subjects, what Lazzarato refers to as 'the indebted man', is in neoliberalism essential to economic growth, meaning that the neoliberal economy is, in many respects, a rent economy. Despite individual, public and political moralizing over debt, then, it is not an impediment to growth but its very condition. For debt to function in this manner, however, individuals, institutions and collectives must actually be indebted. Debt, in this sense, is not only an economic mechanism but also a form of power that represents a specific mode of governance, one that governs, however, through the illusion of freedom. Lazzarato writes:

> The power of debt is described as if it were exercised neither through repression nor through ideology. The debtor is 'free', but his actions, his behavior, are confined by the limits defined by the debt he has entered into. The same is true as much for the individual as for a population or social group. You are free insofar as you assume the *way of life* (consumption, work, public spending, taxes, etc.) compatible with reimbursement'.[44]

What must be emphasized, however, is that such indebtedness is not just a feature of the neoliberal economy but of money itself. This is not to say that the way that credit and debt function in neoliberalism is not heightened, or even unique; it is, rather, to say that that uniqueness is attendant upon what money really is, a social relationship that expresses credit and debt. Thus, although we can speak with Lazzarato of the contemporary indebted subject, it is important to emphasize that it is money itself that enables this condition, albeit in concert with other factors.[45] If Ingham, along with other debt theorists of money, such as Graeber, Michel Aglietta and André Orléan,[46] is correct, then any criticism of the current debt economy must also focus its attention on money – and not just in terms of its financialization but also its origin, historical uses and function in exchange.

Nevertheless, in current economic arrangements, indebtedness functions in tandem with what Lazzarato calls 'machinic enslavement' to capture individuals. Following Deleuze and Guattari, Lazzarato notes that the social subjection that individuals experience through debt is only one side of the coin. We also experience 'machinic enslavement', which unlike social subjection 'occurs via desubjectivation by mobilizing functional and operational, non-representational and asignifying, rather than linguistic and representational, semiotics'.[47] Whereas social subjection via mechanisms such as debt refer to individuals – indeed, for Lazzarato, they *create* individuals – machinic enslavement names the various ways that anonymous flows capture subjects at the molecular level. 'Enslavement does not work with "subjects" and "objects" ', he writes, 'it works on their deterritorialization (or their decodification), that is, with the molecular components, the non-individuated intensive, subhuman potentialities of subjectivity, and the non-individuated, intensive, molecular component parts of potentialities of matter and machines'.[48]

Machinic enslavement, then, is simultaneously less than and more than the various activities that get lumped together under the domain of the conscious, human subject. Lazzarato notes, 'Machinic enslavement activates *pre-personal*, *pre-cognitive*, and *pre-verbal* forces (machinic, linguistic, social, media, economic systems, etc.), which, beyond the subject and individual relations, multiply "possibilities" '.[49] Such machinic enslavement does not run contrary to the representation of the subject at the social level as an indebted subject. The creation of the indebted subject as a means of social subjugation and governance is intertwined with the amorphous and asignifying flows that pulse through subjects at the molecular level. The subject is, to borrow the language of Deleuze and Guattari on which Lazzarato relies, constantly deterritorialized and reterritorialized through molecular and molar movements of credit and debt. Noting the various ways in which the financial system subjects individuals to its logic, Lazzarato comments:

> As an 'investor/debtor', he can be viewed as the very model of subjectivation: the promise he makes to reimburse his debt means that memory and affects (such as guilt, responsibility, loyalty, trust, etc.) must be created to ensure the fulfillment of the promise. But once credit has entered the finance machine, he becomes something else entirely, a mere input of the financial assemblage. Indeed, the credit/debt incorporated into the assemblage loses all reference to the subject who contracted the debt. Credit/debt is literally torn to pieces (in the same way the assemblage tears the subject to pieces) by the financial machine, which the subprime crisis has shown all too well. It is no longer a matter of this or that investment, of this or that debt: the financial assemblage has transformed the subject into a currency that acts as 'capital', into money that generates money.[50]

Although the subject as indebted serves as a vehicle for deterritorialization, so that the subject's debt can be financialized to create more money, the specificity of individual debt and the subject who holds it still matters. Even if debt becomes anonymous and asignifying as capital, the 'promise to pay' at the individual level must remain intact. This was at least part of the issue with the subprime mortgage crisis: toxic debts and the inability to repay threatened to run deterritorialized capital into the ground.

Nevertheless, the interplay that creates indebted subject must also rely on a certain emotional investment on behalf of the subject. Indebtedness as a condition is, of course, not immediately attractive in its own right. No one, in other words, really wants to be indebted, which is why the condition of indebtedness is often supplemented with a moralizing logic. Money, in other words, which is increasingly accessed through debt, must also correspond positively with our lived experience. Martin Konings has recently drawn attention to this aspect of money, noting that it is not just an abstract symbol, or even something that we experience negatively via debt, but is 'a sign that is capable of speaking to our most intensely felt individual needs'.[51] Money, that is, works on us affectively and emotionally, meaning that its power resides at least in part in what it does to and for us in the social field of its own construction, in what it allows access to in that field. Contra Benjamin, who in his fragment emphasizes the element of guilt over atonement, capitalism does, in fact, promise, which is another way of saying that it relies on credit and, of course, debt.

This affective dimension of money accounts for its resiliency, even when money carries along with it negative affects and consequences. Konings notes, for instance, that anxiety about money – an anxiety which, in our debt economy, is all too common – ironically leads one to seek more money. 'We may feel deeply anxious about money, but it is nonetheless likely that our practical attempts to deal with this emotion will be directed to the procurement of money; that is, not the reconsideration of our relationship to money but rather an intensified engagement with it', he writes.[52] Money can do this, of course, because of the power that it holds in the social field. We could always, perhaps, rethink or rework our relationship to money in an attempt to lessen the anxiety that it can and does provoke. We could, in other words, foster some sort of detachment to money, along the lines of Augustine, as mentioned earlier. Such detachment, however, will always remain limited, to the extent that it eventually runs aground on the hard fact that one needs money to gain access to basic needs, wants and desires. Anxiety, in this sense, is not so much about money but life, the way that money mediates life to and for us.

Nevertheless, because it provides access to life, money's attraction also cannot be reduced to its more coercive elements, even when money functions practically more as a problem than a solution. Money is, in other words, alluring, precisely because it provides access to life. Konings writes that

> money's dark side does not negate its binding, generative force: the discontents of capitalist life are inextricably intertwined with the more inviting and alluring aspects of money. Capitalist socialization involves productive mixtures of hope and disappointment, illusion and disillusionment. Although money is a source of tremendous frustration and anxiety, it never fails to excite and motivate us. The anxiety that it engenders paradoxically only strengthens out attachment to it. It is such ups and downs of hope and disappointment – rather than a mechanical pursuit of indifferent utility or a drift into listless alienation – that is characteristic of our financial experience.[53]

Attachment to money, in this sense, takes the form of what Lauren Berlant has called 'cruel optimism', which she defines as a 'relation of attachment to compromised conditions of possibility whose realization is discovered *im*possible, sheer fantasy, or *too* possible, and toxic'.[54]

Such attachments, Berlant stresses, do not necessarily *feel* optimistic; to label these attachments optimistic, rather, refers to the individual's continual gravitation towards the objects in question, even if they operate problematically for the individual. An object of 'cruel optimism' is thus simultaneously 'enabling' and 'disabling'.[55]

Any number of objects can function in this way, but Berlant notes that it is particularly apt in explaining attachment to a particular form of life that we, for whatever reasons, consider good, even if that form simultaneously 'wears out the subjects who, nonetheless, and at the same time, find their conditions of possibility within it'.[56] Such is the case, for example, with life in the contemporary world, especially in nations of relative wealth, where money plays a significant role in structuring social relations: 'The labor of reproducing life in the contemporary world is also the activity of being worn out'.[57]

Nevertheless, if attraction to money cannot be reduced to coercion, coercion always lies behind its attraction, as a means of assuring the continued role of money as the value of values. This is why the power of money does not rely only on belief or faith in order to maintain its position in the social field. Its force as value of values depends on its actual use. Money, that is, can and does function as supreme value, as Mammon, despite individual and collective claims made to the contrary. Even if we consider ourselves outside the grip of money, for religious, moral, political or other reasons, the very acceptance of money in practice, as Goodchild observes, charges it with value and makes us in its image, whether we like it or not. The power of money can be understood, in this respect, through its anticipated or real lack, which presents itself to the subject as a threat to his or her well-being. Goodchild writes:

> Money draws its value from the will to survive that is threatened by a lack of money; money draws its value from a desire for pleasure that is threatened by a lack of money; money draws its value from the promise of advances that that can be made on the speculative anticipation of profits; money draws its value from its creation as debt and from the obligations it imposes to convert value into money to repay loans and interest. Money, as the principle of mediation that makes demands effective, demands that the creation, acquisition, maintenance, and investment of money take priority over all other demands. By all of these means, money becomes the supreme social force.[58]

Goodchild's observation also helps us to understand how the general condition of indebtedness is able to maintain itself. At least in terms of individuals, indebtedness is often, to borrow Lacanian terminology, a forced choice, meaning that choosing to go into debt for access to certain goods and services (education, housing, healthcare, transportation or even basic necessities) is not really much of a choice at all.[59] We do not, however, always and necessarily experience the choice as forced. The weight of debt, its burden, is of course palpable, both psychically and materially, but we also experience the pressure of debt in terms of its opposite, as a promise. We experience debt, in other words, as salvation, but as Benjamin has suggested, it is a salvation that is infinitely postponed.

CONCLUSION: THE DEATH OF MAMMON

Writing in the wake of the financial crisis, Goodchild argues that the latter indicates the dissolution of money as a shared source of value, as the principle, the God, that rules over the world and forms our lives. Just as Mammon once killed God, Mammon now meets a similar fate. 'Mammon has been exposed and killed. Never again can the quest for wealth form the basis of global cooperation', Goodchild writes.[60] Nevertheless, just as news of God's death, God's murder, takes a while to get around, meaning that the name of God continues to circulate in the cultural imaginary, Mammon continues to exercise some hold on individuals and the economy as a whole. 'Mammon is dead and will remain so. Yet it will take decades for this event to reach out ears, even though we have done it ourselves, for we continue to live and worship as though Mammon were alive and well and could still save us from poverty'.[61]

I have outlined earlier some of the ways in which Mammon continues to organize life as the source of its value. Any attempt to shift pieties, to make good on or recognize Mammon's death, then, must find a way to address the components mentioned earlier, specifically the way that money functions economically, affectively, socially and politically, since it is through these means that it maintains itself as the value of values.

Goodchild himself has sought to dissolve the overarching grip that money holds locally and globally over individuals, institutions and political formations by proposing a model of evaluative credit. Such a system, Goodchild speculates, would subordinate credit to evaluation; that is, it would 'enable flows of credit and investment to be directed toward that which matters most', rather than solely towards the financially expedient and profitable.[62] A system of evaluative credit would not supplant the existing economy but supplement it by acting on it parasitically, as a sort of second tier system that would redirect and concentrate flows of credit towards the common good. The implementation of this alternative credit system would require a set of institutions analogous to those currently in place, including banks, investors, evaluators and other sovereign actors, yet it would operate on the basis of different principles, principles not subordinated to Mammon. As Goodchild conceives of it, this system of evaluative credit would also challenge the usual relationship between credit and debt, in effect minimizing the latter. Goodchild writes, for instance, that as fundamentally concerned with the distribution of credit, the structure of evaluative credit would deploy credit as 'neither an instantaneous exchange nor a permanent obligation. It is an act of investment that would endure over time'.[63] He goes on to note:

> Yet if enterprises remain worthwhile, they may continue to attract credit and so may continue to be funded by ever-increasing permanent 'loans'. The ability to command a permanent loan should not be restricted to states and large corporations; it should be possible for any enterprise that is genuinely worthwhile. As the loans increase in size, such enterprises may feel the weight of the responsibility to fulfill their obligations. Yet the worst effects of debt are avoided, since such loans need never to be repaid. Even a loss of credit and a default on the loan leading to the end of the enterprise need not be catastrophic, since it should occur when the service is no longer deemed worthwhile.[64]

Goodchild's system of evaluative credit attempts to shift how we make evaluations, delinking the latter from the logic of money, which inscribes the world in terms of itself. If money 'considers all things insofar as they promise money', Goodchild's system of evaluative credit 'turns its attention outside itself, toward that which matters most'.[65] Goodchild's proposal for evaluative credit, then, seeks to devalue the value of money, through the redirection of time, attention and devotion.

Goodchild, to be sure, acknowledges the provisional nature of his proposal, but what is significant is that it attempts to detach credit from debt, or at least its more deleterious structural, collective and individual effects. Goodchild's proposal, then, is not only a means of rethinking credit but debt, which also means that it gestures towards rethinking money as debt and the role that debt plays economically and subjectively. Nevertheless, any attempt to think along these lines must also consider the affective or emotional dimensions of money as debt, since this is one of the primary means through which money maintains itself as Mammon, as the value of values. It is important to emphasize, however, that affective or emotional detachment from money cannot merely come from an act of will, in a sort of theological reorientation of desire. Even the best of intentions, here, will run aground on the force of money, the simple fact that one has to use it in practice, since it is that use, I have argued, that turns it into an object of belief and desire. Any sort of affective shift in our relationship to money, it seems, would have to occur immanently, in money itself and its actual use.

Again, a focus on debt here is essential for thinking along these lines. Debt, insofar as it relates to consumptive activity, is certainly caught up in the movements of desire. Indeed, capitalism itself can be understood, at least in part, as a machine that generates desire, one that not only harnesses it but creates it for the purposes of production, speculation and capital accumulation. In this sense, it is perfectly appropriate to interrogate the relationship between debt and desire and to speak of the latter's reorientation. But it may also be the case desire itself is no longer the motivating factor in the economy, at least in certain segments and among many individuals. Matthew Tiessen has suggested, for instance, that in economies structured around credit and debt, desire as a source of subjective motivation eventually comes to take a back seat to debt repayment. He notes that 'debt-repayment has – for many – become *the* primary – and perpetual – source of motivation. Debt's appetite, in other words, orients peoples' energies and keeps people working as indentured servants of capital. Debt-free desires are necessarily postponed or abandoned as debt-servicing takes pride of place in an ever shorter list of priorities'.[66] Rather than the constant reproduction of libidinous – or even religious – desire as the engine that drives production, the modern debt economy relies for its repetition on the simple individual and social fact of indebtedness. 'Indeed, these days whether average citizens are careful with their personal finances or not, indebtedness is the condition into which they are born and in which they will inevitably operate (whether it's sovereign debt, ecological debt, student debt, credit card debt, mortgage debt, etc.)', Tiessen writes.[67]

If this is the case, then what Lazzarato refers to as 'the indebted man' names not only a generalized condition of material indebtedness but a subjective relationship to that indebtedness, one that recasts desire accordingly. In a sense, then, a reorientation of desire has already happened, and what remains is the harnessing of this motivation away from repayment and towards refusal. Roberto Esposito has noted that, although indebtedness is the result of relations and flows of power, generalized indebtedness also functions as a means of rendering the relationship between credit and debt inoperative. Esposito notes that the 'fact we are all debtors, or are becoming ones, means that there are no more real creditors. Every creditor is a debtor to another, in a chain whose first link has been lost'.[68] The trick, Esposito writes, is turning 'this oppressive chain into a circuit of solidarity'.[69] Esposito suggests that socializing debt towards the development of socially useful goods would be one way to translate debt into a form of solidarity, and in this much of his suggestion is in line with Goodchild's own call for a system of evaluative credit, at least in terms of its overall thrust. Esposito appeals to the law of jubilee in this respect, speculating that a universalized forgiveness of debt would pave the way to move 'from a sovereign debt to a common debt, to a community of debt, such that the immunitary grip in which the world is suffocating would be broken'.[70] Considering the role that debt currently plays in the economy, in terms of both wealth and subject creation, calls for debt forgiveness may be overly optimistic. Nevertheless, Esposito also suggests that the condition of indebtedness itself may foster forms of resistance towards an 'option of freedom', as he puts it.[71]

Here, it is important to emphasize that just as debt serves as a means to subjugate individuals, institutions and states to the power of Mammon, it also creates the conditions for the latter's disruption in the form of a refusal to pay. Machinic enslavement may anonymize debt for the purposes of wealth creation, but that does not dissolve the subject of debt but rather assumes it: financialization, in other words, depends on a promise to pay as one type of security. Without that promise, through the active negation of that promise, the refusal to pay becomes a means of disrupting the affective, economic and sovereign aspects of money, turning debt into a form of solidarity against debt. It is perhaps in this refusal, and in the solidarity it evokes and organizes, that we can begin to speak of Mammon's real death.

NOTES

1. Quoted in Andrew Clark and Jill Treanor, 'Greenspan – I Was Wrong about the Economy. Sort of', *The Guardian*, 24 October 2008; http://www.theguardian.com/business/2008/oct/24/economics-creditcrunch-federal-reserve-greenspan (last accessed 26 February 2017).

2. Philip Goodchild, 'Exposing Mammon: Devotion to Money in a Market Society', *Dialog* 52.1 (2013): 56.

3. Indeed, if anything, the crisis has only further entrenched the principles and practices that govern the global economy, in effect accelerating neoliberalism. For a discussion along these lines, see Philip Mirowski, *Never Let a Serious Crisis Go to Waste: How Neoliberalism Survived the Financial Meltdown* (London: Verso, 2014).

4. Nietzsche, of course, has the madman say: 'How could we drink up the sea? Who gave us the sponge to wipe away the entire horizon? What were we doing when we unchained this earth from its sun? Whither are we moving? Away from all suns? Are we not plunging continually? Backward, sideward, forward, in all directions? Is there still any up or down? Are we not straying as through an infinite nothing?' See Friedrich Nietzsche, *The Gay Science,* trans. Walter Kaufmann (New York: Vintage Books, 1974), III § 125.

5. Philip Goodchild, *Capitalism and Religion: The Price of Piety* (London: Routledge, 2002), 27.

6. Goodchild, *Capitalism and Religion*, 27.

7. Goodchild, *Capitalism and Religion*, 27.

8. Even for Jesus, allegiance to Mammon signifies an interconnected system of beliefs and practices, which includes not only money and wealth but also work and family, and the investment that we place in these. See, for instance, Matthew 6:25–43 and Luke 18:18–30.

9. Goodchild, *Capitalism and Religion*, 28.

10. Goodchild, *Capitalism and Religion*, 28.

11. Goodchild, *Capitalism and Religion*, 27.

12. Philip Goodchild, *Theology of Money* (Durham, NC: Duke University Press, 2009), 201.

13. See Nietzsche, *The Gay Science*, III § 108, § 343.

14. Slavoj Žižek, *The Sublime Object of Ideology* (London: Verso, 1989), 31; original emphasis.

15. Friedrich Nietzsche, *On the Genealogy of Morals*, in *Basic Writings of Nietzsche*, trans. Walter Kaufmann (New York: The Modern Library, 2000), § 4; hereafter cited as *GM* with section references in the text.

16. Gilles Deleuze, *Nietzsche and Philosophy*, trans. Hugh Tomlinson (New York: Columbia University Press, 1983), 141.

17. Cf. Anselm of Canterbury, 'Why God Became Man', in *Anselm of Canterbury: The Major Works*, ed. Brian Davies and G. R. Evans (Oxford: Oxford University Press, 1998), I/11, II/5.

18. Walter Benjamin, 'Capitalism as Religion', in *Walter Benjamin: Selected Writings, Volume 1: 1913–1926*, ed. Marcus Bullock and Michael W. Jennings (Cambridge, MA: Belknap Press of Harvard University Press, 1996), 288.

19. Benjamin, 'Capitalism as Religion', 288–89.

20. Benjamin, 'Capitalism as Religion', 289; see Daniel Weidner, 'Thinking beyond Secularization: Walter Benjamin, the "Religious Turn", and the Poetics of Theory', *New German Critique* 111, 37.3 (2010): 140–42.

21. Benjamin, 'Capitalism as Religion', 289.

22. Augustine of Hippo, *Confessions*, trans. R. S. Pine-Coffin (London: Penguin Books, 1961), 48/II.5.

23. See Daniel M. Bell, Jr., *The Economy of Desire* (Grand Rapids, MI: Baker Academic, 2012) and William T. Cavanaugh, *Being Consumed* (Grand Rapids, MI: William B. Eerdmans Publishing Company, 2008).

24. Cavanaugh, *Being Consumed*, 14–15.

25. Cavanaugh, *Being Consumed*, 15.

26. William T. Cavanaugh has suggested, for instance, that it is modern consumerism, rather than its critique, that fosters detachment from the material world. He notes, 'What really characterizes consumer culture is not attachment to things but detachment. People do not hoard money; they spend it. People do not cling to things; they discard them and buy other things' (*Being Consumed*, 34.)

27. David Graeber, *Debt: The First 5,000 Years* (Brooklyn, NY: Melville House, 2011).

28. Aristotle, 'Politics', in *The Basic Works of Aristotle*, ed. Richard McKeon (New York: The Modern Library, 2001), 1257a: 35–40. For an excellent discussion of Aristotle's skepticism regarding money and trade in light of his context, and specifically philosophical presuppositions regarding the nature of truth, see Marcel Hénaff, *The Price of Truth: Gift, Money, and Philosophy*, trans. Jean-Louis Morhange (Stanford, CA: Stanford University Press, 2010).

29. Aristotle, *Politics*, 1257b5, 1258a1.

30. See Jacques Le Goff, *Your Money or Your Life*, trans. Patricia Ranum (New York: Zone Books, 1990).

31. Adam Smith, *An Inquiry into the Nature and Causes of the Wealth of Nations* (Edinburgh: Thomas Nelson, 1843), I/2.

32. Smith, *The Wealth of Nations*, I/4.

33. Smith, *The Wealth of Nations*, I/4.

34. Geoffrey Ingham, *The Nature of Money* (Cambridge: Polity, 2004), 25; original emphasis.

35. Ingham, *The Nature of Money*, 12; original emphasis.

36. Ingham, *The Nature of Money*, 12; original emphasis.

37. Ingham, *The Nature of Money*, 74.

38. Ingham, *The Nature of Money*, 74.

39. For a more historically oriented account of the abstract character of money with regard to its Greek origins, see Richard Seaford, *Money and the Early Greek Mind* (Cambridge: Cambridge University Press, 2004).

40. Ingham, *The Nature of Money*, 73.

41. See Martin Konings, *The Emotional Logic of Capitalism* (Stanford, CA: Stanford University Press, 2015), 35.

42. Maurizio Lazzarato, *The Making of the Indebted Man*, trans. Joshua David Jordan (Los Angeles: Semiotext(e), 2011), 19.

43. Lazzarato, *The Making of the Indebted Man*, 20.

44. Lazzarato, *The Making of the Indebted Man*, 31.

45. This is not to say that money is the sole means through which subjects become indebted, that is, that money acts alone in the social field, historically and currently. Graeber, for instance, recognizes various dimensions of exchange

(*Debt*, esp. 89–126). Kojin Karatani's work on 'modes of exchange' is important here as well. In *The Structure of World History: From Modes of Production to Modes of Exchange*, trans. Michael K. Bourdaghs (Durham, NC: Duke University Press, 2014), Karatani recognizes four basic modes of exchange that consist in social formations: reciprocity, plunder and distribution, commodity exchange and what he refers to as 'x', which designates a variety of practices, including 'socialism, communism, anarchism, council communism, [and] associationism' (9). Social formations are characterized, for him, according to which mode is primary, and how it relates to and organizes the other forms.

46. Michel Aglietta and André Orléan, *La violence de la monnaie* (Paris: PUF, 1982).

47. Maurizio Lazzarato, *Signs and Machines: Capitalism and the Production of Subjectivity*, trans. Joshua David Jordan (Cambridge, MA: MIT Press, 2014), 25.

48. Lazzarato, *Signs and Machines*, 27.

49. Lazzarato, *Signs and Machines*, 31.

50. Lazzarato, *Signs and Machines*, 48.

51. Konings, *The Emotional Logic of Capitalism*, 19.

52. Konings, *The Emotional Logic of Capitalism*, 37.

53. Konings, *The Emotional Logic of Capitalism*, 62.

54. Lauren Berlant, *Cruel Optimism* (Durham, NC: Duke University Press 2011), 24; original emphasis.

55. Berlant, *Cruel Optimism*, 25.

56. Berlant, *Cruel Optimism*, 27.

57. Berlant, *Cruel Optimism*, 28.

58. Goodchild, *Theology of Money*, 119.

59. See Jacques Lacan, *The Four Fundamental Concepts of Psychoanalysis*, trans. Alan Sheridan (New York: Norton, 1978), 203–15. As Lacan quips in his discussion of alienation, '*Your money or your life!* If I choose the money, I lose both. If I choose life, I have life without the money, namely, a life deprived of something' (212).

60. Goodchild, 'Exposing Mammon': 56.

61. Goodchild, 'Exposing Mammon': 56.

62. Goodchild, *Theology of Money*, 242.

63. Goodchild, *Theology of Money*, 244.

64. Goodchild, *Theology of Money*, 246.

65. Goodchild, *Theology of Money*, 254.

66. Matthew Tiessen, 'Infinite Debt and the Mechanics of Dispossession', in *Revisiting Normativity with Deleuze*, ed. Rosi Braidotti and Patricia Pisters (London: Continuum, 2013), 124.

67. Tiessen, 'Infinite Debt and the Mechanics of Dispossession', 125.

68. Roberto Esposito, *Two: The Machine of Political Theology*, trans. Zakiya Hanafi (New York: Fordham University Press, 2015), 209.

69. Esposito, *Two*, 209.

70. Esposito, *Two*, 209.

71. Esposito, *Two*, 209.

BIBLIOGRAPHY

AGLIETTA, Michel and André ORLEAN. *La violence de la monnaie*. Paris: PUF, 1982.

ANSELM OF CANTERBURY. *Why God Became Man*. In *Anselm of Canterbury: The Major Works*. Edited by Brian Davies and G. R. Evans. Oxford: Oxford University Press, 1998.

ARISTOTLE. *Politics*. In *The Basic Works of Aristotle*. Edited by Richard McKeon. New York: The Modern Library, 2001.

AUGUSTINE OF HIPPO. *Confessions*. Translated by R. S. Pine-Coffin. London: Penguin Books, 1961.

BELL, Daniel M., Jr. *The Economy of Desire*. Grand Rapids, MI: Baker Academic, 2012.

BENJAMIN, Walter. 'Capitalism as Religion'. In *Walter Benjamin: Selected Writings, Volume 1: 1913–1926*. Edited by Marcus Bullock and Michael W. Jennings. Cambridge, MA: Belknap Press of Harvard University Press, 1996. 288–91.

BERLANT, Lauren. *Cruel Optimism*. Durham, NC: Duke University Press, 2011.

CAVANAUGH, William T. *Being Consumed*. Grand Rapids, MI: William B. Eerdmans Publishing Company, 2008.

CLARK, Andrew and Jill TREANOR. 'Greenspan – I Was Wrong about the Economy. Sort of'. *The Guardian*, 24 October 2008; http://www.theguardian.com/business/2008/oct/24/economics-creditcrunch-federal-reserve-greenspan. Last accessed 26 February 2017.

DELEUZE, Gilles. *Nietzsche and Philosophy*. Translated by Hugh Tomlinson. New York: Columbia University Press, 1983.

ESPOSITO, Roberto. *Two: The Machine of Political Theology*. Translated by Zakiya Hanafi. New York: Fordham University Press, 2015.

GOODCHILD, Philip. *Capitalism and Religion: The Price of Piety*. London: Routledge, 2002.

GOODCHILD, Philip. 'Exposing Mammon: Devotion to Money in a Market Society'. *Dialog* 52.1 (2013): 47–57.

GOODCHILD, Philip. *Theology of Money*. Durham, NC: Duke University Press, 2009.

GRAEBER, David. *Debt: The First 5,000 Years*. Brooklyn, NY: Melville House, 2011.

HÉNAFF, Marcel. *The Price of Truth: Gift, Money, and Philosophy*. Translated by Jean-Louis Morhange. Stanford, CA: Stanford University Press, 2010.

INGHAM, Geoffrey. *The Nature of Money*. Cambridge: Polity, 2004.

KARATANI, Kojin. *The Structure of World History: From Modes of Production to Modes of Exchange*. Translated by Michael K. Bourdaghs. Durham, NC: Duke University Press, 2014.

KONINGS, Martin. *The Emotional Logic of Capitalism*. Stanford, CA: Stanford University Press, 2015.

LACAN, Jacques. *The Four Fundamental Concepts of Psychoanalysis*. Translated by Alan Sheridan. New York: Norton, 1978.

LAZZARATO, Maurizio. *The Making of the Indebted Man*. Translated by Joshua David Jordan. Los Angeles: Semiotext(e), 2011.

LAZZARATO, Maurizio. *Signs and Machines: Capitalism and the Production of Subjectivity*. Translated by Joshua David Jordan. Cambridge, MA: MIT Press, 2014.

LE GOFF, Jacques. *Your Money or Your Life*. Translated by Patricia Ranum. New York: Zone Books, 1990.

MIROWSKI, Philip. *Never Let a Serious Crisis Go to Waste: How Neoliberalism Survived the Financial Meltdown*. London: Verso, 2014.

MITCHELL-INNES, Alfred. 'The Credit Theory of Money'. *The Banking Law Journal* 31 (1914): 151–68.

NIETZSCHE, Friedrich. *The Gay Science*. Translated by Walter Kaufmann. New York: Vintage Books, 1974.

NIETZSCHE, Friedrich. *On the Genealogy of Morals*. In *Basic Writings of Nietzsche*. Translated by Walter Kaufmann. New York: The Modern Library, 2000.

SEAFORD, Richard. *Money and the Early Greek Mind*. Cambridge: Cambridge University Press, 2004.

SMITH, Adam. *An Inquiry into the Nature and Causes of the Wealth of Nations*. Edinburgh: Thomas Nelson, 1843.

TIESSEN, Matthew. 'Infinite Debt and the Mechanics of Dispossession'. In *Revisiting Normativity with Deleuze*. Edited by Rosi Braidotti and Patricia Pisters. London: Continuum, 2013.

WEIDNER, Daniel. 'Thinking beyond Secularization: Walter Benjamin, the "Religious Turn", and the Poetics of Theory'. *New German Critique* 111, 37.3 (2010): 131–48.

ŽIŽEK, Slavoj. *The Sublime Object of Ideology*. London: Verso, 1989.

Section three

SPECULATION AND CRITIQUE

Chapter 9

Impotent signs

Money, speculative subjectivity and the ontological proof

Aidan Tynan

In the late nineteenth century, economics established itself as an independent discipline, with the result that philosophers largely stopped writing about money, a topic that had animated them since the days of Plato and Aristotle. Ole Bjerg, in a recent book dedicated to rectifying this neglect, notes that 'the most curious thing about the contemporary philosophy of money is that it does not exist'.[1] While this is not entirely true, as I will show, it is fair to say, as Bjerg does, that Georg Simmel's *The Philosophy of Money* (1900) marks the end of a certain manner of philosophising about money that includes the work not only of Adam Smith and Karl Marx but also of Kant and Hegel, who either used various conceptualisations of money in their theorising or dealt with monetary issues in their work directly as speculative ones. If, as Marc Shell observes, German philosophers of this time had a 'fascination with money and ontology', it is because 'monetary theory ties together symbol and commodity, as well as universal and particular, in a knotty conception of the relationship between thought and matter'.[2] It is hardly surprising, then, that philosophy has for centuries tended to regard money – located as it is at the intersection of the ideal and the material, the metaphysical and the physical – with both fascination and suspicion, as possessing divine or dissimulating properties connected to power and tyranny.[3]

Economics since Smith, by contrast, has attempted to regard money as a mere expression of the rationality of the social system it serves, and its development as a discipline has consisted in providing the intellectual tools to demystify money of what John Locke once called its 'unnatural' and 'phantastical imaginary value'.[4] This bracketing of the ontological question of money – of what money *is*, of *how* it is – has been seen, since Smith, as necessary for the development of economics as a science.

Marxism, likewise, has sought to demystify money by viewing it as congealed labour power. Both mainstream economics and Marxism, then, naturalise money by avoiding its ontology and viewing it from a purely functional point of view: money is nothing other than the *power* that it grants to its possessor. And yet today, the question of what money is remains as pressing and as open as ever, with money appearing perhaps more fantastical now than it ever has in human history. The notorious financial derivatives associated with the 2007–2008 subprime mortgage crash may or may not be considered money, depending on one's point of view.[5] Similar questions are emerging around the virtual currency Bitcoin. As money appears in more and more sophisticated, technocratic and automated forms, it remains elusive for contemporary consciousness.

Work from the last ten years or so, and in particular since 2008, suggests an approach to the theoretical problem of money, and in particular its ontology, that breaks both with economic orthodoxy and Marxism.[6] This work demonstrates how philosophy, theology and critical theory can function in combination with the social sciences and economics in order to think the problem of money anew in our contemporary climate of seemingly endless crisis. A question that has long been a concern for the philosophy of money is reopened in this recent work: the crucial link between money and religion. Goodchild, a philosopher and theologian, has shown how money – once it becomes identical with credit, as it increasingly does in its capitalist forms – constitutes a promise and an obligation, and is thus best grasped via theology as a religious problem.[7] Money sustains a form of 'piety' in the midst of an increasingly secular society. Graeber, an anthropologist, addresses money in its guise as debt and compares different legal and religious traditions to show how deeply rooted our economic thought is in an ancient moral and theological matrix.[8]

That these recent speculations on money reopen the old (possibly ancient) question of money's theology is significant because it suggests that our current post-secular impasse is related in key ways to the impasses of post-2008 crisis capitalism. Our post-secular condition is, broadly speaking, that the political potency of the religious endures amid the dismantling of religion's traditional institutions.[9] A subjectivity founded on religious concepts such as the law and the state cannot comprehend the death of religion even when it no longer believes in religious authority. Similarly, the inability of most economists to see the 2008 crisis coming suggests that capitalism is incapable of understanding its own death and in the absence of any alternative capitalism endures, zombielike, beyond its effective end as a viable economic system. What I will show here, however, is that these twin impasses can be explained on the basis of a common speculative potency, what I call 'speculative subjectivity', that goes beyond the discrete domains of the economic and the religious. Any properly post-capitalist society must be located beyond the impasses specific to these domains. The theology of money, then, opens onto a more general speculative constitution of reality *that is neither religious nor economic*, and this is what the present chapter will elucidate.

Of course, the link between religion and capitalism has long been recognised by social theory, even if the specific role of money has not always been sufficiently acknowledged. Marx famously insisted that the critique of religion provides the basis for all critique, including the critique of capitalism. If religion is the means by which 'man . . . can objectify his essence only by making it into an *alien*, fantastic being', money is likewise the 'alien substance' by which he objectifies his productive activities, his practical life and daily rituals.[10] Simmel was the first to suggest that capitalism should be understood in terms of its 'spirit', the subjective dispositions it engendered, and emphasised the link to religion in this respect.[11] This idea was taken up by Weber, whose essay *The Protestant Ethic and the Spirit of Capitalism* (1905) is possibly the most famous text in the history of sociology. Weber argues that the Protestant work ethic, and in particular the Calvinist doctrine of predestination, provided the spiritual conditions rendering capitalist accumulation possible: profit stemming from hard work becomes a sign of salvation. He takes Simmel to task for focusing in an overly abstract and ahistorical way on money as distinct from capitalist society.[12] And yet a conception of money as a speculative object *distinct from its social functions* is key to understanding what we mean today when we speak of capitalism in crisis.

In the wake of the economic crises of 2008, it became necessary to attempt to explain both *how* the desires of the masses were drawn into the speculations of financial capitalism and *why* this led the global economy to the brink of collapse. How were low-paid mortgage holders and Icelandic fishermen, among others, able to bring the global economy to its knees despite the sophistications of the financial instruments concocted to integrate them into the system? Many commentators, including Marxists, speak of a crisis of faith brought on by this influx of mass desire via financial credit. Recent trends in economics have seen a return to Keynes's use of the ancient notion of 'animal spirits' as a means of accounting for the spontaneous optimism that sustains (or fails to sustain) economic markets.[13] According to such an approach, economic collapse is explained in terms of a simple psychology of a faith that failed. But this recourse to psychology is, more than anything else, symptomatic of a theoretical impasse that economics by itself cannot remedy.

The real problem lies in articulating how money, in its increasingly abstract, speculative form, can function as an object of faith in the first place, and this can be explained only in terms of a speculative subjectivity. The latter goes far beyond mere psychology, as I will show, in that it is the subjectivity of impersonal, abstract thought. Speculative subjectivity is that aspect of ourselves capable of investing in a reality beyond present states of affairs. It is the mode by which we surpass ourselves in an orientation to pure potentiality or pure futurity in the absence of any 'image' of this future. We can understand both money and religion as means of capturing and policing this speculative capacity. The present socioeconomic constitution of reality depends directly on speculative subjectivity, and in this sense the latter is part of the infrastructure of our world. Nevertheless, this is only the case because the speculative subject has been captured in an objectification, an object-form, namely: money. This capture constitutes the faith, the credo, specific to capitalism. From this point of view, financial crisis is indeed a crisis of faith but one that afflicts the impersonal religion of capitalism rather than the psychology of the believer.

What follows, then, is an attempt to outline how the link between money and religion might ground a conception of post-secular subjectivity in a way capable of orienting us beyond the current impasses of perpetual crisis. I thus argue that the 'theology of money' for which Goodchild calls needs to be supplemented with a new account of subjectivity that takes us beyond the post-secular psychology of the exhausted believer. Articulating an escape from this theopolitical impasse is one of the key challenges for politics today. To this end, my argument will proceed on the basis that the theological critique of capitalism points beyond the distinction between religion and economics as discrete modes of social life. In fact, the key point at which I shall arrive is that the segregation of these domains from one another is source of the twin impasses that are currently preventing us from moving on from the death of God and the death of capitalism. My account of speculative subjectivity is elaborated through readings of key texts in the philosophical discourse on money from Kant to Deleuze and Guattari, passing through psychoanalysis, and drawing on insights from the recent work on the philosophy of money mentioned earlier. My purpose is not to provide a survey of this tradition but to suggest how money and speculative thought share a complexly intertwined history, the ramifications of which, in an age of financial speculation, reach to the subjective core of belief and desire.

THE ONTOLOGICAL QUESTION OF MONEY

Economics sidelines the question of the ontology of money, of what it *is* and *how* it is, in favour of a consideration of its effects and functions, of what it *does*. The reason for this relates to the fact that such ontological questioning lies beyond the mathematical methods that have come to define economics in the twentieth century. But even for Adam Smith, writing in the late eighteenth century, economics could be put on a rational footing only by regarding the power of money in a functional, exchangist manner: 'The powers attributed to money are not inherent in money, but derive from its functions as a means of exchange'.[14] The only way to overcome the illusory powers attributed to money by a tradition of philosophical discourse stretching back to Plato is to identify it with its social power. The ontological question of money is thus suspended so that it may be regarded as the mere expression of the rationality of the social system it serves. This is the bedrock of the modern economic view. For a modern economist, it makes little sense to ask what money is since it is only an efficacy, a power to exchange, measure, store or account for value.[15]

For Marxists also, money remains essentially a power to purchase commodities, most importantly the commodity called labour power. From the Marxist perspective, all commodities, including money, are congealed labour power. Money is unique among commodities, however, because it is the 'universal equivalent' that allows any commodity to be exchanged for any other. For this reason, it also congeals the social relationship between the capitalist who owns the means of production and the worker who owns nothing but labour power. The economic power of money thus translates directly into social power, as Costas Lapavitsas, for example, writes: 'The economic power of money is the source of its social power, making it possible for the owner of money to impose his or her will on others by advancing or withholding money'.[16]

To identify money and power so decisively, however, is problematic because it assumes the power of money instead of explaining it. To say that money only *is* its functions is a purely after-the-fact description. This is a problem shared by mainstream economics and Marxism equally. It is particularly problematic when we consider that the history of money since the establishment of the Bank of England in the seventeenth century has been an increasing abstraction from the material commodity (gold or silver) it was supposed to represent. What an ontology of money needs to address today is this dematerialisation, this spiritualisation, represented by *credit*. The ontological question of money involves an investigation into its *credo*. Since the so-called Nixon Shock of 1971, the dollar has operated as a 'floating' currency, unanchored from any metallic standard and therefore not convertible into anything beyond itself. The modern development of fiat money and credit money, in which monetary value becomes entirely symbolic or 'virtual', grounds the power of money in its value as pure sign operating without referent. A banknote is a promise to pay that can ever be fulfilled only by another promise to pay, in an infinite regress, a chain of signifiers. As Michael Tratner writes, 'To have a dollar is to be owed a dollar: the sign that represents money actually represents that one has the right to another sign'.[17]

This *semiotic* transformation of the global economy – unprecedented in world history – is what facilitated the hegemony of financial capital in the latter half of the twentieth century and precipitated the economic crises that have menaced Europe and the United States since the subprime mortgage crash of 2008. This transformation should not be thought of as a purely economic affair but as a crucial moment in the history of speculative consciousness. It is no coincidence that the poststructuralist theories of the sign that emerged in the 1960s and 1970s with Derrida, Deleuze and others mirror the semiotic transformation of the global economy.[18] Deleuze, for example, tells us that the 'power of language' derives not from its ability to refer to an empirical world outside language but 'to speak infinitely of or about words themselves'. Thought, likewise, has 'no object other than the power of reiteration in indefinite regress (I think that I think that I think. . .) '.[19] Thought frees the *cogito* from empirical reality and language frees the word from the referent, just as money frees value from material commodities. This is not to reiterate the tired argument, most famously put forth by Habermas, that post-structuralist theory is a mere ideological expression of neoliberal capitalism, but to acknowledge the extent to which money and speculative thought share a complexly intertwined history.

What the years since the 2008 crash have shown is that the dematerialisation of money into a pure sign, far from democratising access to it, goes hand in hand with the intensification of money as an instrument of social power. The 1990s in particular saw a trend towards what Randy Martin has called the 'financialization of daily life', in which the management of money as debt and credit – as *risk* – was extended beyond the elite corporate world to include those least insulated against economic precariousness, such as the largely black and Hispanic low-income subprime mortgage holders of Florida and California or the Icelandic fishermen who turned to investment banking in the years prior to 2008.[20] A speculative subjectivity was extended to the masses. The financialisation of the economy offered not just monetary accumulation but what Martin calls 'an acquisition of self', an expansion of subjectivity through a merger of life and business cycles.[21] Money, as a speculative object, as a self-positing sign based on nothing other than a promise of value, determines a corresponding subjectivity, an expanding bubble of desires and beliefs. The crash can thus be seen to represent the bursting of the bubble and the collapse of a certain utopian dream in which even the poorest can act as one-man corporations.

Many explanations of the crash rely on a vague and overly simplistic psychology of faith in the context of an economy overloaded with various forms of credit money. This is true of Marxism as much as of mainstream economics. As the Marxist David Harvey, for example, writes, 'Faith in the system is fundamental and loss of confidence, as happened in 2008, can be fatal'.[22] This reliance on psychology, often gleaned in unreconstructed form from Keynes, glosses over the fundamental point: money is something that can, somehow, compel both belief and disbelief simultaneously in a speculative intermixture of cynicism and hope. Indeed, as David Graeber suggests in his monumental five-thousand-year history of debt, it was not, ultimately, a loss of faith that caused the subprime crash. This was only the *effect*. It was, rather, *too much* faith in an economic system based fundamentally on unpredictability and contingency that was to blame.[23] When the capitalist utopia becomes too believable, something needs to check it, and a sudden demystification of capital's spiritual core is required. In other words, the speculative subjectivity of the masses is something that the financial system, with help of the state, needs not only to draw upon but also to marshal and contain. Money, then, is a sign that compels belief and disbelief, credit and discredit, as part of the means by which capitalism polices and regulates the limits of subjectivity itself.

In order to justify and expand these points I now turn to an essay by the young Marx, collected in *The Economic and Philosophic Manuscripts of 1844*, titled 'The Power of Money in Bourgeois Society'. This text is useful for my discussion because it combines the subjective and the ontological in a way that reveals money to be a form of *self-limiting power*. It avoids the failings of the mature Marx's theory of money as general equivalent, in which money is explained in terms of how commodities become universally exchangeable. In this early piece, the young 'humanistic' Marx is seeking an account of money beginning from 'man's *feelings*, passions, etc.' understood not merely in their 'anthropological' sense but as 'truly *ontological* affirmations of being'.[24] Marx is saying here that human feeling and passion, what we can call desire, only have reality in the various objects that correspond to them; humanity *is* only via these objects. He adds that 'only through developed industry – i.e., through the medium of private property – does the ontological essence of human passion come into being' ('EPM' 322). It is only with capitalism that desire is called upon to constitute social reality directly.

Money thus offers a key to understanding social ontology itself. This is something that Bjerg's recent work has sought to develop. He suggests that the money form provides a way of understanding what Heidegger, writing in the 1920s, famously called Dasein, meaning human existence, the 'to be' of humanity. Heidegger distinguished between Being (*Sein*) and beings (*Seiende*), between the ontological question of Being itself in all its existential significance and the simple 'ontic' being of individual objects.[25] Humanity's tragedy lies in the forgetting of this distinction. While Heidegger and Marx could be no further apart politically, in Marx's account there is nevertheless a similar ontic-ontological distinction: money in capitalist society is not *just* an object, a being, among others but because of its form offers access to Being itself:

> By possessing the *property* of buying everything, by possessing the property of appropriating all objects, *money* is thus the *object* of eminent possession. The universality of its *property* is the omnipotence of its being. It is therefore regarded as an omnipotent being. Money is the *procurer* between man's need and the object, between his life and his means of life. ('EPM' 323)

Money thus comes to occupy the position of the divine. Simmel, in fact, makes a very similar point in *The Philosophy of Money*, where he writes that 'money is the symbol in the empirical world of the inconceivable unity of being, out of which the world, in all its breadth, diversity, energy and reality, flows'.[26] Money is thus both an object and the unity of all objects. It is experienced as an empirical being among others – as gold, coins, banknotes, debts and credits – but also as the transcendental condition for accessing objects in general. As a result of its fundamentally contradicted nature, it perpetrates a universal confusion, an arch-dissimulation that Marx describes with recourse to lines from Shakespeare's *Timon of Athens*:

> Gold? Yellow, glittering, precious gold? No, Gods,
> I am no idle votarist! . . .
> Thus much of this will make black white, foul fair,
> Wrong right, base noble, old young, coward valiant. . . .
> Thou *visible God!*
> That solder'st *close impossibilities,*
> And makest them kiss! ('EPM' 323)

This transformation of things into their contraries is central to the social power of money: if I am ugly, I can nevertheless buy the most beautiful companions. If I am lame, I can buy the best modes of transportation, and so on. Money, Marx writes, can 'transform all my incapacities into their contrary': 'That which I am unable to do as a *man*, and of which therefore all my individual essential powers are incapable, I am able to do by means of *money*' ('EPM' 324–5).

But ultimately, Marx suggests, this power of money is *itself subject to such a transformation into its opposite*, which is to say that money's power is essentially an impotence, a process of self-alienation whereby human capacities are entrusted to an autonomous external agent that stands over and above them. To the extent that money makes desires capable of being realised, to the extent that it gives actuality to desire, no desire may be said even to exist without the money to realise it. Money is thus both power and limitation at once:

> If I have no money for travel, I have no need – that is, no real and realisable need – to travel. If I have the *vocation* for study but no money for it, I have no vocation for study – that is, no *effective*, no *true* vocation. On the other hand, if I have really *no* vocation for study but have the will and the money for it, I have an *effective* vocation for it. *Money* as the external, universal *medium* and *faculty* . . . for turning an *image into reality* and *reality into a mere image*, transforms the *real essential powers of man and nature* into what are merely abstract notions and therefore *imperfections* and tormenting chimeras, just as it transforms *real imperfections and chimeras* – essential powers which are really impotent, which exist only in the imagination of the individual – into *real powers and faculties*.
>
> ('EPM' 325)

What Marx's ontology of money reveals is this intermixture of power and impotence in the translation of the real into the imaginary and back again. As sign, money is the interplay between these registers, a symbolisation of some incapacity that it transforms by giving reality to the abstraction of representation. The consequences of this apparently simple point are startling, because Marx is saying that money is *not* identical to its power since it depends upon those real imperfections that it transforms into faculties. It internalises my impotence and uses it as the basis of its own effectivity. The usual relationship between desire and its objects is then inverted: the object of desire must be made *possible* with money before it can become *desirable* for a subject. Money thus gives concrete reality not only to my desires but also to the limits of my desires and renders these limits impassable by transferring them from the domain of my subjective interiority to the object form. By entering into relations with desire, money can be said to police subjectivity more effectively than the 'pure' power of direct physical coercion, which merely opposes desire from the outside.

But what about the desire for money itself? Noam Yuran makes a crucial point on this when he says that 'the desire for money is not simply a psychological affect but, in a way, is imbedded in the object itself'.[27] He gives the example of Imelda Marcos, who famously owned three thousand pairs of shoes. To amass such a collection of individual *objects* beyond any feasible possibility of using them suggests greed to the point of obsession or madness, whereas the amassing of money to the same excessive degree is seen as a prudent and even a mark of virtue. Whereas one can clearly have too many shoes or cars or any other object, one can never have too much money. The owner of three thousand shoes is seen as mad, or at least eccentric, while the owner of a billion dollars is seen as eminently sane and rational. This point underscores why the psychologism of much contemporary economic discourse is so wrong-headed. Money depsychologises acquisition, giving the desire for it an objective form autonomous of any subjective passion. The greed of the financier is cold-blooded.

Can we not make a similar point about the role of belief? It has become almost a truism since Marx to observe that money is whatever we believe it to be, a secularised God.[28] But we make a serious error when we attribute this belief, this *credo*, to a subject duped by money's dazzling power. The object form of money renders belief impersonal and autonomous of the psychology of the believer, a flow of impersonal credit. Lacan once observed that 'the true formula of atheism is not *God is dead* . . . [but] *God is unconscious*'.[29] Slavoj Žižek helps us to understand this point correctly. It is not that modern secular subjectivity still believes at some deeply buried level in the superstitions it has ostensibly left behind: 'The unconscious is not "deep in me," it is out there, embodied in my practices, rituals, interactions. Even if I subjectively don't believe, I believe "objectively", in and through my acts and symbolic rituals'.[30] Money is the form of this objective belief that is only secured via the empty rituals of economic activity and not by any religious experience.

We might here adapt the theologian Thomas Altizer's claim that in secular society *credo* and *cogito* are 'antithetical acts' in which belief in God requires a leap beyond the limits of knowledge,[31] while knowledge purifies itself of any ideological content.[32] This antithesis has allowed science and religion to sit side by side in the secular world. Money, however, is an object of belief and knowledge *at the same time* in which the act of belief is both determined by and negated by the act of knowledge, and vice versa. It is this antithetical coexistence that defines money as simultaneously imaginary, symbolic and real.[33]

When we talk about the economy in the quasi-theological language of belief, then, this does *not* imply an ideologically blinded subjectivity or the 'false consciousness' of a mystified believer. This is what separates the capitalist religion from all others: it is not possible to escape it through a subjective shift, though a 'raising of consciousness' to a higher level. With capitalism, religious mystification *passes from subject to object*; the act of faith cannot ultimately be distinguished from a cold-blooded rationalism. We can regard this as the capitalist solution to the social problem of atheism, constituting what Deleuze and Guattari, in their discussion of the power of banking and finance, call an 'objective dissimulation' by which the desires and beliefs of the masses are not bewitched but, on the contrary, made into rational investors: 'The Desire of the most disadvantaged creature will invest with all its strength, irrespective of any economic understanding or lack of it, the capitalist social field as a whole'.[34] It is only from the point of view of this objective dissimulation that the vacillations between credit and discredit, faith and the loss of faith, in the semiotic proliferation of the financial economy can be properly understood. But the roots of this idea need to be sought elsewhere, in the history of philosophy and theology.

SPECULATIVE SUBJECTIVITY AND THE ONTOLOGICAL PROOF

I have been arguing that money and speculative consciousness share an intertwined history. As I have suggested, for a post-structuralist philosopher such as Deleuze, subjectivity is defined in relation to an object that eludes it but to which it is also ineluctably drawn. This 'speculative object' is manifested at the level of language by the fact that words don't correspond to their referents in the extra-linguistic world but only to other words in an endless chain. Likewise, the *cogito* of pure reason tells us nothing about external reality but only that thought *is*: it doesn't tell me *what* I think but *that* I think or that some 'thing', some 'other', in me thinks. We should add money here as a third component of what I am calling speculative subjectivity. As with language and the *cogito*, money constitutes value not through reference to any external commodity but solely through its self-referentiality as a sign. A society dominated by credit and finance pushes this to an extreme point at which money becomes godlike, 'the supreme, self-positing substance . . . subject to pure self-affirmation. . . . Its existence flows from its essence'.[35] In each case of language, thought and money, self-limitation is constitutive of a self-positing and self-legitimating power determining of subjectivity; the ability to speak, think and accumulate is knotted together in our constitution as subjects.

For centuries, philosophy and theology have regarded God as a speculative object in the same way that many now understand money in the era of financial capitalism. The ontological proof of God's existence, first put forward by St. Anselm of Canterbury in the eleventh century and revived in different ways in the modern period by Descartes and then Leibniz, states that if God can be conceived as the greatest or most perfect being that can be thought, then he *must* exist since non-existence would be an imperfection and thus a contradiction in terms. In other words, God's existence necessarily flows from his essence. The most important refutation of the ontological proof in modern philosophy comes from Kant, who writes that being is not a 'predicate' contained in the concept of a thing but 'is merely the positing of a thing'.[36] There is no difference between the concept (the representation) of something that exists and the concept of something that does not exist. Existence is, as it were, a non-conceptual matter and thus cannot be proved by reason alone. It is the example that Kant gives in his refutation that is of most concern here:

> A hundred actual dollars do not contain the least bit more than a hundred possible ones. For since the latter signifies the concept and the former its object and its positing in itself, then, in case the former contained more than the latter, my concept would not express the entire object and thus would not be the suitable concept of it. But in my financial condition there is more with a hundred actual dollars than with the mere concept of them (i.e., their possibility).[37]

We should note how Kant's reasoning here is quantitative: a thing's existence does not 'add' anything to the concept or the representation we might have of it, even if its existence *does* make a quantitative difference elsewhere (i.e. in my bank account or wallet). Kant's choice of example is by no means accidental. He ends his refutation by referring to the *value* of the intellectual labour involved in trying to prove the existence of God via pure reason. When it comes to the account book of philosophical speculation, the ontological proof is decidedly unprofitable:

> Thus the famous ontological (Cartesian) proof of the existence of a highest being from concepts is only so much trouble and labor lost, and a human being can no more become richer in insight from mere ideas than a merchant could in resources if he wanted to improve his financial state by adding a few zeros to his cash balance.[38]

We know from elsewhere in his writings that Kant was a staunch advocate of the silver standard at a time when the use of banknotes was increasingly being tried out as a result of shortages of precious metal.[39] Throughout the eighteenth century, the economies of Europe experimented with credit money, regulated by fledgling central banks, but this precipitated a number of catastrophic financial bubbles that caused many, including Kant, to endorse a metallic standard by which money's existence could be materially grounded. Remarking on the speculative fever, driven in large part by colonial expansion, that gripped the European powers during this time, Graeber remarks that 'there had to be some solid, material foundation to all this [financial speculation], or the entire system would go insane'.[40] Kant's comparison of the speculative activity of pure reason and the speculative activity of the merchant who adds zeros to his bank balance is suggestive and is based on real events in the history of European capitalism: as Graeber suggests, eighteenth-century merchants *were* making money, however fraudulently, in a manner similar to the one Kant describes.[41]

An important subtext of Kant's refutation of the ontological proof of God, then, relates to the ontological status of *money*. Indeed, Kant identifies money with pure reason itself when he writes that 'money, as the greatest and most useful means men have for *exchange* of things, called *buying and selling* (commerce)' is comparable to 'a book, as the greatest means for exchanging thoughts'.[42] Thus, even thought has its price; money is 'a thing that, in the circulation of possessions . . ., determines the *price* of all other things (goods), among which even the sciences belong, insofar as they would not otherwise be taught to others'.[43] But money, here, is *silver*, an external materiality acting as referent which contains speculation within proper limits determined by the possibility of an object of experience. As Jean-Joseph Goux remarks, drawing on psychoanalytic ideas, the act of exchange needs to be grounded in something: '*potency* (sexual) is called for. . . . Proof is required, the thing itself, tangible evidence: the agency of force and reference, not reducible to symbolic status'.[44] And yet money, at the time Kant is writing, is heading in the very opposite direction. The link between money as symbol and its metallic referent is becoming tenuous to the point where power and impotence overlap in the sign systems of capital.

For Kant, an entity such a God cannot be proved or disproved and thus remains a pure idea, because it can never be an object of possible experience; it can never claim access to the material potency of the referent. God is what Kant terms a 'transcendental illusion', which he distinguishes from simple empirical illusion. It is one thing to be deceived by objects of possible experience, to suppose, for example, that the moon is made of cheese or that the sun revolves around the Earth. But it is another thing entirely to be misled into believing something on the basis of the laws of reason alone. From the Kantian perspective, God is an objective dissimulation that compels belief via the self-grounding activity of reason rather than through any deception at the level of perception or of the senses. This is why Kant's refutation of the ontological proof does not amount to a denial of God's existence but solely to a bracketing of the question by limiting reason's speculative claims. God, as speculative object, can be said neither to exist or not to exist but can be *assumed* apriori in order to guide morality and regulate behaviours in the practical domain. Knowledge and reason must be kept separate in order to 'make room' for faith. This is the secular solution to the problem of God, but does it not also suggest something about how we treat money, whose intrinsic value we assume, even as we know it to be a mere symbol?

Hegel's response to Kant on the ontological proof amounts at once to a Christian assertion of God's existence and a condemnation of what he sees as Kant's overly pecuniary focus. Far more crucially, perhaps, it attempts to solve the problem of speculative labour power that Kant identified in his refutation. Hegel reiterates Kant's position that 'the possible does not contain more than the actual; a hundred actual dollars do not contain a whit more than a hundred possible ones; – that is, the actual one hundred have no other content determination than the possible'.[45] But he goes on to challenge Kant's representationalism, saying that

> here two kinds of 'states' . . . are *presupposed*: one that Kant calls 'concept', by which we must understand 'representation'; and another, my 'financial state.' . . . 'I', as *possessing* a hundred dollars or as not possessing them, or again, 'I', as *representing* a hundred dollars to myself or as not representing them, is of course a different content.[46]

It is the emphasis on the 'I' as possessor that Hegel takes issue with, since in Kant's refutation it is ultimately 'my financial state' that demonstrates the untenability of the ontological proof. But Hegel argues that the properly Christian attitude should foster an indifference towards whether or not I have the funds to employ the proof's speculative labour. Indeed, the funds are unlimited: the representation or the concept of the 100 dollars is, Hegel says, merely 'on loan' to the object to which it is attributed and the creditor is the 'subjective understanding' itself, a *credo* whose power to transcend the realm of empirical objects should not be limited by any such finite concerns as the state of my finances:

> when a lot of fuss is made about the hundred dollars, that it does make a difference to my financial state whether I *have* them or *not* . . ., we can then be reminded that the human being . . . ought to raise his mind to this abstract universality in which it is in fact indifferent to him whether the hundred dollars . . . are or are not; . . . still more ought the Christian to find himself in this state of indifference.[47]

The irony of this indifference to the finite that Hegel is here saying should define the Christian attitude is, of course, that it amounts to a perfect articulation of how money can work in the absence of a metallic standard and thus take on the kinds of speculative reality that was once only available to God: money's existence flows from its essence, as Goodchild points out. When money becomes credit money, the potency of the external, material referent, the thing itself, is dissipated into a speculative activity by which the subject posits its own reality via, and *no longer in spite of*, the impotence of its concepts or its representations.

Žižek, remarking on this exchange between the two philosophers, argues that their divergence is not simply a question of Hegel's idealism versus Kant's materialism.[48] Rather, Hegel's apparent idealism gives us a superior materialism. For Kant, the link between the representation and the object is assessed on the basis of a subjectivity that can only ever encounter material reality *as* representation and never as it is *in itself*. The representation thus lacks the being of the things to which it can only correspond as a sign does to its referent. But Hegel, Žižek argues, overcomes this by saying that it is this lack, this flaw, in our representations that constitutes, rather than precludes, any viable materialism. The lack of being marking out the object form belongs to the subject who forms the representations, and not to the object itself, while the sign is at once both the lack of being and the materiality of this lack. In short, the materiality of an external reality we might suppose to exist independently of us is, in fact, the product of a self-positing subjective activity because it is the incapacity, the *impotence* of our concepts or representations (or what Hegel calls 'notion', *Begriff*) to grasp anything beyond it that signifies this very materiality:

> With regard to material reality, the ontological proof of God's existence should thus be turned around: the existence of material reality bears witness to the fact that the Notion is not fully actualized. Things 'materially exist' not when they meet certain notional requirements, but when they fail to meet them – material reality is as such a sign of imperfection.[49]

Žižek's reading of Hegel is highly instructive because it draws the necessary link between the *speculative* subjectivity of philosophy (and theology) and the *specular* subjectivity of Lacanian psychoanalysis. In this link, we see clearly that the site of the transcendental illusion is effectively shifted from God to the subjectivity that creates representations but remains essentially opaque to itself, a 'void' or foundational lack.[50] The subject's substantive reality, its object form, is the lack that gives reality to it, like a line of credit it extends to itself. As is well known, Lacan's theory of the self is grounded in constitutive misrecognition: when I see myself in the mirror I acquire a sense of self or a subjective wholeness that is lacking from my immediate embodied existence. For Lacan, we are born prematurely, in a state of bodily helplessness and incoordination. Maturation involves not only physiological development but also a psychical process in which we use internal images to orient us in reality. What Lacan calls 'capture by the image' is the process whereby the ego identifies with its objectification in the mirror in order to remedy the helplessness that characterises our early experiences of embodiment.[51] The image is illusory, but it grants a reality that is otherwise lacking: what I see in the mirror is a fantasy image, an 'ideal', but my (mis)recognition of it *as* the real me constitutes my very selfhood and gives me a place in the order of being.

The gap between imaginary and real is both maintained and overcome, but only through a self-indebtedness, a speculative leveraging of the subject. It is no coincidence that the main clinical problem Freud focused on was guilt, or *Schuld*, a term synonymous with debt. The capitalist solution to the death of God, then, aligns money with subjectivity, even as money performs an objective dissimulation that dispenses with mystified consciousness and thus with any psychology of faith. The problem of adhering to a system of faith in an era of mass cynicism becomes a problem that is solved only by this leveraging of the specular/speculative subject. Goux draws a comparison between Lacan's specular ego and Marx's statement in the opening of *Capital* that 'the body of commodity B acts as a mirror to the value of commodity A'.[52] It is money, as speculative and specular value-form, that secures the universal equivalence of commodities *and* mediates between the real and the fantastical, belief and disbelief, in the order of our subjectivity.

What is missing, however, from the Lacano-Marxism of both Žižek and Goux is a thoroughgoing political critique of subjectivity itself. The Lacanian account offers scant means of addressing the historical and political elements at work in subject formation. The Oedipal family, as crucible of the subject, plays a depoliticising role. Such a critique is needed because psychoanalysis in its theory of the subject simply describes a strategy of containment peculiar to capitalism: what Freud characterised in directly economic terms as libido is a form of desire that, in modern capitalist society, becomes detached from its traditional objects of investment such as religion and the quasi-religious figures of social authority. In Freud's theory, the unconscious remains at a more primitive level and contains inherited beliefs that can be detected in symbolic form (in dreams etc.). The unconscious both desires *and* believes. In this sense, it is not the *actual* father that the infant must negotiate in the perilous course of the Oedipus complex but the archaic, fantastical and terrifyingly punitive father of myth and religion. But if the unconscious believes in the scenes that Freud and others describe, the question is why it becomes a believer in this way.

The only possible answer is that the unconscious has taken on the theological burden that secular capitalist modernity casts off. The analytic method as devised by Freud discovers the unconscious of belief beneath every conscious disavowal. It is in this light that Graeber's counterintuitive suggestion that the crash of 2008 was not caused by a lack but by an *excess* of belief in the financial system appears persuasive. Too much belief, an excess of credit, spurred on by the utopian dream of the unlimited speculative expansion of capitalism, caused the system to reach its limits and come crashing down. To recall Altizer's terms, capitalism cannot, ultimately, resolve the antithesis of *cogito* and *credo*: it passes this antithesis onto the money form in which we simultaneously believe and do not believe and by which we ourselves are both valued and devalued. In this sense, a capitalist crisis is nothing other than a regulatory check to belief, a spectacular reminder to all that money is really not something in which too much faith should be placed.

IMPOTENT SIGNS

I now turn to Deleuze and Guattari's *Anti-Oedipus* (1972), which provides a remarkable and prescient theory of money in the context of financialisation. Deleuze and Guattari's broader theoretical project is oriented around detailing a revolutionary, post-capitalist subjectivity, and for this reason they provide me with key conceptual resources. *Anti-Oedipus* is, ostensibly, a critique of contemporary capitalism that takes psychoanalysis to task for its politically regressive theory of subject formation as a process of socialisation within the nuclear family. Deleuze and Guattari reject the Freudian thesis that unconscious investments of desire are to be understood as fundamentally familial, as in the Oedipus scenario. While Freud believed the Oedipus complex to be an account of how the unconscious is determined by its initial investments in the parental figures, Deleuze and Guattari maintain that Freud simply diagnosed a strategy of containment to which capitalist society has recourse. The family is the agent of a repression that is fundamentally sociopolitical in nature. Oedipus is an apparatus of capture that uses an imaginary familial content to trap desire within a depoliticised familial nexus.

While Deleuze and Guattari criticise Freud's theory of the Oedipus complex, they accept and develop his theory of libido as quantitative (and thus economic) and as abstract (detachable from the objects of its investment). They attempt to push the combination of Freud and Marx as far as it can possibly go by arguing that if psychoanalysis is led, via its clinical work, to such a theory as libido, then it is only because capitalist society increasingly organises itself around abstract quantities instead of meaningful significations. Capitalism is, they assert, the only social formation to base itself on the management of abstract quantities. There is no essential difference between libido and labour power in this respect: both are abstractions that can be quantified and regulated in their concrete forms as sexuality and wage labour, respectively. Marx and Freud discovered the same thing from very different perspectives, but what links them is money, the abstract quantity par excellence. Neurosis is thus desire's commodity form, the mode by which it becomes sellable to the analyst who treats it (*AO* 56). The role of money is central, and it is on this point that Deleuze and Guattari diverge from the Marxist tradition:

> It is unfortunate that Marxist economists too often dwell on considerations concerning the mode of production, and on the theory of money as the general equivalent as found in the first section of *Capital*, without attaching enough importance to banking practice, to financial operations, and to the specific circulation of credit money. (AO 230)

Marxists too often treat money simply as the universal mode of exchange by which all commodities (including labour power) are bought and sold. As I have already suggested, the key problem with this exchangist position is that it identifies economic and social power to such a degree that the fundamental role of money as power is assumed. Whereas Marxism generally attempts to defetishise money by identifying it with purchasing power, Deleuze and Guattari argue that money's true force lies in its semiotic value. This is why banking, finance and credit must feature in any analysis of capitalist social relations, and the monetary dimension cannot simply be reduced to the mode of production. This is heretical for the Marxist point of view, but Deleuze and Guattari insist that if social authority in capitalist society can be maintained in the absence of those potent religious and mythological symbols that societies have traditionally drawn upon to legitimate their authority, then the key to understanding *how* this happens can be found by only looking to the money signs themselves.

The critique of capitalism that Deleuze and Guattari pursue, then, has a fundamental theological component that overlaps with the semiotics of money in a crucial way. They accept the Lacanian idea that the unconscious takes on the burden of repudiated belief (*AO* 307–8). However, they attach a special social significance to this fact. When belief is repudiated, the unconscious emerges as the final believer, the locus of a piety that is sustained in inverse proportion to the semiotic abstraction of money. Whereas all prior social formations depend upon the qualitative process of 'coding', which we can interpret simply as attributing meaning and significance to all phenomena, capitalism is the only society we know of that systematically 'decodes' meanings to the point of terminal disposability. Signs are no longer qualitative but quantitative:

> Above all, there is no longer any need of belief, and the capitalist is merely striking a pose when he bemoans the fact that nowadays no one believes in anything any more. Language no longer signifies something that must be believed, it indicates rather what is going to be done, something that the

> shrewd or the competent are able to decode, to half understand. . . . The person has become 'private' in reality, insofar as he derives from abstract quantities and becomes concrete in the becoming-concrete of these same quantities. It is these quantities that are marked. (*AO* 250)

Capitalism is constituted by this *disenchantment of the sign* that money helps to render possible. Goux remarks that with the 'mindless, desemanticized signs' of modern computerised banking and its virtual money, we are indeed far from 'a hieroglyphic mode of signification, with its blocks of hyperinvested symbols of iconic value recorded in a priestly hand'.[53] And yet, of course, the precapitalist religious and mythopoetic investment in symbols still exists throughout capitalist society, most notably in the contents of the unconscious, in dreams and fantasies. This is why capitalist society, even in its most hypermodern guise, appears haunted by all that it has left behind. The fantasy images that fill the spaces of contemporary culture are frequently primitive, barbarian or feudal in nature, even when they depict utopian or dystopian futures. The unconscious becomes a reservoir of 'semantic surplus', an excess of meaning or significance.[54] But whereas Goux asserts that the religious power of the symbol is *opposed* to the desemanticised monetary signs of capital, Deleuze and Guattari suggest, on the contrary, that the unconscious investment in symbols is quite necessary for the capitalist containment of the belief that has no longer become necessary for maintaining traditional forms of social authority. If we no longer believe, then the unconscious does so in our place.

What Freud diagnosed is the fact that secular subjectivity has not freed itself of its inherited religious and mythic iconography. As we have seen, the psychoanalytic subject describes a structure of disavowal or repudiation: belief becomes unconscious not through a subjective interiority, a psychological depth, but through a *voiding* of this interiority by the object form that strips subjectivity of its meanings: *I don't really believe this, but I act as if I do.* But what Deleuze and Guattari, by way of Graeber, help us to understand is that the unconscious takes on the theological burden of belief in the context of a society that appears threatened by *too much* belief, by an excess of credit that flows through it in the form of a dematerialised economic power. If the subject, as Lacan describes it, is fundamentally split in its specular capture by the 'nothing' that it is and the image that gives it ontological security, then contemporary money is likewise split between the potent void of its referent (the physical place of value, once occupied, however precariously, by gold or silver) and its abstract, impotent sign value.

In opposition to what they see as the Marxist tradition's exchangism, Deleuze and Guattari present a striking and prescient account of money as split into two inconvertible halves. They draw attention to the role of a 'dualism of money', utilising in particular the work of Marxist economist Suzanne de Brunhoff and the post-Keynesian Bernard Schmitt. Both de Brunhoff and Schmitt, despite their different viewpoints, ultimately tell us the same thing: money in capitalist society is fundamentally split into different ontological registers, the mediation between which is central to the regulation of the economy. It is not my goal here to go into the intricacies of Brunhoff and Schmitt nor to assess the fidelity with which Deleuze and Guattari read them.[55] I wish merely to outline the theory of money as Deleuze and Guattari present it in order to draw together the strands of my argument hitherto. The dual aspect of money is summed up as follows:

> It is not the same money that goes into the pocket of the wage earner and is entered on the balance sheet of a commercial enterprise. In the one case, there are impotent money signs of exchange value, a flow of means of payment relative to consumer goods and use values, and a one-to-one relation between money and an imposed range of products . . .; in the other case, [there are] signs of the power of capital, flows of financing. (*AO* 228)

The dualism, then, is between 'the formation of means of payment and the structure of financing, between the management of money and the financing of capitalist accumulation, between exchange money and credit money' (*AO* 229). We have already seen, in Marx, how money is both impotence and power at once. Deleuze and Guattari here develop this insight in a way that encompasses the role of banking and finance. It is money as payment, as ability to exchange, that defines money's impotence. The idea of 'purchasing power' is 'derisory' (*AO* 238). If money's apparent power to exchange must in this respect be called impotent, it is because when money becomes a means of payment it is separated from its *other* aspect, which alone constitutes 'capital's economic force', namely the ability of banks (with the help of the state) to issue money in the form of debt and credit, to create money *ex nihilo* through the manipulation of signs alone. The suggestion that this creative flow is the source of capitalism's economic power may strike us as strange indeed, since we normally associate this with the power to accumulate property and wealth, to buy things. But the flow of pure *credo*, Deleuze and Guattari insist, 'is not assigned to purchases' and is thus 'a pure availability, nonpossession and nonwealth' (*AO* 237). Capitalism may 'in essence' be the mode of production, as Marxism argues, but the economic machine is driven by the 'absurd power' of this 'nonpossessive and non-possessed' flow (*AO* 346).

If banks and financial institutions extend debt and credit to the masses, this flow of signs must be counteracted by another flow, one of payment and income that parcels out the flow of non-possession and non-wealth into assignable property, into possession and into a subject said to possess as its 'own'. Money's Being is actualised in beings. But the two forms of money in the dualism remain incommensurate, inconvertible: there is no identity between the two types of sign, between the sign in its power and in its impotence. An ontological gulf separates them. And yet their intermixture is the key means by which capitalism maintains social order (*AO* 238–9). The fact that the same category, 'money', subsumes both sides of the dualism is the product of an 'objective dissimulation', 'a cosmic swindle' that does not depend on any false consciousness but on the forms of cold-blooded calculation that determine the relationships between the debts and credits created by banks and the forms of payment that correspond to them. It is in this correspondence that financial crisis takes place, since the two sides of the money dualism are both identical and non-identical.

The debt crises affecting much of Europe and North America in recent years have demonstrated the extent to which more and more money needs to be injected into the economy to counteract the effects of expanding debt and the speculative proliferation of financial assets. Money as debt needs to be counteracted by money as payment. Quantitative easing has been used extensively in the US and the UK over the past decade to buy up assets such as mortgage securities from financial institutions and to increase the money supply, but this has had limited success. In this sense, payment money cannot help but strike us as so many impotent signs when contrasted with the economic force of global finance. What the recent crises have shown is exactly what Deleuze and Guattari state plainly: that the banks, positioned as they are between the two forms of money, have a key role in maintaining social authority. Just as religion is positioned at the nodal point between material and spiritual realms, so too are banks positioned between money as payment and money as finance, between payback and creation. Financial crisis thus recasts and exacerbates what Graeber describes as the oldest spiritual dilemma: how can we repay the debt we feel we owe for our very existence? The intractability of this problem has etched itself into both our economic and theological vocabulary: most Indo-European languages contain words in which 'debt' is synonymous with 'sin' and 'guilt'.[56] Such a primordial debt can never be paid off, no matter how many sacrifices, since an ontological gulf separates creator and created, divine and profane. Capitalism secularises this intractability and places it at the very heart of the money form that governs our lives.

CONCLUSION

Since the 2008 financial crisis, the failings of mainstream economics have been widely discussed, with Marxism often claiming legitimacy in the process. Nevertheless, I have shown that the Marxist account needs to be supplemented with work from other traditions encompassing theology and psychoanalysis. I have suggested that Marxism shares with mainstream economics the view that money is identical with its power. This constitutes a peculiar blind spot for contemporary secular consciousness. A return to the early Marx shows that money must, in fact, be viewed as both power *and* power's self-limitation. This is crucial for demonstrating how money's object form maintains intimate ties with subjectivity, and this in turn is how we should understand the self-regulatory dynamics of contemporary capitalist society. Through readings of Kant and Hegel, I was led to suggest that the problem of money overlaps with a concern for the self-positing capacity of the speculative subject. I sketched the outlines of what I call speculative subjectivity, a subjectivity compelled to place trust in an object that eludes it and that forces it to break from a purely empirical consciousness. The psychoanalytic view proved necessary in order to understand how we ourselves are the ultimate objects of this trust.

As self-positing, subjectivity must take itself on faith, since it is at heart nothing at all. The problem of the subject converges, then, on the problem of a theology of money. We are our own piety. As the poet J. H. Prynne put it in his 'Sketch for a Financial Theory of the Self':

> The name of that is of course money, and
> the absurd trust in value is the pattern of
> the bond and contract and interest – just where
> the names are exactly equivalent to the trust
> given to them.
>
> Here then is the purity of
> pragmatic function:
> we give the name of
> our selves to our needs.
> We want what we are.[57]

This literary reference brings to the forefront one of the main theoretical currents of the foregoing discussion: the ontological status of the sign in contemporary society. If religion has, for thousands of years, relied upon the potency of the symbol to ground its reality, secular modernity can be said to mark an impotence of signs, a recognition of their non-identity with their referents. This semiotic detachment from the real also constitutes a state of ontological insecurity. Money here is not just one example of a sign that grounds itself in an 'absurd' trust, but constitutes a power, a 'pragmatic function' centring on economic value, that makes *all* signs as equally impotent, as exiguous as images in a dream.

This splitting of the sign into impotence and power is what Deleuze and Guattari's theory of money allows us to grasp. But this theory sits very well with what the young Marx had already suggested: that money, as sign, constitutes a self-limiting form of power that captures desire. What Deleuze and Guattari add is a critique of subjectivity that proceeds on this basis. If we are, as psychoanalysis argues, half-submerged in a mythico-religious substratum imbued with primordial symbolism, then this fact needs to be historicised in terms of a broader semiotics of capitalism. Without this necessary historicisation, there is a risk that the burden of belief that the unconscious takes on is itself fetishised as an alternative to secular consciousness, and we fail to see how capitalist society depends on the unconscious as a reservoir of surplus meaning, as a final believer in the very midst of disbelief. I have shown how the capitalist solution to the death of God and the spectre of atheism aligned money and subjectivity in such a post-secular fashion. Desire and belief are grounded in a self-positing subject; we want what we are. If, as Weber argued, Calvinism provided the spiritual conditions for industrial capitalism, we might argue that post-secular subjectivity, with its repudiated beliefs, provides the spiritual conditions for financial capitalism.

But if the speculative subject constitutes an insidious mode of self-regulation, it is also the only thing capable of taking us beyond the twin impasses of the contemporary noted at the start of this chapter. It falls to speculative subjectivity to lead us beyond economics and religion as discrete domains of consciousness and of social life. Deleuze and Guattari's conception of desire, stemming as it does from their critique of the Freudian unconscious as the last refuge of belief, is less a means of purging us of religion than of leading us beyond the secular division of the economic and religious passions. Any properly post-capitalist reality is located beyond this division. The concept of speculative subjectivity invoked here provides us with a basis of witnessing this 'beyond' in the signs of money themselves, drained of their mimetic or representational power.

NOTES

1. Ole Bjerg, *Making Money: The Philosophy of Crisis Capitalism* (London: Verso, 2014), 81.

2. Marc Shell, *Money, Language, and Thought: Literary and Philosophic Economies from the Medieval to the Modern Era* (Baltimore: Johns Hopkins University Press, 1982), 151.

3. For the roots of these ideas in ancient philosophy, see Richard Seaford, *Money and the Early Greek Mind: Homer, Philosophy, Tragedy* (Cambridge: Cambridge University Press, 2004), 261.

4. Quoted in Michael Neary and Graham Taylor, 'Marx and the Magic of Money: Towards an Alchemy of Capital', *Historical Materialism* 2.1 (1998): 102.

5. Dick Bryan and Michael Rafferty, *Capitalism with Derivatives: A Political Economy of Financial Derivatives, Capital and Class* (Basingstoke: Palgrave Macmillan, 2006), 155.

6. See, for example, Elie Ayache, *The Blank Swan: The End of Probability* (Chichester: Wiley, 2010); Bjerg, *Making Money*; Philip Goodchild, *Capitalism and Religion: The Price of Piety* (London: Routledge, 2002) and *Theology of Money* (Durham, NC: Duke University Press, 2009); David Graeber, *Debt: The First 5,000 Years* (Brooklyn, NY: Melville House, 2011); Noam Yuran, *What Money Wants: An Economy of Desire* (Stanford, CA: Stanford University Press, 2014); Leonidas Zelmanovitz, *The Ontology and Function of Money: The Philosophical Fundamentals of Monetary Institutions* (Lanham, MD: Lexington Books, 2016). Maurizio Lazzarato's analysis in *The Making of the Indebted Man* (Los Angeles: Semiotext(e), 2012) should also be noted for the way in which it regards indebtedness in contemporary neoliberal society as an existential condition with theological overtones: 'Everyone is a "debtor" accountable to and guilty before capital. Capital has become the Great Creditor, the Universal Creditor' (7). Lazzarato's use of Deleuze and Guattari in his investigation of the subjectivity of indebtedness bears some similarities to my arguments here.

7. Goodchild, *Capitalism and Religion*, 184.

8. Graeber, *Debt*, 8–11.

9. On the politics of post-secularism, see *Political Theologies: Public Relations in a Post-Secular World*, ed. Hent de Vries and Lawrence E. Sullivan (New York: Fordham, 2006).

10. Karl Marx, *Early Writings*, trans. Rodney Livingstone and Gregor Benton (London: Penguin, 1975), 241.

11. Georg Simmel, *The Philosophy of Money*, 3rd ed., trans. Tom Bottomore and David Frisby from a first draft by Kaethe Mengelberg (London: Routledge, 2004), 502.

12. Max Weber, *The Protestant Ethic and the Spirit of Capitalism*, trans. Talcott Parsons (London: Routledge, 1992), 128.

13. George A. Akerlof and Robert J. Shiller, *Animal Spirits: How Human Psychology Drives the Economy, and Why It Matters for Global Capitalism* (Princeton, NJ: Princeton University Press, 2009).

14. Quoted in Neary and Taylor, 'Marx and the Magic of Money', 103.

15. Bjerg, *Making Money*, 82.

16. Costas Lapavitsas, *Social Foundations of Markets, Money and Credit* (London: Routledge, 2003), 67.

17. Michael Tratner, 'Derrida's Debt to Milton Friedman', *New Literary History* 34.4 (2003): 793.

18. The work of Derrida in particular has made important contributions to the twentieth-century philosophy of money. Space prevents me from going into

Derrida's work on this topic, but see his books *Given Time: I. Counterfeit Money*, trans. Peggy Kamuf (Chicago: University of Chicago Press, 1992) and *The Gift of Death*, trans. David Wills (Chicago: University of Chicago Press, 1995). For an accessible, if not altogether sympathetic, reading of Derrida's work in relation to economic ideas, see Tratner, 'Derrida's Debt to Milton Friedman'.

19. Gilles Deleuze, *Difference and Repetition*, trans. Paul Patton (New York: Columbia University Press, 1994), 155.

20. Randy Martin, *Financialization of Daily Life* (Philadelphia: Temple University Press, 2002).

21. Martin, *Financialization of Daily Life*, 3.

22. David Harvey, *The Enigma of Capital: And the Crises of Capitalism* (London: Profile Books, 2010), 114.

23. Graeber, *Debt*, 358–60.

24. Karl Marx, 'Economic and Philosophic Manuscripts of 1844', in *Collected Works, Volume 3: Marx and Engels, 1843–1844*, trans. Clemens Dutt. (New York: International Publishers, 1975), 322; hereafter 'EPM' with page references in the text.

25. Bjerg, *Making Money*, 2–6.

26. Simmel, *Philosophy of Money*, 503.

27. Yuran, *What Money Wants*, 14.

28. See, for example, Kojin Karatani, *Transcritique: On Kant and Marx*, trans. Sabu Kohso (Cambridge, MA: MIT Press, 2003), 212.

29. Jacques Lacan, *The Seminar of Jacques Lacan Book XI: The Four Fundamental Concepts of Psychoanalysis*, ed. Jacques-Alain Miller, trans. Alan Sheridan (New York: W. W. Norton, 1977), 59.

30. Slavoj Žižek, 'Dialectical Clarity versus the Misty Conceit of Paradox', in *The Monstrosity of Christ: Paradox or Dialectic?*, ed. Creston Davis (Cambridge, MA: MIT Press, 2009), 297.

31. Derrida makes similar points in 'Faith and Knowledge: The Two Sources of "Religion" at the Limits of Reason Alone', trans. Samuel Weber, in *Acts of Religion*, ed. and intr. Gil Anidjar (London: Routledge, 2002). See also Milesi's contribution in this volume.

32. Thomas J. J. Altizer, 'Theology and the Death of God', in *Radical Theology and the Death of God*, ed. Thomas J. J. Altizer and William Hamilton (Indianapolis: The Bobbs-Merrill Company, 1966), 96.

33. Jean-Joseph Goux, *Symbolic Economies: After Marx and Freud*, trans. Jennifer Curtiss Gage (Ithaca, NY: Cornell University Press, 1990), 52.

34. Gilles Deleuze and Félix Guattari, *Anti-Oedipus: Capitalism and Schizophrenia*, trans. Robert Hurley, Mark Seem and Helen R. Lane (Minneapolis: University of Minnesota Press, 1983), 229; hereafter *AO* with page references in the text.

35. Philip Goodchild, 'Capital and Kingdom: An Eschatological Ontology', in *Theology and the Political: The New Debate*, ed. Creston Davies, John Milbank and Slavoj Žižek (Durham, NC: Duke University Press, 2005), 142.

36. Immanuel Kant, *Critique of Pure Reason*, trans. Paul Guyer and Allen W. Wood (Cambridge: Cambridge University Press, 1998), 567.

37. Kant, *Critique of Pure Reason*, 567.
38. Kant, *Critique of Pure Reason*, 569.
39. Immanuel Kant, *The Metaphysics of Morals,* trans. Mary Gregor (Cambridge: Cambridge University Press, 1991), 105–6.
40. Graeber, *Debt*, 342.
41. Graeber, *Debt*, 348.
42. Kant, *Metaphysics of Morals*, 103.
43. Kant, *Metaphysics of Morals*, 105.
44. Goux, *Symbolic Economies*, 51.
45. Georg Wilhelm Friedrich Hegel, *The Science of Logic*, trans. George di Giovanni (Cambridge: Cambridge University Press, 2010), 63.
46. Hegel, *The Science of Logic*, 63–4.
47. Hegel, *The Science of Logic*, 65.
48. Slavoj Žižek, *Less than Nothing: Hegel and the Shadow of Dialectical Materialism* (London: Verso, 2012), 404.
49. Žižek, *Less than Nothing*, 405.
50. Žižek, *Less than Nothing*, 145.
51. Jacques Lacan, *Écrits: The First Complete Edition in English*, trans. Bruce Fink with Heloïse Fink and Russell Grigg (New York: W. W. Norton, 2006), 91–2.
52. Quoted in Goux, *Symbolic Economies*, 13.
53. Goux, *Symbolic Economies*, 129–30.
54. Goux, *Symbolic Economies*, 131.
55. Christian Kerslake has admirably accomplished both tasks in his recent article 'Marxism and Money in Deleuze and Guattari's *Capitalism and Schizophrenia*: On the Conflict between the Theories of Suzanne de Brunhoff and Bernard Schmitt', *Parrhesia* 22 (2015): 38–78.
56. Graeber, *Debt*, 59.
57. J. H. Prynne, *Poems* (Newcastle upon Tyne: Bloodaxe, 1999), 19–20.

BIBLIOGRAPHY

AKERLOF, George A. and Robert J. SHILLER. *Animal Spirits: How Human Psychology Drives the Economy, and Why It Matters for Global Capitalism.* Princeton, NJ: Princeton University Press, 2009.

ALTIZER, Thomas J. J. 'Theology and the Death of God'. In *Radical Theology and the Death of God.* Edited by Thomas J. J. Altizer and William Hamilton. Indianapolis: The Bobbs-Merrill Company, 1966. 95–112.

AYACHE, Ellie. *The Blank Swan: The End of Probability*. Chichester: Wiley, 2010.

BJERG, Ole. *Making Money: The Philosophy of Crisis Capitalism.* London: Verso, 2014.

BRYAN, Dick and Michael RAFFERTY. *Capitalism with Derivatives: A Political Economy of Financial Derivatives, Capital and Class.* Basingstoke: Palgrave Macmillan, 2006.

DELEUZE, Gilles. *Difference and Repetition.* Translated by Paul Patton. New York: Columbia University Press, 1994.

DELEUZE, Gilles and Félix GUATTARI. *Anti-Oedipus: Capitalism and Schizophrenia*. Translated by Robert Hurley, Mark Seem and Helen R. Lane. Minneapolis: University of Minnesota Press, 1983.

DERRIDA, Jacques. 'Faith and Knowledge: The Two Sources of "Religion" at the Limits of Reason Alone'. Translated by Samuel Weber. In *Acts of Religion*. Edited and with an introduction by Gil Anidjar. New York and London: Routledge, 2002. 42–101.

DERRIDA, Jacques. *The Gift of Death*. Translated by David Wills. Chicago: University of Chicago Press, 1995.

DERRIDA, Jacques. *Given Time: I. Counterfeit Money*. Translated by Peggy Kamuf. Chicago: University of Chicago Press, 1992.

DE VRIES, Hent and Lawrence E. SULLIVAN (eds.). *Political Theologies: Public Relations in a Post-Secular World*. New York: Fordham, 2006.

GOODCHILD, Philip. 'Capital and Kingdom: An Eschatological Ontology'. In *Theology and the Political: The New Debate*. Edited by Creston Davies, John Milbank and Slavoj Žižek. Durham, NC: Duke University Press, 2005. 127–52.

GOODCHILD, Philip. *Capitalism and Religion: The Price of Piety*. London: Routledge, 2002.

GOODCHILD, Philip. *Theology of Money*. Durham, NC: Duke University Press, 2009.

GOUX, Jean-Joseph. *Symbolic Economies: After Marx and Freud*. Translated by Jennifer Curtiss Gage. Ithaca, NY: Cornell University Press, 1990.

GRAEBER, David. *Debt: The First 5,000 Years*. Brooklyn, NY: Melville House, 2011.

HARVEY, David. *The Enigma of Capital: And the Crises of Capitalism*. London: Profile Books, 2010.

HEGEL, Georg Wilhelm Friedrich. *The Science of Logic*. Translated by George di Giovanni. Cambridge: Cambridge University Press, 2010.

KANT, Immanuel. *Critique of Pure Reason*. Translated by Paul Guyer and Allen W. Wood. Cambridge: Cambridge University Press, 1998.

KANT, Immanuel. *The Metaphysics of Morals*. Translated by Mary Gregor. Cambridge: Cambridge University Press, 1991.

KARATANI, Kojin. *Transcritique: On Kant and Marx*. Translated by Sabu Kohso. Cambridge, MA: MIT Press, 2003.

KERSLAKE, Christian. 'Marxism and Money in Deleuze and Guattari's *Capitalism and Schizophrenia*: On the Conflict between the Theories of Suzanne de Brunhoff and Bernard Schmitt'. *Parrhesia* 22 (2015): 38–78.

LACAN, Jacques. *Écrits: The First Complete Edition in English*. Translated by Bruce Fink with Heloïse Fink and Russell Grigg. New York: W. W. Norton, 2006.

LACAN, Jacques. *The Seminar of Jacques Lacan Book XI: The Four Fundamental Concepts of Psychoanalysis*. Edited by Jacques-Alain Miller. Translated by Alan Sheridan. New York: W. W. Norton, 1977.

LAPAVITSAS, Costas. *Social Foundations of Markets, Money and Credit*. London: Routledge, 2003.

LAZZARATO, Maurizio. *The Making of the Indebted Man: An Essay on the Neoliberal Condition*. Translated by Joshua David Jordan. Los Angeles: Semiotext(e), 2012.

NEARY, Michael and Graham TAYLOR. 'Marx and the Magic of Money: Towards an Alchemy of Capital'. *Historical Materialism* 2.1 (1998): 99–117.

MARTIN, Randy. *Financialization of Daily Life*. Philadelphia: Temple University Press, 2002.

MARX, Karl. *Early Writings*. Translated by Rodney Livingstone and Gregor Benton. London: Penguin, 1975.

MARX, Karl. 'Economic and Philosophic Manuscripts of 1844'. In *Collected Works, Volume 3: Marx and Engels, 1843–1844*. Translated by Clemens Dutt. New York: International Publishers, 1975. 322–25.

PRYNNE, J. H. *Poems*. Newcastle upon Tyne: Bloodaxe, 1999.

SEAFORD, Richard. *Money and the Early Greek Mind: Homer, Philosophy, Tragedy*. Cambridge: Cambridge University Press, 2004.

SHELL, Mark. *Money, Language, and Thought: Literary and Philosophic Economies from the Medieval to the Modern Era*. Baltimore: Johns Hopkins University Press, 1982.

SIMMEL, Georg. *The Philosophy of Money*. Third Edition. Translated by Tom Bottomore and David Frisby from a first draft by Kaethe Mengelberg. London: Routledge, 2004.

TRATNER, Michael. 'Derrida's Debt to Milton Friedman'. *New Literary History* 34.4 (2003): 791–806.

WEBER, Max. *The Protestant Ethic and the Spirit of Capitalism*. Translated by Talcott Parsons. London: Routledge, 1992.

YURAN, Noam. *What Money Wants: An Economy of Desire*. Stanford, CA: Stanford University Press, 2014.

ZELMANOVITZ, Leonidas. *The Ontology and Function of Money: The Philosophical Fundamentals of Monetary Institutions*. Lanham, MD: Lexington Books, 2016.

ŽIŽEK, Slavoj. 'Dialectical Clarity versus the Misty Conceit of Paradox'. In *The Monstrosity of Christ: Paradox or Dialectic?* Edited by Creston Davis. Cambridge, MA: MIT Press, 2009. 234–306.

ŽIŽEK, Slavoj. *Less than Nothing: Hegel and the Shadow of Dialectical Materialism*. London: Verso, 2012.

Chapter 10

Speculation upon speculation; or, a contribution to the critique of philosophical economy*

Josh Robinson

The past decade or so has seen an upsurge of interest in the topic of philosophical speculation, with the publication of numerous and varied (and in many cases conjectural and programmatic) undertakings that seek to probe or assess what it can achieve, or to identify and extend its limits. This concern has taken shape in diverse ways, with frequent acknowledgement that neither a unified notion of speculation nor a single kind of speculative thinking is at work across the range of publications that bear witness to this trend, and indeed recognition that the term might frequently be used in a 'less dignified sense' to refer to kinds of thinking that 'might be giving voice not to knowledge, but to "speculation": to beliefs, surmises, wishes, hopes, imaginings'.[1] More specifically, it has been used to characterize the work of thinkers who 'have begun speculating once more about the nature of reality independently of thought and of humanity more generally',[2] or, in the formulation of a work that is acknowledged as having prompted many of the recent contributions to discussion and theorization of speculation, that kind of thinking that seeks in whatever way to access the absolute.[3]

My concern in this chapter is the relationship between, on the one hand, this renewal of interest in speculation – and in particular those elements of it which are self-avowedly conjectural, and concerned with the anticipation of an otherwise-unknowable future – and, on the other hand, the financial sense of speculation, of buying and selling in order to realize a profit. More specifically, I am concerned with the connections between, on the one hand, the recent proliferation of attention to philosophical speculation and, on the other hand, the ongoing financial and economic crisis that began to manifest itself in 2007–2008 – and, more specifically still, the commonly asserted attribution of this crisis to financial speculation, or investment with the aim of realizing capital appreciation. My own speculatively advanced contention is that investigation of these connections can helpfully illuminate both the limitations and the resources of speculation as a mode of attention to and engagement with the world – and that in doing so, such an investigation can offer an appraisal of both the enterprises and the risks of speculation.

The renewal of interest in speculation is closely linked to a marked shift within continental thought towards the question of the real, an interrogation and ultimately a rejection of anti-realist thought. The editors of one collection of examinations of the resources offered by this concern with speculation for 'continental materialism and realism' (a conjunction that harbours a certain tension) refer to this shift as the speculative turn, a term coined 'as a deliberate counterpoint to the now tiresome "Linguistic Turn"'[4] to bring together in a somewhat artificial grouping a collection of works in which 'one can detect the hints of something new'.[5] This speculative turn is conceived as a departure from what is diagnosed as 'the dominant anti-realist strain of continental philosophy', which, it is claimed, 'has not only reached a point of decreasing returns' but now even 'actively limits the capacities of philosophy in our time'.[6] Others suggest that this tendency might be indicative not only of the emergence of a new trend, but even of a more general paradigm shift within continental thought, raising the questions of whether we are 'in the midst of a philosophical supersession', of whether continental philosophy is 'to become continental realism'.[7]

This shift is presented as a break with a set of procedures and concerns that have become tedious or obsolete: 'By contrast with the repetitive continental focus on texts, discourse, social practices, and human finitude, the new breed of thinker is turning once more toward reality itself'.[8] More specifically, one of its proponents further develops this formulation of continental realism, describing it as 'a middle path that accepts, contra traditionalist continental philosophy, that the natural sciences, realism, and analytic philosophy are not a threat, but aids in the task of first science: *metaphysics*'.[9] The new continental realism, that is, is characterized by a certain methodological pluralism – or perhaps more accurately a pluralism of resources of investigation – and a rejection of what is implicitly presented as the dogmatism of 'traditionalist continental philosophy', the practitioners of which are accused of limiting themselves by rejecting the resources presented by these additional modes of inquiry. Speculative realism claims that it, in contrast with these apparently dogmatic or obsolete approaches, can provide 'the kind of speculation required for grounding realism in philosophical argument'.[10]

The pluralism which Bryant, Srnicek and Harman advocate nonetheless involves an explicit rejection of 'the traditional focus on textual critique' in favour of the resources offered by approaches that include 'notions of noumenal objects and causality-in-itself', turns 'towards neuroscience', the construction of 'mathematical absolutes' and the sharpening of 'the uncanny implications of psychoanalysis' and of 'scientific rationality'.[11] Within this diverse and frequently conflicting repertoire of preoccupations and approaches, what enables these pieces of work to be grouped together under the heading of the speculative turn is what Steven Shaviro identifies as a 'common commitment' that transcends disagreements (including with respect to fundamental principles) to 'metaphysical speculation and to a robust ontological realism',[12] oriented towards the overturning of what Lee Braver characterizes as the Kantian anti-realist claim that 'phenomena depend on the mind to exist'.[13] In this respect, speculation is a resource presented and scrutinized in response to the question of 'how to think the real as a continental philosopher'.[14]

In particular, this orientation finds its expression in a common overarching project of the development of ways in which it might be possible to break the Kantian injunction 'never to venture with speculative reason beyond the limits of experience',[15] an aim which finds its most explicit expression in Shaviro's proclamation that '[p]ace Kant, we *must* think outside of our own thought, and we must positively conceive the existence of things outside our own conceptions of them'.[16] It is the implications of this apparently self-contradictory attempt to develop ways of thinking that are not constrained by thought, ways of conceiving outside conception, that I explore in this chapter. More specifically, I am concerned with the relationship of this attempt to think beyond the bounds of thought to the practice of speculation in search of profit beyond the bounds of what can be realized within the real economy.

I investigate this nexus by means of the exploration of the relationships between speculation, thought, labour and critique, and more particularly of conceptions of the relationship between thought and labour, and of the opposition of the speculative to the productive or real economy. In an approach that is indebted to Marx's mature critical theory, I elucidate and criticize some of the common presuppositions of the most popular and established theories of the ongoing crisis that proliferate across the political spectrum, and bring to light some of the presuppositions they share with versions of the speculative attempt to develop a pure and absolute thought, a thought that is not constrained by the limitations of thought. More specifically, I draw attention to the implications of a tendency of thought to absolutize itself and in doing so, to obscure the extent to which it is permeated by assumptions that are derived from and established by ingrained patterns of social activity, suggest that even the apparently purest metaphysical categories are in fact deeply mediated through social and economic processes of domination. Without confronting, accounting for and seeking to undo this mediation, I suggest, thought cannot become truly speculative.

My starting point is the resonant metaphorical conjunction with which Bryant, Srnicek and Harman's discussion of speculation and its relationship to critique in their introduction to *The Speculative Turn* fleetingly brings together the financial and philosophical senses of speculation:

> This activity of 'speculation' may be cause for concern amongst some readers, for it might suggest a return to pre-critical philosophy, with its dogmatic belief in the powers of pure reason. The speculative turn, however, is not an outright rejection of these critical advances; instead, it comes from a recognition of their inherent limitations. Speculation in this sense aims at something 'beyond' the critical and linguistic turns. As such, it recuperates the pre-critical sense of 'speculation' as a concern with the Absolute, while also taking into account the undeniable progress that is due to the labour of critique. The works collected here are a speculative wager on the possible returns from a renewed attention to reality itself.[17]

This 'speculative wager' already calls to mind what by the late eighteenth century was termed the 'trade of speculation' in which the 'speculative merchant exercises no one regular, established, or well-known branch of business' but rather 'enters into every trade when he foresees that it is likely to be more than commonly profitable', and 'quits it when he foresees that its profits are likely to return to the level of other trades'.[18] For Bryant, Srnicek and Harman the investigation of reality is presented as a wager – the staking of an item of value on a particular outcome, possibly of a chance process, in the pursuit of a return received without further endeavour, a return that takes the form of a reward contingent on the accuracy of a prediction, potentially of a chance event. Insofar as this reward appears as deserved or earned, it does so by virtue of the fact that the speculator accurately predicted something that would come to pass, or took on a certain amount of risk.

The rewards of speculation thus derive from the anticipation of the future, from the fact of having acted in accordance with what would later come to pass, whether by chance or by design. The process of speculation takes into account the contingency of this unknown future, and accepts the risk of losing:

> A bold adventurer may sometimes acquire a considerable fortune by two or three successful speculations; but is just as likely to lose one by two or three unsuccessful ones. This trade can be carried on nowhere but in great towns. It is only in places of the most extensive commerce and correspondence that the intelligence requisite for it can be had.[19]

Smith presents the risks and potential rewards of speculation as equally likely, but nonetheless emphasizes that it requires access not only to the widest markets (and therefore the urban centres of population and trade rather than in 'small towns and country villages'),[20] but also to both information and intelligence. That is to say, the future on which the rewards of speculation depend is presented as at once unknowable and intelligible: speculation is a means of looking into the unknowable, and coming to know it – or perhaps more accurately, behaving as if one knows it, or indeed as if one knew it all along. Even in its financial sense, speculation is 'a matter of knowledge'.[21]

In describing the turn towards reality as a speculative wager, Bryant, Srnicek and Harman draw on precisely this resonance, bringing together the exploration of speculation in the philosophical 'as a concern with the Absolute' with the financial sense of a decision made now that may (or may not) bring future rewards, depending on the outcomes of events that are out of one's own control. This becomes more resonant still as a result of their contrasting of speculation with what is presented as 'the labour of critique'. Here it is not simply the case that speculation is distinguished from critique as two different means or procedures by which knowledge can be produced; the two are rather presented as fundamentally different and incompatible kinds of activity. The speculative wager is presented as offering the potential for an indolent means of attaining knowledge without having to dirty one's hands with the labour of critique.

This metaphor resonates with tendencies that can be observed in the writings both of the proponents of the speculative turn and of its critics. David Golumbia, for example, has offered a critical account of the manufacturing of the dogma of 'correlationism' in order to taint the history of post-Kantian philosophy and thus to dismiss it out of hand without 'having to engage with the voluminous anti-idealist philosophical literature that would make [Meillassoux's] assessments less tractable', resulting in what he terms, in a metaphor pertinent for my purposes here, 'the widespread impression that Meillassoux has conclusively deflated most recent philosophy'.[22] More polemically, Ray Brassier has criticized some of the ways in which speculative realism has been developed and circulated by means of online publicity and discussion, dismissing it as 'a "movement" whose most signal achievement thus far is to have generated an online orgy of stupidity', and objecting to what he identifies as the attempt 'to concoct a philosophical movement online by using blogs to exploit the misguided enthusiasm of impressionable graduate students'.[23] Among the representatives of speculative realism, Harman has made the tongue-in-cheek suggestion that 'a logo . . . designed for projection on PowerPoint screens, accompanied by a few signature bars of smoky dubstep music' would draw attention to the works of speculative realism, the reputation of which 'would stand or fall based on the inherent quality of these works, of which I am confident'.[24] Meanwhile, his blurb to *The Universe of Things* singles out Shaviro's prose as 'devoid of rancor or backstabbing ambition', as if to acknowledge that such characteristics are frequently hallmarks of discussion of speculative realism, whether in its formulations or in the responses to it.

My aim in this chapter, however, is not to draw an opposition between the speculative realists' practices of argumentation, citation and marketing and the supposedly honest labour of philosophical critique, and in doing so to accuse the proponents of the speculative turn of being as it were the neoliberal financiers of philosophy. I should like instead to suggest that the frustration with the apparent limitations of a critique that seems to have 'run out of steam'[25] and with what has been diagnosed and criticized as the (self-)inflationary bombast of some of the 'speculative' responses to it are themselves both symptoms or indices of a more fundamental crisis. This crisis is not merely that philosophy seems not to be making progress with respect to what matters most, but the entanglement of this phenomenon with a decline in the productivity of labour – a decline measured solely in economic terms, and not, importantly, in terms of the goods and services that constitute the material substrate of this production.[26] It is my contention that the malaise at the apparent unproductivity or stuckness of contemporary thought is closely related to this decline in the economic productivity of labour, and to the ongoing financial and economic crisis. This is indicative of a crisis not only insofar as it suggests that thinking might have got stuck, but also, and more importantly, in that it reveals ways in which the absolutes towards which speculative realism orients itself are not absolutes at all, but in fact deeply saturated by ingrained practices and habits based on historically contingent financial relationships of exchange and equivalence.

These relationships, and their implications for speculative thought, are the topic of this chapter – and I investigate them from the perspective of the critique of the conflation of economic value with material wealth. More specifically, I address the possibility that the absolute with which speculative realism is concerned is not in fact outside thought at all, but rather the product or construct of a thought that is itself trapped within ways of thinking that are inescapably in debt to the social and economic relations that constitute the predominant mode of production. My suggestion is that overcoming the obligations of this debt is the condition of the possibility of the development of a speculative thinking that is worthy of the name.

One particularly compelling reason to be suspicious of the opposition of speculation to honest and productive labour is that the distinction between the rewards of speculation and those of labour is reminiscent of the old and malignant opposition of 'creative, productive labour' to 'useless, unproductive speculation', according to which speculation is understood to be parasitic on labour, and which constituted the theoretical foundation of National Socialist economics.[27] Underlying this opposition is something like a 'labour theory of value', according to which labour is the source of all value (in which monetary value represents, corresponds to and is equated with social benefit as such), and the profits made in speculation thus deprive the workers of the monetary reward to which they are entitled, in accordance with the social good that they have produced. Speculation, in this conception, does not produce: no labour is expended, and the profits by virtue of speculation are made not by creating any social benefit, but rather by waiting for changes in price over time. And from the standpoint of labour, speculation appears as a means by which speculators can take wealth that properly belongs to (and that would otherwise remain in the possession of) the workers.

Indeed, for the editors of *The Speculative Turn*, the configuration of the relationship between speculation and labour differs in subtle but significant ways from this. In their appeal to the potential rewards of the speculative wager that they propose, speculation remains defined in opposition to labour, as distinct from labour, but it is not seen as either parasitic or predatory on it. Nor, however, is speculation presented as able to make advances by virtue of the achievements of critique, but rather as a means of attaining knowledge that *takes into account* the achievements of critique. This taking into account is indicative of the rather uneasy relationship between the speculation and critique, as if critique is as much an inconvenience with which a revived, non-dogmatic speculation has to reckon as the shoulders on which it might stand. My contention is that this uneasy relationship is indicative of some of the fundamental workings that underlie prevalent concepts of speculation, and that critical examination of these, including by means of close textual reference to their metaphors and argumentative procedures, can open up avenues for the further development of speculative thought itself.

A comparably uneasy relationship between critique and speculation can be found in Quentin Meillassoux's *After Finitude* (the publication of which the editors of *The Speculative Turn* suggest 'might be called the trigger for the Speculative Realist movement').[28] Meillassoux argues that in order to begin to come to terms with and understand the philosophical implications of natural-scientific claims that pertain to a world before humanity, it is necessary to 'take up once more the injunction to know the absolute, and break with the transcendental tradition that rules out its possibility' (*AF* 28). Speculation is the means by which thought takes up this injunction: it is a particular activity of thought, or more accurately an activity of a certain kind of thought (that is to say, by no means all thought is speculative). More specifically, speculation is that kind of thinking that 'claims to be able to access some form of absolute' (*AF* 34). It is the status of this claim – that thought can somehow transcend its own limitations – with which I am concerned.

Meillassoux's conception of speculation differs from that of Ennis in that for the former this speculative thinking is not identical with metaphysics, which he defines as 'every type of thinking that claims to be able to access some form of absolute being, or access the absolute through the principle of sufficient reason' (*AF* 34). By this definition all metaphysics is speculative, but there remains the possibility of a non-metaphysical speculation: what is at stake in Meillassoux's distinction is the possibility of a means of thinking the absolute without resorting to the principle of sufficient reason, and more particularly, of saving the absolute from the obsolescence of dogmatic metaphysics. The challenge of the arche-fossil provides the motivation for the attempt not only to envisage but also to develop and account for 'an *absolutizing* thought that would not be *absolutist*' (*AF* 34) – that is to say, a way of thinking that can come to know the absolute, without resorting to the assertion that this absolute, 'this God, this world, this history, and ultimately this actually existing political regime necessarily exists, and must be the way it is' (*AF* 34), or what might (albeit not by Meillassoux's definition) be considered a non-dogmatic metaphysics.

Critique, and in particular what he terms 'Kant's Critical de-absolutization' (*AF* 76), was a means of overcoming this absolutism, but at the cost of access to the absolute, and thus the loss of 'the *great outdoors*, the *absolute* outside of pre-critical thinkers: that outside which was not relative to us, and which was given as indifferent to its own givenness to be what it is, existing in itself regardless of whether we are thinking of it or not; that outside which thought could explore with the legitimate feeling of being on foreign territory – of being entirely elsewhere' (*AF* 7). Indeed, Meillassoux recognizes that his attempt to think the absolute, and in particular to defend the thesis that certain (mathematizable) properties of the object 'are effectively in the object in the way in which I conceive them, whether I am in relation with this object or not', is 'almost certain to appear insupportable to a contemporary philosopher', and for the reason that this attempt 'is resolutely *pre-critical* – it seems to represent a regression to the "naïve" stance of dogmatic metaphysics' (*AF* 3). In his diagnosis, the fear of regression to 'a merely dogmatic position' requires that the post-critical philosopher commit in advance to a number of positions as a matter of course, including what he terms 'correlationism' (the maintenance of the unsurpassable character of 'the idea according to which we only ever have access to the correlation between thinking and being, and never to either term considered apart from the other' [*AF* 5]).[29]

These non-negotiable, unquestioned and frequently unacknowledged commitments serve to enable critical philosophy to move away from dogmatism, but at the same time, conversely, they render it defenceless against fanaticism, the (not necessarily religious) belief or emotional commitment founded on dubious or insufficient evidence, against which the Enlightenment took aim:[30]

> It is thanks to the critical power of correlationism that dogmatism was effectively vanquished in philosophy, and it is because of correlationism that philosophy finds itself incapable of fundamentally distinguishing itself from fanaticism. The victorious critique of ideologies has been transformed into a renewed argument for blind faith. (*AF* 49)

Critique enables philosophy to set itself free from dogmatism; however, it does so at the cost not only of abandoning the attempt, let alone claim, to know the absolute, but also of having unquestioningly to adhere to the conviction that the absolute not be thinkable. It is for this reason that contemporary fanaticism is diagnosed not as a reaction against critical reason, but rather as 'the *effect* of critical rationality, and this precisely insofar as . . . this rationality was *effectively emancipatory*' (*AF* 49): the success of critique in destroying dogmatism paves the way for a revived obscurantist fanaticism.

Like the editors of *The Speculative Turn*, Meillassoux accepts the undeniable progress made by critique and explicitly argues against any suggestion that breaking with the transcendental tradition that rules out the possibility of knowing the absolute might involve any kind of attempt to revert to a pre-critical framework:

> Is this to say that we must once again become pre-critical philosophers, or that we must go back to dogmatism? The whole problem is that such a return strikes us as strictly impossible – we cannot go back to being metaphysicians, just as we cannot go back to being dogmatists. On this point, we cannot but be heirs of Kantianism. (*AF* 28–29)

It is not the case that critique is to be rejected in favour of a reversion to metaphysical dogmatism, but rather that it is impossible to act as if the critical revolution did not happen. Indeed, part of the problem is that it did not go far enough, that despite its aspirations, critique continues to harbour certain prejudices. That is to say, for Meillassoux the problem of critique is in a sense that it is not critical enough, that 'critical potency is not necessarily on the side of those who would undermine the validity of absolute truths, but rather on the side of those who would succeed in criticizing *both* ideological dogmatism and sceptical fanaticism' (*AF* 49).

I share with Meillassoux the importance of ensuring that critique is adequately critical – and indeed of working towards its becoming more so. I also share with the proponents of the speculative turn a conviction as to the importance not only of recognizing the limits to critique, but also of developing and revitalizing speculative procedures by means of which these limits can be transcended. However, such a project brings with it certain dangers, for the development of such speculative resources – procedures by which we might come to know that which with the current intellectual resources appears to be unknowable – runs the risk of their conflation with either the overreaching assertion that one knows what one does not in fact know, or the inadequately critical conviction that one is coming to know the absolute, when this absolute is not absolute at all, but in fact something not only already established and known to critical thought, but even something that an enhanced critique could reveal to be pre-critical. The pressing question, then, is that of what it might mean fully to take into account the resources not only of critique but also of critique's relationship to the potential for fully speculative thinking.

This is what is at stake when Alain Badiou in his preface to *After Finitude* refers to Meillassoux's 'remarkable "critique of critique"' (*AF* vii). Meillassoux's project is presented as a matter not simply of mobilizing speculation against critique, or even of rescuing the absolute from the critical prohibition on attempts to know it, but rather of mobilizing a critical potency beyond the limits of a critique that 'has not been critical enough in spite of all its sore-scratching',[31] to the extent that it is possible to ask, however polemically, after 'the real difference between conspiracists and a popularized, that is a teachable version of social critique inspired by a too quick reading of, let's say, a sociologist as eminent as Pierre Bourdieu'.[32] This is why Meillassoux's 'critique of the de-absolutizing implication' (*AF* 49) (that is to say, of the throwing out of the baby of the absolute along with the dogmatic metaphysical bathwater) leads towards the possibility of envisaging what he terms 'a speculative critique of correlationism' as the only way of breaking with the latter's fidelity to the principle of reason (AF 63).

Labour, however, enters Meillassoux's conceptual web in a fundamentally different way from that of Bryant, Srnicek and Harman, as can be seen from its fleeting appearance in his dense and enigmatic explanation of why it is that he sees in Hegel the necessity of contingency derived from an external principle, an ontologically superior Whole, rather than solely from contingency itself. The assertion that contingency is necessary (as distinct from his own claim that *only* contingency is necessary) 'is in fact entirely compatible with metaphysics' (*AF* 80):

> Hegelian metaphysics thus sustains the necessity of an irredeemably contingent moment in the process of the absolute: a moment deployed in the

> very heart of nature through which the infinite, in order to contain nothing of the external which would limit it and thereby finitize it, passes, via a pure contingency, a reality without effectivity, a pure finitude, inaccessible in its disorder and gratuity, to the labour of the concept.[33]

Meillassoux's argument here – and it is worth observing Slavoj Žižek's claim in his interview with Ben Woodard that concludes *The Speculative Turn* that Meillassoux here 'crucially simplifies the properly Hegelian relationship between necessity and contingency'[34] – is that the contingency identified here is not necessary because it is contingency as such, but rather because it 'is deduced from the unfolding of the absolute, which in itself, qua rational totality, is devoid of contingency' (*AF* 80). Hegel's thought thus remains (for Meillassoux, and in Meillassoux's terms) metaphysical rather than non-metaphysically speculative.[35]

Meillassoux also silently dissents from Hegel in his account of the workings of conceptuality. More specifically, he does not adequately distinguish the Hegelian account of the concept from the Kantian, according to which (in Meillassoux's characterization) 'the subject of a proposition can never impose its existence upon thought solely by virtue of its concept, for being is never part of the concept of the subject, it is never its predicate – it is added to this concept as a pure positing' (*AF* 32). Such a pure positing remains present in Meillassoux's claim that 'for Hegel, the fact that nature only partially corresponds to the Hegelian concept of nature is the mark of the former's necessary defectiveness' (*AF* 80). This characterization differs significantly from Hegel's account, according to which concepts develop within a process of judgement, out of the process of abstraction, in which the differentiated moments from which it is to be abstracted are posited as existing on their own account and reflected into themselves, at which point the universality of the abstraction itself – the very thing that makes it a concept – is lost:

> The concept as this relation of its *independent* determinations has lost itself; for it is thus no longer their *posited unity*, and they no longer exist as its *moments*, as its *appearance*, but as existing in and for themselves. As individuality the concept returns to itself in its determinateness; with this the determinate has itself become a totality. Its return to itself is thus the absolute, original *division of itself* – or in other words, as individuality it is posited as a *judgement*.[36]

The concept that Meillassoux attributes to Hegel remains a posited unity – that is to say, for Hegel it would not yet be a concept but rather something like a conception or immediate abstraction. In Hegel's terms, it is still lost; it has not undertaken the return to itself that would enable it to become determinate. Meillassoux's version of Hegel is one in which the concept 'thus excludes the *universal* from itself';[37] in contrast, the Hegelian concept that has developed out of this conception is not something to which being is merely posited, but rather something that is active, not simply a conception created by us that remains inert (hence Hegel's acceptance, contra Kant, of the ontological argument).

While acknowledging that the 'Hegelian metaphysics' to which Meillassoux objects is not founded on a Hegelian account of the concept, Meillassoux's reference to the labour of the concept is nonetheless of particular interest, for the concept is at the heart of Hegel's speculative thinking, even if in Meillassoux's characterization this speculation remains metaphysical: at the end of the first part of *The Science of Logic*, before moving to discuss subjective logic or the theory of the concept, Hegel describes the concept as 'the realm of *subjectivity* or of *freedom*'.[38] Meanwhile, in his enclosure sent with his October 1812 letter to Niethammer discussing the teaching of philosophy to schoolchildren, he asserts that 'only the *grasped* [*das* Begriffene], and that means the speculative, which proceeds from the dialectic, is the philosophical in the *form of the concept*'.[39]

The labour to which Meillassoux refers is the end point of the infinite's passing through the heart of nature. Indeed, this labour is precisely what distinguishes the Hegelian concept from the dogmatic and rigid conceptions that we form ourselves. That is to say, the recognition of the labour of the concept is already to describe thinking as labour. Just as importantly, this labour is carried out by the concept, rather than by the subject with the help of the concept: for Hegel the concept is no mere tool that is distinct from the person who thinks with it, as can be seen most clearly from his ridiculing in a letter to Niethammer of 10 October 1811 of the idea that concepts are '*aids* to the understanding in *thinking*', a conception he equates to the notion that 'chewing and swallowing were merely an aid in eating, as if the understanding did many other things besides thinking'.[40]

The speculative thinking of the concept, then, is for Meillassoux not only not sharply distinguished from labour, but even identified with it, an implication which finds an echo in the somewhat surprising place of Alberto Toscano's critique of speculation from the perspective of a critical materialism influenced by Lucio Colletti, for whom 'speculation, conceived as the pretension of philosophical thought to logically encompass being, is fundamentally incompatible with materialism'.[41] Toscano summarizes the Hegelian position that Colletti diagnoses as 'contempt towards the isolated thing and the thought that thinks it (mere intellect as opposed to reason)': the 'labour of speculative reason (*Vernunft*), as opposed to the intellect or understanding (*Verstand*), is to traverse the various configurations of the finite and to undo its separateness'.[42] Here again – and again in a discussion of Hegel – labour is used to refer to the achievements or tasks of a faculty of cognition, and in this instance it is associated unambiguously with speculative reason, rather than with the movement of the Hegelian concept. This conjunction helps to reveal what Meillassoux misses: that the absolutely contingent reality of nature, a reality which has no need of the human to think it, is itself nothing other than the inscription of the subject into the intrasubjective reality of labour that is oriented towards the production of abstract value – a labour that is social only in the constrained and constraining sense of the sociality of the commodity form.

Other representatives of the so-called speculative turn work with or refer to less differentiated conceptions of labour. In his critique of *After Finitude*, for example, Peter Hallward argues that Meillassoux's critique of causality relies on a conflation of metaphysical and natural necessity, which leads him erroneously to infer from the critique of metaphysical necessity that there is 'no cause or reason for anything to be the way it is', including in the natural or physical world:

> Meillassoux's acausal ontology, in other words, includes no account of an actual process of transformation or development. There is no account here of any positive ontological or historical force, no substitute for what other thinkers have conceived as substance, or spirit, or power, or labour. His insistence that anything might happen can only amount to an insistence on the bare possibility of radical change.[43]

Here labour seems to be a relatively undetermined category, an as it were interchangeable term for an 'ontological or historical force', a human intervention into the world, which can thus be equated with spirit. Levi Bryant works with a similar conception of labour in discussing the 'transportation of difference', the term he uses to refer to the action of one object on another (an example given is 'the manner in which a flower transports the differences of sunlight'), which 'never takes place in a smooth, frictionless space, but always requires labour or work'.[44] Once again, labour is used here to refer relatively generally to activity that brings about change, and that encounters resistance as it does so.

In his discussion of what he terms Hegel's analysis of the passage from labour to thought, Slavoj Žižek presents an account of how thought develops out of precisely such conception of labour, which is defined as human activity directed towards the production of an object that someone (whether oneself or another) will consume. And following Gérard Lebrun, Žižek recognizes that this labour, importantly, is not all-powerful, but rather indicates a limit of human endeavour: 'As an aggressive activity deployed by a finite being, labour signals above all man's impotence to integrally take possession of nature'.[45] Žižek distinguishes Hegel's response to this finitude from those of Kant and Fichte, which he characterizes as philosophies of struggle to overcome both these external obstacles and (as a result) the subject's own nature. In Hegel, in contrast, Žižek identifies the remedy to what he characterizes as this 'pathological particularity', namely that the universal subject has gone through some kind of therapeutic procedure that makes it self-secure in its knowledge that its 'thought already is the form of reality', with the result that 'it can renounce enforcing its project on reality, it can let reality be the way it is'.[46]

This, for Žižek, provides the explanation for the truth in abstraction, as if the criterion of such a truth consists solely in the extent to which it is compatible with the motivations of an as it were personified subjectivity:

> This is why labour gets all the more close to its truth the less I work to satisfy my need, i.e., to produce an object I will consume. This is why industry which produces for the market is spiritually 'higher' than production for one's own needs: in market-production, I manufacture objects with no relation to my needs. The highest form of social production is therefore that of a merchant.[47]

The quotation provided in support of this claim – 'the merchant is the only one who relates to the Good as a perfect universal subject, since the object in no way interests him on behalf of its aesthetic presence or its use value, but only insofar as it contains a desire of an other'[48] – is from Lebrun rather than Hegel, who does not refer to the merchant or to trade in the section of the *Phenomenology* on lordship and bondage (or indeed anywhere else in the *Phenomenology*). That is to say, both the affective, motivational explanation of the truth and the exposition of its implications are Žižek's additions to Hegel's account, the latter via Lebrun.

This introduction of the affective element in Žižek's version of Hegel – as if the Kantian-Fichtean and Hegelian subjects were actually existing human beings, and as if the Hegelian had in some sense been cured of its Kantian-Fichtean neurosis, and were thus able contentedly to accept its limitations and thus to let the world be (even if not had necessarily actively or consciously chosen this path) – posits a kind of affective subjectivity within the subject that can be content, resigned or dissatisfied. This affective subjectivity, which governs the development of the subject, is at the same time not accounted for – that is to say, there is no account of why it should be the case that the affective constitution of the Hegelian subject differs from the Kantian-Fichtean. The only way around this – which is of course the point – is for one version to be diagnosed as pathological, and the other to represent the cure to this pathology.

This begins to make clear what is at stake in Žižek's claim that labour is 'simultaneously the (trans)formation of external objects and the disciplinary self-formation/education (*Bildung*) of the subject itself':[49] this self-formation and education can only consist in the taming and treatment of the affective subjectivity-within-the-subject, the result of which is the cured Hegelian (in fact Žižekian) subject. What Žižek presents is in a sense an internalization of the Hegelian account he is analysing – what Žižek refers to as labour in general is in the Hegelian account from which he takes his cue the much more specific activity (under the much more specific conditions) of the bondsman's service to the lord. That is to say, what Žižek theorizes as the indeterminate human activity directed towards the production of any object that will be consumed, whether by the person who expends this labour or by somebody else, is not the production of goods for sale on an anonymous market, but rather the specific case of labour expended in the service of a particular other. Indeed, the first appearance of the term *Arbeit* in the *Phenomenology* after the preface (which was of course written after the rest of the book had been finished) is in the very extract that Žižek cites, and is used as a synonym for the work carried out by the bondsman in service of the lord.[50] This labour is indeed indeterminate in its content, and also with respect to its product, but it takes place under a very specific social relationship.

This has significant implications for the conclusion Žižek draws as to the relationship between labour and the subject, with particular respect to the abstraction of labour:

> And this is also why, in order to arrive at the 'truth' of labour, one should gradually abstract from the (external) goal it strives to realize. The parallel with war is appropriate here: in the same way that the 'truth' of the military struggle is not the destruction of the enemy, but the sacrifice of the 'pathological' content of the warrior's particular Self, its purification into the universal Self, the 'truth' of labour as the struggle with nature, its stuff, is also not victory over nature, it is not to compel nature to serve human goals, but the self-purification of the labourer itself.[51]

Here it is worth observing that Žižek's claim, that the truth of labour is attained by means of abstraction from its goal, is asserted, but not in the form of an assertion – instead it is expressed by means of the recurring 'this is why' formulations (the one cited here is the third within four sentences) that serve to create the argumentative impression that the relevant propositions have been put beyond question, even though their veracity has by no means been established. This claim is presented, that is, as if it is being deduced and explained by means of a critical explication of Hegel, as if the assertion cannot admit to being speculative, and rather requires or seeks refuge in the garb of the labour of critique.

The truth of labour to which Žižek refers is the development out of labour by means of this abstraction of thought, as the realization of labour in self-reflexive thinking without an object: labour 'achieves its *telos* in thinking which no longer works on an external stuff, but is already its own stuff, or, which no longer imposes its subjective/finite form onto external reality, but is already in itself the infinite form of reality'.[52] This truth is actualized in the distinction between finite and infinite or speculative thought:

> For the finite thought, the concept of an object is a mere concept, the subjective goal one actualizes when, by way of labour, one imposes it onto reality. For the speculative thought, on the contrary, thought is not merely subjective, it is in itself already objective, i.e., it renders the objective conceptual form of the object.[53]

Here the relationship between 'labour' and thought begins to become clear, but once again Hegel is referring to labour within the specific context of servitude. So when Žižek argues that Hegel 'celebrates precisely the alienated and alienating character of labour', which 'forces me to submit to artificial discipline, to renounce my innermost immediate tendencies, to alienate myself from my natural Self', he is once again, as was the case with the introduction of production for sale on a market, quietly admitting into the discussion a conceptual repertoire that only develops with the rise of Marxism, such that, for example, the Hegelian sense of alienation, which with respect to labour refers to the creation by one's labour of something outside oneself of which one can subsequently dispose, is conflated with the Marxist.[54]

This goes hand in hand with Žižek's expansion of the concept of labour, opening up Hegel's concept of the work carried out specifically within service to include all work carried out to produce something that will be consumed, no matter by whom. Žižek thus goes well beyond the Hegelian account of the indifference to the particularity of the product and the activity that makes it with respect to the particularity of the relationship under which it is produced, and instead displays an indifference towards this relationship – the very factor that is central to Hegel's account. In doing so Žižek deploys – but does not formulate or account for – a concept of labour that is not only indistinct (because it does not distinguish between the production of objects for one's own consumption and that for the use of another) and premature (by virtue of the fact that it also includes the abstract labour of industrial production, including in its detailed division), but that also, because it does not recognize the specificity of the value-producing character of capitalist labour, silently projects this character back across time.

This is to make the same mistake as orthodox or traditional Marxism, which identifies labour as the source of all social wealth ('value' here is understood transhistorically), and argues that this value should be equitably distributed to its producers – that is to say, it objects to the skimming off of the surplus value by the capitalist in the form of profit. In fact, as Moishe Postone demonstrates, this transhistorical, positive conception of labour as the source of all social wealth is not Marxian at all, but rather a theory common to bourgeois political economy and social critique alike, which 'dates at least as far back as John Locke's writings and found its most consistent expression in Ricardo's political economy'.[55] In doing so, traditional Marxism misrecognizes what is specific to the Marxian conception of labour, namely its double character: that it is at once 'presupposed as the labour of the isolated individual', and 'becomes social in that it takes on the form of its immediate opposite, the form of abstract universality'.[56] Contra Marx, traditional Marxism assumes that labour is always already social, and that this sociality is mediated by the market and private property, and that 'overcoming capitalism would involve the supersession of a mediated form of social relations by a direct unmediated form'.[57]

The concepts of value and labour that underlie Marx's mature critique of capitalism are in fact highly critical, even if in Marx's work this critique is developed only incipiently, and at times ambiguously or even contradictorily. This critical character is illuminated more clearly when they are considered from the perspective of the distinction between material wealth and economic value, where the former consists in everything – experiences as well as resources – that improves and enhances the experience of life, the latter the measurable quantity in which wealth can be produced, accumulated and hoarded in its capitalist form. Labour in Marx is thus not a transhistorical conception of all activity oriented towards the production of material wealth (whether for oneself or another), or even the particular capitalist manifestation of this production-oriented activity, but rather an 'oppressive, inhumane, and antisocial activity that both is determined by and produces private property'.[58] As such the Marxian critique of capitalist labour is not the critique 'of the private character of labor from the standpoint of directly social labor', but rather the more thoroughgoing critique of their relation to one another, 'a critique of private labor and immediately social labor as complementary, as one-sided terms of an elemental opposition that characterizes capitalist society'.[59]

The social force of the institution of labour is evident not only in the extent to which it dominates our lives, but also in the very difficulty of thinking of labour as a historically specific formation, of not conceiving of it except as a transhistorical constant. It is not simply an abstraction that results from thinking a range of different kinds of labour together under a single concept, but rather, as Marx argues, a way of thinking that has its roots in the way in which society is organized:

> [T]his abstraction of labour as such is not the intellectual result of a concrete totality of labours. The indifference to particular labour corresponds to a social form in which individuals move from one labour to another with ease, and the particular kind of labour is coincidental to them – thus they are indifferent to it. Here labour has become, not only in its concept but also in reality, a means of creating wealth as such, and has ceased to be entangled with individuals in their particularity as a determination.[60]

This abstraction that develops from social praxis is what Alfred Sohn-Rethel terms an *actually existing* or '*real abstraction* resulting from spatio-temporal activity', and thus an abstraction which 'does not originate in men's minds but in their actions'.[61] Or in Žižek's paraphrase, advanced in his discussion of Sohn-Rethel's account of the particular real abstraction of the commodity, '[b]efore thought could arrive at pure abstraction, the abstraction was already at work in the social effectivity of the market'.[62] The ways in which we behave – in which we are forced to behave – create abstractions that precede and exist outside our conceiving of them. As Ernst Lohoff argues in his account of the historical development of the category of abstract labour, the category of abstract labour is 'not simply a prerequisite of the capital relation, but rather, at least in its more developed form, its product'.[63]

What is characteristic of this real, lived abstraction of labour is not that it is activity oriented towards the improvement of human life, towards the production of something that will be consumed, whether by the labourer or by another, but rather that it is, in Marx's terms, a 'means of creating wealth as such' – not material wealth as such, the improvement of life in the world, but wealth determined in its capitalist form of value. Abstract labour is defined not according to its product, nor according to any criterion of use or benefit (however defined), but with respect solely to the fact that it produces abstract value. It is characterized by the wage relation and is the site of production of exchange value – and, most importantly, of surplus value, which enables the generation of profit and drives cycles of accumulation.

This, of course, contrasts with another way of trying to make a profit: speculation, or 'buying with the hope to sell at a gain'.[64] The institutionalization of this practice has resulted in the emergence of what has been termed a 'speculation economy', in which 'business management focused on production is replaced with business management focused on stock price'.[65] Indeed, this economy has grown in both volume and significance to the extent that some argue that the United States 'no longer is a capitalist country', and that while capitalism 'still characterizes a portion of the American economy', it 'has become subordinated to a new economic order', financialism, in which 'the financial markets exist primarily to serve themselves'.[66] This system is one in which 'capital is raised for the purpose of creating, selling, and trading securities and derivative securities that do not finance industry but rather trade within markets that exist as an economy unto themselves'.[67]

The problem here diagnosed is that economic resources have been diverted 'from capitalist production in the real economy to satisfy the demand of financial claimants, primarily stockholders',[68] and that as a result 'financialism threatens to rob the patrimony of future generations for the profit of the present and damages our national security by forcing us to outsource the production of our most essential goods and services'.[69] According to this account, the imperative to maximize stockholder profit 'keeps managers' and stockholders' focus on the short term',[70] a situation in which management has little choice but 'to do what it has to do in order to meet the market's expectations, no matter how unrealistic those expectations may be'.[71] The result is a system in which the principal incentives and motivations are short-term pressures which 'are designed to lead to long-term disaster'[72] – to 'layoffs, plant closings, alienated workers, unsafe products, and a polluted environment, all in the name of today's profit'.[73]

From the perspective of Mitchell's critique of financialism, the contemporary economy 'is characterized not simply by the triumph of finance over business, but by the domination of a stock market that has followed the logic of a widespread common stock structure to largely detach itself from business'.[74] Contrasting financialism with capitalism's 'ability to stimulate economic growth, the creation and distribution of wealth, and the sustaining of that wealth over time', he claims that we have made a transition away from capitalism to 'a system in which the present generation robs future generations of their economic patrimony and national security'.[75] Mitchell's distinction – between the 'special moral role' capitalism plays within society and the 'intrinsically immoral' financialism that has replaced it[76] – structurally resembles the infamous National Socialist distinction between, on the one hand, the productive, creative capital of the state that is 'indispensable for the life of the nation', and, on the other hand, the destructive, rapacious, parasitic-predatory capital of the market. This market capital 'does not work productively', but rather works its way into production solely in order to take its cut: 'Its principal bearer is Jewish high finance, which aspires to let the productive nations work for it, and thereby to trouser the yields of their work'.[77]

Critics of the financial economy, whether liberal-capitalist, socialist or National Socialist, appear to agree on two things: that the speculative economy as it exists (or existed) came about because of a decisive shift;

and that extent of speculation needs to be curbed, whether by the reversing of this shift or (more commonly) by the introduction of (frequently unspecified) new measures. In Mitchell's liberal-capitalist account there is a tension between the claim on the one hand that the transition from capitalism to financialism is a recent one, and, on the other hand, that 'finance had completed its triumph over industry and everything necessary for the modern market was in place by 1919'.[78] He identifies a 'speculation intrinsic in the capital structure of American corporations', which 'permanently changed American business and the way it was regulated' by creating 'an economy inseparable from speculation', an economy that 'was embedded in a market characterized by increasing numbers of small common stockholders'.[79] He charts the 'increasing popular interest in speculation' over the first decade of the twentieth century, which marked a shift from conservative investment (based on judging earning potential) to speculation (based on anticipating price fluctuation).[80]

Arguing from a socialist perspective, Costas Lapavitsas locates the cause in political decisions made in the late twentieth century, particularly in the shift away from Keynesianism. His claim is that financialization 'represents a transformation of mature capitalism resting on the altered conduct of non-financial enterprises, banks and households', which 'has taken place during the last four decades within a "channel of accumulation" determined by neoliberal ideology and shaped through deregulation of labour and financial markets'.[81] Meanwhile Feder, whose economic views predominated within the NSDAP of the 1920s, saw the problem in the fact that '[d]uring the course of the development of high capitalism, the essential function of the large banks consisted solely in the fact that they enabled, by means of *the creation of additional fiat money beyond their own means and deposits* – and in some circumstances beyond the assets of the economy! – the financing of all great technical innovations and inventions, just as purely speculative and in some cases fraudulent manipulations could be financed'.[82]

It is worth observing that these explanations are not necessarily mutually incompatible, but focus on different aspects of the conjuncture that enabled the growth of the speculative economy. Moreover, the proposed liberal-capitalist and socialist solutions bear considerable resemblance to one another, both involving some kind of state regulation. Mitchell, who insists that we 'must destroy financialism for the sake of capitalism', argues that 'meaningful reform can be achieved only by reforming the market, by reforming finance itself to create the incentives for stockholders and managers to relearn the lesson that profits come from industrial production, not from the breeze that blows toward tomorrow'.[83]

Meanwhile, Lapavitsas argues that the solution consists in 'accepting that public authorities have the right and the obligation to intervene in the economy in the interests of the many', which provides the basis for devising 'policies that could re-establish control over capital domestically and internationally', which he insists is 'part of the struggle for socialism'.[84] Of course, one reason why the courses of action look similar is the fact that the policies that would bring about these reforms remain undefined – but this is perhaps also indicative of the paucity of thought being undertaken in this direction.

There have been a great many attempts to account for the ongoing financial and economic crisis in terms of the distinction between real and speculative or financial capital. Indeed, Mitchell's explanation simply asserts that there can be no doubt 'that speculation caused the financial crisis of 2008, first in housing, and then in derivative securities'.[85] In this version of the explanation this crisis represents the culmination of a process whereby finance came to triumph over industry, the inevitable deserved, self-incurred and predictable (and, indeed, predicted) consequence of 'the short-term pressures that the modern construct of the stockholder puts on corporate management', which are 'designed to lead to long-term disaster'.[86] Lapavitsas seems to share a foundational belief in what he terms 'the tendency to crisis that has characterized financialization since its inception', arguing that 'the great crisis that broke out in 2007' is 'a systemic crisis that reflects the advancing penetration of financial relations into the operations of enterprises and households, in part due to the transformation of banks', which has brought about a complex and deep 'interpenetration of financial and real accumulation' in the mature capitalist economies.[87]

This is not an explanatory base I share. Just as Postone's development of the Marxian critique of capitalist labour is not a critique of private labour from the standpoint of immediately social labour, but rather the fundamental critique of their relation to one another, I do not conceive the relationship between labour and speculation as one of opposition, or indeed of exploitation, whether predatory or parasitic. Speculation rather *anticipates* the future value of the commodities produced by labour. However, as labour is increasingly expelled from the process of production in the quest for efficiency and savings, the mass of surplus value produced in the world tends towards zero, with the result that capital is increasingly unable to attain valorization within the productive economy – what Marx and others have identified as capitalism's tendency towards crisis.[88]

The massive expansion in the speculative trade in what Ernst Lohoff and Norbert Trenkle term second-order commodities – that is, commodities 'which demonstrate the specific use-value of representing *future* value' – is a means of compensating for this 'melting away of the mass of value', and in doing so of deferring the crisis.[89] The particular means by which this happens is what Marx terms fictitious capital, the phenomenon whereby a single bond or security can itself serve as a guarantee for further investment: this fictitious capital thus seems to multiply as it comes into the possession of different people. From this perspective, the deregulation in the 1970s that Lapavitsas claims is the indirect cause of the crisis was in fact the means of overcoming the crisis of over-accumulation of the 1970s, and indeed enabled the post-Fordist boom.[90] According to this account the volume of speculative transactions is not the cause of the crisis, but an index of its magnitude.

Speculation is not the cause of the crisis, but the refuge in which capital takes flight when it can no longer reliably attain valorization within the real economy. It is not parasitic on labour, but its emergence coincides with the demise of labour, which is increasingly becoming unproductive – not, however, with respect to its ability to produce material social wealth, but rather as a means of producing abstract value, because of the decreasing rate of surplus value that results from the expulsion of labour from the process of production as a result of mechanization and automation. In opposing speculation to the real economy and blaming the former for any crises within capitalism, these liberal-capitalist, socialist and National Socialist critics of speculation conflate abstract value and material social wealth. Their critiques share a single mechanism: they latch onto a single phenomenon of capitalist society and criticize it from the perspective of another. In doing so they fail to recognize that the fundamental problem consists in the fact that the interactions and tensions between these phenomena are allowed to appear as totality: that the capitalist sphere of reference is taken to be the full extent of reality. This real is that of centrist realism.[91]

I should like to suggest that the sense of the limitedness of critique to which many of the works associated with the so-called speculative turn testify is closely related to the increasing irrelevance of abstract labour to the process of valorization (and thus the increasing divergence of the production of abstract value from that of social, material wealth) – and the recourse to speculation analogously related to the flight of capital from production to speculation in the quest to maintain profitability. And for all of the speculative realists' care to differentiate their positions from those of a 'naïve' realism (pace Harman's observation that the phrase tends to pose 'as the name for one type of realism while really insinuating that *all* realism is naive'),[92] there has been remarkably little attention to the extent and quality of the mediation of the real with which they are concerned through the categories, practices and real abstractions of capital.[93] Without attention to this mediation, from the perspective of its ruthless critique, any concern with the absolute runs the risk of absolutizing the real abstractions of capital.

The concepts within and with which we think require further interrogation, particularly with respect to their mediation through economic categories, transactions and behaviours – one starting point here might be a thoroughgoing investigation of the implications and effects of categories such as the real economy, real subsumption, real accumulation, real value. I share with many of the proponents of the speculative turn a sense of the urgency of speculation. In particular, while critique can help us ascertain the limits of instrumental reason, going beyond these limits cannot but require procedures of thought that are emphatically speculative. Such a speculation, however, requires not the abandonment of critique, but its renewal and reinvigoration – a renewed critique of actually existing metaphysics, and of the extent to which its categories are themselves bound up with and mediated by the constraints of frequently unobserved or unacknowledged real abstractions. Without the commitment to such a renewal of critique, speculative thought can never be speculative enough.

NOTES

* I should like to express my thanks to all those who have shared their comments on this chapter as it developed, especially to Christopher Müller and to Jennifer Yusin. I am particularly grateful for the discussion and critique of an earlier draft of this chapter at a workshop hosted by the Inter-Chicago Circle for Experimental Critical Theory at the University of Illinois at Chicago: my thanks to Jen Hawe, Peri Johnson, Adam Kotsko, Davis Smith-Brecheisen and above all to Anna Kornbluh.

1. Simon Jarvis, 'What Is Speculative Thinking?', *Revue Internationale de Philosophie* 227.1 (2004): 70.
2. Levi Bryant, Nick Srnicek and Graham Harman, 'Towards a Speculative Philosophy', in *The Speculative Turn: Continental Materialism and Realism*, ed. Levi Bryant, Nick Srnicek and Graham Harman (Melbourne: re.press, 2011), 3.
3. Quentin Meillassoux, *After Finitude: An Essay on the Necessity of Contingency, with a Preface by Alain Badiou*, trans. Ray Brassier (London and New York: Bloomsbury Academic, 2008), 38; hereafter *AF* with page references in the text.
4. Bryant, Srnicek and Harman, 'Towards a Speculative Philosophy', 1.
5. Bryant, Srnicek and Harman, 'Towards a Speculative Philosophy', 3.
6. Bryant, Srnicek and Harman, 'Towards a Speculative Philosophy', 3.

7. Paul J. Ennis, *Continental Realism* (Winchester and Washington: Zero Books, 2011), 1.

8. Bryant, Srnicek and Harman, 'Towards a Speculative Philosophy', 3.

9. Ennis, *Continental Realism*, 1.

10. Tom Sparrow, *The End of Phenomenology: Metaphysics and the New Realism* (Edinburgh: Edinburgh University Press, 2014), 3.

11. Bryant, Srnicek and Harman, 'Towards a Speculative Philosophy', 3.

12. Steven Shaviro, *The Universe of Things: On Speculative Realism* (Minneapolis: University of Minnesota Press, 2014), 5.

13. Lee Braver, *A Thing of This World: A History of Continental Anti-Realism* (Evanston, IL: Northwestern University Press, 2007), 39.

14. Ennis, *Continental Realism*, 2.

15. Immanuel Kant, *Kritik der reinen Vernunft*, ed. Wilhelm Weischedel, Werkausgabe in 12 Bänden, 3, 2 vols (Frankfurt a.M.: Suhrkamp, 1992), I, 29–30.

16. Shaviro, *The Universe of Things*, 67.

17. Bryant, Srnicek, and Harman, 'Towards a Speculative Philosophy', 3.

18. Adam Smith, *An Inquiry into the Nature and Causes of the Wealth of Nations: A Selected Edition*, ed. Kathryn Sutherland (Oxford: Oxford University Press, 1998), 111.

19. Smith, *An Inquiry*, 111–12.

20. Smith, *An Inquiry*, 111.

21. Lawrence E. Mitchell, *The Speculation Economy: How Finance Triumphed over Industry* (San Francisco: Berrett-Koehler, 2008), 104.

22. David Golumbia, '"Correlationism": The Dogma That Never Was', *Boundary 2* 43.2 (2016): 3, 9.

23. Ray Brassier, 'I Am a Nihilist Because I Still Believe in Truth: Ray Brassier Interviewed by Marcin Rychter', *Kronos*, 4 March 2011; http://web.archive.org/web/20110310062157/http://kronos.org.pl/index.php?23151,896 (last accessed 28 February 2017).

24. Graham Harman, 'On the Undermining of Objects: Grant, Bruno, and Radical Philosophy', in *The Speculative Turn: Continental Materialism and Realism*, ed. Levi Bryant, Nick Srnicek and Graham Harman (Melbourne: re.press, 2011), 21.

25. Bruno Latour, 'Why Has Critique Run Out of Steam? From Matters of Fact to Matters of Concern', *Critical Inquiry* 30.2 (2004): 225–48.

26. Indeed, it is not simply the case that the real-terms decline in the economic productivity of labour is unrelated or indifferent to what happens in the material substrate, but rather that the fall in economic productivity is a necessary consequence of the rise in material productivity which results from the 'permanently functioning compulsion to reduce labor time' in pursuit (at least in the short term) of higher profit; cf. Claus Peter Ortlieb, 'A Contradiction between Matter and Form: On the Significance of the Production of Relative Surplus Value in the Dynamic of Terminal Crisis', in *Marxism and the Critique of Value*, ed. Neil Larsen et al. (Chicago and Alberta: MCM', 2014), 91–105.

27. Gottfried Feder, *Kampf gegen die Hochfinanz: eine Hauptquelle zur Ideengeschichte und Frühzeit des Nationalsozialismus* (Bremen: Roland Faksimile,

2003; facsimile of the Munich edition of 1935; first edition published 1933), 167. Unless otherwise stated, translations are my own.

28. Bryant, Srnicek and Harman, 'Towards a Speculative Philosophy', 8.

29. For a persuasive critique of Meillassoux's diagnosis of the contamination by correlationism since Kant, see Golumbia, 'Correlationism', 5–7.

30. Here fanaticism and its French counterpart *fanatisme* are the most common translations of the German *Schwärmerei*, one of the mentalities, along with materialism, fatalism, atheism and free-thinking unbelief which Kant considers generally dangerous, and which critique alone is able to cut off at the root; Immanuel Kant, *Kritik der reinen Vernunft*, ed. Wilhelm Weischedel, Werkausgabe in 12 Bänden, 3, 2 vols (Frankfurt a.M.: Suhrkamp, 1974), I, 35; cf. *Critique de la raison pure*, trans. Claude-Joseph Tissot, 2 vols (Paris: Librairie de Ladrange, 1835), I, 27; *Critick of Pure Reason*, trans. Francis Haywood (London: W. Pickering, 1838), xxvi; *Critique of Pure Reason*, trans. J. M. D Meiklejohn (London: Henry G. Bohn, 1855), xxxvii; *Critique de la raison pure*, trans. Jules Barni, 2 vols (Paris and London: Germer-Baillière, 1869), I, 38; *Critique de la raison pure*, trans. A. Tremesaygues and B. Pacaud (Paris: Félix Alcan, 1905), 32; *Critique of Pure Reason*, trans. by Norman Kemp Smith (London: Macmillan, 1929), 32. Kant, who takes the term from Luther's polemical coinage to designate the swarming confusion of his opponents (and particularly those who did not share his understanding of the divinely ordained relationship between internal faith and external action), uses it to refer to those under the delusion that it is possible to attain access to the transcendent by means of sensory experience (that is to say, for Kant the concept contains a theoretical component, a moment of epistemic failure, as a counterpart to the practical stance or attitude connoted by the English term); cf. Amy Nelson Burnett, 'Luther and the *Schwärmer*', in *The Oxford Handbook of Martin Luther's Theology*, ed. Robert Kolb, Irene Dingel and L'ubomír Batka (Oxford: Oxford University Press, 2014), 512–13; Rachel Zuckert, 'Kant's Account of Practical Fanaticism', in *Kant's Moral Metaphysics: God, Freedom, and Immortality*, ed. Benjamin J. Bruxvoort Lipscomb and James Krueger (Berlin and New York: De Gruyter, 2010), 292–97.

31. Latour, 'Why Has Critique Run Out of Steam?', 232.

32. Latour, 'Why Has Critique Run Out of Steam?', 228–29.

33. Quentin Meillassoux, *Après la finitude: Essai sur la nécessité de la contingence* (Paris: Seuil, 2006), 108. I have returned to the French here in part to avoid the misleading use of notion to translate the German *Begriff* (concept), in part because the more literal translation I have offered, considerably less fluent than Ray Brassier's rendering of Meillassoux's sentence, helps more clearly to identify the stages to which Meillassoux is referring in his characterization of Hegel.

34. Slavoj Žižek and Ben Woodard, 'Interview', in *The Speculative Turn: Continental Materialism and Realism*, ed. Levi Bryant, Nick Srnicek and Graham Harman (Melbourne: re.press, 2011), 414.

35. This is more or less the same criticism that Adorno makes of Hegel when arguing that he 'takes sides with the universal' by virtue of the fact that he 'does not deal with the particular as particular, but merely with particularity, which is already something conceptual'. Theodor W. Adorno, *Negative Dialektik*

(Frankfurt a.M.: Suhrkamp, 1966), 322. Conversely, Gillian Rose levels at Adorno the charge that he 'confines himself to "dialectic", which is the second, negative stage of reason', and as a result 'remains within the dialectical antinomies of subject and object, particular and universal, individual and state', without relating 'these oppositions to each other as they come to light in a dynamic historical development' but instead arguing 'that they are frozen'; Gillian Rose, 'From Speculative to Dialectical Thinking – Hegel and Adorno', in *Judaism and Modernity: Philosophical Essays* (Oxford and Cambridge, MA: Blackwell, 1993), 61. The distinction with which Rose is working here is Hegel's between abstract, dialectical and speculative methods and souls of philosophy: the first, merely abstract stage of philosophy 'holds determinations fast and comes to know them in their fixed distinctions'; the second, dialectical stage 'is the movement and confusion of such fixed determinations; *negative* reason'; the speculative, in contrast, is 'the positive-rational, the *spiritual*, it alone is truly philosophical' – it consists in 'knowledge of *what is opposed in its unity* – or more precisely, that in their truth opposites are one'; Georg Wilhelm Friedrich Hegel, 'Ueber den Vortrag der philosophischen Vorbereitungswissenschaften auf Gymnasien. Privatgutachten an Immanuel Niethammer vom 23. Oktober 1812', in *Nürnberger Gymnasialkurse Und Gymnasialreden (1808–1816). Beilagen Und Anhang*, ed. Klaus Grotsch, Gesammelte Werke, 10, 2 vols (Hamburg: Meiner, 2006), II, 830–31. For defences of the speculative character of Adorno's thought against this charge, cf. Jarvis, 'What Is Speculative Thinking?', and my own 'Dialektik und Spekulation. Über die Grenzen der spekulativen Vernunft', in *Probleme der Dialektik heute*, ed. Stefan Müller (Wiesbaden: VS Verlag für Sozialwissenschaften, 2009), 229–46.

36. Georg Wilhelm Friedrich Hegel, *Wissenschaft der Logik*, ed. Eva Moldenhauer, Werke in 20 Bänden, 6 (Frankfurt a.M.: Suhrkamp, 1986), II, 301.

37. Hegel, *Wissenschaft der Logik*, II, 301.

38. Hegel, *Wissenschaft der Logik*, II, 240.

39. Hegel, 'Ueber den Vortrag der philosophischen Vorbereitungswissenschaften auf Gymnasien. Privatgutachten an Immanuel Niethammer vom 23. Oktober 1812', 832.

40. Georg Wilhelm Friedrich Hegel, *Briefe von und an Hegel: 1785 bis 1812* (Hamburg: Meiner, 1969), 389.

41. Alberto Toscano, 'Against Speculation, Or, a Critique of the Critique of Critique: A Remark on Quentin Meillassoux's *After Finitude* (After Colletti)', in *The Speculative Turn: Continental Materialism and Realism*, ed. Levi Bryant, Nick Srnicek and Graham Harman (Melbourne: re.press, 2011), 89.

42. Toscano, 'Against Speculation', 88.

43. Peter Hallward, 'Anything Is Possible: A Reading of Quentin Meillassoux's after Finitude', in *The Speculative Turn: Continental Materialism and Realism*, ed. Levi Bryant, Nick Srnicek and Graham Harman (Melbourne: re.press, 2011), 138, 139.

44. Levi Bryant, 'The Ontic Principle: Outline of an Object-Oriented Ontology', in *The Speculative Turn: Continental Materialism and Realism*, ed. Levi Bryant, Nick Srnicek and Graham Harman (Melbourne: re.press, 2011), 275, 277.

45. Gérard Lebrun, *L'envers de la dialectique: Hegel à la lumière de Nietzsche*, ed. Paul Clavier and Francis Wolff (Paris: Seuil, 2004), 207; cited in Slavoj Žižek, 'Is It Still Possible to Be a Hegelian Today?', in *The Speculative Turn: Continental Materialism and Realism*, ed. Levi Bryant, Nick Srnicek and Graham Harman (Melbourne: re.press, 2011), 209.

46. Žižek, 'Is It Still Possible to Be a Hegelian Today?', 209.

47. Žižek, 'Is It Still Possible to Be a Hegelian Today?', 209.

48. Lebrun, *L'envers de la dialectique*, 206; cited in Žižek, 'Is It Still Possible to Be a Hegelian Today?', 209.

49. Žižek, 'Is It Still Possible to Be a Hegelian Today?', 209.

50. Georg Wilhelm Friedrich Hegel, *Phänomenologie des Geistes*, Werke in 20 Bänden, 3 (Frankfurt a.M.: Suhrkamp, 1986), 153; cf. Žižek, 'Is It Still Possible to Be a Hegelian Today?', 210.

51. Žižek, 'Is It Still Possible to Be a Hegelian Today?', 209.

52. Žižek, 'Is It Still Possible to Be a Hegelian Today?', 210.

53. Žižek, 'Is It Still Possible to Be a Hegelian Today?', 210.

54. Žižek, 'Is It Still Possible to Be a Hegelian Today?', 209.

55. Moishe Postone, *Time, Labor, and Social Domination: A Reinterpretation of Marx's Critical Theory* (Cambridge and New York: Cambridge University Press, 2003), 53–54.

56. Karl Marx, *Januar 1859–Februar 1860*, Karl Marx, Friedrich Engels: Werke, 13 (Berlin: Dietz, 1972), 21.

57. Postone, *Time, Labor, and Social Domination*, 47.

58. Karl Marx, 'Über Friedrich Lists Buch *Das nationale System der politischen Ökonomie*', *Beiträge zur Geschichte der Arbeiterbewegung* 14.3 (1972): 436.

59. Postone, *Time, Labor, and Social Domination*, 48.

60. Marx, *Januar 1859–Februar 1860*, 635.

61. Alfred Sohn-Rethel, *Intellectual and Manual Labour: A Critique of Epistemology*, trans. Martin Sohn-Rethel (Atlantic Highlands, NJ: Humanities Press, 1978), 20.

62. Slavoj Žižek, *The Sublime Object of Ideology* (London and New York: Verso, 1989), 17.

63. Ernst Lohoff, 'Die Kategorie der abstrakten Arbeit und ihre historische Entfaltung', *Marxistische Kritik* 1 (1986): 51.

64. A. Stockbroker, 'What Is Speculation in Stocks?', *Wall St Journal*, 16 (October 1909): 6.

65. Mitchell, *The Speculation Economy*, x.

66. Lawrence E. Mitchell, 'Financialism: A (Very) Brief History', in *The Embedded Firm: Corporate Governance, Labor, and Finance Capitalism*, ed. Cynthia A. Williams and Peer Zumbansen (Cambridge and New York: Cambridge University Press, 2011), 42.

67. Mitchell, 'Financialism: A (Very) Brief History', 42.

68. Mitchell, 'Financialism: A (Very) Brief History', 51.

69. Mitchell, 'Financialism: A (Very) Brief History', 43.

70. Lawrence E. Mitchell, *Corporate Irresponsibility: America's Newest Export* (New Haven, CT: Yale University Press, 2001), 5.
71. Mitchell, *The Speculation Economy*, 271.
72. Mitchell, *Corporate Irresponsibility*, 153.
73. Mitchell, *Corporate Irresponsibility*, 5.
74. Mitchell, *The Speculation Economy*, 278.
75. Mitchell, 'Financialism: A (Very) Brief History', 59.
76. Mitchell, 'Financialism: A (Very) Brief History', 59.
77. Joseph Goebbels, *Der Angriff. Das kleine abc des Nationalsozialisten* (Berlin: Kampf-Verlag, 1929), 12.
78. Mitchell, *The Speculation Economy*, 269.
79. Mitchell, *The Speculation Economy*, 3–4.
80. Mitchell, *The Speculation Economy*, 104–5; the distinction comes from Edward Sherwood Meade, *Trust Finance: A Study of the Genesis, Organization, and Management of Industrial Combinations* (New York: Appleton, 1913), 115–16.
81. Costas Lapavitsas, *Profiting without Producing: How Finance Exploits Us All* (London and New York: Verso, 2014), 323.
82. Feder, *Kampf gegen die Hochfinanz*, 323.
83. Mitchell, 'Financialism: A (Very) Brief History', 59; *The Speculation Economy*, x.
84. Lapavitsas, *Profiting without Producing*, 327.
85. Lawrence Mitchell, 'Financial Speculation: The Good, the Bad and the Parasitic', *The Conversation*; http://theconversation.com/financial-speculation-the-good-the-bad-and-the-parasitic-33613 (last accessed 28 February 2017).
86. Mitchell, *Corporate Irresponsibility*, 153.
87. Lapavitsas, *Profiting without Producing*, xvi, 271.
88. Karl Marx, *Theorien über den Mehrwert*, Karl Marx, Friedrich Engels: Werke, 26 (Berlin: Dietz, 1967), 508–18; cf. Ortlieb; Robert Kurz, 'The Crisis of Exchange Value: Science as Productive Force, Productive Labor, and Capitalist Reproduction', in *Marxism and the Critique of Value*, ed. Neil Larsen et al. (Chicago and Alberta: MCM', 2014), 17–75.
89. Ernst Lohoff and Norbert Trenkle, *Die große Entwertung: warum Spekulation und Staatsverschuldung nicht die Ursache der Krise sind* (Münster: Unrast, 2012), 19, 97.
90. Lohoff and Trenkle, *Die große Entwertung*, 213–14.
91. I am grateful to Adam Kotsko for suggesting this formulation.
92. Graham Harman, 'The Assemblage Theory of Society', in *Towards Speculative Realism: Essays and Lectures* (Winchester: Zero Books, 2010), 171.
93. Indeed, what acknowledgement there has been has come from the standpoint not of a critique that seeks to overcome this mediation, but of a philosophy that seeks less to overcome than to take into account the fact that the world of capitalist decision 'constitutes the Real in its own inescapable terms'. Nick Srnicek, 'Capitalism and the Non-Philosophical Subject', in *The Speculative Turn: Continental Materialism and Realism*, ed. Levi Bryant, Nick Srnicek and Graham Harman (Melbourne: re.press, 2011), 175.

BIBLIOGRAPHY

ADORNO, Theodor W. *Negative Dialektik*. Frankfurt a.M.: Suhrkamp, 1966.

BRASSIER, Ray. 'I Am a Nihilist Because I Still Believe in Truth: Ray Brassier Interviewed by Marcin Rychter'. *Kronos*, 4 March 2011; http://web.archive.org/web/20110310062157/http://kronos.org.pl/index.php?23151,896. Last accessed 28 February 2017.

BRAVER, Lee. *A Thing of This World: A History of Continental Anti-Realism*. Evanston, IL: Northwestern University Press, 2007.

BRYANT, Levi, Nick SRNICEK and Graham HARMAN. 'Towards a Speculative Philosophy'. In *The Speculative Turn: Continental Materialism and Realism*. Edited by Levi Bryant, Nick Srnicek and Graham Harman. Melbourne: re.press, 2011. 1–18.

BRYANT, Levi. 'The Ontic Principle: Outline of an Object-Oriented Ontology'. In *The Speculative Turn: Continental Materialism and Realism*. Edited by Levi. Bryant, Nick Srnicek and Graham Harman. Melbourne: re.press, 2011. 261–78.

BURNETT, Amy Nelson. 'Luther and the *Schwärmer*'. In *The Oxford Handbook of Martin Luther's Theology*. Edited by Robert Kolb, Irene Dingel and L'ubomír Batka. Oxford: Oxford University Press, 2014. 511–24.

ENNIS, Paul J. *Continental Realism*. Winchester and Washington: Zero Books, 2011.

FEDER, Gottfried. *Kampf gegen die Hochfinanz: eine Hauptquelle zur Ideengeschichte und Frühzeit des Nationalsozialismus*. Bremen: Roland Faksimile, 2003.

GOEBBELS, Joseph. *Der Angriff. Das kleine abc des Nationalsozialisten*. Berlin: Kampf-Verlag, 1929.

GOLUMBIA, David. ' "Correlationism": The Dogma That Never Was'. *Boundary* 2.43 (2016): 1–25.

HALLWARD, Peter. 'Anything Is Possible: A Reading of Quentin Meillassoux's *After Finitude*'. In *The Speculative Turn: Continental Materialism and Realism*. Edited by Levi Bryant, Nick Srnicek and Graham Harman. Melbourne: re.press, 2011. 130–41.

HARMAN, Graham. 'The Assemblage Theory of Society'. In *Towards Speculative Realism: Essays and Lectures*. Winchester: Zero Books, 2010. 170–98.

HARMAN, Graham. 'On the Undermining of Objects: Grant, Bruno, and Radical Philosophy'. In *The Speculative Turn: Continental Materialism and Realism*. Edited by Levi Bryant, Nick Srnicek and Graham Harman. Melbourne: re.press, 2011. 21–40.

HEGEL, Georg Wilhelm Friedrich. *Briefe von und an Hegel: 1785 bis 1812*. Hamburg: Meiner, 1969.

HEGEL, Georg Wilhelm Friedrich. *Phänomenologie des Geistes*. Werke in 20 Bänden, 3. Frankfurt a.M.: Suhrkamp, 1986.

HEGEL, Georg Wilhelm Friedrich. 'Ueber den Vortrag der philosophischen Vorbereitungswissenschaften auf Gymnasien. Privatgutachten an Immanuel Niethammer vom 23. Oktober 1812'. In *Nürnberger Gymnasialkurse und Gymnasialreden (1808–1816). Beilagen und Anhang*. Edited by Klaus Grotsch. Gesammelte Werke, 10. 2 vols. Hamburg: Meiner, 2006. II, 823–32.

HEGEL, Georg Wilhelm Friedrich. *Wissenschaft der Logik*. Edited by Eva Moldenhauer. Werke in 20 Bänden, 6. Frankfurt a.M.: Suhrkamp, 1986. II.

JARVIS, Simon. 'What Is Speculative Thinking?' *Revue Internationale de Philosophie* 227.1 (2004): 69–83.

KANT, Immanuel. *Critick of Pure Reason*. Translated by Francis Haywood. London: W. Pickering, 1838.

KANT, Immanuel. *Critique de la raison pure*. Translated by Claude-Joseph Tissot. 2 vols. Paris: Librairie de Ladrange, 1835. I.

KANT, Immanuel. *Critique de la raison pure*. Translated by Jules Barni. 2 vols. Paris and London: Germer-Baillière, 1869. I.

KANT, Immanuel. *Critique de la raison pure*. Translated by A. Tremesaygues and B. Pacaud. Paris: Félix Alcan, 1905.

KANT, Immanuel. *Critique of Pure Reason*. Translated by J. M. D Meiklejohn. London: Henry G. Bohn, 1855.

KANT, Immanuel. *Critique of Pure Reason*. Translated by Norman Kemp Smith. London: Macmillan, 1929.

KANT, Immanuel. *Kritik der reinen Vernunft*. Edited by Wilhelm Weischedel. Werkausgabe in 12 Bänden, 3. 2 vols. Frankfurt a.M.: Suhrkamp, 1974. I.

KANT, Immanuel. *Kritik der reinen Vernunft*. Edited by Wilhelm Weischedel. Werkausgabe in 12 Bänden, 3. 2 vols. Frankfurt a.M.: Suhrkamp, 1992. I.

KURZ, Robert. 'The Crisis of Exchange Value: Science as Productive Force, Productive Labor, and Capitalist Reproduction'. In *Marxism and the Critique of Value*. Edited by Neil Larsen, Mathias Nilges, Josh Robinson and Nicholas Brown. Chicago and Alberta: MCM', 2014. 17–75.

LAPAVITSAS, Costas. *Profiting without Producing: How Finance Exploits Us All*. London and New York: Verso, 2014.

LATOUR, Bruno. 'Why Has Critique Run Out of Steam? From Matters of Fact to Matters of Concern'. *Critical Inquiry* 30 (2004): 225–48.

LEBRUN, Gérard. *L'envers de la dialectique: Hegel à la lumière de Nietzsche*. Edited by Paul Clavier and Francis Wolff. Paris: Seuil, 2004.

LOHOFF, Ernst. 'Die Kategorie der abstrakten Arbeit und ihre historische Entfaltung'. *Marxistische Kritik* 1 (1986): 46–69.

LOHOFF, Ernst and Norbert TRENKLE. *Die große Entwertung: warum Spekulation und Staatsverschuldung nicht die Ursache der Krise sind*. Münster: Unrast, 2012.

MARX, Karl. *Januar 1859–Februar 1860*. Karl Marx, Friedrich Engels: Werke, 13. Berlin: Dietz, 1972.

MARX, Karl. *Theorien über den Mehrwert*. Karl Marx, Friedrich Engels: Werke, 26. Berlin: Dietz, 1967.

MARX, Karl. 'Über Friedrich Lists Buch *Das nationale System der politischen Ökonomie*'. *Beiträge zur Geschichte der Arbeiterbewegung* 14 (1972): 423–46.

MEADE, Edward Sherwood. *Trust Finance: A Study of the Genesis, Organization, and Management of Industrial Combinations*. New York: Appleton, 1913.

MEILLASSOUX, Quentin. *After Finitude: An Essay on the Necessity of Contingency, with a Preface by Alain Badiou*. Translated by Ray Brassier. London and New York: Bloomsbury Academic, 2008.

MEILLASSOUX, Quentin. *Après la finitude: Essai sur la nécessité de la contingence*. Paris: Seuil, 2006.
MITCHELL, Lawrence E. *Corporate Irresponsibility: America's Newest Export*. New Haven, CT: Yale University Press, 2001.
MITCHELL, Lawrence E. 'Financialism: A (Very) Brief History'. In *The Embedded Firm: Corporate Governance, Labor, and Finance Capitalism*. Edited by Cynthia A. Williams and Peer Zumbansen. Cambridge and New York: Cambridge University Press, 2011. 42–59.
MITCHELL, Lawrence E. 'Financial Speculation: The Good, the Bad and the Parasitic'. *The Conversation*; http://theconversation.com/financial-speculation-the-good-the-bad-and-the-parasitic-33613. Last accessed 28 February 2017.
MITCHELL, Lawrence E. *The Speculation Economy: How Finance Triumphed over Industry*. San Francisco: Berrett-Koehler, 2008.
ORTLIEB, Claus Peter. 'A Contradiction between Matter and Form: On the Significance of the Production of Relative Surplus Value in the Dynamic of Terminal Crisis'. In *Marxism and the Critique of Value*. Edited by Neil Larsen, Mathias Nilges, Josh Robinson and Nicholas Brown. Chicago and Alberta: MCM', 2014: 77–121.
POSTONE, Moishe. *Time, Labor, and Social Domination: A Reinterpretation of Marx's Critical Theory*. Cambridge and New York: Cambridge University Press, 2003.
ROBINSON, Josh. 'Dialektik und Spekulation. Über die Grenzen der spekulativen Vernunft'. In *Probleme der Dialektik heute*. Edited by Stefan Müller. Wiesbaden: VS Verlag für Sozialwissenschaften, 2009. 229–46.
ROSE, Gillian. 'From Speculative to Dialectical Thinking – Hegel and Adorno'. In *Judaism and Modernity: Philosophical Essays*. Oxford and Cambridge, MA: Blackwell, 1993. 53–63.
SHAVIRO, Steven. *The Universe of Things: On Speculative Realism*. Minneapolis: University of Minnesota Press, 2014.
SMITH, Adam. *An Inquiry into the Nature and Causes of the Wealth of Nations: A Selected Edition*. Edited by Kathryn Sutherland. Oxford: Oxford University Press, 1998.
SOHN-RETHEL, Alfred. *Intellectual and Manual Labour: A Critique of Epistemology*. Translated by Martin Sohn-Rethel. Atlantic Highlands, NJ: Humanities Press, 1978.
SPARROW, Tom. *The End of Phenomenology: Metaphysics and the New Realism*. Edinburgh: Edinburgh University Press, 2014.
SRNICEK, Nick. 'Capitalism and the Non-Philosophical Subject'. In *The Speculative Turn: Continental Materialism and Realism*. Edited by Levi Bryant, Nick Srnicek and Graham Harman. Melbourne: re.press, 2011. 164–81.
STOCKBROKER, A. 'What Is Speculation in Stocks?' *Wall St Journal*, 16 October 1909: 6.
TOSCANO, Alberto. 'Against Speculation, or, a Critique of the Critique of Critique: A Remark on Quentin Meillassoux's *After Finitude* (After Colletti)'. In *The Speculative Turn: Continental Materialism and Realism*. Edited by Levi Bryant, Nick Srnicek and Graham Harman. Melbourne: re.press, 2011. 84–91.

ŽIŽEK, Slavoj. 'Is It Still Possible to Be a Hegelian Today?' In *The Speculative Turn: Continental Materialism and Realism*. Edited by Levi Bryant, Nick Srnicek and Graham Harman. Melbourne: re.press, 2011. 202–23.

ŽIŽEK, Slavoj. *The Sublime Object of Ideology*. London and New York: Verso, 1989.

ŽIŽEK, Slavoj and Ben WOODARD. 'Interview'. In *The Speculative Turn: Continental Materialism and Realism*. Edited by Levi Bryant, Nick Srnicek and Graham Harman. Melbourne: re.press, 2011. 406–15.

ZUCKERT, Rachel. 'Kant's Account of Practical Fanaticism'. In *Kant's Moral Metaphysics: God, Freedom, and Immortality*. Edited by Benjamin J. Bruxvoort Lipscomb and James Krueger. Berlin and New York: De Gruyter, 2010. 291–318.

Chapter 11

Believing in deconstruction

Laurent Milesi

> What is usually called deconstruction would not be possible if there was no money and no capital.[1]

Do you believe in deconstruction? And what does deconstruction believe (in)?

'I don't know, one has to believe' (*il faut croire*), Jacques Derrida might have responded again, as he did by way of a final answer to the returning, initial question 'Do you believe this?', *Vous croyez?* (but also 'do you (really) think so?'), in the last lines of *Memoirs of the Blind*.[2] Contemporaneous with 'Circumfession' (1989–1990), Derrida's first explicit engagement with the question of faith as well as with his own special blend of religiosity and atheism, this sustained reflection on self-portraiture adumbrated the necessity of conceiving faith as a blind faith when knowledge fails (cf. *faut*: *falloir*, i.e. necessity but also, especially if on its own, *faillir*: to fail, fall, lapse) and the subject cannot confidently fall back on any credit. But he might have responded in translation, in the impregnable singularity of another idiom, which would thus tie our experience of faith as 'simply a speech act'[3] – the believer pledges his or her belief the moment he or she utters *credo* – with issues of linguistic difference and alterity within the proper 'itself' (*idion*).

Indeed, the etymological (hence historical, genealogical as well as linguistic) determinations of what is called 'belief' cannot satisfactorily conjure up and capture the whole economic palette of the French *croire* and *croyance*, in particular their consonance with 'credit', so that 'credence' would be a more appropriate term in English to start answering what Derridean deconstruction believes that belief means. Belief in translation, therefore, in tune with Derrida's oft-repeated claim that deconstruction is indissociable from the aporetic experience of the untranslatable.[4] And at the crossroads of the experience of rethinking belief in deconstruction in translation, there would be not only faith and even fidelity (faithfulness), credit and credence (*croyance*), and trust(worthiness) (*fiabilité*), but also more generally:

1 the various Derridean inflections of a 'religion without religion', such as the messianic (messianicity without messianism), or that 'waiting without horizon of expectation' introduced towards the end of *Specters of Marx*, which characterizes the fundamental relationship to the other and to futurity-to-come (*l'avenir*),[5] as well as the reformulation of the social bond as interruptive unbinding (*déliaison*[6]);
2 the crucial link with technicity in the two 'spontaneous', 'mechanical' sources of the religious in 'Faith and Knowledge . . .';[7]
3 even the principle of 'abstraction' from an absolute God, related to the vexing relationship between various forms of negative theologies and deconstruction's own kenotics of discourse as the emptying out of any ontological, essentializing substratum.[8]

This chapter will thread its way through this nexus of densely interrelated themes in order to show how, well before the enduring current convergence between a crisis of faith and a crisis in economic belief and credit, Derridean deconstruction had not only alerted us to the common foundations and mechanisms of religion and economics but had also endeavoured to retrieve a pre-critical, aneconomic impetus at the root of the most elementary faith, unbinding it from an economics of credit in order to save the 'speculative act' from and against itself. In so doing, while paying attention to the themes outlined earlier, it will excavate several so far uncharted origins for Derrida's singularly speculative construction of 'faith' and 'belief' in order to highlight the ways in which Derridean thought attempts to gesture towards a more primordial *coup de don* stripped from a grounding in credit and (re)appropriation. This reconstruction of the generalized logic of faith and credit in Derridean deconstruction will end with a conclusion ('Money talks') which will probe the relevance of Derrida's more specific reflections on money for today's crisis. Coming full circle, like the form which Derrida ascribed to economics (see *infra*), it will offer some speculative thoughts about the renewed relation between cruelty, the crude and creed, already highlighted in the etymological cruxes of 'Circumfession', in the rise of fundamentalist terrorism and in our times of 'credit crunch'.

RAW BELIEF: BEFORE FAITH-AS-CREDIT

According to Emile Benveniste's *Vocabulaire des institutions indo-européennes*, the semantics of Latin *fides*, from which 'faith' was derived, covered the spectrum from confidence (trust: French *confiance*) to credit; the confidence A has in B matching the credit the latter has with the former but in inverse relation to that which presides over our usual notion and semantic construction of 'confidence'. Thus, *fides est mihi apud aliquem* meant literally 'I have credit [credit is to me] with somebody'; that is, somebody has confidence in me, rather than the expected 'I have confidence (faith) in somebody'. In this asymmetrical bond, the exchange hinges on the credit I have with somebody who thus invests me with/invests in me a confidence which I therefore have at my disposal, the preposition *apud* marking that possession. In French, *donner sa foi à*, literally: to give one's faith to, is what one does when one has confidence in somebody (*avoir confiance en*), whose credit therefore one has in one's trust. This prompts Benveniste to ask how one can at once give and have the same thing in this 'economic' relation, a dilemma which the semantics of *habere – fidem habere alicui*, from which the French *avoir foi en* was derived – elucidate: the Latin verb was used in several idiomatic locutions where its meaning ranged from 'to have' to 'to give' to 'to attribute'.[9] Enlisting another study of Benveniste ('Don et échange dans le vocabulaire indo-européen') in *Given Time*, his first full-length attempt to save the gift from the strictures of economics that annul it in the circle of exchange, returns, gift and countergift, debt and acknowledgement, Derrida similarly notes that the root *dö* does not properly signify 'to give' but either 'to give' or 'to take', depending on the syntactical construction.[10] Later, in 'Fidélité à plus d'un', he will recall this paradoxical gift in Lacan's borrowed formula about love as giving what one does not have, already evoked in *Given Time*.[11]

However, in Benveniste's conclusion, the history of *fides* extends well beyond its etymological kinship, as the abstract substantive of a different verb: *credo* (from which comes 'credit', or the confidence in somebody's solvency). As Antoine Meillet has shown,[12] the former linkage between *credo* and *fides* was revived in the Christian era, when *fides*, then a profane term, shifted towards the meaning of 'religious faith', and *credere*: to believe, towards that of confessing one's *fides* (and *credo* then became used as the performative symbol of apostolic faith and creed).

The first of the fifty-nine 'periods' of Derrida's semi-autobiographical 'Circumfession' not only tacitly revisits this dense etymological crux but also adds some of its own via the near-untranslatable chance felicities (cf. '*veine*') of homophony in French, in which I will therefore quote this passage alongside Geoffrey Bennington's English rendering:

> Le vocable cru, lui disputer ainsi le cru . . ., comme si je tenais à lui pour lui chercher querelle quant à ce que parler cru veut dire, comme si jusqu'au

sang je m'acharnais à lui rappeler, car il le sait, *cur confitemur Deo scienti*, ce qui nous est par le cru demandé, le faisant ainsi dans ma langue, l'autre . . ., n'ayant jamais aimé que l'impossible, le cru auquel je ne crois pas, et le mot cru laisse affluer en lui par le canal de l'oreille, une veine encore, la foi, la profession de foi ou la confession, la croyance, la crédulité, comme si je tenais à lui pour lui chercher dispute en opposant un écrit naïf, crédule, qui par quelque transfusion immédiate en appelle à la croyance du lecteur autant qu'à la mienne, depuis ce rêve en moi depuis toujours d'une autre langue, d'une langue toute crue, d'un nom à demi fluide aussi, là, comme le sang . . ., la surabondance d'une crue . . ., la cruauté surtout, encore le sang, *cruor*, *confiteor*, ce que le sang aura été pour moi, je me demande si Geoff le sait.

The crude word, fight with him in this way over what's crude . . ., as though I were attached to him so as to look for a fight over what talking crude means, as though I were trying relentlessly, to the point of bloodshed, to remind him, for he knows it, *cur confitemur Deo scienti*, of what is demanded of us by what's crude, doing so thus in my tongue, the other one . . ., having never loved anything but the impossible, the crudeness I don't believe in, and the crude word lets flow into him through the channel of the ear, another vein, faith, profession of faith or confession, belief, credulity, as though I were attached to him just to look for a quarrel by opposing a naive, credulous piece of writing which by some immediate transfusion calls on the reader's belief as much as my own, from this dream in me, since always, of another language, an entirely crude language, of a half-fluid name too, there, like blood . . ., superabundance of a flood . . ., cruelty above all, blood again, *cruor*, *confiteor*, what blood will have been for me, I wonder if Geoff knows it.[13]

Written against Geoffrey Bennington's *théologiciel* (the 'theological software' called 'Derridabase' in the French original, initialled by a G[od] – hence Augustine's '*cur confitemur Deo scienti*': why we confess to God, when he knows), the unquenchable periodic overflow (*crue*, from *croître*[14]) and meandering syntax of Derrida's circumfession leads to 'the continuous flowing of blood, absolute, absolved'. The *cru* emerges as the common spring at the origin (of the circumfession), for crudeness and belief (*croire*, past participle *cru*), (the) past (of) belief in its crude (raw) state, from which 'faith, profession of faith or confession, belief [*croyance*], credulity' are *derived* by etymological kinship. Through Derrida's impossible idiom, like the most impossible of belief (cf. 'having never loved anything but the impossible, the crude (belief) I don't believe in'), 'another language, an entirely crude language, . . . like blood', what is believed (*cru*) can be only the utmost speculative wager, violently conflated with raw cruelty uttered in the performative of a Christ-like self-sacrifice. *Hoc est enim cruor meus, confiteor*: this is my red blood, I confess, flowing in and out of (the body or corpus of) my writing – *cruor* also means the blood shed as in a cruel battle, and here the blood sacrificially spilt at circumcision – the 'veins' of which (blood and writing) course in unison by a stroke of luck (*veine*)[15] and substitute a more archaic, raw '*cruor, confiteor*' for *credo* and *fides*. As we shall see later, Derrida's opening circumfessional creed or profession of faith harbours the seeds of an *ab-solved* (i.e. etymologically, unbound) as much as absolute 'religion' whose atheological rationale is glossed in period 30, which anticipates the double source of 'religion' (*religare, relegere*) in 'Faith and Knowledge . . .' (see *infra*) and weaves a bond between religion and writing, both being bound by the sacrality of the letter, my 'graphic writing':

> almost with every letter, . . . bound [*lier*] better and better but . . . read [*lire*] less and less well over almost twenty years, like my religion about which nobody understands anything, any more than does my mother who asked other people a while ago . . . if I still believed in God . . ., but she must have known that the constancy of God in my life is called by other names, so that I quite rightly pass for an atheist, the omnipresence to me of what I call God in my absolved, absolutely private language being neither that of an eyewitness nor that of a voice . . ., nor a transcendent law or an immanent *schechina*[16]

'Circumfession' insistently beats about (*circum-*) the 'bush' of Derrida's own circumcision and turns around it incessantly in a prior act of *con-version*: 'Sa circoncision avant toute foi possible' (His circumcision before any possibility of faith), writes Hélène Cixous in *Portrait of Jacques Derrida as a Young Jewish Saint*, which wields the pen-as-scalpel to turn around and return to 'Circumfession', in a passage playing on the return of *foi* (faith) as several *fois* (times).[17] Underwriting faith (*foi*) as a covenant each time (*chaque fois*) renewed is a 'cruder' – that is, at once more raw and more cruel – sacrificial performative whose originary technicity binds as it unbinds (*ab-solves*), to which I would now like to turn.

ABSOLUTE *TEKHNÈ* AND THE TWO SOURCES OF 'RELIGION'[18]

In 'Faith and Knowledge: The Two Sources of "Religion" at the Limits of Reason Alone', Derrida's fullest meditation on the 'return of the religious' and the rise of fundamentalism in the 1990s, religion, often singled out by quotation marks in the text, is framed within the conceptual space staked out by faith and knowledge, belief and science, in the gap 'between believing one knows and knowing one believes' ('FK' § 35). Despite the difficulty of rigorously adhering to conceptual differences (e.g. 'FK' § 16) – including in a discussion of Kant, in whose German *Glaube* translates both 'faith' and 'belief' – Derrida *paradoxically* strives to prize open the linkage between faith (*foi*) and credence (*croyance*), *fides* and *credo*, by dissociating faith as the performative, testimonial experience of the 'holy' (*saint*), the 'unscathed' (*indemne*, i.e. not being damned or damaged), the 'safe and sound' ([*sain et*] *sauf*), the 'sacred', from religion as institutionalized creed ('FK' § 12, etc.), noting also that faith is not reducible to the dogma or *doxa* of a belief ('FK' § 11).[19] (About the same time, in a round-table discussion at Villanova University that was to instigate a set of three conferences centred on religion, Derrida reiterated this basic distinction, before citing Kierkegaard as an example: 'I would distinguish between religion and faith. If by religion you mean a set of beliefs, dogmas, or institutions – the church, e.g. – then I would say that religion as such can be deconstructed, sometimes in the name of faith.'[20])

Compounding in its title Kant's *Religion within the Limits of Reason Alone*, Hegel's own *Faith and Knowledge* – whose final movement, like that of the section on 'Religion' in *The Phenomenology of Spirit*, proclaims ontotheology as that 'which determines absolute knowledge as the truth of religion' (see 'FK' § 17[21]) – and Bergson's *The Two Sources of Morality and Religion*, Derrida's essay repeatedly 'bifurcates' the origin of *religio* and analyses the mechanical 'bond of repetition to itself' ('FK' § 26) between these 'two sources' – what, in 'Fidélité à plus d'un', he designates as the *retenue*, or 'the bond but also the scruple which unbinds while holding at a distance' ('F' 227; cf. also 'FK' § 20). In particular, Derrida recalls religion's two overlapping derivations or etymological sources ('FK' §§ 33–34), again following Benveniste in *Le Vocabulaire des institutions indo-européennes*, who gives '*recollecter*' as his own translation and bond between *lecture* and election, *lire* and *lier*:

- *relegere*, from *legere*: to pluck [flowers], gather [flowers into a bunch] – what reading (*legere*) also does; thus one cannot read, let alone re-read (*re-legere*), without being re-ligious, patience or even *passion* characterizing 'proper' reading for Derrida – hence 'bringing together in order to return and begin again; whence *religio*, scrupulous attention, respect, patience . . . ' (the Ciceronian filiation);
- *religare*, from *ligare*: to tie, bind – in French: *lier*, *relier* – an etymology invented by Christians, Benveniste adds, 'linking religion to the *bond* . . ., to obligation, ligament, and hence to duty, to debt etc., between men or between man and God' (Lactantius and Tertullian) ('FK' § 34; translation emended).

What facet of the religious these filiations or genealogies shed light on and what they have in common as linguistic praxes endowed with interpretative effects (rather than as foundations of the 'true' sanctified by unthought etymologism; 'FK' § 33) is, for Derrida, 'a persistent bond that bonds itself first and foremost to itself', 'a resistance or a reaction to disjunction. To ab-solute alterity' ('FK' § 34). As we shall see later, it is this iterative bond economically returning to the self that 'Faith and Knowledge. . .' wishes to unbind or *ana-lyse*, (dis)solve and 'ab-solve'. To this effect, Derrida discriminates between the experience of belief, credit, trust and the sacred, the unscathed and the auto-immune double bind of the *sauf*, then proposes the *déliaison* (unbinding, or binding without bond) as a new, looser form of social contract and community. To put it in provisional terms at this stage of my argument and taking into account Derrida's view that '[a]s soon as there is a social bond there is faith':[22] there would be in Derrida's invented ante-primal idiom or *avant-première langue*[23] a more originary *cru*, a mixture of raw belief stripped of (*sans*) credit and 'bonds', and sacrificial blood (*sang*) shed before established religion, whose ordeal and experience would testify to the precondition for any faith.

Towards the end of *Specters of Marx*, in a dense, proleptic reflection clearly awaiting to be further teased out, Derrida had already broached the possibility of thinking together in a singular configuration Religion and Technics – alongside production, hence fetishism, idealization, autonomization and automatization, but also the messianic and the eschatological, crucial for his attempt to rethink the political – and hinted at the 'return of the religious'.[24] In a section of 'Faith and Knowledge. . . ' which tacitly invites a parallel between justice and law on the one hand and faith and religion on the other, some of those technical concerns will reappear and shape the 'mystical' alliance within the religious between 'the fiduciary or the trustworthy' and foundational knowledge, between belief or credit and performativity or 'technoscientific or tele-technological performance' ('FK' § 22), when religion founds itself as religious law.[25]

If religion mediates between faith and knowledge, it is therefore caught between fidelity and technology, as Derrida's challenging analysis of the complicity between the most fundamentalist forms of religious belief and globalized media technologies, the alliance between the tele-technoscientific and the two sources of religion ('FK' § 46), also reminds us. Bernard Stiegler saw this complicity more generally as the dual articulation of deconstruction, both as 'a thinking of technics, of tele-technologies. . ., of the "media" in all its guises – beginning with the most primal traces that launch the process of hominization . . . and extending as far as the Web and all forms of technical archiving and high-fidelity [*sic*] recording, including those of the biotechnologies', and 'a thinking of *fidelity*, of fidelity to the past, of memory and of heritage – that is, fidelity in the Law. And, in this sense, a thinking of faith, of truth and religion.'[26] About Derrida's essay more specifically, he observes:

> 'Faith and Knowledge' calls upon and testifies to that which precedes science and religion qua their common possibility of believing – in the truth. The possibility of believing common to faith and knowledge is that of an initial *yes* contained in every assertion, in every word which promises.[27]

In this repetition (cf. 'FK' § 22: '*"religion" can only begin and begin again*') – which is also that of its overlapping sources ('FK' § 33) – lies the quasi-primordiality of technicity for faith according to Derrida: 'No faith . . . nor future without everything technical, automatic, machine-like supposed by iterability. In this sense, the technical is the possibility of faith, indeed its very chance' ('FK' § 38).[28]

Religion, therefore, is the response to faith and technology; indeed '"Religion is **the response**"' ('FK' § 29), that is, etymologically 'to swear – the faith' ('FK' § 31), a guarantee or promise 'in return' to a pledge or *sponsio*; religion as the automatic, machinic, spontaneous (*sponte sua*) response to an inaugural *spondeo*, therefore an iterative re(-)sponse. As Derrida adds, borrowing from Benveniste's article on '*Sponsio*':[29] '*Respondeo, responsum*, is said of the interpreters of the gods, of priests, notably of the haruspices, *giving a promise in return for the offering*, depositing a security in return for a gift' ('FK' § 21).

But if religion is the response in return for an offering or a gift, a more primordial faith waged on a belief without the possibility of credit (*croyance sans crédit*) must be sought that could be aligned with the Derridean endeavour to think a more inaccessible gift without return. While 'Faith and Knowledge. . . ' and, more indirectly, 'Circumfession' have now imposed themselves as incontrovertible signposts in Derrida's reflection on the religious, and *Given Time*, then *The Gift of Death*, as the most sustained treatments of the impossibility, yet necessity of the gift, it is in the formidable edifice of *Glas* (1974) that the vestigial traces of an *aneconomic* thinking about both must be discovered, more precisely in the splendid exegesis of the first, original moment of natural religion (before aesthetic, then revealed religion) in Hegel's tripartite philosophy of religion, pertaining to the self-giving of the luminous essence (*Lichtwesen*).[30]

COUP DE DON: THE GIFT OF BLIND FAITH

Referring to Benveniste's discussion of 'Religion' in *Le Vocabulaire des institutions indo-européennes*, 'Faith and Knowledge. . . ' recalls, in a section on the '*phenomenology of religion, religion as phenomenology*'[31] ('FK' § 8; cf. also §§ 10, 36), that the 'proper meaning' of the archaic root for 'God' (*deiwos*) is 'luminous' and 'celestial' ('FK' § 8), before conjuring up a '*Nocturnal light . . . , more and more obscure*' as a metaphor for the 'retreat', through thought, to '*a certain desert*', a 'more than *archi-originary*' 'third place' ('FK' § 20).[32] In the originary moment of Hegel's natural religion evoked by Derrida, the pure *phainesthai* or phenomenological self-giving of 'pure light' as pre-ontotheological being is said to occur 'in the night of its essence' (*die Nacht seines Wesens*). Consuming itself spontaneously and invisibly as soon as it rises, it self-sacrificially 'burns itself in the all-burning [*le brûle-tout*]' (*G* 238a) or *holocaust* (from Greek *holos* and *kaustos*, denoting '[a] sacrifice wholly consumed by fire, a whole burnt offering'[33]). The *logic* of the all-burning which characterizes the sacrifice is conveyed in economic terms, as 'the double register of its accounting, accountable calculus [*calcul comptable*]' (*G* 241a).

For Derrida, what is at stake in the 'essenceless by-play' (*wesenloses Beiherspielen*) of the self-annulling holocaust of the originary sun before it 'occidentalizes itself' (*wesen, west*) is the unthought possibility of a 'pure' (also Greek *pur*: fire) gift, the self-sacrifice, but also, concomitantly, the stricture of self-binding which initializes the (anniversary) *return*,[34] the countergift as exchange, the debt in the very moment of its self-conscious annulment, the bond, and ultimately religion's revealed truth. This spontaneous, self-sacrificial holocaust, or 'holocaust of the holocaust', describes 'the process of the gift (before exchange)' (*G* 242a) since '[t]he gift can be only a sacrifice, that is the axiom of speculative reason' (*G* 243a). Shedding a retrospective sidelight on Derrida's later reflections on the Kantian distinction between 'reflecting faith' (*reflektierender Glaube*) and 'dogmatic faith' ('FK' § 15), *Glas* exhumes the aneconomic spending always already at work at the dawn of consciousness and subjectivity before so-called 'revealed religion'. It articulates the religious-cum-economic determinations of 'speculation' and attempts to point to a prior performative act called the *coup de don*, after Stéphane Mallarmé's famous *coup de dés* (dice throw) randomly cast by thought:[35]

> This reflection (in both senses of the word) of the holocaust engages history, the dialectic of sense, ontology, the speculative. The speculative is the reflection [*speculum*] of the holocaust's holocaust. . . . The dialectic of religion,

> the history of philosophy (etc.), produces itself as the reflection-effect of a *coup de don* [the gift's blow, stroke, time, etc.] as/in holocaust. (*G* 242a)

All speculation is always already a derived by-product whereby thought attempts to calculate and capitalize on the chances of its returns. Similarly, the gift cannot exist without knowledge (*connaissance*) and acknowledgement (*reconnaissance*), therefore without immediately being reinscribed within the space of the debt, (re)appropriation and accountability. It thus annuls itself as it 'contracts' into the *annulus* of circular returns (*G* 243a, 244a),[36] the odyssey of the circle being the narrative and movement of economics par excellence for Derrida.[37]

During a round-table discussion on the gift at the Villanova conference on 'Religion and Postmodernism' (1997), Derrida's take on the impossibility, yet necessity of the pure gift opposed him to Jean-Luc Marion's 'phenomenological' emphasis on originary (Husserlian) *Gegebenheit* in their approach to faith. Against the givenness of faith for Marion, Derrida proposed to think faith as aporetically as the (im)possibility of the gift, the gift of faith whose thinking can begin only with the attempt to think the possibility of their impossibility, and which, unlike the being-given, does not exist and appear as such.[38]

Returning to the demarcation between faith and religion in 'Fidélité à plus d'un', Derrida implicitly aligns faith with the gift: 'Maybe there is "religion" . . . at the moment when this supposition of knowledge is produced . . ., at the moment of the *determination* of the gift, and therefore of the appropriation of the gift by such and such a doxic or dogmatic institution of faith' ('F' 238). Swearing faith, that is, answering 'yes' to blind belief through a performative act (*credo*), offers the glimpse of a gift. Conversely, once faith as belief (*croire*) is waged on *credit*, it is *de facto* inscribed within a (re)appropriative, fiduciary economy, including in institutionalized forms of (revealed) religion: 'What one calls credit in capitalism, in economics, has to do with faith, and the economists know that. But this faith is not or should not be reduced or defined by religion as such.'[39]

In *H. C. for Life, That Is to Say. . .*, the first of two book-length tributes to Hélène Cixous, Derrida returns to the various forms and strengths of the singular, yet equivocal French verb *croire* – to believe something, what somebody tells me, to believe *in* somebody's word, which 'has to do with the act of faith in the given word'; among iterative phatic phrases like 'I believe', 'believe me' and so on – and tests its 'metal' (the book frequently speaks jointly of alliances and alloys[40]) against the subjunctive mood 'would that I might believe. . . ', 'which seems to play between the possible and the impossible' (*HC* 3), when our powers of belief are indeed tested to the limits of (in)credulity.[41] In keeping with 'vintage deconstruction' and its generalizable structure of reversal,

> [a]bsolute belief is only truly itself . . . where it does not believe only what is possible, and where it is possible to believe. . . . To believe when it is possible and measurable only by the yardstick of the possible, is not yet to believe. If one hears the full might of meaning this word has, to believe should then lie and only reside in this impossible faith in the impossible. Then one could believe only in miracles. And to believe *would* be the miracle, the magical power of the miracle. The miracle would be the ordinary of belief. (*HC* 4)

Therefore, '[t]he only possibility of faith is in the *epoché*',[42] the absolute suspension of belief – or perhaps Coleridge's 'willing suspension of disbelief'.[43] If deconstruction, as Derrida often maintains, is 'an experience of the impossible', of the aporetic possibility of the impossible qua possible,[44] 'belief in deconstruction' begins only when it is impossible to believe, to lend fiduciary trust to something or someone, when one must take a speculative leap of faith without the promised certainty of speculation yielding a return or credit. Only on this structural precondition can belief be(come) a 'pure' performative event and act of faith (rather than institutionalized 'articles of faith'; 'FK' § 47), an advent of the radically unanticipatable future-to-come (*avenir*) and messianic guise of the *arrivant*, as much as an invention (of the truth or of the other).

Their very aporia and impossibility is the condition under which one can begin to think both the gift and a faith stripped from credit: the gift begins with the impossibility of giving without receiving in exchange, and faith when one is called upon to believe and trust in the impossible without the safe return of a credible and creditable knowledge. Derrida explicitly made the parallel on several occasions, especially in 'Fidélité à plus d'un' ('F' 237, 238): commensurate with the incommensurable gift is the act of faith 'which renounces trying to know whether there has been a gift. The gift forever belongs to the order of faith, it opens the order of faith, of a law irreducible to any knowledge'. In this movement from economics to aneconomics, or back to an originary aneconomics, what is at stake is the liberation or 'abs-traction' of the gift and faith from what, in a different context, the essay 'Speculate – On Freud' called 'bindinal economy':[45] the economy of the tie, of the bond, whether in *religio* or a *socius*, denoting a shared idiom and a community (cf. 'FK' § 47). This 'abs-traction' or unbinding (*déliaison*) is articulated to a dual operation in 'Faith and Knowledge. . . ': that of the ambidextrous *sauf*, which defines the paradoxical logic of auto-immunity and is introduced into community (as 'auto-co-immunity'; 'FK' § 40) in order to deconstruct its common, shared assumptions and premises, and the particle *sans*, first explored in the earlier writings on Maurice Blanchot gathered in *Parages*, which I will now briefly analyse.[46]

SANS: UNBINDING 'FAITH' FROM FAITH, OR THE INTERRUPTION OF RELIGION

Unbinding faith and religion from their concrete anchoring in a historical, revealed figure (Messiah), having faith and believing even when there is nothing or nobody to believe in yet, when it is said to be impossible to believe ('I cannot believe this'), Derrida wishes not only to withdraw 'religion' from religion, uprooting its institutionalized constructs and tangled sources, or even faith from religion, as we saw, but also to wrench a more radical faith from faith-as-invested trust or *confiance*, to abs-tract or ab-solve faith from any residual economics of common credit and solvency. Before the *con-fiance* (con-fidence: trust) of the social pact as bond of *Mitsein* waged on credit or credence, there would be, in Derrida's invented, ante-primal idiom, an as-yet underived *fiance*.

The nonce word *fiance*, for which I risked the translation 'fiding' in *H. C. for Life, That Is to Say. . .* – *HC* 125: 'an act of faith in fiding', required when belief has to be at its strongest[47] – comes before any (dis)trust, positive *confiance* or negative *méfiance*,[48] just as there is always already a more originary, performative, iterative 'yes (yes)' prior to any (affirmative or negative) response and responsibility.[49] It spontaneously springs at the root of the chain belief-trust(worthiness) – *fiabilité* – fidelity-fiduciary-faith ('FK' § 29; also § 47) and could operate as the *ur*-matrix for a new alliance or covenant: another, looser, auto-(co-)immune social nexus.

In their introduction to *God, the Gift, and Postmodernism*, Caputo and Scanlon note that

> in Derrida we encounter the kenotics of faith, of a groping blindness, like a blind man feeling his way with a stick or a stylus, 'writing in the dark'. The mistake would be to treat this blindness, as do deconstruction's critics, as so much nihilism and despair, instead of seeing there exactly the opposite, a work of faith, of hope, and desire for a future to come.[50]

Rather than the spontaneous occidentalization which precipitated the originary gift of luminous essence of the religious towards subjectivity in Hegel's *Phenomenology* (cf. *G* 239a), we are witnessing here a new 'orientation' (from *oriri*, hence 'origin'; cf. 'FK' §§ 9, 10, 20, 36), which would be found in a raw alliance, a new fiduciary bond severing the communal tie, one so precarious and fragile that the endeavour to think it through is compared to wandering in a desert or retreating to a nocturnal light.

The contaminative principle of auto-immune auto-indemnification at the heart of religion-as-gathering is similarly at work within society and what is called a 'community', hence Derrida's coinage '*auto-co-immunity*': 'Nothing in *common*, nothing immune, safe and sound, *heilig* and holy, nothing unscathed in the most autonomous living present without a risk of auto-immunity' ('FK' § 37). Derrida's 'religion', the religious without religion or faith without fiduciarity, would therefore aim to be a performative *credo* without credit, an originary binding without bond (*déliaison*) that would make possible the (belief in) gathering together without/before a community or sociality that erases subjectivities in the name of promised collectivity. Just as *fiance* endeavours to think through the fiduciary without (*sans*) the bond of a *con-*, the social bond (*nexus* or *desmos*) should be rethought as dis-sociation and interruption,[51] and society as a loose 'collection' of *plus d'un*:

> [*Another 'tolerance'*] . . . *would respect the distance of infinite alterity as singularity. And this respect would still be* religio . . . *as* . . . *reticence, distance, dissociation, disjunction, coming from the threshold of all religion in the* bond of repetition to itself, *the threshold of every social or communitarian bond.* ('FK' § 25)

> There [in the dimension of the promise each time I speak to the other], before all religion, we are in the order of faith, the one which constitutes social bond in general, simultaneously . . . as being-with and as un-binding, relation without relation. ('F' 264; insertion mine)[52]

In Caputo's words, Derrida wishes for a 'universal, transnational . . ., purely rational religion, by proposing a certain desertification of religion, but without . . . excluding faith' – abstracting it from place and localisms while remaining faithful to the sacrality of the (bound) letter in translation: 'Religion as a universal messianicity despoiled of all messianism, as a faith without dogma advancing in the risk of absolute night'.[53]

DECONSTRUCTING SPECULATION IN TIMES OF CRISIS

I recalled from the outset that, in 'Fidélité à plus d'un', Derrida remarked once more that deconstruction has always been linked to the question of the untranslatable ('F' 253), therefore bound up with the singularity of an idiom ('F' 221) – which for him dictates two fidelities: respecting the irreducible untranslatability of the idiom while apprehending it otherwise, as a provocation, a test from the call to translate, an engagement to translate within the experience of the untranslatable ('F' 224). Indeed, no such radical uprooting of tradition, no such long-suffering crossing of the desert which the 'miracle of translation' promises,[54] would be conceivable without this singular reinvention of the *tout autre* but also of language, from the innermost conviction of an insuperable, radical alterity within one's 'own' language as the language of the other: the remaining, habitable singularity of the *mono-* even in the *plus d'une langue* of deconstruction.[55] For Derrida, the idiom 'inscribes a distance within itself' which 'conditions its irreducible economy in a language at the same time as it announces, without waiting . . ., the work of translatability.' It is this expropriation from/within itself which aligns it with the problematic of *déliaison* as the attempt to free singularities from their subjugation within the communal: 'One could then say about the idiom itself what was said about social binding or unbinding' ('F' 224).

In rethinking and 'translating' religion, faith and belief, Derridean deconstruction performs, as it usually does, a 'retreat' ('FK' § 20) to the 'pre-critical' state of what remains unthought or needs undoing by thought. If, as Heidegger provocatively stated at the beginning of *What Is Called Thinking?*, we are not yet capable of thinking and must still learn to do so,[56] for Derrida a similar injunction could apply to what is called 'speculation', let alone in times of the crisis of capitalism.[57] In this respect, we should bear in mind that Derridean deconstruction is, among other things, an attempt to demarcate itself from philosophies of 'reflection' (as well as self-reflexivity), to retreat 'before' specular reflexivity,[58] which takes the same form as, and runs parallel to, his critique of the reappropriative circularity of economics, the law (*nomos*) that circuitously brings everything back home (*oikos*), to the self and to the proper. If 'speculation' is to be saved from and against itself for Derrida, it is as 'pure' or 'blind', aneconomic speculation, which, like the risk of thought in Mallarmé's *coup de dés*, would entail thinking while sacrificing the hope of a return. 'Thinking blind', without the implication of egological self-reflection in a mirror (*speculum*), before the 'critical'[59] moment of enlightenment and decision making, requiring a blind faith.[60]

In removing the economic foundations of credence and the shared communality of trust (*confiance*), Derrida's belief without belief-as-credit is not an apocalyptic move symptomatic of our times of enduring crisis and vacillating faith; rather, paradoxically as it may seem, it is an affirmative gesture pointing to a possible hope for the future while restoring a more archaic, pre-critical covenant of faith.

CONCLUSION: 'MONEY TALKS'

As early as an interview for *La Quinzaine littéraire* published in August 1983, in which he had already hinted at the 'return of the religious', Derrida was asked what his thoughts were about 'the idea that the present world is in crisis'.[61] Emphasizing first the impossibility to do justice to such a complex question, let alone so economically ('in two pages'), Derrida then dwelt, in the second of his six 'times', on the unavailability of 'a *principle of response*, a discourse sure enough of its legitimacy (foundation, axiomatics, certitude, or truth) that it could authorize the *response in principle*' ('EC' 69). The next four replies or 'economies' focused, *inter alia*, on the enduring, predominantly Western, 'modern' notion of crisis, including its own very crisis throughout twentieth-century thought (Valéry, Husserl), as well as on the 'provisional, accidental, unintelligible' essence of crisis.

Underlying Derrida's thinking and circumspect response was what I would designate as a principle of incalculability ('unintelligible') that chimes with the end of 'Faith and Knowledge. . . ' ('FK' § 50) and must be envisaged alongside deconstruction's emphasis on the chance operations of *différance* and on an aneconomics of expenditure. Such a principle of chance, *différance* (which implies both temporization and temporalization[62]) and incalculability – the necessity, as it were, to take incalculability into account – precisely affect what is called 'money' (possibly derived from Latin *monere*: to warn, remind), and the failure to understand or factor in this radical principle and dynamics of uncertainty and indeterminacy is arguably conducive to what is termed a (financial as much as fiduciary) 'crisis'.

In November 2001, under the joint auspices of the Collège international de philosophie and the Institut CDC pour la recherche, de la Caisse des dépôts et consignations (the national French savings and banking institution which manages National Savings Bank funds and local community funds), a conference gathered philosophers, economists, anthropologists and psychanalysts around the theme of money. Grouped under the heading 'The Spirit of Money' (*L'esprit de l'argent*), Derrida's little-known exchanges with Christian Arnsperger, Egidius Berns, Simon Critchley, Marcel Drach and Jean-Joseph Goux developed four main interrelated motifs in response to four series of questions: money as sign and *fait de langage*; belief; justice; the incalculable.[63] I would like to return to this nexus of themes and later extend its relevance to our paradoxical times of crisis in belief as well as of religious fundamentalism.

In 'On the "Priceless", or the "Going Rate" of the Transaction' (1991), first given as a talk in a session on 'the spirit of the market', Derrida had already developed the equation between monetary and linguistic signs, giving substance to an association which he had already made in the 'Différance' essay:

> There is nothing fortuitous, in fact, about our having so often used the model of tender [*du numéraire*] and of monetary sign to analyze the functioning of language – or of a system of signs in general.

> . . . money's belonging to the illimitable order of language or inscription – of the mark – is precisely that which overflows monetary calculation or economic objectivity. Money drags this calculation toward infinity or toward the incalculable, toward the abyss of a speculation that is no longer strictly that of the stock exchange or contained within the institutions of economic transactions.[64]

In his preamble and first question during the exchange with Derrida on money, Jean-Joseph Goux recalls the conceptual and epochal convergence between the deconstructive critique of the (structuralist) sign and the logic as well as practice of the monetary sign, both tending towards inconvertibility.[65] As soon as a sign is deemed to be referential and differential – and money, like language with which it shares a symbolic nomenclature, circulates as such a sign – something called 'credit' or 'public faith'[66] sets in a principle of belief (even before the historical advent of money's fiduciary dimension) whose non-stabilizable volatility undermines what would be its purely material economic value. Thus, the question of money cannot be conceived without a process of idealization,[67] and '[a]s soon as there is monetary sign . . . that is, differance and credit, the *oikos* [of eco-nomics] is opened and cannot dominate its limit'.[68] This is why Derridean deconstruction cannot rest content with economic calculability, with the restricted space of an *oikos*, to which it opposes a more generalizable speculative aneconomics whose incalculable 'standard' would be the undetermined place of a gift-without-return. The 'spirit of money' radically compromises the possibility of any autonomous theory of money since the endless circulation of the monetary sign, waged on an unfathomable belief, forever defers encounter with the Husserlian illusion of the 'thing itself'. Not unlike Freudian analysis, whose mantra 'Where the id was, there shall I be' (*Wo Es war, soll ich werden*) aims to record the impossibility to arrive at a stable transaction within the subject-as-being, speculation becomes interminable. What further exceeds calculability in intersubjective exchanges is the priceless price or worth (Kant's *Würde* or *Würdigkeit*) of the other, to whom one responds and in whom one must believe unreservedly: being as the ultimate 'resource' of general equivalence.[69] The calculability of money stems from an originary, equivocal incalculability and returns to it (rather than guarantees returns waged on fixed values). The price without (market) price, or pricelessness, is that of the relationship to the absolute other, whose other name is an incalculable, unconditional justice (*dikè*) based on interruption and dissociation. At its paradoxical core lies the invaluable value of the other, the pricelessness of Kantian *Würde* or dignity beyond calculation which sets in motion the movement of speculation and is opposed to the pricing of commodities as well as to the sovereign authority of whoever has power to decide on the worth of a currency. Therein lies also the mystical 'sprit of money':

> Money as *spirit* of the market would be what, in the market and even in exchange in general, is *either* no longer a matter of economics in a strict sense of a restricted economy and no longer reducible to the circumscribable field of a theory, as objective, material, technically masterable calculability, *or else* what, without exceeding economics in general, would overflow the strict and cold monetary accounting of material interests, of exchanges, or of the production of useful goods.[70]

What at once guarantees and threatens money-as-sign is its nature as a 'symbol', a pact or contract binding two (or more) parties. Yet, as Derrida explains, for money to work in economic transactions, it has to rest on the ultimately intangible, immaterial, consensual credit which a community accords it. When credit wanes and a crisis of belief sets in – or when money is counterfeited – the groundlessness of its 'authority' is revealed as that of a simulacrum.[71]

In what may seem like a bold – or, indeed, highly speculative – conclusive gambit, one perhaps requiring a blind leap of faith, I would like to hazard a connection between the groundlessness of money thus laid bare and the deconstruction of 'foundations', in 'religion' but also in law-as-justice (versus justice *à venir*),[72] as what '*founds in foundering, wherever it steals away under the ground of what it founds*' ('FK' § 22), which in 'Faith and Knowledge. . .' Derrida analyses in relation to a generalizable notion of the rise of 'fundamentalisms' ('FK' §§ 5, 28) in the so-called return of the religious.

Reared on disregard for the pricelessness of human dignity, 'fundamentalism' harbours no doubts about its own *grounds*: those of the pure, archaic, orthodox foundations it wants to restore as well as the fanatical grounds for exterminating, in the name of its one-sided divine justice, whoever would oppose its creed. It raises the issue of another meaning of 'blind faith', in the name of whose *credo* cruelty is perpetrated and raw blood crudely shed as the price to pay for refusing to be bound to somebody's fundamental beliefs. Although Derrida's meditation early in 'Circumfession', recalled at the beginning of this chapter, predates the contemporaneous context of the 'return of the religious' in 'Faith and Knowledge. . .', the chance etymological double vein of French *cru*, both 'believed' and 'raw'/'crude', returns to haunt us here as we piece together what binds the economic crisis in fiduciarity to a spiritual crisis, and the increasingly felt precariousness of safe financial returns to the threatening payload of the 'return of the religious'. When our assumed belief in the material foundations of intangible money melts away, we all become doubting Thomases longing for some quasi-sensorial proof of its indestructible relation to the infungible thing-in-itself. A painstakingly patient study would be needed to uncover what secret ties might be holding together the erosion or ruination of (Western) trust inaugurated by the 'credit crunch' and the phenomenal upsurge of (especially Islamic) radicalism in the first decade of the twenty-first century. Signs of the times, and an infinite regressive semiosis of the invaluable and the incredible...

NOTES

1. Jacques Derrida, in *L'argent. Croyance, mesure, spéculation*, ed. Marcel Drach (Paris: La Découverte, 2004), 228; translation mine.

2. Jacques Derrida, *Memoirs of the Blind: The Self-Portrait and Other Ruins*, trans. Pascale-Anne Brault and Michael Naas (Chicago and London: University of Chicago Press, 1991), 1, 129. More generally this text deals with what happens (to belief) if power and knowledge, when conferred by the senses, fail. The decision to remove the direct object of the question of belief ('this') in the return of the question is addressed in the two translators' staged dialogue entitled 'To Believe: An Intransitive Verb? Translating Scepticism in Jacques Derrida's *Memoirs of the Blind*', *Paragraph* 20.2 (1997): 101–19.

3. John D. Caputo, Kevin Hart and Yvonne Sherwood, 'Epoché and Faith: An Interview with Jacques Derrida', transcribed by Brooke Cameron and Kevin Hart, in *Derrida and Religion: Other Testaments*, ed. Yvonne Sherwood and Kevin Hart (London: Routledge, 2005), 45.

4. See, for instance, 'Fidélité à plus d'un. - mériter d'hériter où la généalogie fait défaut', *Cahiers Intersignes* no 13: 'Idiomes, nationalités, déconstructions. Rencontre de Rabat avec Jacques Derrida' (Paris/Casablanca: Intersignes/Toubkal, 1998), 253; hereafter 'F' with page references in the text and in my own translation. This crucial 'motif' of deconstruction was first broached in 'Des tours de Babel' (1980), trans. Joseph F. Graham, in *Psyche: Inventions of the Other, Volume I*, ed. Peggy Kamuf and Elizabeth Rottenberg (Stanford, CA: Stanford University Press, 2007), 191–225.

5. Jacques Derrida, *Specters of Marx: The State of the Debt, the Work of Mourning, and the New International*, trans. Peggy Kamuf, intr. Bernd Magnus and Stephen Cullenberg (London: Routledge, 1994), 168. See also 'F' 246. For an excellent collection of essays on Derridean messianicity, see *The Politics to Come: Power, Modernity and the Messianic*, ed. Arthur Bradley and Paul Fletcher (London: Continuum, 2010).

6. The term first appeared more casually in *Glas* (1974) – trans. John P. Leavey, Jr., and Richard Rand (Lincoln, NE and London: University of Nebraska Press, 1986), 98b – and *La Vérité en peinture* (Paris: Flammarion, 1978), 389;

translated as 'unboundness' in *The Truth in Painting*, trans. Geoff Bennington and Ian McLeod (Chicago and London: University of Chicago Press, 1987), 341 – before being increasingly thematized in numerous texts as the interruption of a bond. See also *Adieu à Emmanuel Levinas* (Paris: Galilée, 1997), 127: 'la déliaison de ce « sans »'; compare with *Adieu to Emmanuel Levinas*, trans. Pascale-Anne Brault and Michael Naas (Stanford, CA: Stanford University Press, 1999), 70: 'unbinding'.

7. Jacques Derrida, 'Faith and Knowledge: The Two Sources of "Religion" at the Limits of Reason Alone', trans. Samuel Weber, in *Acts of Religion*, ed. and intr. Gil Anidjar (New York and London: Routledge, 2002), 42–101; hereafter 'FK' with section references in the text. I have subsequently silently substituted 'bond' for 'link' in Weber's translation for reasons of linguistic and thematic consistency whenever necessary.

8. See, for instance, 'How to Avoid Speaking: Denials', trans. Ken Frieden and Elizabeth Rottenberg, in *Psyche: Inventions of the Other, Volume II*, ed. Peggy Kamuf and Elizabeth Rottenberg (Stanford, CA: Stanford University Press, 2008), 143–95, and the three 1993 essays gathered as *On the Name*, ed. Thomas Dutoit, trans. David Wood et al. (Stanford, CA: Stanford University Press, 1995).

9. Emile Benveniste, *Le Vocabulaire des institutions indo-européennes*, vol. 1. Economie, parenté, société, chap. 8: 'La fidélité personnelle' (Paris: Minuit, 1969), 115 ff.

10. Jacques Derrida, *Given Time: I. Counterfeit Money*, trans. Peggy Kamuf (Chicago and London: University of Chicago Press, 1992), 78–79.

11. 'F' 236–37, and Derrida, *Given Time*, 2.

12. See Benveniste's footnote in *Le Vocabulaire des institutions indo-européennes*, 120, referring to Antoine Meillet's pioneering work published in the *Mémoires de la Société de Linguistique de Paris* in 1922.

13. Jacques Derrida, 'Circonfession', in *Jacques Derrida*, ed. Geoffrey Bennington and Jacques Derrida (Paris: Seuil, 1991), 7–8; Jacques Derrida, 'Circumfession', trans. Geoffrey Bennington, in *Jacques Derrida*, ed. Geoffrey Bennington and Jacques Derrida (Chicago and London: University of Chicago Press, 1993), 3–4, 6.

14. For a more explicit instance of the play on *croire* and *croître*, see Jacques Derrida and Elisabeth Roudinesco, *For What Tomorrow. . . : A Dialogue*, trans. Jeff Fort (Stanford, CA: Stanford University Press, 2004), 44.

15. Cf. also 'la veine de ce mot' in 'Circonfession', 18, period 3. The 'vein' receives a similar chance polysemic treatment in *H. C. for Life, That Is to Say. . .*, trans., with additional notes, by Laurent Milesi and Stefan Herbrechter (Stanford, CA: Stanford University Press, 2006), 39; hereafter *HC* with page references in the text.

16. Derrida, 'Circumfession', 154–55; French insertions mine.

17. Hélène Cixous, *Portrait of Jacques Derrida as a Young Jewish Saint*, trans. Beverley Bie Brahic (New York: Columbia University Press, 2004), 82. In *H. C. for Life, That Is to Say. . .*, Derrida had already praised Cixous's writing thus: 'The event, and the poetics of the event we are attempting to think here, can only happen at this price: faith yet each time renewed [*la foi chaque fois toutefois*]' (95).

18. Michael Naas's comprehensive study, *Miracle and Machine: Jacques Derrida and the Two Sources of Religion, Science, and the Media* (New York: Fordham University Press, 2012), has made it difficult to add new interpretative angles to Derrida's landmark intervention; yet it is hoped that, from this point onwards, the argumentative trajectory of the present study will manage to do so. For another detailed analysis of Derrida's essay, see John D. Caputo, *The Prayers and Tears of Jacques Derrida: Religion without Religion* (Bloomington and Indianapolis: Indiana University Press, 1997), 151–59, § 11. A forthcoming collection of essays on Derrida's 'Faith and Knowledge. . .', based on the One-Day Workshop at the University of Nottingham in June 2015 and co-edited by Agata Bielik-Robson and Arthur Bradley, will be published in the 'Futures of the Archive: Theory, Criticism, Crisis' series at Rowman & Littlefield International.

19. This goes against Hart's strange reading of an alignment of faith ('testimonary credence') with belief (*croyance*) rather than with the more literally expected *foi* of the title in Derrida's text. See Kevin Hart, '"Absolute Interruption": On Faith', in *Questioning God*, ed. John D. Caputo, Mark Dooley and Michael J. Scanlon (Bloomington and Indianapolis: Indiana University Press, 2001), 188, 191.

20. *Deconstruction in a Nutshell: A Conversation with Jacques Derrida*, ed. John D. Caputo (New York: Fordham University Press, 1997), 21. Those three conferences were on 'Religion and Postmodernism', in 1997 (published as *God, the Gift, and Postmodernism*, 1999) and in 1999 (*Questioning God*, 2001), as well as a third event on 'Circumfession' and Augustine's *Confessions* in 2001 (published as *Augustine and Postmodernism: Confessions and Circumfession*, 2005).

21. Derrida further comments: 'Distinct from faith, from prayer or from sacrifice, ontotheology destroys religion, but, yet another paradox, it is also perhaps what informs, on the contrary, the theological and ecclesiastical, even religious, development of faith' ('FK' § 18).

22. Caputo et al., 'Epoché and Faith', 45.

23. Translated as 'prior-to-the-first' in Jacques Derrida, *Monolingualism of the Other; or, The Prosthesis of Origin*, trans. Patrick Mensah (Stanford, CA: Stanford University Press, 1998), 61, 62, 64, 65.

24. Derrida, *Specters of Marx*, 166–67.

25. See Jacques Derrida, 'Force of Law: The "Mystical Foundation of Authority"', ed. Anidjar, trans. Mary Quaintance, in *Acts of Religion*, 230–98. Of particular relevance for our argument is the following: 'The word *credit* carries all the weight of the proposition and justifies the allusion to the mystical character of authority. The authority of laws rests only on the credit that is granted them. One believes in it; that is their only foundation. This act of faith is not an ontological or rational foundation. Still one has yet to think what *believing* means' (240).

26. Bernard Stiegler, 'Derrida and Technology: Fidelity at the Limits of Deconstruction and the Prosthesis of Faith', in *Jacques Derrida and the Humanities: A Critical Reader*, ed. Tom Cohen (Cambridge: Cambridge University Press, 2001), 239, and 257: 'The question of passive synthesis is immediately that of the trustworthiness of the message and of the messenger, of news and media, of belief

and credit – a question . . . of fiduciary capital, of tele-technologies, of faith and incarnation.'

27. Stiegler, 'Derrida and Technology', 257.

28. This statement is echoed by Stiegler's '*Technics is the condition as much of science and knowledge as of religious faith*' ('Derrida and Technology', 259). For a similar view of the technical as the very condition of fidelity and of the very relation between religion and technology as itself originarily technical, see Arthur Bradley, 'The Letter Giveth', in *Mind Factory*, ed. Louis Armand (Prague: Litteraria Pragensia, 2005), 114–15.

29. Benveniste, *Le Vocabulaire des institutions indo-européennes*, vol. 2. Pouvoir, Droit, Religion (Paris: Minuit, 1969), 215.

30. See Jacques Derrida, *Glas*, trans. John P. Leavey, Jr. and Richard Rand (Lincoln, NE and London: University of Nebraska Press, 1986), 237a–44a; hereafter *G* with page and column references in the text.

31. Let us also recall that 'phenomenology' etymologically means 'the science of what appears in the light (*phos*)'.

32. I shall briefly return to the relation between this desert and the experience of translation in a later section of this chapter. For an account of the desert (within the desert) as a third place related to Plato's *khora* and the messianic in 'Faith and Knowledge. . . ' as well as in Derrida's earlier texts, see also my 'Thinking (through) the Desert (la pensée du désert) with(in) Jacques Derrida', in *The Politics of Deconstruction: Jacques Derrida and the Other of Philosophy*, ed. Martin McQuillan (London and Ann Arbor, MI: Pluto Press, 2007), 173–91.

33. *The Oxford English Dictionary*, 2nd ed. on CD-ROM (v. 4.0.0.2) (Oxford: Oxford University Press, 2009), s. v. 'holocaust, *n.*, 1. Let us note in passing that Derrida avails himself of a translinguistic pun on German *Opfer*: sacrifice, and French *s'offrir* in his rendering of the phenomenological problematic of self-giving as self-sacrificing in this primal scene of Hegel's *Phenomenology* ('*gibt sich dem Fürsichsein zum Opfer*': 's'offre en holocauste au pour-soi'; *Glas* [Paris: Galilée, 1974], 268a).

34. The analysis of the *annulus* or circular *return* of any anniversary *date* (from Latin *datum*: given), inaugurated in *Glas* (see especially 244a), is continued in, for example, 'Shibboleth: For Paul Celan', trans. Joshua Wilner, rev. Thomas Dutoit, in *Sovereignties in Question: The Poetics of Paul Celan*, ed. Thomas Dutoit and Outi Pasanen (New York: Fordham University Press, 2005), 1–64.

35. See Stéphane Mallarmé, 'Un coup de dés jamais n'abolira le hasard', in *Collected Poems and Other Verse*, trans. with notes by E. H. and A. M. Blackmore, intr. Elizabeth McCombie (Oxford: Oxford University Press, 2006), 139–59 (161–82 for the English translation, which ends: 'Every Thought Emits a Dice Throw').

36. This annular movement is also the constitution of the *Selbst*, which 're-stricts the general economy . . . into a circulating economy' (*G* 244a) – whose first formulation can be found in the essay in *Writing and Difference* pitching Georges Bataille's generalizable aneconomics against the restricted economy of Hegel's speculative dialectics. See Jacques Derrida, 'From Restricted to General

Economy: A Hegelianism without Reserve', in *Writing and Difference*, trans., with an introduction and additional notes, by Alan Bass (London: Routledge, 2001 [1978]), 317–50. For an attempt to trace Derrida's différance to Bataille's 'systemic expenditure' and other conceptualizations of effects of temporality in relation to concepts of money and economy in the 1930s and 1940s, see Nadja Gernalzick, 'From Classical Dichotomy to Differantial Contract: The Derridean Integration of Monetary Theory', in *Metaphors of Economy*, ed. Nicole Bracker and Stefan Herbrechter (Amsterdam and New York: Rodopi, 2005), 55–67.

37. See Derrida, *Given Time*, 24, 101, and also 7, about the analogy between the law of economy and the Hegelian dialectic of Absolute Knowledge: 'The being-next-to-self of the Idea in Absolute Knowledge would be odyssean in this sense, that of an economy and a nostalgia, a "homesickness," a provisional exile longing for reappropriation.'

38. See 'On the Gift: A Discussion between Jacques Derrida and Jean-Luc Marion, Moderated by Richard Kearney', *God, the Gift, and Postmodernism*, ed. John D. Caputo and Michael J. Scanlon (Bloomington and Indianapolis: Indiana University Press, 1999), 54–78 (especially 59). For an excellent development on Marion's 'heterology of donation' and how his misconstruction of Derrida's position on the gift relates to his alignment of deconstruction with the *via negativa*, see Hent de Vries, *Philosophy and the Turn to Religion* (Baltimore and London: Johns Hopkins University Press, 1999), especially 53–54, 79–80.

39. 'The Villanova Roundtable: A Conversation with Jacques Derrida', in *Deconstruction in a Nutshell*, ed. Caputo, 23.

40. Like money, words can be 'coined' or 'minted', and (in French) *de bon aloi*, that is, of the right kind and proportion of alloy, 'sterling'.

41. Compare with Mark 9:24: 'I believe; help thou mine unbelief' (*KJV*).

42. Caputo et al., 'Epoché and Faith', 47, and also 30–31.

43. Compare with Derrida, *The Gift of Death*, 115: 'The irreducible experience of belief, between credit and faith, the *believing* suspended between the credit [*créance*] of the creditor ([*créancier*] *Gläubiger*) and the credence ([*croyance*] *Glauben*) of the believer [*croyant*].'

44. See, for example, Jacques Derrida, 'Psyche: Invention of the Other', trans. Catherine Porter, in *Psyche: Inventions of the Other, Volume I*, ed. Kamuf and Rottenberg, 15; *Aporias*, trans. Thomas Dutoit (Stanford, CA: Stanford University Press, 1993), 70–7; 'Force of Law' and 'Hostipitality', trans. Gil Anidjar, in *Acts of Religion*, ed. Anidjar, 243, 244, 364; and *God, the Gift, and Postmodernism*, ed. Caputo and Scanlon, 72.

45. Jacques Derrida, *The Post Card: From Socrates to Freud and Beyond*, trans., with an introduction and additional notes, by Alan Bass (Chicago and London: University of Chicago Press, 1987), 389.

46. This, and similar Blanchotian operators, is analysed in 'Pas', in *Parages* (Paris: Galilée, 1986), 19–116; translated by John P. Leavey as '*Pace* Not(*s*)', in *Parages*, ed. John P. Leavey, trans. Tom Conley et al. (Stanford, CA: Stanford University Press, 2011), 11–101. See, especially for our argument, the structure of 'X without X' as 'ce re-trait laisse tout intact (sauf, indemne) en apparence' (91;

cf. 78 in English). See also Arleen Ionescu, 'Pas-de-noms / Plus de noms. Derrida and Blanchot', *Word and Text: A Journal of Literary Studies and Linguistics* 1.1: 'Names in Culture and Daily Life' (2011): 59–69.

47. See also *HC* 95. Translated as 'fidence', the word first occurs in *The Politics of Friendship* (1994), trans. George Collins (London and New York: Verso, 2005 ed.), especially 14, 194, where it is used as the common denominator upstream of critical distinctions between confidence, faith, fidelity and credence.

48. Whether the latter takes the form of disbelief (*mécréance*) or discredit, according to Bernard Stiegler's analyses of the political desire to believe in the face of lack of credibility. See especially *The Decadence of Industrial Democracies Disbelief and Discredit, Volume 1*, trans. Daniel Ross and Suzanne Arnold (Cambridge: Polity, 2011).

49. See, for example, Jacques Derrida, 'Ulysses Gramophone: Hear Say Yes in Joyce' (orig.: 1984), trans. François Raffoul, in *Derrida and Joyce: Texts and Contexts*, ed. Andrew J. Mitchell and Sam Slate (Albany, NY: SUNY Press, 2013), 41–86.

50. *God, the Gift, and Postmodernism*, ed. Caputo and Scanlon, 8.

51. Cf. 'The Villanova Roundtable', *Deconstruction in a Nutshell*, 15: 'Dissociation is the condition of community, the condition of any unity as such', and 'F' 224: 'The social bond supposes, even requires interruption'. Derrida makes a similar point about justice (*dikè*) in the exchange about money to which I shall return in conclusion; see *L'Argent. Croyance, mesure, speculation*, ed. Drach, 218.

52. In a famous passage of *Totality and Infinity*, Levinas had already written that '[f]or the relation between the being here below and the transcendent being that results in no community of concept or totality – a relation without relation – we reserve the term religion.' See Emmanuel Levinas, *Totality and Infinity: An Essay on Exteriority*, trans. Alphonso Lingis (The Hague: Martinus Nijhoff, 1979), 80, and compare with 'FK' § 49, which refers to Blanchot and Levinas. The locution 'relation without relation' had already cropped up repeatedly in Jacques Derrida and Pierre-Jean Labarrière, *Altérités* (Paris: Osiris, 1986), translated in *Parallax* 10.4, ed. Stefan Herbrechter (2004): 17–76.

53. Caputo, *The Prayers and Tears of Jacques Derrida*, 154, 155.

54. Derrida, *Monolingualism of the Other*, 72.

55. That is, more than one/no more of one, according to the well-known, minimal definition of deconstruction given by Derrida himself in *Mémoires for Paul de Man*, rev. ed., trans. Cecile Lindsay et al. (New York: Columbia University Press, 1989 [1986]), 15.

56. Martin Heidegger, *What Is Called Thinking?*, trans. Fred D. Wieck and J. Glenn Gray, intr. J. Glenn Gray (New York: Harper & Row, 1968), 3 (Part One, Lecture I).

57. Lyotard's consonant remark, in 'The Sublime and the Avant-Garde', is worth noting here: 'There is something of the sublime in capitalist economy. . . . It is, in a sense, an economy regulated by an Idea – infinite wealth or power. It does not manage to present any example from reality to verify this Idea. In making science subordinate to itself through technologies, especially those of language,

it only succeeds, on the contrary, in making reality increasingly ungraspable, subject to doubt, unsteady.' See Jean-François Lyotard, *The Inhuman: Reflections on Time*, trans. Geoffrey Bennington and Rachel Bowlby (Cambridge: Polity, 1991), 105.

58. See, for instance, 'Letter to a Japanese Friend', trans. David Wood and Andrew Benjamin, and, more indirectly, 'Désistance', trans. Christopher Fynsk, in *Psyche: Inventions of the Other, Volume II*, ed. Kamuf and Rottenberg, 4 and 222, respectively. The canonical work of reference on this issue is, of course, Rodolphe Gasché's *The Tain of the Mirror: Derrida and the Philosophy of Reflection* (Cambridge, MA and London: Harvard University Press, 1986). It is also in this sense that one must understand Derrida's insistence on the spectral, that is, that which fails to return an image, rather than the specular in *Specters of Marx* and elsewhere.

59. In an essay on Mallarmé, Derrida defined the 'crisis' as 'the moment when simple *decision* is no longer possible, where the choice between opposing paths is suspended. A crisis, therefore, of criticism, which will always use judgment *to decide* (*krinein*) on value and meaning, to distinguish between what is and what is not, what has value and what has not, the true and the false, the beautiful and the ugly, all signification and its opposite.' See Jacques Derrida, 'Mallarmé', trans. Christine Roulston, in *Acts of Literature*, ed. Derek Attridge (New York: Routledge, 1992), 113.

60. In 'Hospitality, Justice and Responsibility: A Dialogue with Jacques Derrida', in response to a question, about both *The Truth in Painting* and *Memoirs of the* Blind, as to how painting can lead us towards a new vision or another kind of faith, Derrida reiterated the necessity for faith to be blind to be what it is. See *Questioning Ethics: Contemporary Debates in Philosophy*, ed. Richard Kearney and Mark Dooley (London and New York: Routledge, 1999), 80.

61. Translated by Peggy Kamuf as 'Economies of the Crisis' and collected in *Negotiations: Interventions and Interviews, 1971–2001*, ed., trans. and intr. Elizabeth Rottenberg (Stanford, CA: Stanford University Press, 2002), 69–73; hereafter 'EC' with page references in the text.

62. Jacques Derrida, 'Différance', in *Margins of Philosophy*, trans., with additional notes, by Alan Bass (Brighton: Harvester, 1982), 8. This principle will allow Derrida to reverse the classical formula 'time is money' into 'money is time', money as 'time won, time saved', and as '*an economy of time*': 'As substitute or equivalent in general, [money] begins by economizing on the time of exchange of things and goods; it accelerates circulation to infinity'; see 'On the "Priceless", or the "Going Rate" of the Transaction', in *Negotiations*, 322–23.

63. See *L'argent. Croyance, mesure, spéculation*, ed. Drach, 16–17 for a summary of the exchange. Derrida prefaced his replies by inscribing money – in French *argent*, whose linguistic semi-inconvertibility or semi-untranslatability he recalls both here (203) and also earlier in 'On the "Priceless", or the "Going Rate" of the Transaction' (*Negotiations*, 319) – within a complex network of themes and problematics: the question of the gift, hospitality, debt, belief (*croyance*) and credit (203).

64. Derrida, in *Negotiations*, 318, 320. See also 'Différance', in *Margins of Philosophy*, 9.

65. See *L'argent. Croyance, mesure, spéculation*, ed. Drach, 202. Goux's own early work in *Économie et symbolique* (Paris: Seuil, 1973), then, one decade later, on André Gide in *Les Monnayeurs du langage* (Paris: Galilée, 1984), predisposed him to pointing out this convergence in the thinking of Jacques Derrida, who had himself been influenced by Goux's two-part essay 'Numismatiques' (*Tel Quel*, 1968–1969), on the structural homology between money and language, the notion of value across Freud, Nietzsche, Marx and Saussure, and money as a privileged standard for the principle of general, symbolic equivalences and exchanges.

66. The phrase is Derrida's in 'On the "Priceless", or the "Going Rate" of the Transaction', in *Negotiations*, 317.

67. Derrida, in *L'argent. Croyance, mesure, spéculation*, ed. Drach, 204. Such a process of idealization or abstraction occurs the moment a sign is put into circulation, with (dis)credit, devaluation or inflation accruing according to movements and exchanges (205, about 'deconstruction' taken as such a verbal and monetary sign).

68. Derrida, *Given Time*, 15; insertion mine.

69. Derrida glossing Goux, in *L'argent. Croyance, mesure, spéculation*, ed. Drach, 206. See already in 'Faith and Knowledge. . .': The price of human life, which is to say, of anthropo-theological life, the price of what ought to remain safe (*heilig*, sacred, safe and sound, unscathed, immune), as the absolute price, the price of what ought to inspire respect, modesty, reticence, this price is priceless. It corresponds to what Kant calls the dignity (*Würdigkeit*) of the end in itself, of the rational finite being, of absolute value beyond all comparative market price (*Marktpreis*).' ('FK' § 40).

70. Derrida, 'On the "Priceless", or the "Going Rate" of the Transaction', in *Negotiations*, 315–16. See also *L'argent. Croyance, mesure, spéculation*, ed. Drach, 212, 219.

71. Derrida in *L'argent. Croyance, mesure, spéculation*, ed. Drach, 211. Soon after Marcel Drach's evocation of *Given Time: I. Counterfeit Money*, Derrida insists that 'fake money' is only so insofar as it is held to be authentic and therefore is an undetected simulacrum of authenticity: there cannot be any authentic money without the possibility of falsification, and thus counterfeitability belongs intrinsically to money's 'authenticity'.

72. See Derrida, 'Force of Law', in *Acts of Religion*, ed. Anidjar, 230–98.

BIBLIOGRAPHY

BENVENISTE, Emile. *Le Vocabulaire des institutions indo-européennes*. Volume 1. Economie, parenté, société. Paris: Minuit, 1969.

BENVENISTE, Emile. *Le Vocabulaire des institutions indo-européennes*. Volume 2. Pouvoir, Droit, Religion. Paris: Minuit, 1969.

BRADLEY, Arthur. 'The Letter Giveth'. *Mind Factory*. Edited by Louis Armand. Prague: Litteraria Pragensia, 2005. 106–119.

BRADLEY, Arthur and Paul FLETCHER. *The Politics to Come: Power, Modernity and the Messianic*. London: Continuum, 2010.

BRAULT, Pascale-Anne and Michael NAAS. 'To Believe: An Intransitive Verb? Translating Scepticism in Jacques Derrida's *Memoirs of the Blind*'. *Paragraph* 20.2 (1997): 101–119.

CAPUTO, John D. (ed.). *Deconstruction in a Nutshell: A Conversation with Jacques Derrida*. New York: Fordham University Press, 1997.

CAPUTO, John D. *The Prayers and Tears of Jacques Derrida: Religion without Religion*. Bloomington and Indianapolis: Indiana University Press, 1997.

CAPUTO, John D., Mark DOOLEY and Michael J. SCANLON (eds.). *Questioning God*. Bloomington and Indianapolis: Indiana University Press, 2001.

CAPUTO, John D., Kevin HART and Yvonne SHERWOOD. 'Epoché and Faith: An Interview with Jacques Derrida'. Transcribed by Brooke Cameron and Kevin Hart. In *Derrida and Religion: Other Testaments*. Edited by Yvonne Sherwood and Kevin Hart. London: Routledge, 2005. 27–50.

CAPUTO, John D. and Michael J. SCANLON (eds.). *Augustine and Postmodernism: Confessions and Circumfession*. Bloomington and Indianapolis: Indiana University Press, 2005.

CAPUTO, John D. and Michael J. SCANLON (eds.). *God, the Gift, and Postmodernism*. Bloomington and Indianapolis: Indiana University Press, 1999.

CIXOUS, Hélène. *Portrait of Jacques Derrida as a Young Jewish Saint*. Translated by Beverley Bie Brahic. New York: Columbia University Press, 2004.

DE VRIES, Hent. *Philosophy and the Turn to Religion*. Baltimore and London: Johns Hopkins University Press, 1999.

DERRIDA, Jacques. *Adieu à Emmanuel Levinas*. Paris: Galilée, 1997.

DERRIDA, Jacques. *Adieu to Emmanuel Levinas*. Translated by Pascale-Anne Brault and Michael Naas. Stanford, CA: Stanford University Press, 1999.

DERRIDA, Jacques. *Aporias*. Translated by Thomas Dutoit. Stanford, CA: Stanford University Press, 1993.

DERRIDA, Jacques. 'Circonfession'. In *Jacques Derrida*. Edited by Geoffrey Bennington and Jacques Derrida. Paris: Seuil, 1991. 7–291.

DERRIDA, Jacques. 'Circumfession'. Translated by Geoffrey Bennington. In *Jacques Derrida*. Edited by Geoffrey Bennington and Jacques Derrida. Chicago and London: University of Chicago Press, 1993. 3–315.

DERRIDA, Jacques. 'Des tours de Babel'. Translated by Joseph F. Graham. In *Psyche: Inventions of the Other, Volume I*. Edited by Peggy Kamuf and Elizabeth Rottenberg. Stanford, CA: Stanford University Press, 2007. 191–225.

DERRIDA, Jacques. 'Désistance'. Translated by Christopher Fynsk. In *Psyche: Inventions of the Other, Volume II*. Edited by Peggy Kamuf and Elizabeth Rottenberg. Stanford, CA: Stanford University Press, 2008. 196–230.

DERRIDA, Jacques. 'Economies of the Crisis'. Translated by Peggy Kamuf. In *Negotiations: Interventions and Interviews, 1971–2001*. Edited, Translated and with an introduction by Elizabeth Rottenberg. Stanford, CA: Stanford University Press, 2002. 69–73.

DERRIDA, Jacques. 'Faith and Knowledge: The Two Sources of "Religion" at the Limits of Reason Alone'. Translated by Samuel Weber. In *Acts of Religion*. Edited and with an introduction by Gil Anidjar. New York and London: Routledge, 2002. 42–101.

DERRIDA, Jacques. 'Fidélité à plus d'un - mériter d'hériter où la généalogie fait défaut'. *Cahiers Intersignes* 13: 'Idiomes, nationalités, déconstructions. Rencontre de Rabat avec Jacques Derrida'. Paris and Casablanca: Intersignes/ Toubkal, 1998.

DERRIDA, Jacques. 'Force of Law: The "Mystical Foundation of Authority"'. Translated by Mary Quaintance. In *Acts of Religion*. Edited and with an introduction by Gil Anidjar. New York and London: Routledge, 2002. 230–98.

DERRIDA, Jacques. 'From Restricted to General Economy: A Hegelianism without Reserve'. In *Writing and Difference*. Translated, with an introduction and additional notes, by Alan Bass. London: Routledge, 2001 [1978]. 317–50.

DERRIDA, Jacques. *Given Time: I. Counterfeit Money*. Translated by Peggy Kamuf. Chicago and London: University of Chicago Press, 1992.

DERRIDA, Jacques. *Glas*. Translated by John P. Leavey, Jr. and Richard Rand. Lincoln, NE and London: University of Nebraska Press, 1986.

DERRIDA, Jacques. *H. C. for Life, That Is to Say. . .*. Translated, with additional notes, by Laurent Milesi and Stefan Herbrechter. Stanford, CA: Stanford University Press, 2006.

DERRIDA, Jacques. 'Hostipitality'. Translated by Gil Anidjar. In *Acts of Religion*. Edited and with an introduction by Gil Anidjar. New York and London: Routledge, 2002. 358–420.

DERRIDA, Jacques. 'How to Avoid Speaking: Denials'. Translated by Ken Frieden and Elizabeth Rottenberg. In *Psyche: Inventions of the Other, Volume II*. Edited by Peggy Kamuf and Elizabeth Rottenberg. Stanford, CA: Stanford University Press, 2008. 143–95.

DERRIDA, Jacques. *La Vérité en peinture*. Paris: Flammarion, 1978.

DERRIDA, Jacques. 'Letter to a Japanese Friend'. Translated by David Wood and Andrew Benjamin. In *Psyche: Inventions of the Other, Volume II*. Edited by Peggy Kamuf and Elizabeth Rottenberg. Stanford, CA: Stanford University Press, 2008. 1–6.

DERRIDA, Jacques. 'Mallarmé'. Translated by Christine Roulston. In *Acts of Literature*. Edited by Derek Attridge. New York: Routledge, 1992. 111–26.

DERRIDA, Jacques. *Margins of Philosophy*. Translated, with additional notes, by Alan Bass. Brighton: Harvester, 1982.

DERRIDA, Jacques. *Mémoires for Paul de Man*. Revised Edition. Translated by Cecile Lindsay et al. New York: Columbia University Press, 1989 [1986].

DERRIDA, Jacques. *Memoirs of the Blind: The Self-Portrait and Other Ruins*. Translated by Pascale-Anne Brault and Michael Naas. Chicago and London: University of Chicago Press, 1991.

DERRIDA, Jacques. *Monolingualism of the Other; or, the Prosthesis of Origin*. Translated by Patrick Mensah. Stanford, CA: Stanford University Press, 1998.

DERRIDA, Jacques. *On the Name*. Edited by Thomas Dutoit. Translated by David Wood et al. Stanford, CA: Stanford University Press, 1995.

DERRIDA, Jacques. 'On the "Priceless", or the "Going Rate" of the Transaction'. In *Negotiations: Interventions and Interviews, 1971–2001*. Edited, Translated and with an introduction by Elizabeth Rottenberg. Stanford, CA: Stanford University Press, 2002. 315–28.

DERRIDA, Jacques. '*Pa*ce Not(*s*)'. Translated by John P. Leavey. In *Parages*. Edited by John P. Leavey. Translated by Tom Conley et al. Stanford, CA: Stanford University Press, 2011. 11–101.

DERRIDA, Jacques. 'Pas'. In *Parages*. Paris: Galilée, 1986. 19–116.

DERRIDA, Jacques. *The Politics of Friendship*. Translated by George Collins. London and New York: Verso, 2005.

DERRIDA, Jacques. *The Post Card: From Socrates to Freud and Beyond*. Translated, with an introduction and additional notes, by Alan Bass. Chicago and London: University of Chicago Press, 1987.

DERRIDA, Jacques. 'Psyche: Invention of the Other'. Translated by Catherine Porter. In *Psyche: Inventions of the Other, Volume I*. Edited by Peggy Kamuf and Elizabeth Rottenberg. Stanford, CA: Stanford University Press, 2007. 1.47.

DERRIDA, Jacques. 'Shibboleth: For Paul Celan'. Translated by Joshua Wilner, rev. Thomas Dutoit. In *Sovereignties in Question: The Poetics of Paul Celan*. Edited by Thomas Dutoit and Outi Pasanen. New York: Fordham University Press, 2005. 1–64.

DERRIDA, Jacques. *Specters of Marx: The State of the Debt, the Work of Mourning, and the New International*. Translated by Peggy Kamuf. Introduction by Bernd Magnus and Stephen Cullenberg. London: Routledge, 1994.

DERRIDA, Jacques. *The Truth in Painting*. Translated by Geoff Bennington and Ian McLeod. Chicago and London: University of Chicago Press, 1987.

DERRIDA, Jacques. 'Ulysses Gramophone: Hear Say Yes in Joyce'. Translated by François Raffoul. In *Derrida and Joyce: Texts and Contexts*. Edited by Andrew J. Mitchell and Sam Slate. Albany: SUNY Press, 2013. 41–86.

DERRIDA, Jacques and Pierre-Jean LABARRIÈRE. *Altérités*. Paris: Osiris, 1986.

DERRIDA, Jacques and Pierre-Jean LABARRIÈRE. *Alterities*. Translated by Stefan Herbrechter. *Parallax* 10.4. Edited by Stefan Herbrechter (2004): 17–76.

DERRIDA, Jacques and Elisabeth ROUDINESCO. *For What Tomorrow. . . : A Dialogue*. Translated by Jeff Fort. Stanford, CA: Stanford University Press, 2004.

DRACH, Marcel (ed.). *L'argent. Croyance, mesure, spéculation*. Paris: La Découverte, 2004.

GASCHÉ, Rodolphe. *The Tain of the Mirror: Derrida and the Philosophy of Reflection*. Cambridge, MA and London: Harvard University Press, 1986.

GERNALZICK, Nadja. 'From Classical Dichotomy to Differantial Contract: The Derridean Integration of Monetary Theory'. In *Metaphors of Economy*. Edited by Nicole Bracker and Stefan Herbrechter. Amsterdam and New York: Rodopi, 2005. 55–67.

GOUX, Jean-Joseph. *Économie et symbolique*. Paris: Seuil, 1973.

GOUX, Jean-Joseph. *Les Monnayeurs du langage*. Paris: Galilée, 1984.

GOUX, Jean-Joseph. 'Numismatiques (I-II)'. *Tel Quel* 35 (1968): 64–89; 36 (1969): 54–74.

HEIDEGGER, Martin. *What Is Called Thinking?* Translated by Fred D. Wieck and J. Glenn Gray. Introduction by J. Glenn Gray. New York: Harper & Row, 1968.

IONESCU, Arleen. 'Pas-de-noms/Plus de noms. Derrida and Blanchot'. *Word and Text: A Journal of Literary Studies and Linguistics* 1.1: 'Names in Culture and Daily Life' (2011): 59–69.

KEARNEY, Richard and Mark DOOLEY (eds.). *Questioning Ethics: Contemporary Debates in Philosophy*. London and New York: Routledge, 1999.

LEVINAS, Emmanuel. *Totality and Infinity: An Essay on Exteriority*. Translated by Alphonso Lingis. The Hague: Martinus Nijhoff, 1979.

LYOTARD, Jean-François. *The Inhuman: Reflections on Time*. Translated by Geoffrey Bennington and Rachel Bowlby. Cambridge: Polity, 1991.

MALLARMÉ, Stéphane. *Collected Poems and Other Verse*. Translated with Notes by E. H. and A. M. Blackmore. With an introduction by Elizabeth McCombie. Oxford: Oxford University Press, 2006.

MILESI, Laurent. 'Thinking (through) the Desert (la pensée du désert) with(in) Jacques Derrida'. In *The Politics of Deconstruction: Jacques Derrida and the Other of Philosophy*. Edited by Martin McQuillan. London and Ann Arbor, MI: Pluto Press, 2007. 173–91.

NAAS, Michael. *Miracle and Machine: Jacques Derrida and the Two Sources of Religion, Science, and the Media*. New York: Fordham University Press, 2012.

STIEGLER, Bernard. 'Derrida and Technology: Fidelity at the Limits of Deconstruction and the Prosthesis of Faith'. In *Jacques Derrida and the Humanities: A Critical Reader*. Edited by Tom Cohen. Cambridge: Cambridge University Press, 2001. 238–70.

STIEGLER, Bernard. *The Decadence of Industrial Democracies Disbelief and Discredit, Volume 1*. Translated by Daniel Ross and Suzanne Arnold. Cambridge: Polity, 2011.

Section four

FUTURE REVELATIONS

Chapter 12

Credit and investment: A matter of faith

Philip Goodchild

THE FUTURE OF CAPITALISM: HOW FAITH EXCEEDS KNOWLEDGE

One day capitalism will come to an end. This end might be benign: another socio-economic system might emerge within capitalism,[1] whether leaving capitalist formations as mere archaic residues, or directly expunging them, or allowing them to fade into insignificance as something that no longer matters.[2] This end might also be malignant: human economic activity could be massively reduced by a natural disaster, a plague or meteorite, or a human-made catastrophe, such as climate change, runaway artificial intelligence or nanotechnology, global war or anarchy. The economy might fall prey to a peril of its own making, such as hyper-inflation or a debt-deflationary spiral. At any rate, whether the end is benign or malignant, we can be relatively certain, even if it endures as long as the lifetime of the sun, that capitalism will one day come to an end. If the approach of that end is recognised, then people will anticipate a time when investments will no longer yield a profit, debts will no longer be repaid and work will no longer yield wages.[3] In other words, if the existence of the end is recognised, capitalism will destroy itself on the penultimate day: the confidence required for daily economic interactions will evaporate. The end will come before it has arrived. Then if we recognise that it should end on the penultimate day, should we not also recognise this the day before, and so bring the end a day closer, and then the day before that, and again and again until we reach our present day? One day capitalism will come to an end. Should that knowledge not be sufficient to destroy capitalism here and now? Why, then, does it appear to continue as before? Or could it be the case, by contrast, that what we take as capitalism is now a collective illusion, a shared belief system that guides conduct within a broader ecological, economic and psychological reality whose grounds are already far from capitalist? Has capitalism ended already?

Both the self-destruction of capitalism and its postponement depend upon belief. What do people really believe about the end of capitalism? Do they believe it is immortal, simply in order to go about their business from day to day, disavowing any certainty they might have of its end?[4] Or do they believe that if they act as though the end will not come yet, then collectively they can succeed in postponing the end, perhaps beyond their own lifetimes, beyond those of their children and beyond their immediate circle of care and concern? The situation is analogous to those who consciously invest in an inflated market: they know the trend of rising prices will eventually come to an end, but, for now, it looks set to continue, and it seems worth taking the risk that one can sell at a higher price than one has bought. As such, these investors contribute to the continuing trend of rising prices – but also, in their efforts to sell once the collapse begins, to the collapse itself. So is capitalism itself a bubble? Are we all speculators who take a gamble on its continuation? Is it such a gamble that keeps capitalism alive? Is capitalism itself the gamble that its benefits can be enjoyed now while its costs will be borne by others?

Such reflections are merely speculative: who knows what is really in people's hearts? What is believed by us is perhaps least known to ourselves.[5] Others may infer what a person believes from their behaviour, at the cost of inaccuracies brought about through excessive generalisation, but a person has little access to what they have disavowed. Nevertheless, speculations on the beliefs of others cannot be laid aside by any person of influence who makes a public pronouncement, for the effect of a pronouncement depends on how people react to it, which depends in turn on what is in people's hearts.[6] We are familiar with the way in which the pronouncements of central bankers are capable of moving markets, for what can be said is strictly constrained by anticipations of how the markets might respond to it.[7] Nevertheless, few can anticipate exactly what that response will be, so financial stability is best ensured by saying as little as possible so as to provoke as little reaction as possible. The mood of the market can only be read with hindsight: all explanations of price fluctuations have to be given after the event as subsequent rationalisations.

The point of these speculative reflections is simply this: there is a discrepancy between knowledge and belief when it comes to the future. It is possible to know that capitalism will end, yet to act as though it will not come to an end, perhaps in the hope that through such action the end might yet be averted. This discrepancy between knowledge and belief is not a familiar one. It is normal to regard belief as falling short of knowledge on the grounds that it lacks justification: it may not be grounded in the evidence.[8] It is also possible to regard knowledge as falling short of belief insofar as it is not inwardly appropriated: the classic example here is knowledge of one's own death, a knowledge that can be disavowed or alternatively resolutely appropriated, affecting everything that one does.[9] In capitalism, however, belief has a causal efficacy that exceeds knowledge: every time one enters a contract, makes an investment or takes out a debt, one does so in the faith that one will be capable of discharging obligations, that one's counterparties will in turn discharge their obligations and that the entire economic system – including, for example, the value of money – will remain stable enough for the transaction to be completed over time. One believes in the possible, not the necessary. Knowledge relates only to the past and the present; it is belief that searches out fixed points of reference in the future in order to guide conduct in the present.[10] This belief may be deemed 'rational' if it is guided in accordance with existing knowledge: the past is treated as a guide to the future. Even so, it is still a case of believing, even if one attempts to subordinate belief to knowledge. But such is hardly a rational assumption, for many investment vehicles are legally required to state this mantra: 'past performance is not a reliable indicator of future results'.[11] While present knowledge comes about as a result of past events, future events come about as a result of present beliefs; often, the course of events refutes the beliefs that have generated it, as in financial crises. Yet the mismatch of belief and reality can also be positive. Belief seems 'irrational' when it goes against the evidence; yet it may be precisely this resistance to a negative reality which wards off its occurrence.[12]

Economic agents, in this respect, are not rational actors: the future that they anticipate depends upon their own actions, as well as the anticipations and actions of others. Sir Mervyn King, the governor of the Bank of England 2003–2013, explains that a monetary economy behaves very differently from the textbook description of a market economy because it introduces radical uncertainty – there are no rational expectations about the future under conditions of uncertainty.[13] As he puts it, 'Radical uncertainty drives a gaping hole through the idea of complete and competitive markets'.[14] The future markets needed to produce an equilibrium simply cannot and do not exist. 'The market economy cannot, therefore, coordinate spending plans. There are too many missing markets'.[15] Instead of the wisdom of crowds converging around a fixed point of future equilibrium, the future is path-dependent, and radically different outcomes are possible depending on the state of anticipation here and now. In the behaviour of crowds, foolishness, mean-spiritedness and fatalism may be compounded, just as much as irrational exuberance: markets have their bears and bulls.

If people act out of hope for a particular outcome, a different outcome will be produced from one if they had acted out of fear for another.[16] The world is made not simply by what people do, nor simply by how they reason, but by how they believe. The 'healthiness' of a belief is then not merely a product of its realism, its conformity to reality, because the reality it seeks to conform to does not yet exist; a belief is healthy insofar as its outcome is positive, whether or not it produces the outcome it believes in.[17] Realism may correspond to a fatalism that fails to imagine anything could possibly be different.[18]

The purpose of this chapter is to explore this faith-dimension implicit in the future orientation of credit and investment. It seeks to explore a discrepancy between what is commonly believed by economic agents – as is evident from their practice – and the economic reality by which they live, for people treat economic reality as though it were a market, a sum of exchanges; they treat debts as though these have to be repaid, so that they will have become exchanges. Yet, in the meantime, economic reality is constituted as a set of obligations together with conduct guided by faith. A central part of faith in markets is not only their just and efficient distribution of resources to those best able to make use of them but also their tendency towards equilibrium, their stability. The context of this discussion is, of course, the aftermath of the credit crisis of 2007–2008 which demonstrated the real possibility of an imminent economic apocalypse. What is now widely accepted is that capitalism can come to an end. A faith in the stability of markets is demonstrably misplaced.[19] So what happens to the faith necessary to sustain everyday economic conduct when its evidence basis refutes it? I shall argue that where this faith fails to conform to reality, reality itself must be modified to approximate to faith. The aim is to simulate an efficient and stable market, and in doing so, to ward off the possibility of an imminent economic apocalypse. One has to repay debts, not simply so that they will appear as market exchanges with hindsight, but so that default does not spread by contagion. Where this faith was previously underwritten by economic theory, it is now underwritten by privileged and centralised institutions: only central banks are capable of absorbing bad debts and defaults without passing them on. Central banks offer redemption from debt; without this, approximation to a market is impossible. Our economic reality cannot be accurately described as 'free market capitalism', even if it depends on a belief in this;[20] like a traditional religion, economy is a matter of faith, depending on hierarchy and acts of redemption. As such, it has to be understood according to categories of faith rather than acts of exchange. The task that lies before us, then, is to indicate what these categories might be: it is to substitute philosophy of religion for market economics in the articulation of current economic reality.

VARIETIES OF FAITH: ALTERNATIVE APPROACHES TO EXISTENTIAL CATEGORIES

In order to distinguish states of the heart, it is necessary to distinguish between fundamental orientations for desire, investment, attention and perhaps even devotion. Familiar philosophical approaches in modern thought may offer an initial categorisation. According to an old Platonic formulation, what is desired is always the good:[21] if one desires a particular thing, then it is always as a means towards an end – a particular food is desired if it brings about a state of satisfaction or health. If such a desire is ignorant, and the food one craves is in fact unhealthy after all, then it mistakes the path to the end, not the end itself. Desire has to be criticised by objective reality, but unless we have absolute certainty about the objective good, we have to guide our conduct by faith in such a reality. By contrast, according to a modern Kantian formulation, things in themselves are neither good nor bad: only a human will can be good because it alone may be judged by a moral law.[22] Where the classical Platonic perspective finds good outside in the surrounding world, the Kantian perspective finds good only within a possibility for the will: this perspective is uprooted from the world, turned in on itself subjectively. A faith is still required, but now this is a faith in the moral principles that judge the will. A third perspective on the good is presented by the utilitarian consumer who finds good in what is purchased and owned according to his or her subjective estimation, and subjective satisfaction becomes the index of the good. While the Kantian subject may still criticise herself according to her conscience, by the moral law, a utilitarian subject cannot criticise his own preferences, but only the rationality of his choices to maximise his utility. The utilitarian, like the Platonist, is turned outwards towards the world, but instead of being drawn outward to discover what is really good in things, he draws the world back into himself, in a progressively re-ordered fashion, subject entirely to his own mastery, to maximise his existing sense of satisfaction. The utilitarian judges by taste, but guides conduct entirely through faith in the accuracy of such a taste. Such, then, is a traditional categorical scheme for the fundamental orientations of desire: the Platonic, the Kantian and the utilitarian. Faith is placed in either objective ends, subjective principles or the sense of taste.

Contemporary capitalism would seem to require faith in the sovereignty of the consumer and the principle of taste.[23] Self-criticism is disavowed. Yet the variety of life choices actually taken would seem to suggest that not only do people have different natures and so different desires, and not only do people construct different preferences for themselves in path-dependent choices, but people also largely have little idea of what is actually good for them, both in terms of the goods of which they remain in radical ignorance as a result of the choices they have taken and in terms of the harms which excessive and repeated choices might also accomplish. For taste, satisfaction and dissatisfaction tell us comparatively little of our real conditions of existence. According to this scheme, then, what we most lack is self-criticism: for the good life, consumer existence should be supplemented by Platonic and Kantian dialectics, by inquiries into objective goods and moral principles.

Can criticism save us? Or must we look outside ourselves, whether to central banks or religious redeemers? One problem with this scheme of desire is that it is itself too Kantian: it distinguishes states of the heart according to their inner structure, not according to the good that is desired. It assumes that the heart determines itself from within, rather than having its orientation given and its attention attracted from without. It assumes that faith is shaped within the limits set by reason alone, rather than faith exceeding all reason. It can offer only an imbalanced and incomplete set of categories. As we will see, modern thought in both its empiricist and its critical formulations is insufficient to attain reality. An alternative, and more Platonic scheme, can distinguish fundamental orientations according to the kinds of good that are desired rather than the orientation of the will. In this less familiar categorisation, there are competitive goods, objects of appropriation, things that can be mine insofar as they are not yours. These include such things as food, property, land, financial assets, children, affection from lovers, honours, status and competitive prizes. Yet if much human endeavour aims at success in appropriation, this is by no means the sum total of endeavour, for there are also cooperative goods, objects of participation, things that can be mine insofar as they are also yours.[24] These include such things as environments, freedom from pollution, roads, communications, markets, governments, institutions, cultures, marriages, families, contracts, laws, freedoms and rights. Much human endeavour either presupposes such participation or endeavours to make such participation possible.[25] In relation to these two kinds of good, entirely different kinds of ethics are possible: with goods of acquisition, one has a simple choice between being self-centred or altruistic. With goods of participation, one has a simple choice between being responsible, conserving, transmitting or enhancing such goods, or being irresponsible, a 'free rider'. Nevertheless, individual human responsibility is strictly limited, and in most respects one can do no more than receive the benefits of existing participatory goods, at best with sufficient gratitude and respect to signal the significance of these human activities which are beyond our individual control. While subjective estimations of wealth tend to focus on the satisfactions afforded by competitive goods, insofar as these are capable of exchange, and thus pricing and measurement, a much richer account of wealth is given by accounting for those goods that are cooperative and participatory, which offer enduring benefits to a succession of generations. One might seek to assess the market capitalisation of a mutual society, a university, a school or a hospital, but this offers no real measure of the benefits that such institutions provide through participation rather than exchange.

Simply pointing out the existence and inevitability of participation is enough to demonstrate that our world has never been fully capitalist: *far from coming to an end, capitalism has never even properly begun.* Modernisation and rationalisation, insofar as they seek to reorganise society on the basis of evidence, tend to turn attention towards the measurable and comparable, even if only in order to gather subjective assessment of their benefits.[26] The measurable and comparable is, by its very nature, only that which admits of exchange; actual participation in certain kinds of institution is not comparable because it requires commitment. Institutions are exclusive in an inverse sense to competition: I can belong to one family only if I do not belong to another. Goods of participation require commitment and obligation; if a subject might initially choose between institutions or between contracts, once the choice has been taken, then such institutions and contracts impose commitments and obligations. Even economic life is concerned with debts and obligations more than it is concerned with subjective preferences. The rationality for assessing responsible participation is entirely different from that assessing the maximisation of utility. In this respect, an economic discipline focused on the 'evidence', on values alone, only engages with a pale fragment of reality, for all economic forms of life other than pure bilateral exchange – and here one might consider markets, contracts, laws, corporations, banks, rating agencies, etc. – belong to the political and ethical spheres of participation rather than the purely economic sphere of competition. To the extent that modern 'rationalisation' forgets this and offers a distorted vision of institutions according to criteria of pricing, measurement and performance, and especially insofar as it endeavours to reconstruct such institutions so that they can be subject to such criteria, then capitalism will hasten its self-destruction. As in relation to the external environment, the realms of culture, the realms of nurturing, personal care and unpaid labour, capitalism bites the hand that feeds it.[27]

Nevertheless, a division between competitive and cooperative goods is incomplete. There is a further dimension of reality the existence of which simply requires pointing out. There are also renunciative or distributive goods, goods of offering, goods that I can only possess insofar as I give them away.[28] Time itself is a good of offering: the only time I have is the time I spend. Even if I spend that time 'on myself', or by myself, the time that I have spent is time I have no longer. I cannot save time, for time will continue to pass. Although one speaks of 'having time' and one imagines participating in an event, the language of appropriation and participation is not strictly accurate for time, for a moment of time is presented to us only on the condition that it is immediately removed into the past; at the same time, we experience this time only if we pay attention to something else for a time. Desire, investment, attention, devotion and life itself are goods of offering: independently of any participation in relations or appropriation of satisfactions, these goods that characterise the human 'heart' are essentially oriented outwards and only exist in their enactment. They are essentially temporal goods. The life one has lived is the life that one has spent. In some respects, one essentially desires neither satisfaction nor participation: one desires a life.[29] Yet insofar as the life one lives is constituted not only by the satisfactions that it affords, and not only by institutions and cultures in which it participates, but also by what is venerated, what is attended to, what is invested in and desired, then such a life is determined not merely by an economic rationality that seeks to maximise utility, not merely by a political and ethical rationality that seeks to maximise participation, but also by a religious rationality that seeks to venerate what is most worthy of veneration, to spend its time on that which matters. This is true not simply for some private, religious compartment of life concerned with secret thoughts. The whole of life is life in time: it is true for the economic life of credit and investment, even if it is short-circuited by a veneration for satisfaction or status, or a veneration for markets and capitalism, for, as we have seen, even these involve a faith. Faith is a universal condition of human life: it is simply a matter of orientation towards the future.

THE FUTURE OF A DELUSION: CAPITALISM AND SECULARISATION

Søren Kierkegaard once remarked that life can be understood only backwards, but has to be lived forwards.[30] The financialisation of everyday life, the encroachment of debt as the dominant relationship for ensuring predictable behaviour[31] and the apparent unexpectedness[32] of the recent credit crisis have all enforced this existential realisation for the current generation: past performance cannot be taken as a reliable guide to future results. It is no longer sufficient to live according to moral principles, to maintain warm interpersonal relationships, to gain a particular training, to participate in an enduring institution, to offer one's services to those in need: none of this is sufficient to provide economic security. Instead, one has to become an entrepreneur of oneself, a speculator and risk-taker, constructing networks to create opportunities, seizing opportunities to maximise one's security and evading or bouncing back from the blows of misfortune when they strike. Being oriented to the future is crucial, even if the future only offers uncertainty. The customs, structures and institutions bequeathed to us from the past may no longer be relevant or effective. Planning for the future involves creative destruction of our inheritance from the past: the institutions established through the efforts of past generations may no longer serve us, so we no longer serve them. As such, the future orientation generates instability in a self-fulfilling anxiety: our forefathers have betrayed us, or perhaps we have betrayed them. At any rate, we hasten our own uprooting: we no longer have a real, active and organic participation in the life of a community which is focused on preserving the treasures of an ordered social and economic life from the past for the sake of the future.[33] Participation is replaced by achievement and appropriation. Nevertheless, this orientation towards the future is tremendously thin: lacking the depth of history, composed of real events and named individuals, the future can only be anticipated in vague outline, never known. We cannot feed on the future in the same way that we may receive from and feed off the past. The future offers us nothing to enrich and empower our lives; on the contrary, it is we who in order to build it have to offer our very lives.[34]

Now, insofar as religion consists in a communal life, preserving the treasures of the past to regulate personal conduct and interpersonal relationships, then it enters into a complex relation with a 'capitalist' society. On the one hand, it trains people to be honest economic agents, enthusiastic, sincere and committed, and spirituality offers an ideal preparation for becoming an entrepreneur of the self. Religion itself survives well within 'capitalism', enabling the formation of capitalist 'faith'.[35] On the other hand, its total claims are implicitly rejected: the repayment of debts is seen as more urgent than fulfilling one's religious obligations, and hardly incompatible. Moreover, religious formations of society offer little guidance for the effective performance of one's professional role in a highly rationalised and networked society: the past is not a guide to the future. In this respect, religious guidance seems to be redundant and irrelevant. Most significantly, religious emphases on personal obligations are at odds with consumer emphases on guiding conduct by taste. In these respects, narratives of secularisation that accompany modern rationalisation and consumerism are not entirely out of place. Religion offers little in the way of evidence for rationality, expertise in constructing and performing new roles and immediate personal satisfaction.

Now, one of the great theorists of secularisation, Sigmund Freud, defined religion not in terms of knowledge as an error, but as an illusion, a belief that is held to fulfil wishes irrespective of whether it is true.[36] He distinguished an illusion, which is derived from human wishes and cannot be verified, from a delusion, which is a belief held in direct contradiction to reality.[37] Religion, which for him expressed the infantile wish for security found in a father-figure, was expected to expire as more rational and scientific means for fulfilling the pleasure-principle were established. Here we may note that such a confidence in secularisation is itself a delusion: the neurotic attempt to reconstruct reality so that it may be known purely through the evidence of the facts is a wilful denial of the existence of goods of participation, which preserve the legacy of the past, and the goods of offering, which pose the problem of the future. Capitalism itself, likewise, is an obsessive compulsive disorder that seeks to provide economic security by progressively dismantling it. The more it succeeds in undermining security, the more patently its remedies are required, and the more it persuades itself of its own delusional world view.[38] Now while the future continuation of religion in some shape or form need hardly be debated – it is imposed upon us by the structure of time that we have to make an offering of our lives rather than an exchange – the future of the existence of the delusion of capitalism is a much more pertinent issue, for the question is not whether there exists a faith through which we offer ourselves for the sake of a future, but what that faith is.

In this respect, the recent credit crisis both discloses the enduring significance of faith and expresses a significant mutation, for if the credit crisis was caused by a collapse in both the demand for risk and the supply of insurance,[39] leading to a loss in value of securitised debt, then it exposed the extent to which finance is a form of economic behaviour that expresses a faith in the existence, rationality and justice of a market. When a market threatens injustice, when its invisible hand becomes malign, rewarding the risk-takers and punishing tax-payers, when it becomes irrational, governed by wild swings in prices, and when it dissolves completely, leaving 'toxic assets' that cannot be disposed of, then it exposes such faith as an illusion.[40] Perhaps few investors still hold to the 'efficient market hypothesis'.[41] Nevertheless, faith in the ideal of a market can still remain robust in spite of the overwhelming evidence to the contrary in the form of the frequency of financial crises:[42] it simply mutates to a conditional. 'If we can build and ensure a secure market, then it will deliver efficiency, rationality and justice'. Faith in the market has always been aspirational. It is such a faith that endeavours to build and maintain a market; while it is possible to imagine that there were few economic relations of production at all prior market relations, as though the market were the only basis for a productive reality, in practice market reforms are largely introduced to replace inefficient relations of production based around planned or centralised forms of redistribution. The customs and norms that governed economic life prior to its reorganisation around the state and the market were primarily underpinned by religious guides to conduct.[43] One can therefore offer a simple set of contrasts between the ideal of a secular, democratic market and the older, religious forms of social life that it seeks to replace. Markets are based on the ownership of private property, as guaranteed by the state, while religious obligations regard wealth as something to be offered. Markets are based on freedom of contract and exchange between equals, while hierarchy is sanctioned by religious status. Markets are characterised by transparency and availability of information, while religious ceremonies conducted in temples are characterised by secrecy. Reward in markets is given on the basis of merit, while under religious auspices patronage is more frequent. Markets offer a mechanism for balancing supply and demand, while custom or priestly wisdom is required for centralised redistribution. Lastly, markets are oriented towards equilibrium in exchange, while centralised redistribution, conducted out of charity, is always far from equilibrium.

Such a set of contrasts disclose how a faith in markets is in part a faith in empowerment by making all behaviour transparent and predictable. Obligations are to be rendered finite and manageable, as are the demands of authority which become delimited by employment and contract. The vagaries of the human heart, its desires and its good will, can be rendered reliable insofar as they are combined through the law of large numbers into aggregate demand, becoming predictable and even pliable. Reward, by contrast, is offered purely on the basis of merit. Each of these is an item of faith; or, rather, faith is an attempt to realise the truth of these by constructing an ideal market. Nevertheless, such an ideal can exist only within an imaginary present, where the past and future are entirely discounted. The market ideal is a delusion: a contradiction of known reality. In reality, the past and the future count – and cannot simply be counted as if they are a former or future present.

COUNTING IN TIME: RETHINKING BASIC ECONOMIC CATEGORIES

The fundamental illusion arises from regarding the economy as a market in terms of exchanges, as though we were isolated individuals as producers, consumers and owners of property. This offers a purely synchronic perspective: at any instant of time, an account book can record wealth in terms of stocks or assets or cash owned, minus any liabilities – where such obligations are priced at what they would be worth if paid in full at the right time, as though an exchange has taken place and is complete. But economic reality is made up of enduring obligations that exist through time, a network of credits and debts, as well as of regular payments that become due, such as taxes, rents, interest, dividends and bills; all this is alongside clearly temporal activities of working and producing, providing services, negotiating contracts and exchanges and consuming products. To represent these temporal realities as a synchronic snapshot is to set aside all the driving processes, needs and obligations that make up economic reality as such in favour of a set of abstract quantifications of purely symbolic realities such as claims to property. Of course, there is no need to deny the role of individual human needs, preferences and aspirations in driving economic activity, nor the role of individual craving for recognition and status achieved through competition. But the experience of living in a world composed of knowledge, institutions and resources constructed for us by other people suggests that the temporal and social experiences of debt and obligation may have a decisive role in determining our activity and our cooperation: we are oriented towards the future by our relations to others and to the past.

This temporal and social perspective can be applied to formulate some basic economic categories for wealth accumulated in the past, measured in the present and anticipated in the future. Wealth accumulated in the past is present to us as *stocks*, or as *capacities*, or as *institutions*. Stocks are competitive in exchange: if I receive more of your goods, you have less of them. Capacities, by contrast, are non-competitive and are often communicable goods: your understanding of processes of production does not restrict my understanding, but enhances it. Institutions, in turn, are inherently collective: I can only belong to an institution such as a corporation, a hospital or a university, if my colleagues do as well. When it comes to rationalising and so measuring wealth in the present, by contrast, we require a different perspective, for economic contributions have to be related to the needs and preferences of others. The wealth of stocks is measured in *prices*, as value in exchange, in terms of what others are willing to pay. The wealth of capacities can be measured by salaries, wages or credit ratings, indicating the amounts that others are willing to pay or trust. The wealth of institutions may be measured by *asset values*, but note that here, as before with prices and salaries, we are dealing with mere representations of wealth. A share in a corporation may be an asset, but a corporation in turn holds a corresponding obligation to its shareholders. When we are concerned with purely financial assets, then there are only mirroring credits and debts. For every financial asset there is an equal and offsetting liability: if I have a claim on you, such as a share, a bond or a contract, you have a corresponding obligation. While past accumulation of stocks, capacities and institutions may be considered forms of positive wealth, since there is apparently no corresponding liability as we do not measure our debts to the past, they only enter into relations of production and distribution in actuality through the medium of obligations, credits and debts. In exchange, there is no net creation or destruction of represented wealth but a nominal equivalence. Overall financial assets and liabilities across all institutions balance out to zero.

This offers a further suggestion about the dynamic of secularisation: it derives from rationalisation though bookkeeping, treating reality as through it is what can be estimated in the present, for as long as we seek to maximise profits, or wealth measured in terms of accounts, then there is no possible way in which we can measure our debt to the past. We no longer count our inherited obligations, when all we can consider is what others may pay for in the future. The intrinsic nature and value of our goods is not represented in itself, but insofar as others are willing to recognise, prefer and pay for them: we even lose access to the present. We forget what true wealth might be.

How, then, are we to consider wealth creation, the provision of wealth for the future? Again, it can only be properly counted if it is anticipated and measured in terms of what another might be willing to pay for it. And every financial investment produces a corresponding financial obligation or *debt*. But a debt does not merely have a price, even if it can be valued, bought and sold: a debt is an obligation to repay a certain amount by a certain date, even if that date is often postponed.[44] This temporal dimension of wealth is irreducible in promises, contracts, debts, futures, options and derivatives. So while balance sheets record the present value of a debt – what it will have been worth once it has been paid, with a deduction in price to account for risk – temporality reintroduces uncertainty. We do not know what things will really be worth. Moreover, while some debts derive from an exchange – a loan is an exchange of equivalent amounts of money separated in time, with interest as a payment for the time – others are obligations that are simply imposed (e.g. taxes), or inherited (e.g. national debts), or undertaken (e.g. voluntary contracts). In all these cases, the role of obligations is obscured by counting a debt as a present value, as though debts were reducible to exchange.

Economic life, therefore, does not consist simply in a series of exchanges, and any attempt to model economic life based on the reductive illusions recorded in account books will produce fantastic and wildly inaccurate forecasts. Our temporal relations to the past and future – including inheritance, obligation and belief – cannot be rationalised so easily. If we study the economy purely in terms of money, as though we could see the whole economy with hindsight as a series of exchanges, then we repress the experience that economic life is always lived forwards, in uncertainty, guided by inheritance, obligation, creativity and belief. *Credit has a different ontology and experience from exchange,* for credit is a belief system that posits itself in opposition to its own knowledge: we have to treat economic realities as though they could all be given a present value, priced in money, rather than treating them as temporal realities extended through time. Participation in financial markets requires a considerable degree of repression. In the first place, such a belief system is founded on the circular logic of self-assertion: as long as there is confidence, there is liquidity, and as long as there is liquidity, there is confidence. This faith is grounded in nothing outside of itself, a pure assertion of will: it is a nihilistic faith.[45] In the second place, it is founded on an internal, practical contradiction: money can only store value and so be a basis for confidence in liquidity if it is not spent; at the same time, money can be liquid only if it is spent rather than being used as a store. Similarly, ongoing temporal and uncertain investments are made only if they can be instantly exchanged for a secure store of value, while investments are actually sold only if one is uncertain about their future value. There is an inconsistency between 'the liquidity of a security (which can readily be sold in order for another to be bought) and the structural non-liquidity of the capital represented by that security'.[46] In the third place, it is founded on a fourfold repression.[47] One represses the reality that financial investments are ongoing temporal relations of risk and responsibility and that the pricing and liquidity of risks merely passes them on, without in any way reducing the underlying uncertainty. In this respect, secondary markets which increase overall investment also increase overall risk; secure risk management increases the capacity to take risks, and so ensures that risks will be undertaken until defaults are realised.[48] Similarly, one represses the reality that the financial sector is structured by ongoing credit relations rather than simply by private ownership and exchange of assets, so that default does not merely result in a loss of wealth for some, but spreads by contagion. One represses the reality that the market only exists as an act of will, a moral postulate, and that risk is only priced accurately insofar as there remains a market. What remains uncertain is whether there will be any buyers at all or whether an asset will have any price. Finally, one represses the reality that there is no real money in the financial sector, including no true store of value and no true market: there are only debts and the swapping of debts issued by one institution for another. Faith in money values is misplaced because what we take as money is in fact debt. Far from being simply an object of appropriation or a commodity, money is the correlate of an obligation, a duty of offering.

Here, faith in the existence, rationality and justice of markets has to be assisted by a supplement: there is an obligation to repay debts. This is simply a moral obligation. In the system as a whole, all credits and debts must balance each other out: one person's liability is always another person's asset.[49] Credit and debt, then, cannot be conceived as positive assets or the basis for market forces, and yet they have a real influence on economic behaviour. They are virtual assets. To have faith in a system of financial assets is to have faith that debts will be repaid (or can be insured against default). In essence, then, faith in the economic system involves trust in the efficiency and effectiveness of markets as well as a moral compunction: debts must be repaid. This is necessary in order to reduce the future to the present: the pricing of the risk of default, which reduces a future event to a present price, is achievable only if all are simultaneously under an obligation to repay debts, so that any investment or lending will prove to have been an exchange.

The recent financial crisis has appeared to challenge that faith. In a global financial economy supported by bubbles in speculative assets such as property, not all debts can be repaid. For once a bubble bursts, and people seek to sell their assets to repay their debts, then the market price drops significantly. The assets used to guarantee loans against default hold insufficient value, and access to income is no longer available, so debt spreads by contagion. There are apparently only three solutions available in the system as a whole, each concerning money: a devaluation of the currency in which debts are denominated, which only works at the expense of debts in other currencies; inflation, or a generalised devaluation of currencies in relation to assets, which reduces the relative values of debts in relation to current assets and income; or some kind of default or debt write-off, which spreads to others by contagion.[50] Each of these is problematic, but only the last option has been treated as viable. What we have learned from the recent crisis, however, is that not all debts have to be repaid: even if sovereign governments are held hostage by their bond markets, central banks, working together in cooperation, have taken over bad debts without their stability being threatened. We thus have a situation where a belief in repaying debts is the condition for all financial activity, alongside a belief that certain institutions do not have to repay debts. The mutation in capitalist belief is one in which faith in central bank intervention replaces faith in markets, for if faith in markets is essentially a matter of faith in money; the nature of money will specify the form of capitalist faith at work in credit and investment. The institutional arrangements surrounding central banks determine what money actually is.

RESPONDING TO THE CRISIS: CENTRAL BANKS AS REDEEMERS

Since debts are priced in money and have to be repaid in money, the very nature of debt, of a financial obligation to the future, is determined by the nature of money itself – not as a putative 'thing-in-itself', as if that nature could be determined either by science or by taste, nor as a mere social practice or description of conduct, as though money was simply a convention – but as a partially binding formation of social and temporal relations,[51] a specific and complex institutional arrangement that needs to be specified.

What is money? This is an immense question, the history of which cannot be reviewed here.[52] Instead, I shall sketch out the nature of the institutional arrangements through which money is created and maintained in existence. Instead of money having a single essence, it is effectively produced by a conjuncture of three levels of a pyramid of institutional arrangements, involving three kinds of money. Modern money is not to be identified with any one kind, but with the entire pyramid itself – money is in fact a differential relation between three kinds of money, none of which can retain its function as money without the others. These institutional arrangements, as we shall see, are fundamentally supported by faith in central banks. It is only in financial crisis, threatened by a contagion of defaults, that the nature of this support becomes evident: capitalism would have come to an end were it not for the role of central banks.

The commonsense view of money is that it is an accumulated stock: it has to be accumulated through income so as to enable expenditure. But neither of these is strictly true for those who are able to perpetually increase their leverage or debt – they have a privileged relation to money. The illusion of money as a finite stock was exposed by the global financial crisis of 2007–2008. For if there were a finite amount of money distributed in the global economy, even if this money was initially created through borrowing, how could there ever be a global credit crisis?[53] For if the excess borrowing of financial institutions, governments and consumers had already been spent, then it should have been sitting in someone's bank account somewhere – perhaps in money market funds – and the banks who took these deposits should have had no shortage of deposits to underwrite their loans. In the financial crisis, it was the price of assets that fell in the panic, while the stock of money ought to have been unchanged. Yet what actually happened is that banks and financial institutions had borrowed over the short term in order to lend over the long term – that is the essence of their business practice, what a bank actually is rather than a simple error of judgement[54] – and in the crisis, lending from the money markets and other banks dried up so that debts that were about to expire could not be rolled over and renewed. While we can say that the credit crisis happened because financial institutions ran out of money – they have to balance their books and treat money as though it was an accumulated stock, even though it was evaporating before their eyes like a stock of champagne at a party – in reality, they ran out of time and confidence. So we find a striking paradox: the basis of financial morality, which involves matching assets to liabilities, income to expenditure, consists in treating money as an accumulated stock like coins or gold. If one treats money prudently in that way, one gains access to credit; yet credit is a financial asset that is offset by one's own liability. They cancel out, leaving only time and trust.[55]

At the next level of the pyramid, we might suppose that money is essentially a credit, a financial asset created by institutions that are willing to lend. For in reality, over 97% of what is used as money in exchange does not take the form of coins or notes, but is simply recorded electronically: your asset of holding money in your bank account is the bank's liability to you, or your overdraft or loan is your liability to the bank and the bank's asset.[56] In the system as a whole, credits and debts cancel each other out. Similarly, at the end of the day when all payments in an economy are made as transfers between bank accounts, there are no truckloads of notes and coins travelling between major banks – for most such transactions cancel each other out, and the excess can simply be transferred from the reserves that clearing banks hold at the central bank to the reserve account of another bank.[57] So if our electronic money is a token of something of value, it is a token of reserves held at a central bank. Clearing banks hold a privileged place in the hierarchy in virtue of being able to participate in the clearing system. In fact they buy notes and coins for distribution by paying with the central bank reserves they hold, indicating that reserves are apex of the monetary system.[58]

What, then, are central bank reserves? We like to think of them as stocks of gold or foreign currency. Yet while these certainly exist, in practice reserves held at a central bank simply consist in a closed accounting system. Clearing banks, various foreign central banks and national governments hold reserve accounts at the central bank, and these are the only institutions permitted to hold an account in the reserve currency. What are these assets? They are loans made to the privileged institutions by a central bank at a given rate of interest in exchange for something of value – almost always treasury bonds – lent by the privileged institutions to the central bank, and usually an equivalent rate of interest is paid on these deposits.[59] These are time-limited loans, subject to a rate of interest, that are simply bilateral swaps. They do not circulate outside the account books of the central bank. More than two parties are involved, however, for one could not make such a swap without some asset to swap, yet in this case the object that is swapped is a treasury bond, the debt of a national government. A treasury bond, in turn, is also a bilateral swap: a financial institution lends central bank reserves (not money per se) to a government in exchange for owning a debt paying a fixed rate of interest (paid in central bank reserves). The creation of 'money' in this way has limited inflationary effects for the reserves never circulate outside of the central bank. Moreover, it is simply a network of cancelling assets and liabilities: the net stock of money produced through these transactions amounts to zero. Similarly, if all governments were to pay off their debts and reclaim all their treasury bonds, there would be no reserves at the central bank, no basis for the money system and no global financial system at all.[60] Once created, central bank reserves have to be treated as financial assets, just as deposit money has to be treated as an accumulated stock; yet in the act of creation of a mutual liability, there is no counterparty to the increase in overall reserves in the central banking system. Similarly, there is no counterparty to the overall existence in the financial system of over $700 trillion of complex derivatives such as credit default swaps – these are simply swaps and could vanish overnight without anything being affected. Central bank reserves are simply mutual credits, and yet they are the basis for money units of account, means of payment, stores of value and standards for future payments.

This pyramid, then, consists in three heterogeneous, and often inconvertible, kinds of money: money as a stock of notes and coins, money as a financial asset offset by another's liability and money as a credit capable of being created out of nothing, such as central bank reserves. The practical inconvertibility of central bank reserves, for all but privileged and trusted institutions, ensures that a hierarchy exists throughout the financial system. This hierarchy is disclosed to have significance when it comes to the need to default on debt: ordinary economic agents are expected to repay their debts' actual money – but, practice, this means through transferring deposits between bank accounts; banks may operate at perpetual leverage, never repaying all their debts, for their debts are simply others' assets – but, in a financial crisis, the entire system has to be supported by central banks; and central banks are the debtors of last resort, creating monetary reserves at will. It is the need for a central bank to deal with the contagion of default that gives a unity to the economic system.

Let me explain. An economic agent is required to act as if economic values should be judged in terms of prices, discounting the time, as well as to act as if one should always repay one's debts, including interest to compensate for risk. This is all to the good: a culture where all take the repayment of debts seriously is one where rash promises will be few and far between, while faith in the capacities of others to deliver encourages mutual cooperation. Debts are undertaken in good faith that others will in turn deliver on their promises, and the entire economic system functions as a network of contracts, debts and obligations. The level of debt in the economy is identical to the level of credit: in some respects, it can be taken as a measure of our trust and cooperation. But should some event cause several of these economic agents to default – such as a rise in interest rates – then the cumulative effect is a whole series of defaults that could threaten to bring down the entire economic system. Credit itself, the condition for future-oriented economic activity and the expression of the degree of mutual trust and cooperation in the economy, becomes seen as debt, enforcing austerity upon all. An invisible hand pulls the lever, and there is a sudden change in perspective: credit discloses that it has always already been debt. What we discover is that economic contracts are inherently rash promises because it is impossible to represent economic reality as a whole, including the future. So long as contracts are promises to deliver money or commodities, they cannot fully represent networks of production and dependency, externalised costs and risks, nor future threats and possibilities. All promises are in some sense rash promises, even if it may be more imprudent not to promise at all. We therefore arrive at a curious dilemma: all debts ought to be repaid, yet all debts are to some degree imprudent, and impractical; some debts are unpayable. How may this be resolved?

Only a central bank can save us: the system is saved by its exceptions. As lenders of last resort, central banks have discovered their ability to buy up toxic assets, using their own reserves; in doing so, they take debts upon themselves that will never be repaid, functioning as debtors of last resort. For in turn, they are permitted to issue fresh central bank reserves to purchase such toxic assets, without any requirement that such reserves should be repaid to anyone. The overall quantity of central bank reserves in the clearing system might increase, but this has strictly limited effects upon the wider economy apart from offering financial stability. For since these reserves are only held in the accounts of a few privileged institutions at the central bank, where they are transferred but never leave, then there are no concerns about over-supply. The clearing system does not operate as a market. Financial markets are themselves guaranteed by a non-market system: we do not exist under 'free market capitalism' – on the contrary, we are only able to sustain the illusion of 'free market capitalism' to the extent that central banks operate outside of market exchange where debts are repaid. In each of its strategies for intervention, whether setting interest rates, determining the money supply, purchasing 'troubled' assets, in quantitative easing, or merely in providing economic forecasts, the central bank operates as an exception to market relations. Central bank operations express hierarchy, secrecy, privilege, patronage and special 'wisdom'; they treat their wealth as something to be offered for the sake of stability. Only by conforming to a religious rationality, determining where credit and relief is to be offered, can they play the role of redeemers of markets.

CONCLUSION: A CRISIS OF KNOWLEDGE

The progressive rationalisation, marketization and globalisation of the world have produced a crisis of knowledge first discerned in the 1930s by Simone Weil: 'In almost all fields, the individual, shut in within the bounds of a limited proficiency, finds himself caught up in a whole which is beyond him, by which he must regulate all his activity, and whose functioning he is unable to understand'.[61] Specialisation leads to the subordination of those who execute to those who coordinate,[62] and yet even those who coordinate find it increasingly difficult to understand the whole. When knowledge grows increasingly specialised, it becomes harder to discern how different aspects of life interrelate and harder to discern the future.[63] All market participants are ignorant of the true workings of the system in which they participate. Although an initial experiment with constructing free markets and laissez-faire economics had collapsed into the disasters of world war, depression and totalitarianism,[64] the free market was resurrected as a solution to the crisis of knowledge.[65] Where, individually, people are unable to calculate the coordination of forces, the mechanism of market pricing was invoked to coordinate action by balancing supply and demand. Eventually, the market came to be seen as a saviour, capable of delivering the best of all possible worlds.

The fundamental problem with this faith is that economic choices have to be taken on the basis of what will happen in the future.[66] Where guesses about the present can balance each other out, such as a crowd guessing the number of beans in a jar by taking the mean value of the guesses, guesses about the future are more problematic: while the future may be forecasted, it is not seen, so there is no force leading towards a mean value; moreover, the actual future depends on current guesses.[67] Here faith in the market is given a second lease of life: if all economic agents believe in the efficiency and effectiveness of the market mechanism, they will determine their conduct accordingly and the future will become predictable because the behaviour that is producing it will itself be predictable. In this way, it is simply sufficient to have a faith in the market mechanism, rather than an effective market mechanism itself, to produce stability. Once there is stability, then it seems as though assets have determinate prices, and forecasts can be made.

Nevertheless, the fundamental problem remains: if no individual can accurately foresee the future, neither can the crowd. There is no access to knowledge of external reality; instead, one can only observe the crowd, and the signs to which the crowd is likely to respond.[68] Economic reality becomes essentially specular, where a crowd consists of a multitude of individuals who simply watch each other, subject to wild fluctuations caused by a contagion of hope and fear, rather than sharing in a collective perception of an external reality.[69]

What has been lost in the recent credit crisis is the belief that the market is self-stabilising. It is now evident that the market can compound errors. Positive feedback loops, driving wild variations, can predominate over negative feedback loops. There is no true estimation of risks. In such circumstances, the market requires the presence of a leader, one who sees and acts accordingly irrespective of market sentiment. Predictability can be restored by the leader who pronounces on the reliability of forecasts. Central banks, because of their unique position in relation to markets, are placed in this leadership role by markets themselves. For this, the market can forgive them for conduct that would be punished in the case of others: central banks do not need to repay their debts. Since they speak and act for the sake of financial stability alone, then it is usually sufficient for the market to pay attention to them to be restored to stability. There is still the illusion that the market is operating as it should, but instead of simply operating as a balancing mechanism, nor simply operating as a belief system ensuring uniformity and predictability, it acts as a system of submission to the judgements of the expert leader: the central bank and its monetary policy committee.

This might seem to be a minor and technical mutation in and of itself. It does, however, signal a fundamental shift in the relationship between faith and knowledge. For a faith in markets as sources of stabilisation is combined with a faith in empiricism: markets are filled with agents who sift through the evidence and come to a balanced judgement. What is now accepted is that capitalism can come to an end. The threat of a debt-deflation spiral, triggered by a bursting bubble or a default on debt, is a real and present danger. If central banks are able to function as a lookout, watching for signs of financial instability, and if their pronouncements are sufficient to modify market values sufficiently to restore a kind of stability, then the market can forgive them any debt for that. An empiricist faith has been replaced by a kind of apocalyptic faith. It is not enough to read the evidence; one has to judge the signs of the times. Capitalism will come to an end, certainly, but if central banks can postpone the end, they may be recognised as redeemers. Any price can be paid for the postponement of an economic apocalypse.

It also marks a shift in economic morality. It used to be the case that one had to repay debts and balance the books as a matter of faith in the market: transactions had to be conducted so that, with hindsight, they will have become exchanges. Derivatives were invented to give assets liquidity, ensuring the existence of a market.[70] Now, however, there is a far greater danger than a return to the inequalities, inefficiencies and relations of patronage characteristic of the past. For if default on debt cannot be effectively insured against, spreading risk through the system as a whole, because default itself spreads by contagion to the system as a whole, then there is always the danger that any one failure to repay debt might be part of this process of contagion, a harbinger of economic apocalypse. One repays one's debts to postpone the apocalypse.

Let me conclude, then, by summarising this somewhat complex argument: for like life itself, this chapter has to be read forward, yet can only be understood backward. The credit crisis can only be understood with hindsight as a fundamental mutation of belief. For all the questions raised about the mispricing of risk, the stability of financial markets, the practices of banking including securitisation and the multiplication of derivatives, the perverse incentives and even challenges raised to the legitimacy of economics as a discipline, it would seem that economic life has continued much as before. What has changed, as a result of crisis, is the faith that underpins economic reality. Instead of that taking the form of faith in the secular utopia of markets, supported by the public production of knowledge as evidence, faith is now placed in the uniformity of faith itself, as guaranteed by the stabilising intentions of central banks. Instead of being guided by hope for the future, the 'market' now seeks to postpone the economic apocalypse.

A different relationship to the future has become predominant: instead of guiding present conduct by forecasts derived from past performance, conduct is guided by a fear of instability. There is a fundamental discrepancy between what we know of the past and what might happen in the future. This faith manifests itself as a faith in markets to organise behaviour around imitation and so provide a measure of predictability and instability; it also manifests itself as a faith in the obligation to repay debts, which increases the opportunities to become indebted in the present, so that future behaviour will be predictable. As such, this faith is a hope that life may be understood, if life is reduced to the quantification of exchange and debt.

Nevertheless, this faith is deeply misguided and will no doubt generate further instability as a result of its repression of reality. For reality itself cannot be reduced to exchange. Instead, there are dimensions of participation, inheriting the institutions created in the past, and renunciation, offering the time that is present. These entire dimensions of reality are obscured by the faith in exchange. Yet they remain present in the institutions of economic life, and dramatised by the redemptive activities of central banks, providing the one remaining source of stability. If the aim of economic life was considered as including more than merely competition and appropriation, recognising that it includes participation and offering, then economic reality could be understood once more on religious terms. How this religious orientation would be formulated has yet to be seen – for it may well be that dominant global religions, formulated for an entirely different organisation of economic life, do not provide an adequate account without further adaptation. Yet until a mutual accommodation can be found between economics and theology, between credit and faith, then their mutual discrepancy can only lead to instability and potential catastrophe.

NOTES

1. Paul Mason, *Postcapitalism* (London: Allen Lane, 2015).

2. While this might be hard to imagine now, it is the fate that has overtaken some previous social systems, such as Christian churches in Europe.

3. Jean-Pierre Dupuy, *Economy and the Future: A Crisis of Faith*, trans. M. B. DeBevoise (East Lansing: Michigan State University Press, 2014), 65.

4. As suggested by Dupuy, *Economy and the Future*, 85.

5. Those who gather survey data on what we say we believe may have little better access to what people do in fact believe.

6. Simone Weil envisaged an extraordinary process of intelligence gathering during the occupation of France in which the Free French were to formulate their policy by listening to people's 'secret thoughts' in order to offer France as an inspiration before restoring it as a nation. See Simone Weil, *The Need for Roots: Prelude to a Declaration of Duties towards Mankind*, trans. Arthur Wills (London: Routledge and Kegan Paul, 1952), 189–91.

7. For a definitive study, see the dissertation by Liesbeth Noordegraaf-Eelens, *Contested Communication: A Critical Analysis of Central Bank Speech* (Rotterdam: Erasmus University, 2010), available at: repub.eur.nl/pub/21061/EPS2010209MKT9789058922540.pdf (accessed 17 August 2015).

8. The classic statement is by Plato, 'Theaetetus', trans. M. J. Levett, in *Plato: The Complete Works*, ed. John M. Cooper (Indianapolis: Hackett, 1997), 201d.

9. Søren Kierkegaard, *Concluding Unscientific Postscript*, trans. David F. Swenson and Walter Lowrie (Princeton, NJ: Princeton University Press, 1968), 147–52; Martin Heidegger, *Being and Time*, trans. John Macquarrie and Edward Robinson (Oxford: Blackwell, 1962), 274–311.

10. Dupuy, *Economy and the Future*, 21, 36.

11. UK's Financial Conduct Authority, *Conduct of Business Sourcebook* 4.6.2 (4); https://fshandbook.info/FS/html/FCA/COBS/4/6 (last accessed 26 February 2017).

12. Dupuy, *Economy and the Future*, 87 adapts Günther Anders's reflections on the possibility of global destruction in an atomic age for the predicament of capitalism. Anders, 'Theses for an Atomic Age', *The Massachusetts Review* 3.3 (1962): 493–505.

13. Mervyn King, *The End of Alchemy: Money, Banking and the Future of the Global Economy* (London: Little, Brown, 2016), 42.

14. King, *The End of Alchemy*, 129.
15. King, *The End of Alchemy*, 301.
16. George A. Akerlof and Robert J. Schiller, *Animal Spirits: How Human Psychology Drives the Economy, and Why It Matters for Global Capitalism* (Princeton, NJ: Princeton University Press, 2010).
17. See, for example, Ernst Bloch, *Spirit of Utopia* trans. Anthony A. Nassar (Stanford, CA: Stanford University Press, 2000); Jürgen Moltmann, *Theology of Hope*, trans. James W. Leitch (London: SCM Press, 1967).
18. Dupuy, *Economy and the Future*, 96–104.
19. Note that this does not mean the end of the political promotion of market solutions. See, for example, Philip Mirowski, *Never Let a Serious Crisis Go to Waste: Neoliberalism Survived the Economic Crisis* (London: Verso, 2013).
20. Ha-Joon Chang, *23 Things They Don't Tell You about Capitalism* (London: Penguin, 2010), 1–10.
21. Plato, 'Symposium', trans. Alexander Nehemas and Paul Woodruff, in *Plato: The Complete Works,* ed. Cooper, 206a; 'Republic', trans. G. M. A. Gruber, in *Plato: The Complete Works*, ed. Cooper, 505d-e (Indiapolis, IN: Hackett, 1997).
22. Immanuel Kant, 'Groundwork for the Metaphysics of Morals', in *The Cambridge Edition of the Works of Immanuel Kant: Practical Philosophy*, ed. Mary J. Gregor (Cambridge: Cambridge University Press, 1996), 50.
23. See Stefan Schwarzkopf, 'The Political Ontology of Consumer Sovereignty', *Theory, Culture and Society* 28:3 (2011): 106–29.
24. Alasdair MacIntyre, *Dependent Rational Animals* (London: Duckworth, 1999), 119.
25. Luigi Bruni explores how economics focuses on *eros*, obscuring *philia* and *agape*. See Luigi Bruni, *The Wound and the Blessing*, trans. N. Michael Brennen (New York: New City Press, 2012).
26. André Gorz, *Critique of Economic Reason*, trans. Gillian Handyside and Chris Turner (London: Verso, 1989), 109.
27. Maria Mies and Veronika Bennholdt-Thomsen, *The Subsistence Perspective*, trans. Patrick Camiller, Maria Mies and Gerd Weih (London: Zed Books, 1999).
28. Kierkegaard explained the attitude to life formed from this perspective: 'He bears in mind that he owns nothing except what is given to him and owns what is given to him not for him to keep but only on loan, as a loan, as entrusted property'. Wealth is not to be rich oneself, but to make others rich. Søren Kierkegaard, *Christian Discourses*, trans. Howard V. Hong and Edna H. Hong (Princeton, NJ: Princeton University Press, 1997), 29, 114.
29. Gilles Deleuze, *Pure Immanence: Essays on a Life*, trans. Anne Boyman (New York: Zone Books, 2001).
30. Søren Kierkegaard, *Journals and Papers*, trans. Howard V. Hong and Edna H. Hong (Bloomington: Indiana University Press, 1967), I. 1025.
31. Maurizio Lazzarato, *The Making of Indebted Man*, trans. Joshua David Jordan (New York: Semiotext(e), 2012).
32. The events themselves fitted perfectly with Steve Keen's mathematical models; see Steve Keen, *Debunking Economics* (London: Zed Books, 2012). Even

some non-economists were willing to launch into print to predict the coming crisis: Ann Pettifor, *The Coming First World Debt Crisis* (Basingstoke: Palgrave Macmillan, 2006); Philip Goodchild, *Theology of Money* (London: SCM Press, 2007).

33. Weil, *The Need for Roots*, 41

34. Weil, *The Need for Roots*, 48.

35. William B. Connolly, *Capitalism and Christianity, American Style* (Durham, NC: Duke University Press, 2008).

36. Sigmund Freud, 'The Future of an Illusion', in *The Penguin Freud Library, 12: Civilization, Society and Religion,* trans. James Strachey, ed. Albert Dickson (London: Penguin, 1991), 179–241.

37. Freud, *The Future of an Illusion*, 213.

38. Capitalism is best understood as a world view or moral obligation, rather than as an incomplete economic practice: it is the social system in which capital is measured as an accumulated quantity in terms of exchange value. See Goodchild, *Theology of Money*, 84.

39. Joseph Stiglitz, *Freefall: Free Markets and the Sinking of the Global Economy* (London: Penguin, 2010), 28.

40. John Cassidy, *How Markets Fail: The Logic of Economic Calamities* (London: Penguin, 2009).

41. For a decisive refutation, see George Cooper, *The Origin of Financial Crises* (Petersfield: Harriman House, 2008).

42. Charles P. Kindleberger, *Manias, Panics and Crashes: A History of Financial Crises* (New York: John Wiley & Sons, 2000).

43. Karl Polanyi cites three principles: reciprocity, redistribution and householding. *The Great Transformation* (Boston, MA: Beacon Press, 2001), 48–56. For the religious underpinning of these, see Polanyi, *The Livelihood of Man* (New York: Academic Press, 1977).

44. For the significance of the conversion of uncalculated credit into a calculable debt, see David Graeber, *Debt: The First 5,000 Years* (New York: Melville, 2011), 386.

45. Massimo Amato and Luca Fantacci, *The End of Finance* (Cambridge: Polity, 2012), 220.

46. Amato and Fantacci, *The End of Finance*, 19.

47. Amato and Fantacci suggest that the rationalization of this neurotic repression is expressed in the Black-Scholes formula for pricing options. See *The End of Finance*, 57.

48. A mathematical model of the asset-inflation and debt-leverage vicious circle (initially described by Keynes, Schumpeter and Minsky) has been constructed by Keen, *Debunking Economics*, chap. 14.

49. L. Randall Wray, *Modern Money Theory* (Basingstoke: Palgrave Macmillan, 2012), 1.

50. Note that each of these can be challenged as an effective policy option: Adair Turner rejects each in turn as resulting in the increase of sovereign or private debt. See Adair Turner, *Between Debt and the Devil: Money, Credit and Fixing Global Finance* (Princeton, NJ: Princeton University Press, 2016), 224.

51. For accounts of money involving social and temporal formations, see Nigel Dodd, *The Social Life of* Money (Princeton, NJ: Princeton University Press, 2014); Joseph Vogl, *The Specter of Capital*, trans. Joachim Redner and Robert Savage (Stanford, CA: Stanford University Press, 2015).

52. A useful collection of arguments and perspectives is offered by Geoffrey Ingham (ed.), *Concepts of Money: Interdisciplinary Perspectives from Economics, Sociology and Political Science* (Cheltenham: Edward Elgar, 2005). My previous study refused to answer this, preferring instead to explore money in its external and internal relations: an ecology, politics and theology of money. See Goodchild, *Theology of Money*.

53. This problem is discussed, if somewhat inadequately, by Philip Coggan, *Paper Promises: Money, Debt and the New World Order* (London: Allen Lane, 2011), 134–35.

54. King describes this process as financial alchemy: 'By alchemy I mean the belief that all paper money can be turned into an intrinsically valuable commodity, such as gold, on demand and that money kept in banks can be taken out whenever depositors ask for it. The truth is that money, in all forms, depends on trust in its issuer. Confidence in paper money rests on the ability and willingness of governments not to abuse their power to print money. Bank deposits are backed by long-term risky loans that cannot quickly be converted into money. For centuries, alchemy has been the basis of our system of money and banking'. King, *The End of Alchemy*, 8.

55. 'Circulation does not involve a series of progressive compensations but rather the endless proliferation of a nondischargeable debt. As a result of this temporalization, which makes available what is unavailable, interminability is programmed into the functional operations of the system'. Vogl, *The Specter of Capital*, 56.

56. Andrew Jackson and Ben Dyson, *Modernising Money* (London: Positive Money, 2012), 60.

57. For this essential function of credit creation operating through the clearing system, see Richard A. Werner, *New Paradigm in Macroeconomics* (Basingstoke: Palgrave Macmillan, 2005), 171–80.

58. L. Randall Wray, *Modern Money Theory*, 86.

59. Josh Ryan-Collins et al., *Where Does Money Come From? A Guide to the UK Monetary and Banking System* (London: New Economics Foundation, 2012), 70–72.

60. Mary Mellor, *The Future of Money* (London: Pluto Press, 2010), 28.

61. Simone Weil, *Oppression and Liberty*, trans. Arthur Wills (London: Routledge & Kegan Paul, 1958), 13.

62. Weil, *Oppression and Liberty*, 42.

63. Gorz, *Critique of Economic Reason*, 32.

64. Polanyi, *The Great Transformation*, 22.

65. F. A. Hayek, 'Economics and Knowledge' and 'The Use of Knowledge in Society', in *Individualism and the Economic Order* (Chicago: University of Chicago Press, 1948), 33–56, 77–91; Milton Friedman and Rose Friedman, *Free to Choose* (London: Secker & Warburg, 1980), 15.

66. As Vogl points out, supply and demand mechanisms only work where there are fixed budgets, not when future expectations and the creation of debts are in play. Vogl, *The Specter of Capital*, 112.

67. Dupuy, *Economy and the Future*, 27–28.

68. Joan Robinson, *Economic Philosophy* (Harmondsworth: Penguin, 1964), 48–49.

69. André Orléan, *The Empire of Value: A New Foundation for Economics*, trans. M. B. DeBevoise (Cambridge, MA: MIT Press, 2014), 50–61.

70. Vogl argues that financial derivatives create their own conditions of possibility, appealing to the market to make their claim to economic rationality come true, by calculating unpredictable future prices on the basis of unpredictable past prices. See Vogl, *The Specter of Capital*, 73–74.

BIBLIOGRAPHY

AKERLOF, George A. and Robert J. SCHILLER. *Animal Spirits: How Human Psychology Drives the Economy, and Why It Matters for Global Capitalism*. Princeton, NJ: Princeton University Press, 2010.

AMATO, Massimo and Luca FANTACCI. *The End of Finance*. Cambridge: Polity, 2012.

ANDERS, Günther. 'Theses for the Atomic Age'. *The Massachusetts Review* 3.3 (1962): 493–505.

BLOCH, Ernst. *Spirit of Utopia*. Translated by Anthony A. Nassar. Stanford, CA: Stanford University Press, 2000.

BRUNI, Luigi. *The Wound and the Blessing*. Translated by N. Michael Brennen. New York: New City Press, 2012.

CASSIDY, John. *How Markets Fail: The Logic of Economic Calamities*. London: Penguin, 2009.

CHANG, Ha-Joon. *23 Things They Don't Tell You about Capitalism*. London: Penguin, 2010.

COGGAN, Philip. *Paper Promises: Money, Debt and the New World Order*. London: Allen Lane, 2011.

CONNOLLY, William B. *Capitalism and Christianity, American Style*. Durham, NC: Duke University Press, 2008.

COOPER, George. *The Origin of Financial Crises*. Petersfield: Harriman House, 2008.

DELEUZE, Gilles. *Pure Immanence: Essays on a Life*. Translated by Anne Boyman. New York: Zone Books, 2001.

DODD, Nigel. *The Social Life of* Money. Princeton, NJ: Princeton University Press, 2014.

DUPUY, Jean-Pierre. *Economy and the Future: A Crisis of Faith*. Translated by M. B. DeBevoise. East Lansing: Michigan State University Press, 2014.

FREUD, Sigmund. *The Future of an Illusion*. Translated by James Strachey. In *The Penguin Freud Library, 12: Civilization, Society and Religion*, ed. Albert Dickson. London: Penguin, 1991, 179–241.

FRIEDMAN, Milton, and Rose FRIEDMAN. *Free to Choose*. London: Secker & Warburg, 1980.
GOODCHILD, Philip. *Theology of Money*. London: SCM Press, 2007.
GORZ, André. *Critique of Economic Reason*. Translated by Gillian Handyside and Chris Turner. London: Verso, 1989.
GRAEBER, David. *Debt: The First 5,000 Years*. New York: Melville, 2011.
HAYEK, F. A. *Individualism and the Economic Order*. Chicago: University of Chicago Press, 1948.
HEIDEGGER, Martin. *Being and Time*. Translated by John Macquarrie and Edward Robinson. Oxford: Blackwell, 1962.
INGHAM, Geoffrey (ed.). *Concepts of Money: Interdisciplinary Perspectives from Economics, Sociology and Political Science*. Cheltenham: Edward Elgar, 2005.
JACKSON, Andrew and Ben DYSON. *Modernising Money*. London: Positive Money, 2012.
KANT, Immanuel. *Groundwork for the Metaphysics of Morals*. In *The Cambridge Edition of the Works of Immanuel Kant: Practical Philosophy*. Edited by Mary J. Gregor. Cambridge: Cambridge University Press, 1996.
KEEN, Steve. *Debunking Economics*. London: Zed Books, 2012.
KIERKEGAARD, Søren. *Christian Discourses*. Translated by Howard V. Hong and Edna H. Hong. Princeton, NJ: Princeton University Press, 1997.
KIERKEGAARD, Søren. *Concluding Unscientific Postscript*. Translated by David F. Swenson and Walter Lowrie. Princeton, NJ: Princeton University Press, 1968.
KIERKEGAARD, Søren. *Journals and Papers*. Translated by Howard V. Hong and Edna H. Hong. Bloomington: Indiana University Press, 1967.
KINDLEBERGER, Charles P. *Manias, Panics and Crashes: A History of Financial Crises*. New York: John Wiley & Sons, 2000.
KING, Mervyn. *The End of Alchemy: Money, Banking and the Future of the Global Economy*. London: Little, Brown, 2016.
LAZZARATO, Maurizio. *The Making of Indebted Man*. Translated by Joshua David Jordan. New York: Semiotext(e), 2012.
MACINTYRE, Alasdair. *Dependent Rational Animals*. London: Duckworth, 1999.
MASON, Paul. *Postcapitalism*. London: Allen Lane, 2015.
MELLOR, Mary. *The Future of Money*. London: Pluto Press, 2010.
MIES, Maria and Veronika BENNHOLDT-THOMSEN. *The Subsistence Perspective*. Translated by Patrick Camiller, Maria Mies and Gerd Weih. London: Zed Books, 1999.
MIROWSKI, Philip. *Never Let a Serious Crisis Go to Waste: Neoliberalism Survived the Economic Crisis*. London: Verso, 2013.
MOLTMANN, Jürgen. *Theology of Hope*. Translated by James W. Leitch. London: SCM Press, 1967.
NOORDEGRAAF-EELENS, Liesbeth. *Contested Communication: A Critical Analysis of Central Bank Speech*. Dissertation. Erasmus University, Rotterdam, 2010. repub.eur.nl/pub/21061/EPS2010209MKT9789058922540.pdf. Last accessed 17 August 2015.

ORLÉAN, André. *The Empire of Value: A New Foundation for Economics*. Translated by M. B. DeBevoise. Cambridge, MA: MIT Press, 2014.

PETTIFOR, Ann. *The Coming First World Debt Crisis*. Basingstoke: Palgrave Macmillan, 2006.

PLATO. *Republic*. Translated by G. M. A. Grube. In *Plato: The Complete Works*. Edited by John M. Cooper. Indianapolis, IN: Hackett, 1997. 971–1223.

PLATO. *Symposium*. Translated by Alexander Nehemas and Paul Woodruff. In *Plato: The Complete Works*. Edited by John M. Cooper. Indianapolis, IN: Hackett, 1997. 457–505.

PLATO, *Theaetetus*. Translated by M. J. Levett. In *Plato: The Complete Works*. Edited by John M. Cooper. Indianapolis, IN: Hackett, 1997. 157–234.

POLANYI, Karl. *The Great Transformation*. Boston, MA: Beacon Press, 2001.

POLANYI, Karl. *The Livelihood of Man*. New York: Academic Press, 1977.

ROBINSON, Joan. *Economic Philosophy*. Harmondsworth: Penguin, 1964.

RYAN-COLLINS, Josh et al. *Where Does Money Come From? A Guide to the UK Monetary and Banking System*. London: New Economics Foundation, 2012.

SCHWARZKOPF, Stefan. 'The Political Ontology of Consumer Sovereignty'. *Theory, Culture and Society* 28.3 (2011): 106–29.

STIGLITZ, Joseph. *Freefall: Free Markets and the Sinking of the Global Economy*. London: Penguin, 2010.

TURNER, Adair. *Between Debt and the Devil: Money, Credit and Fixing Global Finance*. Princeton, NJ: Princeton University Press, 2016.

UK'S FINANCIAL CONDUCT AUTHORITY. *Conduct of Business Sourcebook* 4.6.2; https://fshandbook.info/FS/html/FCA/COBS/4/6. Last accessed 26 February 2017.

VOGL, Joseph. *The Specter of Capital*. Translated by Joachim Redner and Robert Savage. Stanford, CA: Stanford University Press, 2015.

WEIL, Simone. *The Need for Roots: Prelude to a Declaration of Duties towards Mankind*. Translated by Arthur Wills. London: Routledge and Kegan Paul, 1952.

WEIL, Simone. *Oppression and Liberty*. Translated by Arthur Wills. London: Routledge & Kegan Paul, 1958.

WERNER, Richard A. *New Paradigm in Macroeconomics*. Basingstoke: Palgrave Macmillan, 2005.

WRAY, L. Randall. *Modern Money Theory*. Basingstoke: Palgrave Macmillan, 2012.

Chapter 13

How do we know we have a future?

Richard Dienst

Opening a conversation about 'the future' is an invitation to all kinds of confusion, cliché and platitude. Everybody is supposed to know that there will be a future – it may be catastrophic or glorious or boring – but beyond that nobody really knows anything. Vague certainty alongside strict ignorance: both parts of this age-old consensus are open to question. Maybe we know quite a bit about what is going to happen, and that is why the open-ended idea of the future seems to have outlived its usefulness. Maybe it will turn out that 'the future' is just a name for the place where a special kind of unfinished knowledge and a certain kind of would-be collectivity are supposed to meet some day, under the banner of faith or science or history. As soon as there is no 'we' in the present moment, every kind of futural knowledge, along with the people hoping or dreading to embody its truth, will spin away from the assigned meeting place. Maybe the idea that there could be a shared future – carried forward by an ever-expanding collective learning process – has been roundly repudiated not because it is a distant fantasy, but because its arrival is always announced too soon.

A long line of philosophers have tried to strip the future of its remoteness, its inaccessibility or inevitability, which underwrites a kind of authority invoked by divine and secular rulers alike. For ancient materialists like Lucretius, the antidote was simple: through contemplation of an endlessly changing cosmos we can be cured of the illusion that the future somehow already exists. Change, rhythm, repetition, multiplicity: none of these attributes of existence require the notion of the future as an ulterior reality. A more modern strategy has been to refine the notion of 'knowledge' to exclude anything like speculation, guesswork or routine. As David Hume famously argued, we think we have a future because we think we know that the sun will rise tomorrow. Because we've seen it rise every day so far, we expect it to do so again. But for Hume this answer, though based on solid experience, involves no knowledge. As he puts it, '[i]f there be any suspicion, that the course of nature may change, and that the past may be no rule for the future, all experience becomes useless'.[1] Hume's position remains agnostic: all we can say is that yes, we have a future, for the time being, until we know otherwise. From that fact, from that 'matter of fact', nothing follows: the everyday impression that 'there's always a future' is no guarantee of anything, neither about the course of nature nor about the rules of knowledge. Moreover, any effort to endow that lack of knowledge with pathos of one kind or another is a mistake. Spinoza argued that hope and fear, the basic future-oriented affects, arise strictly through inadequate knowledge and thus will be necessarily dispelled when the proper exercise of reason has removed our doubts. For all of these thinkers, there is no prestige in ignorance, no matter who wants to convince us otherwise. That is why the philosophical refusal of futurity is often condemned as a nihilist, and the notions of 'belief' and 'faith' continue to be prescribed against the 'presentism' of active thought, as if knowledge needs such supplements to avoid starving from what it does not yet know.

Of course, it is not true that the future is completely unknown. In fact, it would be hard to define any kind of knowledge, even and especially scientific knowledge, that does not already contain within it the principles and protocols for extending present certainties into otherwise uncertain contexts. And this kind of futurity must be at work elsewhere, too: even language seems to dictate a forward propulsion, so that, as Kleist once described, simply starting to speak a sentence to a listener calls forth its eventual completion. It is not possible to articulate a thought without turning 'forward' in some sense. Moreover, all of our usual ways of defining a statement, an action or a form of life somehow acknowledge this essential aspect, whether expressed in terms of transitoriness, impermanence, potentiality or some other open-ended term.

But the current repudiation of the future has little to do with these old philosophical debates. Instead, the driving forces are cultural and political, that is to say, historical. The older demystifying critiques had made it possible to think realistically and strategically about the future, and it is precisely that attitude, with all its variants, that now seems to have lost its way. Those who failed to see the failures of modernity were condemned to repeat them as post-modernity; now that the cycles of failure and disillusionment have run through a few more rounds, disappointment is chronic and exhaustion is pandemic. There is a widespread feeling that the whole vocabulary of future-oriented thinking, even the future tense itself, has been absorbed into one or another form of oppression and exploitation. There are right-wing versions of this argument aimed against the remnants of liberalism, and there are left-wing versions aimed at market hype and the capitalist democracy. In both cases, it is a matter of rejecting every program or process that would require the wrong kind of obligation, commitment or indebtedness. At the microsocial level, psychic investments are being withdrawn, mutual responsibilities are being scaled back and everyday expectations for minimal sociability are crashing. At the macrosocial level, one can only wonder if there is a macrosocial level after all.

It would be very difficult to track all the variants of this crisis in futurity, which traverses both structures of feeling and structures of governance. (The refrain that everything is always 'in crisis' is just another version of the phenomenon.) For the moment, it will be more useful to examine a couple of very specific examples, outlining the concrete parameters of our questions about the future without having to use overly general diagnostic tools. At the same time, we can investigate the often-overlooked practical aspects of our need for knowledge. For the moment, the best answers to the question 'how do we know we have a future?' are probably 'who wants to know?' followed by 'what's it to you?' In asking what we think we know about the present, let alone the future, we should never forget to ask how we go about trying to know anything in the first place, and why.

If someone asks you to explain exactly how you have acquired a sense of history or an understanding of the world, what could you say? It is not as if 'history' and 'world' are steady, clear-cut reference points; most of the time they are invoked casually, whenever one wants to invoke some 'big picture'. And that raises another question: under what circumstances do we actually attempt to summon up 'the big picture' in any detail? Is it not more likely to be a vague horizon glimpsed fleetingly when we are trying to think about something else?

Sometimes you just have to open the newspaper. Media theorists like Benjamin and Sloterdijk have commented on the complicated mixture of focus and distraction that is produced in the construction of 'news'. The apparently simple act of navigating a newspaper requires both tightly framed acts of concentration and aggressive forms of ignoring, forgetting and disconnecting one piece after another. If we actually tried to read a newspaper, watch a news broadcast or follow a Reddit feed by paying careful attention to every item and then synthesizing all of them into a coherent story or picture, our thoughts would spin off into the void. Everyday news consumption requires a more-or-less fine-tuned practice of hermeneutic triage, deploying what we think we already know to select, reject, ingest, absorb and expel morsels of never-really-new morsels of news. Meanwhile the manufacturers of news have proliferated both in number and in variety, a development that has tended to favour ever cheaper and faster forms of diffusion and recycling. If it has always been true that the scope and complexity of our 'world picture' depends on the quality of ingredients on offer and the robustness of our intellectual metabolisms, the current situation could be seen as a public health crisis, where poorer provisions and imbalanced diets threaten the ongoing existence of that imaginary ecosystem about which the news was supposed to inform us.

How then do we ever get the impression that we know what is going on? No critic has ever managed to inventory the full range of maneuvers in play, criss-crossing the terrain between the obvious and the unnoticed, the desirable and the doubtful, the familiar and the baffling. Wishful thinking of every kind threads through it all, absorbing shocks and steering around sinkholes. In other words, the composition of a 'world picture' is always a kind of transindividual dream work in progress, from which we never wake up. Sometimes, however, we get the impression that things make a little more sense, if only for a moment or two.

Here I want to examine just one inconspicuous moment of vexed worldliness and endangered futurity. It flashed up in *The New York Times* at the end of April 2014. Like many major newspapers, the *Times* publishes a massive Sunday edition, divided into various formats and sections. On some weekends, there are hundreds of pages of material, which increasingly resembles a digest of the website offerings. To state the obvious: the whole package is not designed to produce a narrative, or an overview, or a synthesis. Invariably there will be echoes and repetitions: a news story in one section might be discussed in another; a celebrity mentioned in one context might reappear elsewhere. The most regular feedback loop crosses between advertising and editorial content; after a few scattered iterations, any name, product or brand will acquire the hazy aura of significance. Newspapers, even in the form of old-fashioned bundles of paper, thus demonstrate a general principle of contemporary media: the prevailing order prefers to express itself as redundant profusion.

The Sunday, 20 April 2014 edition included a long piece on the front page of the Business section headlined 'Taking on Adam Smith (and Karl Marx)', by Stephen Erlanger, the Paris bureau chief. It offers a long profile of Thomas Piketty, the French economist whose just-published book *Capital in the Twenty-First Century* had become a surprise best seller in the US. The article appeared in the midst of a Piketty wave in the *Times*: no fewer than nine pieces on the economist would be published in the week before and the week after 20 April. Those pieces included opinion columns by the liberal Paul Krugman and the conservative David Brooks, a Fashion & Style piece on Piketty's visit to New York, and articles about the popularity of the book in the Books section and the statistics-driven Upshot section. Erlanger's piece appears in the midst of full-spectrum coverage of Piketty – and not only in the *Times* but also in all the major news outlets in the US (but especially those based in Washington, New York, Boston and Los Angeles).

Here is how Erlanger describes the significance of Piketty's book:

> His book punctures earlier assumptions about the benevolence of advanced capitalism and forecasts sharply increasing inequality of wealth in industrialized countries, with deep and deleterious impact on democratic values of justice and fairness.[2]

A sentence like that should stop readers in their tracks. It presents a verdict on capitalism that has been circulating around the radical left for decades. In this context, however, this position is treated strictly as a scholarly argument, a proposition to be debated by professionals. Erlanger does not address whether the argument is true; instead, he asks what kind of an economist could say such a thing. The main focus of the article is Piketty's career, grounded in his academic discipline and framed as a challenge to 'Marxism and laissez-faire economics' alike. The posture of the book is presented as the product of his biography, marked by his distaste for post-68 radicalism and a successful career at the top French and US institutions. His credentials are based not on the bleakness of his view of contemporary capitalism, but on the immense statistical database he assembled in order to chart the long-term dynamics of the system.

We'll return to Piketty's book in a moment. For now, we have to continue browsing through the Sunday paper. In the glossy Magazine section, there was a long article titled 'It's the End of the World as We Know It. . . and He Feels Fine'.[3] The author of the piece, Daniel Smith, offers a sympathetic profile of the English writer Paul Kingsnorth. The piece revolves around Kingsnorth's decision to break from environmental activist groups like Earth First and 350.org, on the grounds that he could no longer believe that ecological catastrophe could be averted. In 2009, he and Dougald Hine published a 7,000-word manifesto titled *Uncivilisation*, which sparked a debate in the UK about the possibilities of stopping climate change and mass extinction. The article marked the first time Kingsnorth's name had appeared in *The New York Times*; at the time, none of his books had been published in the US. The Dark Mountain Project he co-founded in 2009 – a 'network of writers, artists and thinkers who have stopped believing the stories our civilisation tells itself', according to its self-description – produces a series of 'Uncivilised' hardbacked books, as well as collections of music and a website of digital material. In other words, he is a fringe figure whose main claim on our attention is his principled repudiation of ecological hope.

In keeping with its personality-centered approach, Smith's profile treats Kingsnorth's departure from environmental activism as a drama of emotion and choice. His life story is retold in a way that pivots around personal crises, and his political experiences are cast as a cycle of radical awakenings and dashed hopes. If such a dedicated, informed and experienced activist could change his mind so drastically – we are prompted to think – surely his decision should be respected. The profile ends with a brief discussion of *The Wake*, a novel Kingsnorth had just published through the crowd-funding publisher Unbound. Written in a deliberately fabricated version of Old English, the novel reanimates the lost cause of Saxon resistance to the Norman invasion of 1066, not as an exercise in guerrilla nostalgia but in order to see its failure close-up. The newspaper profile does not grapple with the complexity of the novel, focusing instead on its mood of bewilderment in the face of immense loss, so that 1067 mirrors 2014 rather closely. In the end, the *Times* presents Kingsnorth's story as an irreversible turn from the (grand but illusory) political to the (intimate and honest) aesthetic, from wishful thinking to deep grief and disabused defiance.

At first it seems that Piketty and Kingsnorth do not have much in common, except that both of them are addressing problems on a planetary scale. The first is presented as a serious but loyal critic of the capitalist market system, speaking from a position of institutional authority. The other is positioned (quite literally, in a large photograph) as an isolated figure in the woods, paradoxically attracting attention for having rejected not only the civilization of 'ecocide' but also the major ecological movements trying to prevent it. What becomes visible in their conjuncture, however, is something else. They circumscribe two limits of contemporary discourse about the future of the planet. On one hand, each offers a devastating critique of the present order, which could be answered only by denial and deception; on the other hand, each refuses to call for any new transformational project capable of altering the current course. Even if they are not talking about the same 'thing', each operates within the parameters of an unhappy enlightenment: no game-changing event or paradigm-shifting rethink is on the horizon. And so we are left to ask: what could be more dire than knowing the worst and not being able to do anything about it?

One of the main arguments of Thomas Piketty's instantly famous book *Capital in the Twenty-First Century* follows his demonstration, through extensive data, of the propensity of capital to reproduce itself faster than the growth of incomes and outputs. His conclusion, though ringed with qualifications, is that slower global output over the next few decades will be accompanied by even greater concentrations of wealth, including ever larger private fortunes and more voracious sovereign wealth funds. 'Once constituted, capital reproduces itself faster than output increases. The past devours the future'.[4] Such an outcome portrays a capitalism currently in the very pink of health, monstrously alive, and for Piketty it remains 'hard to imagine [this future] in the framework of existing political institutions unless there is a particularly effective system of repression or an extremely powerful apparatus of persuasion, or perhaps both' (*CTC* 439). This could be stated a little differently: it is indeed very easy to imagine such a future, because powerful systems of repression and persuasion are already being expanded and updated. Perhaps there remains some doubt about the precise proportions of these two systems (more of one, less of the other), but it is hard to doubt that the two of them together can manage a situation of increasingly extreme inequality.

The predictive aspect of Piketty's argument is remarkably muted. For a book about capitalism 'in the twenty-first century', it makes few statements about the next eighty or so years. Instead the book builds up a kind of projective momentum from the way it accumulates evidence, registering at the level of prose and statistics the uneven but apparently unstoppable accumulation of capital. When speaking about how capital captures the future, it is not its 'spectrality' that matters but its stubborn embeddedness, its persistence and its historicity. Piketty's analysis collects an unprecedented array of historical evidence: step by step, he illustrates how inequality becomes 'built in' to the system of wealth accumulation at various levels, both in the tendency for returns on capital to outpace returns on labour and in increasingly large differentials of labour income itself. (Piketty finds no evidence that these huge gaps correspond to any 'rational productivity justification' [*CTC* 334].) There were a few post-war decades when growth of capital and growth of income were converging (a brief respite in a longer historical pattern of capital's ascendancy), but those days are behind us, Piketty argues. A greater 'intensity' of capital everywhere, slower growth, stagnating incomes for most of those who live on their labour: these are the key features of the decades leading to 2100.

Contrast this account with Immanuel Wallerstein's contribution to the collective volume titled *Does Capitalism Have a Future?* His answer is pretty emphatic: no, capitalism has no future.[5] It has expended its powers of growth and reproduction. It has reached the limits of its ability to harness governments to stabilize the political and social conditions of reproduction. In more or less drastic terms, these propositions are widely accepted, and not only on the left: capitalism cannot keep going on like this, it has stopped doing what it was built to do, modernization is over, development is over, the terminal crisis is here and so on. And yet, at the same time, capitalism isn't really dead; in fact, it's doing everything it can to secure a future for itself, to secure 'the' future for itself. It does this throughout its operations, however you describe them: through the rule of its laws, the rationality of its investments, the restructuring of social relationships through its law of value, the injection and projection of indebtedness through its apparatus of capture – all of these techniques and assemblages work to ensure the specifically capitalist character of every future currently on offer.

Such analyses generate a peculiar rhetorical situation. First, a convincingly broad and complex world picture is produced, showing a bleak, even unthinkable future. This outcome can be blocked only through fundamental change at the level of global economic governance. (Piketty's solution is based on a global tax on wealth, which would require far-reaching mechanisms of coordination and enforcement.) The specific proposals, however, are deemed in advance to be both inadequate and unlikely. The provisional sense of empowerment that comes with better knowledge is thus spiked with a bitter recognition of the immense difficulty of change. That difficulty might spark some readers to call for more resolute and radical efforts than the author himself has proposed. Other readers, no matter how convinced, will quite rationally decide that no systemic change is possible. The more powerful the text, in other words, the less universal its reception will be, unless it can carry out a discursive revolution along with its analytic one. Otherwise, a sweeping and convincing argument will have the paradoxical effect of disarming opposition to the current state of affairs. (This is the most damning charge offered by Yanis Varoufakis in his review of Piketty.[6]) This booby-trapped dynamic is familiar from discussions around climate change and ecological destruction. We live in an era when taking the long view seems to be especially crippling.

In fact, we should note that Piketty treats the topic of climate change – or, as he puts it, 'the possibility of deterioration of humanity's natural capital' – in just three pages out of 600, very near the end of the book. 'If we take a global view', he writes, 'then this is clearly the world's principal long-term worry'. (*CTC* 567) He pauses to consider various estimates of the damage and different plans for addressing the problem. He quickly decides that 'no one knows for now how these challenges will be met' (*CTC* 569). And yet, whether one tries to estimate the losses from climate disruption or to propose vast investments to ameliorate the problems, the course of capital accumulation, with its attendant inequality, that is projected in Piketty's core model will be much more turbulent.

At this point it is worth quoting the famous lines from Fredric Jameson's *The Seeds of Time* (1994): 'It seems to be easier for us today to imagine the thoroughgoing deterioration of the earth and of nature than the breakdown of late capitalism; perhaps that is due to some weakness in our imaginations'.[7] Twenty years on, it might be added that we have gotten even better at imagining the ruin of the planet, while losing even the feeling of rueful regret about the permanence of capital's dominion.

Mike Davis, in his 2010 *New Left Review* essay 'Who Will Build the Ark?', rehearses the intellectual response to such end-game scenarios with dogged fidelity. In a deliberately schizoid construction, Davis writes his essay twice, offering both worst-case and best-case scenarios. In the first part, he presents 'arguments for believing that we have already lost the first, epochal stage of the battle against global warming. . . . In a warmer world, socio-economic inequality will have a meteorological mandate'.[8] In the second part of his essay, by contrast, he enjoins us to 'start thinking like Noah', assembling new visions of collective living that would inevitably be centered in cities. Let me quote his appeal at length: we must

> think beyond the horizon of neoliberal capitalism toward a global revolution that reinvigorates the labour of the informal working classes, as well as the rural poor, in the sustainable reconstruction of their built environments and livelihoods. Of course this is an utterly unrealistic scenario, but either one embarks on a journey of hope . . . or one submits to a future in which designers are just the hireling imagineers of elite alternative existences.[9]

There's something weird about the rhetorical address here, where the alternative between a journey of hope and a hireling existence are horribly mismatched, in terms of both affect and agency. Davis exhorts his readers to be 'designers' – engineers as much as activists – of a new way of life, and his call for 'explicitly utopian thinking' is grounded in a principled refusal to accept the conclusions mapped out by all of the evidence he presented earlier.

So: how do we know we have a future? For Piketty and Davis, everything we know about the future has to be inflected (or discounted) by some kind of moral or political commitment drawn from a realm outside the situation being described. Piketty remains a pragmatist about changing capitalism, *in spite of everything*, and Davis remains an idealist about fighting climate change, *in spite of everything*. What makes such attitudes seem resolute and hopeful, rather than cynical? As long as we are willing to take some action, as long as we have not simply given up, we feel we can avoid the comfortable passivity of cynicism. And yet we have to keep wondering: what is it about our awful situation that makes us think we can do anything about it?

Paul Kingsnorth and Dougald Hine's manifesto *Uncivilisation* announces the collapse of civilization itself.[10] It is an old story, they admit, but this time will be the last: civilizations have collapsed before, but now it is time to rid ourselves of the wish to save even the idea of saving it. 'We do not believe that everything will be fine. We are not even sure, based on the current definitions of progress and improvement, that we want it to be'. Their litany of woes and disappointments is meant to be comprehensive. They briefly take note of the faltering global economy, but the word 'capitalism' appears only once, in a sentence bidding farewell to (ecological) politics: 'Capitalism has absorbed the greens, as it absorbs so many challenges to its ascendancy'. Once they have stamped out all the embers of optimism and the ground has been cleared of all the old allegiances, they want to regroup with like-minded people. Yet, unlike other manifestos of the moment (such as *The Coming Insurrection,* with which *Uncivilisation* shares its no-future attitude and its rugged self-sufficiency), the Dark Mountain text is notable for the way it turns to art and writing as the last refuge of sociability. Its emphatically post-human–centric vision is grounded in the conviction that storytelling can create a new sense of coherence. The text ends: 'The end of the world as we know it is not the end of the world full stop. Together, we will find the hope beyond hope, the paths which lead to the unknown world ahead of us'.

As these lines demonstrate, it is hard to give up the words 'hope' and 'world' without surrendering the minimum requirements of political speech, at least in a radical vein. From the 'end of the world' to 'the unknown world ahead', from the loss of hope to the 'hope beyond hope', the words struggle mightily to say something positive without sounding duped by the old charms. To be sure, the impulse to jettison these keywords can be seen in various radical movements these days: 'hope' is denounced as a pacifying slogan, and 'world' is repudiated as a more-or-less explicitly imperialist totalization. What makes Kingsnorth a plausible emblem of the Zeitgeist, then, is the way his writing reconciles the melancholy of widespread defeat, failure and loss with the stoic courage of a campaigner. Perhaps this complex attitude is more adequately expressed in his first novel, *The Wake*. (It has given Kingsnorth some glimpses of mainstream fame, having been longlisted for the Man Booker Prize and optioned for a movie by Mark Rylance.) The novel thoroughly dismantles the temptation to hanker after radical heroes or to seek comfort in past glories.[11] The first-person narration is delivered in a stripped-down and modernized version of Old English (or is it a scuffed-up and de-Normanized version of modern English?) whose initial impression of wonderful strangeness turns sour over the course of the book, like an incantation losing its power to conjure magic. The traumas of invasion are real, but what seemed 'good' and 'triewe' about the old ways turns out to be neither, and everything ends in fire and madness.

Kingsnorth has expressed his dissent from never-say-die optimism in other venues as well. In a recent review of George Marshall's *Don't Even Think about It: Why Our Brains Are Wired to Ignore Climate Change* and Naomi Klein's *This Changes Everything: Capitalism vs. the Climate*, he lays out not only the scientific evidence of worsening ecological conditions, but also the apparently unavoidable dead ends in attempts to mount an adequate response.[12] Kingsnorth deploys Marshall to explain our paralysis and then holds up Klein as an example of the way the paralysis gets worse when we try to fight it with the usual existential exhortations and political prescriptions. 'We have failed to act on climate change not because we don't know enough about it, or because we don't know how to prevent it: we have failed to act on it because at one level we don't want to act on it. And we don't want to act on it because we don't want to believe it's really happening'. The problem with our thinking about the problem is not just a failure of imagination or ideological distortion, but some kind of cognitive inhibition, which manifests itself in a host of reasonable arguments for doing nothing. That is where, for Klein, political movements can intervene, by overwriting individual dispositions with collective learning processes. Klein calls for a new mass movement for the planet, far beyond the anti-globalization protests of fifteen years ago: only a concerted mobilization could overcome the neural inertia or willful ignorance that has stunted green politics for decades. But that is exactly where Kingsnorth makes two objections: the left simply does not know how to scale up its mobilizations to the necessary size, and every effort to claim the climate as a specifically leftist cause will further 'entrench the cultural polarisation' rather than overcome it. So he strikes a third position beyond Marshall and Klein: we should not ignore the bad news about climate change no matter how distressing it is, and we should stop expecting a political or technological solution to problems created by the whole political and technological system in the first place.

And so the general outlook shaping the Sunday newspaper experience becomes a little clearer. We know enough about the future to know that nothing will ever get much better, and it might get much worse; the real challenge is finding a way to be okay with that. On one hand, there appears to be no future because capitalism can't be reined in; on the other, there is no future because climate change has already happened. There are a few people who will say to Piketty: your reforms are admirable but impossible, which is why a more radical solution, although it seems even more impossible, is nevertheless necessary. Likewise, there are some people who will reply to Kingsnorth: all is not lost; this is no time to back away from the fight. The false hopes are not entirely false: it will just take more work to make them true. And there are plenty of people who won't be shocked or upset about the prospect of greater inequality and imminent ecocide, because somehow they knew it all along.

Of course, a newspaper, no matter how thick, provides only a limited view of any historical moment. There are countless other paths we could have taken through that edition of *The New York Times*: browsing the real estate section, scanning the bond prices and exchange rates, working through the news and the sports and the movies. But it is doubtful that lingering over the daily news will make us feel any closer to the world, no matter how carefully we draw connections. That is because 'the world' is not a picture built up from innumerable snapshots and data points, although that is precisely how money presents its domain, as if its universal circulation guaranteed some kind of coherence. Instead, the world, if it still exists, appears only as a matter of belief, as Deleuze once said, which is nothing other than a belief in the body itself.[13] The belief that sustains money touches upon neither of these substances, neither the world as it is nor the body as it is lived. Instead it counterfeits each to the other. In the midst of this incessant trafficking in ordinary hopes and fears, the stories about Piketty and Kingsnorth stood out for a moment precisely because a link could be drawn between them, connecting economic totality and biological destiny under the sign of futurity. Although that glimpse seems to trace the farthest outline of the world we are living in now, it becomes visible only because we cannot believe in it.[14]

To outline a brief theoretical response to this impasse, we can return to the work of Fredric Jameson, who proposes a mode of thinking and knowing – sometimes called 'the dialectic', sometimes 'Utopia', sometimes simply 'theory' – that promises to undo the double binds we've outlined so far. In order to grasp this aspect of Jameson's work, it is necessary to recognize and follow through a basic principle: even when there is nothing to look forward to, there is no going back. The feeling that we live in a perpetual present does not mean that all thought and action has stopped. This is a hard position to practice, because we are so used to going back to historical models, or to old beliefs, or to golden ages, just as we are prone to invoke the possibility of something better just ahead. Every form of historicism, like every form of leftist resistance to capitalism, remains 'backward looking' or 'reactionary' if it does not orient itself towards the 'ceaseless transformation of all things'. In fact, Jameson 'goes back' to Marx only in order to show how Marx himself had already articulated this theoretical orientation on a world scale. In *Representing 'Capital'*, Jameson writes: 'Marx alone sought to combine a politics of revolt with the "poetry of the future", and applied himself to demonstrate that socialism was more modern than capitalism and more productive. To recover that futurism and that excitement is surely the fundamental task of any left "discursive struggle" today'.[15] And in *Valences of the Dialectic*, at the end of a magnificent evocation of the thoroughly human, thoroughly historical world in which we now find ourselves, he adds: 'Only Marx theorized this historically original secular totality, which is henceforth the horizon of our being, all the absolutes invented within it are at one and the same time an acknowledgement of that ceiling itself, a recognition of our ultimate Being as History'.[16]

And yet the recognition that we are condemned to a future of our own making does not mean that we are equipped to control it. For the left and the right alike, the failure to acknowledge the unknown quality of the future is manifested in the privilege and pride of so-called strategic thinking. Armed with an organon of political and economic causality, each camp issues calls to action and awaits the day when the correctness of their line is vindicated by events. By contrast, Jameson speaks on behalf of 'those few remaining Utopian idealists who may still harbor the conviction that what is unrealized is better than what is real or even than what is possible'.[17]

In today's 'discursive struggles', such a position is virtually unheard of. It demands that we wean ourselves away from various consolations, including those of specialist expertise, ideological correctness, faithful inheritance and, yes, strategic acumen. It sets itself beyond worn-down cynicism on one hand and radical good conscience on the other. It refuses to dwell either in the experience of defeat or in the principle of hope, although it is intimately familiar with both. What is required is a Utopian 'method' or 'prospective hermeneutic' that is capable of '[changing] the valences on phenomena which so far exist only in our own present; and experimentally to declare positive things which are clearly negative in our own world, to affirm that dystopia is in reality Utopia if examined more closely, to isolate specific features in our empirical present so as to read them as components of another system'.[18] Are there utopian possibilities in Wal-Mart? What about universal conscription? Such exercises and experiments are not, Jameson insists, in themselves a political programme; they are at best the resuscitation of the urge to develop such a programme in an era that appears to have lost the taste for it. As we survey the academy, the media, the movements, the social networks and elsewhere, we have to wonder: who will undertake such exercises, both worldly and unworldly, engaged and disengaged, defiant and patient? Is this work happening already, or will it have to be invented from scratch? If the question of the future can still be posed, where will the questioning happen? Will it happen in books and essays, in recordings and transmissions, in gatherings and scatterings, in short bursts and long unfoldings? If there is no future, what will happen instead?

How will we know?

NOTES

1. David Hume, *An Enquiry Concerning Human Understanding*, ed. and intr. Peter Millican (Oxford: Oxford University Press, 2007), 27 ('Sceptical Doubts Concerning the Operations of the Understanding', Part II).

2. Steven Erlanger, 'Taking on Adam Smith (and Karl Marx)', *New York Times*, 19 April 2014, http://www.nytimes.com/2014/04/20/business/international/taking-on-adam-smith-and-karl-marx.html; in print: 20 April 2014, BU1 (last accessed 26 February 2017).

3. Daniel Smith, 'It's the End of the World as We Know It. . . and He Feels Fine', *The New York Times*, 17 April 2014, http://www.nytimes.com/2014/04/20/magazine/its-the-end-of-the-world-as-we-know-it-and-he-feels-fine.html (last accessed 26 February 2017); in print: *The New York Times*, 20 April 2014: 28–33, 46–47. The reader responses to Smith's profile of Kingsnorth offer an approximation of the current common sense:

> 46% yes, we're doomed
> 27% Kingsnorth is irresponsible, we can still save the planet
> 11% Humans will go extinct, the planet will go on without us
> 8% People have been crying wolf about the end of the world for centuries; we'll be fine
> 8% population control is the only hope

See The Staff, 'Analytics: Is Doomsday Coming?', *The New York Times*, 3 May 2014, http://6thfloor.blogs.nytimes.com/2014/05/03/analytics-is-doomsday-coming/ (last accessed 26 February 2017).

4. Thomas Piketty, *Capital in the Twenty-First Century*, trans. Arthur Goldhammer (Cambridge, MA: Harvard University Press, 2014), 571. Henceforth cited in text as *CTC*.

5. Immanuel Wallerstein, 'Structural Crisis, or Why Capitalists May No Longer Find Capitalism Rewarding', in *Does Capitalism Have a Future?* ed. Immanuel Wallerstein et al. (New York: Oxford University Press, 2013), 9–35.

6. Yanis Varoufakis, 'Egalitarianism's Latest Foe: A Critical Review of Thomas Piketty's *Capital in the Twenty-First Century*', *Real-World Economics Review* 69 (2014): 18–35, http://www.paecon.net/PAEReview/issue69/whole69.pdf (last accessed 26 February 2017). This article appears in a special issue on Piketty, where many other left-of-centre economists take issue with the book.

7. Fredric Jameson, *The Seeds of Time* (New York: Columbia University Press, 1994), xii.

8. Mike Davis, 'Who Will Build the Ark?', *New Left Review* 61 (January–February 2010): 29.

9. Davis, 'Who Will Build the Ark?', 45.

10. Paul Kingsnorth and Dougald Hine, *Uncivilisation: The Dark Mountain Manifesto*. http://dark-mountain.net/about/manifesto/ (last accessed 26 February 2017).

11. Paul Kingsnorth, *The Wake* (London: Unbound Books, 2014). But an earlier piece displays signs of old-fashioned leftist heroism, focused on the real-life Saxon fighter Hereward. See Paul Kingsnorth, 'Bring Back the English Resistance', *The Idler* 42: 'Smash the System' (Idler Books, 2009): 61–69.

12. Paul Kingsnorth, 'The Four Degrees', *London Review of Books* 36.20 (23 October 2014): 17–18.

13. Gilles Deleuze, *Cinema 2: The Time-Image*, trans. Hugh Tomlinson and Robert Galeta (Minneapolis: University of Minnesota Press, 1989), 171–73.

14. This tendency is not limited to the major newspapers. There has been a recent spate of works by radical leftists disowning the very idea of the future. See, for example, Franco Berardi, *After the Future*, ed. Gary Genosko and Nicholas Thoburn (Edinburgh: AK Press, 2011), and T. J. Clark, 'For a Left with No Future', *New Left Review* 74 (March–April 2012): 53–75.

15. Fredric Jameson, *Representing 'Capital': A Reading of Volume One* (London and New York: Verso, 2011), 90.

16. Fredric Jameson, *Valences of the Dialectic* (London and New York: Verso, 2009), 608.

17. Jameson, *Valences of the Dialectic*, 369.

18. Jameson, *Valences of the Dialectic*, 434.

BIBLIOGRAPHY

BERARDI, Franco. *After the Future*. Edited by Gary Genosko and Nicholas Thoburn. Edinburgh: AK Press, 2011.

CLARK, T. J. 'For a Left with No Future'. *New Left Review* 74 (March–April 2012): 53–75.

DAVIS, Mike. 'Who Will Build the Ark?' *New Left Review* 61 (January–February 2010): 29–46.

DELEUZE, Gilles. *Cinema 2: The Time Image*. Translated by Hugh Tomlinson and Robert Galeta. Minneapolis: University of Minnesota Press, 1989.

ERLANGER, Steven. 'Taking on Adam Smith (and Karl Marx)'. *New York Times*, 19 April 2014. http://www.nytimes.com/2014/04/20/business/international/taking-on-adam-smith-and-karl-marx.html. In print: 20 April 2014. BU1. Last accessed 26 February 2017.

HUME, David. *An Enquiry Concerning Human Understanding*. Edited and Introduced by Peter Millican. Oxford: Oxford University Press, 2007.

JAMESON, Fredric. *Representing 'Capital': A Reading of Volume One*. London and New York: Verso, 2011.

JAMESON, Fredric. *The Seeds of Time*. New York: Columbia University Press, 1994.

JAMESON, Fredric. *Valences of the Dialectic*. London and New York: Verso, 2009.

KINGSNORTH, Paul. 'Bring Back the English Resistance'. *The Idler* 42: 'Smash the System' (Idler Books, 2009): 61–69.

KINGSNORTH, Paul. 'The Four Degrees'. *London Review of Books* 36.20 (23 October 2014): 17–18.

KINGSNORTH, Paul. *The Wake*. London: Unbound Books, 2014.

KINGSNORTH, Paul and Dougald HINE. *Uncivilisation: The Dark Mountain Manifesto*. http://dark-mountain.net/about/manifesto/. Last accessed 26 February 2017.

NEW YORK TIMES STAFF. 'Analytics: Is Doomsday Coming?' *New York Times*, May 3, 2014. :http://6thfloor.blogs.nytimes.com/2014/05/03/analytics-is-doomsday-coming/. Last accessed 26 February 2017.

PIKETTY, Thomas. *Capital in the Twenty-First Century*. Translated by Arthur Goldhammer. Cambridge, MA: Harvard University Press, 2014.

SMITH, Daniel. 'It's the End of the World as We Know It. . . and He Feels Fine'. *New York Times,* 17 April 2014. http://www.nytimes.com/2014/04/20/magazine/its-the-end-of-the-world-as-we-know-it-and-he-feels-fine.html. In print: *New York Times*, 20 April 2014: 28–33, 46–47. Last accessed 26 February 2017.

VAROUFAKIS, Yanis. 'Egalitarianism's Latest Foe: A Critical Review of Thomas Piketty's *Capital in the Twenty-First Century*'. *Real-World Economics Review* 69 (2014): 18–35. http://www.paecon.net/PAEReview/issue69/whole69.pdf. Last accessed 26 February 2017.

WALLERSTEIN, Immanuel. 'Structural Crisis, or Why Capitalists May No Longer Find Capitalism Rewarding'. In *Does Capitalism Have a Future?* Edited by Immanuel Wallerstein et al. New York: Oxford University Press, 2013. 9–35.

Index

abstraction, 24, 28, 87–88, 90, 94–95, 103–5, 109, 119, 129, 133–35, 137, 140, 177, 186, 192–94, 197, 215, 219, 227–28, 249, 252–53, 255–56, 260, 272, 295n67, 314
Abu Ghraib, 161
acceleration, 90–91, 101–2, 106, 111, 120
accelerationism, 66, 72–73, 78–79, 82n33, 121, 175–76. *See also* sovereign, sovereignty: sovereign acceleration
accreditation, 91, 94, 102, 133. *See also* credit
accumulation, 9, 29, 31–32, 35n32, 155, 160, 172, 175–76, 201, 213, 216, 221, 230, 255–56, 259–61, 339–40
Adorno, Theodor, 263n35, 264n35; and Horkheimer, Max, 171
Agamben, Giorgio, 9, 17n9, 42, 47, 54, 56, 75–76, 79n2, 176; *Homo Sacer*, 61n39
Aglietta, Michel, 195
Akerlof, George A., 234n13
alienation, 164, 198, 205n59, 219, 254
Altizer, Thomas, 5, 220, 227
American Declaration of Independence, 143
Anders, Günther, 110–11, 121, 125n48, 325n12
Andrew, Major John, 130
aneconomics, 272, 278–79, 281, 284–86
angel, angelic, 121, 178–79, 182n31
anorexic, 178
Anselm of Canterbury, 189, 221
anti-Christ, 65, 67–71, 76–77
anxiety, 49, 163, 197–98
apocalypse, 70, 73, 78, 323, 342, 342, 346n3; economic, 306, 323–24
architecture, 87, 88, 95, 106, 125n43
Arendt, Hannah, 139
Aristotle, 154–55, 191, 204n28, 211
Arnold, Benedict, 130
Arnsperger, Christian, 285
art: American, 137–42; as commodity, 138–39, 141. *See also,* market: art market
Artforum, 141
artificial intelligence, 303
assets, 2, 231, 258, 314–19, 321–23; toxic, 312, 321
atheism, 3–4, 7, 9, 220, 233, 263n30, 271
atonement, 197
Augustine of Hippo, 67–68, 174, 197; *Confessions,* 190

auto-immunity, 277, 281, 283
automation, 6, 260, 278; of speculation, 114
Ayache, Elie, 234n6
Avanessian, Armen, 82n33
Avant-Garde (journal), 137–38

Bacon, Francis, 154
Badiou, Alain, 17n9, 79n2, 178–79, 248
Bakunin, Mikhail, 76–77
bank, 6, 230–31
banking, 21–22, 26–27, 29–30, 32, 154, 164, 220, 229–30; central bank, 132, 136, 304, 306, 308, 317–21, 323–24; infrastructure, 88, 91; system of, 87
banknote, 215, 218, 222
Bank of England, 87–88, 90–91, 94–95, 98–102, 106, 110–11, 114, 121, 122n3, 123n30, 125n43, 125n45, 215
bankruptcy, 162
barter, 132, 135, 151, 191–93
Barth, Karl, 5
Barthes, Roland, 112
Bataille, Georges, 3, 162, 176, 291n36
Bauer, Bruno, 164
Bauman, Zygmunt, 41, 54–56, 58n1; liquidity, 41, 54; liquid modernity, 55
Beckett, Samuel, 73, 159
belief, 3, 6–7, 39, 51, 99, 123n26, 188, 214, 217, 220, 221, 223, 226–29, 239, 271–95, 304, 324; vs. knowledge, 88, 95, 104, 119–21, 194, 275, 304, 324, 333–34; raw, 272, 277. *See also* Derrida, Jacques: 'Faith and Knowledge'
Benjamin, Walter, 1, 8–10, 76–77, 105, 110, 121, 176, 197, 199, 335; 'Capitalism as Religion', 189–90
Bennington, Geoffrey, 273–74
Benveniste, Émile, 272–73, 276, 278–79
Bergson, Henri, 276
Berlant, Lauren, 5, 198
Berns, Egidius, 285
Bethlehem, 69, 76–78
biopolitics, 40–41, 50, 57–58, 66, 69, 78
Bitcoin. *See under* currency
Bjerg, Ole, 211, 217, 234n6
Blair, Tony, 79
Blanchot, Maurice, 282, 292n46
Blanton, Ward, 80n7
Bloch, Ernst, 76
blood, 40–41, 50, 53, 56–57, 62n48, 274–75, 277
Bodin, Jean, 22–24
body, 40–41, 47–54, 56, 88, 154, 156–63, 170–73, 175, 177–78, 180, 344
body politic, 40, 50–51, 53
Boggs, J. S., 141
bond, 6, 150, 159–63, 166, 260, 272–73, 275–77, 279, 281–82, 289n6, 293n51, 319
Bourdieu, Pierre, 248
Bradley, Arthur, 291n28
Brassier, Ray, 121, 243, 263n33
Brault, Pascale-Anne, 288n2
Braver, Lee, 241
Brecht, Berthold, 110
Bretton Woods agreement, 129, 131–32, 139
British Empire. *See* imperialism
Brooks, David, 336
Bruce, Steve, 16n3
Brunhoff, Suzanne de, 230
Bryan, Dick, 234n5
Bryant, Levi, 16n1, 240, 242–43, 248, 251, 261n2, 261n4, 261n5, 261n6, 262n8; *The Speculative Turn: Continental Materialism and Realism*, 16n1, 240, 242, 245, 248–49, 261n2
Burnett, Amy Nelson, 263n30

Cacciari, Massimo, 79n2
calculation, 2, 40, 43–44, 49, 72, 173, 231, 280, 286–87. *See also* incalculabe

Calvinism, 233
capital, 5, 7, 9, 22, 27–32, 40, 54, 56, 58n1, 153, 170, 172–73, 177–80, 216, 223, 229, 240, 259–60, 338–40
capitalism, 1, 6–10, 58, 82n33, 132, 163, 166, 169–70, 175–76, 195, 212–14, 216–17, 220–21, 223, 226–31, 256–61, 284, 303–7, 309, 312, 337, 339–40, 342–43; emergence of, 29–30, 189; end of, 303, 318, 323; as faith, 185, 188, 311, 322; free market capitalism, 306; as machine that generates desire, 202; religious structure of, 105, 186–90, 197; ritual dimension of, 99–100, 104–5, 186–88, 197, 311–13, 344
Caputo, John D., 4, 282–83, 290n18
Carl V, 28–29
cartoons, 135–36
Casa di San Giorgio, 29–30
Castelli, Leo, 141
catastrophe, 222; ecological, 337–43
Cavanaugh, William T., 190, 204n26
Charles V, 21–22
chrematistics, 154, 156–57, 159
Christ, 9, 51, 164, 186, 188–89, 274; resurrection of, 189
Christianity, 9, 68, 75, 149–51, 156, 159, 161–62, 164, 166, 188–90
Cicero, 276
circulation, 50, 223, 228, 295n67
Cixous, Hélène, 275, 280
Claire Fontaine, 178
climate change, 58n1, 303, 343, 341. *See also* ecocide; environmentalism
coinage, 283, 292n40; prerogative, 22–25, 27
coins, 25–27, 95, 100–101, 104, 123n33, 133, 135–38, 218, 319–20
Coleridge, Samuel Taylor, 281
Colletti, Lucio, 250
The Coming Insurrection (Invisible Committee), 342
commodity, 49, 54, 153–54, 166, 192, 211, 215–17, 221, 226, 228, 259
communism, 171, 204n45
confidence, 8, 273, 316, 318; loss of, 217. *See also* trust
consumerism, 44
consumption, 8, 40, 44, 49, 53, 190–92, 194–95, 254, 307, 308, 318
corporation, 62n48, 77, 216, 258, 314
correlationism, 243, 246–48, 263n29
counterfeiting, 287, 295n70
countergift, 273, 279
coup de don (Derrida), 272, 279. *See also* gift
credence, 152–53, 271–72, 276, 282, 284, 290n19, 293n47
credit, 7, 9, 87–88, 100–102, 105, 123n33, 124n36, 153, 155–57, 159, 163–67, 193–95, 212–13, 215–18, 220–22, 224–26, 228–29, 231, 272–73, 277, 280–83, 286–87, 294n63, 314–21; alternative credit systems, 200–202; credit card, 98, 111, 167, 194–95, 201; creditor-debtor relationship, 8, 21–23, 150, 188, 193–202; credit system, emergence of, 21–23, 28–30, 100–105, 133; interpersonal, 100–101, 193; metaphysical dimension of, 101–2
credit crunch, 272, 288. *See also* 2007–08 financial crash
credo, 7, 9, 153, 214–15, 220, 224, 227, 230, 271, 273, 276, 283. *See also* belief; faith
creed, 272
crisis, 1–16, 121, 133, 170, 180, 212–14, 216, 227, 231, 239, 244, 259–60, 272, 283–85, 287, 294n59, 312, 335, 339; of futurity, 334–35, 339; of imagination, 110, 121, 334, 340–41; of knowledge, 322; *krisis*, 90, 94, 98, 120; public health, 336; of representation, 130
Critchley, Simon, 285

cru (crude, believed), 274, 277, 287
crude, 272, 274. *See also* raw
cruel, cruelty, 150, 198, 272, 275
currency, 26–27, 88, 94–95, 100–103, 112, 131, 136, 139, 160, 171, 196, 215, 287, 317, 319; Bitcoin, 212; dollar, 129–31, 134–38, 140–41, 154, 215–16, 222, 224; living currency, 170–75, 177–80. *See also* money
cynicism, 217, 226, 341

Danto, Arthur C., 141
Dark Mountain Project, 337, 341
Davis, Mike, 341
debt, 6–9, 21–22, 28, 31, 150, 159, 167, 188–90, 193, 197–99, 212, 216, 218, 226, 231, 231, 244, 273, 279, 280, 294n63, 303, 305–6, 309, 312–24; cancellation of, 21; default on, 200, 306, 316–17, 320–21, 323–24; experience of, 194–99; forgiveness of, 21–22, 202; infinite, 28; national, 9, 21, 23, 28, 30, 32, 87–88, 101–2; repayment, 320; social structure of, socialization of, 29, 202; sovereign, 28, 201–2, 327n50; toxic, 197. See also *Schuld*
deconstruction, 271–95; and translation, 271–72
Defoe, Daniel, 88, 95, 100–102, 105, 112, 123n33, 124n36; *Daniel Defoe and the Bank of England* (Hamilton and Parker), 122n3
Delessert, Etienne, 138
Deleuze, Gilles, 3–4, 46, 189, 214, 216, 220–21, 344; *Anti-Oedipus*, 4, 227; and Guattari, Félix, 4, 46, 176, 196, 214, 220, 227–31, 233
déliaison (Derrida), 272, 277, 281, 283–84, 289n6
Derrida, Jacques, 3–4, 7, 154–55, 167n11, 216, 234n18, 235n18, 235n31, 271–95; 'Circumfession', 271–73, 275, 278, 287; 'Différance', 285, 294n62, 295n64; 'Economies of the Crisis', 294n61; 'Epoché and Faith', 288n3, 290n22, 292n42; 'Faith and Knowledge', 98, 123n24, 235n31, 272, 275, 277–79, 281, 285, 287, 291n32, 295n69; 'Fidélité à plus d'un', 272, 276, 280–81, 283, 288n4; *The Gift of Death*, 235n18, 278, 292n43; *Given Time: I. Counterfeit Money*, 17n15, 154–55, 235n18, 273, 278, 289n10, 292n37, 295n68, 295n70; *Glas*, 278–79, 288n6, 291n33, 291n34; *H. C. for Life, That Is to Say . . .*, 280, 282, 289n15; *Memoirs of the Blind*, 271; 'On the "Priceless", or the "Going Rate" of the Transaction', 285, 294n62, 294n63, 295n66, 295n70; *Specters of Marx*, 272, 277. See also *coup de don*; *déliaison*; future-to-come *(see under* future*)*; religion without religion
Descartes, René, 221
desire, 40, 44–45, 110, 155–61, 170–73, 176–79, 186, 190–91, 197, 199, 201–2, 213–14, 217, 219–21, 226–28, 233, 307, 308, 310
destruction, 68, 78, 171, 304, 309–11, 315, 325n12. *See also* money: destruction of; ruin
devaluation, 295n67
différance, 155, 285, 292n36
Dillon, Michael, 77–78, 80n15, 81n31
disaster, 159, 303, 322
disbelief: 58, 217, 226, 233, 263, 281, 292n41, 293n48. *See also* faith: lack of
discredit, 217, 221, 293n48, 295n67
dollar. *See under* currency
Douglas, Mary, 5
Doyle, Jennifer, 139
Drach, Marcel, 285; *L'argent. Croyance, mesure, spéculation*, 288n1, 293n51, 294n63, 295n65, 295n67, 295n69, 295n70, 295n71
Drucker, Johanna, 134

Dumont, William, 130
dystopia. *See* utopia, utopianism

ecocide, 338, 341–43. *See also* climate change; environmentalism
economics, 1–16, 44, 151, 154, 211–15, 217, 232, 245, 273, 281–82, 284; economic theory, 31, 136; New Economic criticism, 133
economy, 44, 50, 58, 159, 173–74, 185, 192, 200, 217, 220–22, 231, 241, 260, 292n36, 314, 315, 324, 325; debt economy, 194–95, 197, 201–2, 287; economic sphere, 309; libidinal, 169–70, 172, 174–79, 256–58; as market, 313; as matter of faith, 306
Edelman, Lee, 179
Ennis, Paul J., 246, 262n7, 262n9
environmentalism, 337–38. *See also* climate change; ecocide
equivalence, 9, 172, 226, 244, 286, 315, 319; law of, 94–95, 101, 103–5, 109, 119–21
Erlanger, Stephen, 336–37
eschatology, 41, 57, 67–70, 72, 75–76, 78, 277
Esposito, Roberto, 69, 76, 79n2, 202
ethics, 178
etymology, 151, 271–74, 276–76, 278
Eucharist, 165
exchange, 1–16, 26, 27, 30, 44, 49, 53, 134, 139, 140–41, 142, 172, 180, 187, 191–94, 204n45, 215, 217, 225, 228, 230, 244, 273, 279, 281, 287, 293n51, 295n65, 295n67, 314–15, 317, 323–24; systems of, 171–72; unexchangeable, 172
exploitation, 56–57, 77, 163, 171–72, 180, 259

faith, 1–3, 5–8, 40–42, 44, 51–52, 54, 56–58, 66, 177–80, 185, 187, 213–14, 217, 221, 223, 226, 232, 271–78, 280–84, 287, 293n47, 294n60, 312, 315, 322, 324; automatic, 6; blind, 279, 284, 287, 294n60; lack of, 9, 58, 217, 226, 233, 263n30. *See also* capitalism: as faith
fatalism, 263n30, 305–6
Feder, Gottfried, 258, 262n27
Federal Reserve, 185
feedback loops, 323, 336
Félibien, André, 21–22
fetish, fetishism, 139–42, 166, 187, 191, 228
Feuerbach, Ludwig Andreas von, 164
Fichte, Johann Gottlieb, 252
fidelity, 272, 277–78, 282, 291n28, 293n47
finance, 23, 25, 32, 114, 196, 221, 228, 230–31, 258–59, 312; finance capitalism, 8, 23–25, 159, 164, 196; financial markets, 1, 26–27, 30; financialization, 21–35, 195–96, 202
Fiskus, 23–25, 30, 33n10, 33n16. *See also* treasury
Fort-Da, 153, 163
Foucault, Michel, 40, 44–45, 50, 53–54, 56, 176
Fourier, Charles, 171–72
Francis I, 23, 28
freedom, 102, 105, 125n48, 190, 194–95; of choice, 120, 194–95
Freud, Sigmund, 160–61, 226–27, 229, 233, 286, 295n65, 311, 312
Freyer, Hans, 74
Friedman, Milton, 132, 142
Fuggers, 21–22, 29
fundamentalism, 1, 272, 275, 287
future, 49, 52, 57–58, 68, 76–79, 121, 195, 229, 243, 259, 278, 282, 284, 304, 305, 310, 314, 317, 320–22, 324, 333–34, 338–41, 343–45; as collective vision, 333; future-oriented thought, 321, 334; future-to-come (*avenir*) (Derrida), 281–82; recovery of, 344; uncertainty and unknowability of, 6, 103, 111–12, 239, 242, 281, 305, 311, 333–34, 345

gambling, 160, 163, 304. *See also* speculation
Gandy, Joseph Michael: *An Imagined View of Soane's Bank of England in Ruins*, 95–98, 103, 106, 110–11, 121, 125n43, 125n45
Gasché, Rodolphe, 294n58
Gellius, Aulus, 160
Gernalzick, Nadja, 292n36
Gersten, Gerry, 138
Gibbon, Edward, 75
Gide, André, 295n65
Gierke, Otto von, 23–24
gift, 142, 273, 278, 280–82, 286, 292n38
Gillies, John, 167n10
globalization, 39, 41, 54–55, 57, 59n2, 163, 213, 216, 277
God, 2, 8–9, 41–42, 51, 56, 67, 98–99, 154, 164–66, 173–74, 176, 186–89, 214, 220, 222–26, 233, 272, 274, 279; death of, 3–4, 98–100, 103, 105, 120, 186–87, 199; Kingdom of, 42, 51–53, 58
Goebbels, Joseph, 265n77
gold standard, 114, 129, 131–32, 154, 215. *See also* precious metals
Golumbia, David, 243, 263n29
Goodchild, Philip, 5, 7, 185–86, 198–200, 212, 214, 224, 234n6; *Capitalism and Religion*, 99–100, 103, 120, 123n33, 186–87; *Theology of Money*, 187
Goodwin, Jason, 143n3
Goux, Jean-Joseph, 223, 226, 229, 285–86, 295n65, 295n69
government, 30, 40, 77, 101–2
grace, 22
Graeber, David, 6–8, 191–92, 195, 204n45, 212, 217, 222–23, 226, 229, 234n6
Greenspan, Alan, 185
Groh, Ruth, 80n8
Grossheutschi, Felix, 70, 80n8
growth, 110–11, 195, 257–58, 339
Guggenheim, The, 137–38
guilt, 5, 8–9, 149–50, 160, 163, 188–90, 196–97, 226, 231. See also *Schuld*
Gunder, Andre, 35n32
Guyotat, Pierre, 179

Habermas, Jürgen, 216
Habsburgs, 21, 29
Hallward, Peter, 251
Hardt, Michael, 52
Harman, Graham, 240, 242–43, 248, 260, 261n2, 261n4, 261n5, 261n6, 262n8
Harper's Magazine, 136
Hart, Keith, 133
Hart, Kevin, 290n19
Harvey, David, 130, 217
Hegel, Georg Wilhelm Friedrich, 73, 164, 211, 224–25, 232, 248–54, 263n35, 264n35, 265n60, 276, 278–79, 282, 291n36, 292n37; *The Phenomenology of Spirit*, 276, 282
Heidegger, Martin, 3, 4, 152–53, 164–65, 217–18, 284
Hell, Julia, 75, 80n15
Hippolytus, 68
Hobbes, Thomas, 39–62; *Leviathan*, 39–62
Hoelzl, Michael, 80n15
Holy Roman Empire. *See* imperialism
Hooker, William, 81n16
hope, 198, 217, 284, 304, 306, 323–24, 341–43
Hume, David, 333–34
Hundred Years' War, 28
Husserl, Edmund, 280, 285–86
hyper-complexity, 110

ideology, 187, 194–95
imperialism: American, 137–38, 141–42; British Empire, 65, 71, 100; Holy Roman Empire, 23, 68, 72; Roman Empire, 23, 65–66, 68, 81n19
incalculable, 3, 285–86
individuation, 46, 194–97, 199

Industrial Revolution, 100, 110
inflation, 95, 295n67, 303, 304, 317–19, 327n48
Ingham, Geoffrey, 9, 192–94
institution, 3, 5, 26, 87–91, 100–102, 110, 122n14, 172, 185–87, 193, 195, 200, 202, 212, 231, 306, 308–11, 314–20, 324, 338–39; institutionalization, 10, 28–30, 88, 91, 102, 256, 276, 280–82
interest rates, 321
investment, 153, 159, 199, 305–6, 310, 315–17
Ionescu, Arleen, 292n46
Islamism, 5

Jambet, Christian, 179
Jameson, Fredric, 340, 344–45; *The Seeds of Time*, 340–41
Jarvis, Simon, 261n1, 264n35
Jennings, Theodore Jr., 80n7

Kant, Immanuel, 4, 161, 171, 211, 214, 222–25, 232, 241, 246, 249–50, 252, 262n15, 263n29, 263n30, 276, 279, 286, 295n69, 307, 308
Karatani, Kojin, 204n45, 235n28
Katechon, 65–82
Keane, Webb, 134
Kennedy, John F., 136
Kerslake, Christian, 236n55
Keynes, John Maynard, 2, 136, 213, 217
Kienholz, Edward, 138
Kierkegaard, Søren, 276, 310
King, Sir Mervyn, 305, 328n54
Kingsnorth, Paul, 337–38, 342–43, 346n3; *The Wake*, 338, 342
Klee, Paul, 121
Klein, Naomi, 343
Kleist, Heinrich von, 334
Klossowski, Pierre, 169–78; *The Baphomet*, 173–74; *La monnaie vivante*, 169–70
Konigs, Martin, 197–98
Kotsko, Adam, 266n91
Kracauer, Siegfried, 90, 110–11
Krämer, Sybille, 8, 91, 94, 104, 122n14
Krugman, Paul, 336
Kurz, Robert, 265n63, 266n88

Labarrière, Pierre-Jean, 293n52
labour, 67–68, 163–64, 172, 186, 222, 241–60, 262n26, 303, 314; division of, 191–92; power, 49, 56, 171, 212, 215, 224, 227–28; living labour, 170–71; wage labour, 169, 227
Lacan, Jacques, 3–4, 171, 199, 205n59, 220, 225–26, 228–29, 273
Lactanius, 276
Lanier, Jaron, 114
Lapavitsas, Costas, 215, 258–60
Lardreau, Guy, 179
Latour, Bruno, 262n25, 263n31, 263n32
Lazzarato, Maurizio, 5, 194–96, 202, 234n6; *The Making of the Indebted Man,* 194–96, 202, 234n6
Le Bret, Cardin, 22
Lebrun, Gérard, 251–52
Leibniz, Gottfried Wilhelm, 221
Lekachman, Robert, 136
Levinas, Emmanuel, 3, 155, 294n52
Levine, Les, 138
liberalism, 40, 42–43, 334
Lipman, Jean, 137
liquidity, 316, 323. *See also* Bauman, Zygmunt
loan, 153, 156–57, 224, 319
Locke, John, 42, 155, 211, 255
Lohoff, Ernst, 256, 259, 266n89, 266n90
Loyseau, Charles, 22
Lucretius, 333
Luther, Martin, 263n30
Lyotard, Jean-François, 75, 293n57, 294n57

machine, 98, 109, 114, 201, 230, 278
machinic enslavement, 196–97, 202

Mackay, Robin, 82n33
Mallarmé, Stéphane, 279, 284, 294n59
Mammon, 185–90, 198–99, 202
Marcos, Imelda, 219
Marion, Jean-Luc, 280
market, 2, 7, 26–31, 99, 105, 110–11, 120, 133, 135–37, 151, 156, 163, 166, 176, 186, 191–94, 213, 243, 252–58, 287, 304–6, 312–13, 316–18, 321–24; art market, 138–39, 141; non-market system, 321
Marshall, George, 343
Martin, Randy, 216
Marx, Karl, 1, 9, 31, 58, 139, 154–55, 163–66, 211, 213, 217–20, 226–27, 233, 255–56, 260, 265n56, 295n65, 344–45; *Capital*, 17n23, 163–66, 226, 230, 232, 241;*The Economic and Philosophic Manuscripts of 1844*, 217
Marxism, 82n33, 212, 215, 217, 228, 229–30, 232, 255, 337
materialism, 178–79, 225, 240, 250, 263n30
Maurer, Bill, 133, 135
Mauss, Marcel, 5, 162
Meier, Heinrich, 80n8
Meillassoux, Quentin, 243, 246–51, 263n29, 263n33; *After Finitude*, 245, 248, 251, 261n3, 263n33
Meillet, Antoine, 273
mercy, 149, 151, 161, 167n11
Messiah, 67–69, 71
messianic, messianicity, messianism, 66, 76, 78–79, 272, 277, 281, 283
McGann, Jerome, 134
Milesi, Laurent, 235n31, 291n32
Mill, James, 164
minting. *See* coinage
Mitchel-Innes, Alfred, 194
Mitchell, Lawrence E., 257–59, 262n21, 265n65, 265n66, 265n67, 265n68, 265n69, 266n70, 266n71, 266n72, 266n73
Mitchell, William, 112, 114
modernity, 1–3, 10, 30, 33n16, 41, 44, 54–55, 56–57, 120–21, 186, 226, 232, 334
monetization, 27, 30, 95, 103, 111–14
money, 1–3, 5–8, 27, 39–62, 90, 94–95, 132–33, 142–43, 149–67, 191–92, 197–200, 205n59, 211–36, 272, 285–88, 292n36, 292n40, 293n51, 294n62, 295n65, 295n70, 317, 318, 319, 320, 344; accreditation of, 26; affective dimension of, 197–98, 201; as animating force, 90, 101, 111, 121; circulation of, 39, 40, 286; dematerialization and spiritualization of, 88, 91, 98, 100, 102–3, 111, 119–20, 130, 215–16, 229; destruction of, 142; electronic, 319; indifference of, 102, 120–21, 122n17; interaction with, 198; as life-giving force, 197–99, 205n59; materiality of, 91, 94, 100, 103–4, 114, 124n38, 130, 133–35, 137–38, 142, 187, 192; as mediator, 90, 94–95, 103–4, 111, 122n17, 132–33, 137, 191–93; paper money, 26, 30, 87, 95, 100, 102, 114, 119, 124n38, 130–32, 139–40, 142–43, 143n3, 320; sacrificial logic of, 119; social aspects of, 99, 103–4, 111, 114, 124n38, 133, 137, 140–41; as social relation, 193–99, 204n45; speculative nature of, 88, 94, 98, 104–5, 111, 114, 119, 193, 195; as technology, 98, 104, 114, 11, 194–95; value of, 25–26, 88, 91–95, 98, 104–5, 120, 131, 136–37, 192–93, 198–200, 305, 320; visual representation of, 134–42. *See also* currency
morality, 8, 102, 105, 149–67, 188–89, 197, 223, 318, 323; moral law, 307; moral obligation, 316, 320, 321; moral principle, 310

Morris, Robert, 138
Moses, 51

Naas, Michael, 288n2, 290n18
nature, 8, 42, 47, 77, 102, 106, 119–20, 157–58, 166, 219, 249–51, 253, 340; natural law, 7, 106, 119–20; natural law of gravity, 91, 106, 125n48
Neary, Michael, 234n4, 234n14
Negri, Antonio, 52
neoliberalism, 195
news, 335–36
New Yorker, 135
New York Times, 136, 336–38, 344
Niethammer, Friedrich Immanuel, 250
Nietzsche, Friedrich, 3–4, 8–9, 42, 58, 61n40, 99, 101–3, 110, 149–51, 154, 159–62, 166, 173, 186–90, 295n65; *On the Genealogy of Morality,* 17n24, 149, 159–60, 167n1, 188
nihilism, nihilist, 175, 176–78, 316, 334
9/11, 1, 4
Nixon, Richard M., 129, 136, 138; Nixon Shock, 130, 136, 215
Noah, 341
North, Lord, 100, 102–3
nostalgia, 114, 136, 338

Oakeshott, Michael, 59n9, 60n24
obligation, 7, 212, 244, 259, 276, 305, 314
oikonomia (Aristotle), 154, 156
ontological proof, 211, 221–25
Orléan, André, 195
Ortlieb, Claus Peter, 262n26, 266n88

pagan, paganism, 75, 68, 173–74
parasite, parasitic, 62n48, 170, 189–90, 245, 259–60
Pasolini, Pierre Paolo, 171
Peirce, Charles Sanders, 134
perception, 110–11, 121, 223, 323
performativity, 78, 101, 273–74, 276–77, 279, 280–83
Peterson, Eric, 80n14
photography, 90, 91, 98, 110–14, 120, 140; analogue, 91, 112–14; digital, 91, 112–14; photographic image, 110–14; silver-based film, 111–14
Piketty, Thomas, 336, 343; *Capital in the Twenty-First Century*, 336–40
Piranesi, Giovanni, 95
Plato, 211, 215, 291n32, 307, 308
pleasure, 151, 161, 172
Poe, Edgar Allen, 124n38
politics: political economy, 21, 23, 30, 44, 163–64, 255; political theology, 4, 42, 65–82; political theory, 31, 66
Polybius, 75
polytheism, 173
Poovey, Mary, 133–34
Pope Innocent the Third, 161
Popper, Karl, 55
pornography, 139
Postone, Moishe, 255, 259, 265n57, 265n59
post-secular, 3
power, 5, 8, 22–32, 39–58, 61n39, 65, 102, 136, 161, 185, 188–95, 202, 215–33, 251, 287; imperial, 24, 70–71, 75; seignioral, 30–32; sovereign, 22, 25–28, 30, 39–62; state power, 23–24, 30–31, 39–62, 66, 68, 73–74, 103, 119, 135, 137
powerlessness, 110, 161
precious metals, 25, 49, 91, 94, 100, 112, 137, 192, 222, 224; gold, 30, 49, 88, 91, 95, 100, 114, 129, 137, 156, 192, 215, 218, 229; silver, 29–30, 49, 91, 100, 112, 114, 137, 156, 191–92, 215, 222–23, 229. *See also* gold standard
price, 94, 105, 120, 135, 150, 223, 245, 258, 286–87, 295n69, 304, 309, 312, 314–18, 320, 323, 329n70; market price, 286, 295n69

priceless, 286–87, 295n69. *See also* Derrida, Jacques: 'On the "Priceless", or the "Going Rate" of the Transaction'
privatization, 4, 27, 29, 31–32, 43
progress, 58, 111, 119–21, 161
promise, 6, 51–52, 57–58, 149, 154, 156, 160, 212, 215–16, 278, 283–84, 315, 320–21
property, 52, 77, 218, 231; private, 24, 31, 33n10, 186, 217, 255, 313
prostitution, 139, 164, 169, 175, 177–80
Proudhon, Pierre-Joseph, 164
Prynne, J. H., 232
Pryor, Robert, 136
purity, 95, 109, 112, 119

quantification, 94–95, 98, 104–5, 109, 120, 134, 151, 155, 193, 222, 227–29, 255, 314, 324, 327n38
queer, 139, 142, 179

Rafferty, Michael, 234n5
raw, 274, 275, 282, 287. *See also* belief; crude; raw
Reagan, Ronald, 142
redeemer, 322, 323
redemption, 9, 188–90, 306, 324. *See also* salvation
reification, 110, 155
religion, 1, 42, 164, 212–14, 220, 226, 231, 233, 272, 275–80, 282–84, 287, 291n28, 310, 312; religion without religion (Derrida), 3, 272, 283; return of the religious, 277, 284, 287–88
Renaissance, 26, 31
Ricardo, David, 255
risk, 3, 44, 78, 132, 216, 240, 242–43, 284, 310, 312, 315–17, 320–21, 323–24, 328n54
ritual, 4, 6, 99. *See also* capitalism: ritual dimension of
Roman Empire. *See* imperialism
Romanticism, 106, 119, 125n48
Ronell, Avital, 59n8
Rose, Gillian, 264n35
Roudinesco, Elisabeth, 289n14
ruin, 95, 98, 103, 106–7, 112, 119–21, 125n48, 341; as Romantic trope, 106–7, 119, 125n48. *See also* destruction; Simmel, Georg: 'The Ruin'

sacrality, sacred, 3, 10, 24–25, 33n16, 70, 112, 120–21, 275, 276–77, 283
sacrifice, 8–9, 188, 231, 274–75, 277, 279, 284, 291n33; logic of, 8; self-sacrifice, 9, 279, 291n33. *See also* money: sacrificial logic of
Sade, Marquis de, 171
Saint Paul, 66–70, 72–73, 77–78, 80n7, 150; 'First Letter to the Thessalonians', 66–68, 80n6; 'Second Letter to the Thessalonians', 67–68, 77, 79n6
Saint-Simon, Henri de, 164
salvation, 189, 199, 202, 213, 321. *See also* redemption
sans (without), 282–83, 289n6
Saussure, Ferdinand de, 134, 295n65
Scanlon, Michael J., 282
Schmitt, Bernard, 230
Schmitt, Carl, 40, 42–45, 52–53, 56, 59n6, 60n36, 65–82, 172; 'Accelerator despite Itself', 65–66, 70–73; *Political Theology*, 59n6, 76
Schuld (guilt, debt), 8, 150, 160, 188–89, 226. *See also* debt; guilt
Scooby Doo, 131–32
Seaford, Richard, 234n3
secularism, secularization, 3–5, 90, 103–5, 119–21, 189, 226, 311, 312
security, securization, 28, 31, 43, 46, 50, 52, 55–56, 66–67, 73, 77–78, 81n31, 82n31, 202, 229, 257, 278
seigniorage, 25–27, 30, 137, 140. *See also* power: seignioral
self-sacrifice. *See* sacrifice
sexuality, 139, 178–79, 227
Shakespeare, William, 149–67, 218; *The Merchant of Venice*, 149–67;

Shylock, 149–51, 155, 166; *Timon of Athens,* 218
Shaviro, Steven, 241, 244
Shell, Marc, 131–32, 156, 211
Shiller, Robert J., 234n13
sign, signification, 6–17, 23–26, 70–71, 91, 105, 111, 114, 131, 134–35, 138, 155, 170, 172, 174–75, 186–87, 194, 197, 211–36, 286–88, 295n67
Simmel, Georg, 1, 211, 213, 218; *The Philosophy of Money*, 88, 105–6, 119–20, 122n7, 122n17, 211, 218; 'The Ruin', 106, 119–20, 125n48
simulacra, 172, 175
sin, 8–9, 188–90, 231
Sloterdijk, Peter, 335
Smith, Adam, 123n30, 191–92, 211, 215, 243, 262n18, 262n19, 262n20
Smith, Ernie, 138
Soane, Sir John, 88, 95, 106
Sohn-Rethel, Alfred, 256
Sontag, Susan, 112
sovereign, sovereignty, 21–28, 30–32, 39–62, 70, 76–79, 153, 193, 186, 307, 317; sovereign acceleration, 66. *See also* power: sovereign power
speculation, 1–16, 112, 153, 212–14, 223, 239–66, 257–58, 279, 280–81, 283–84, 286, 310. *See also* gambling; money: speculative nature of
speculative realism, 2, 240, 243–44
speculative subjectivity, 211–12, 214, 216–17, 221, 225, 232–33
speculative turn, 240–41, 244, 247–48, 251, 261
Spengler, Oswald, 75
Spinoza, Baruch, 334
spirituality, spiritualization, 13, 88, 98, 100, 150–51, 161, 311. *See also* money: dematerialization and spiritualization of
Srnicek, Nick, 240, 242–43, 248, 261n2, 261n4, 261n5, 261n6, 262n8, 266n93
state, 3, 6, 24, 26, 28, 30–32, 42–43, 54, 58n1, 61n39, 65, 87, 91, 100–101, 134–37, 176, 212, 230, 258, 313. *See also* power: state power
Stiegler, Bernard, 277, 291n28, 293n48
Stockbroker, A., 265n64
stock exchange, 285
stocks and shares, 314

Taubes, Jacob, 66, 68, 70, 73, 76, 80n14
tax, taxation, 22, 25, 28–29, 31–32, 34n23, 35n35, 53, 138, 312
Taylor, Charles, 139
Taylor, Graham, 234n4, 234n14
technics, technicity, 272, 275, 277–78
technology, technologization, 88, 91, 110–15, 277, 291n28
Terpstra, Marin, 80n14
Tertullian, 68, 70, 276
theology, 5, 8, 10, 58, 65–82, 105, 121, 172, 175, 190, 212, 221, 225, 232; Christian, 169, 185, 188; of money, 213–14; natural, 174
Third Reich, 65–66, 71–72
Tiessen, Matthew, 201
Tiqqun, 170, 176–78; *Preliminary Materials for a Theory of the Young-Girl*, 176–78
Toscano, Alberto, 250
trade, 43–44, 59n2, 101, 102, 123n33, 150–51, 191–92, 204n28, 242–43, 252, 257, 259
tragedy, 95, 106–7, 120, 125n48
transcendence, 100, 103, 175
translation, 49, 111, 283, 284, 291n32. *See also* deconstruction: and translation
transubstantiation, 180
Tratner, Michael, 216, 235n18
treasury, 23–25, 33n16. See also *Fiskus*
Trenkle, Norbert, 259, 266n90
Trump, Donald, 58n2

trust, 2, 8, 101–3, 154, 160, 164, 232–33, 272–73, 277, 281–82, 284, 288, 314, 317, 319–21, 328n54. *See also* confidence
2007–08 financial crash, 1, 5, 170, 185, 196–97, 199, 212–13, 216–17, 226, 232, 239, 259, 306, 317, 318, 323, 324. *See also* credit crunch

unbelief. *See* disbelief
uncertainty, 193, 285, 315. *See also* future: uncertainty and unknowability of
Uncivilisation (Paul Kingsnorth and Dougald Hine), 337, 341–42
Unisys Corporation, 77–78, 81n31
usury, 154
utilitarianism, 307
utopia, utopianism, 52, 58, 76, 120–21, 171–72, 174, 216–17, 226, 229, 341, 344–45; and dystopia, 229

Valéry, Paul, 285
value, valuation, 6, 25, 49–50, 98, 105, 119–20, 139, 150, 165, 170, 172, 185–90, 198–201, 211, 216, 221, 223, 227, 229, 244, 254–61, 286, 294n59, 309, 315–16, 319–20, 340; exchange value, 172, 230, 256, 314, 327n38; surplus value, 172, 255–56, 259–60. *See also* money: value of
Varoufakis, Yanis, 340
Vattimo, Gianni, 4
Vietnam War, 138
Virno, Paolo, 79n2
vitalism, 178
Vogl, Joseph, 328n55, 329n69, 329n70
Volney, Comte de, 75
Vries, Hent de, 292n38

Wallerstein, Immanuel, 339
Warhol, Andy, 138–43; *Campbell's Soup,* 140; *Making Money,* 141; *Two-Dollar Bill,* 140
Washington, George, 134, 136, 138
waste, 157, 172
wealth, 56, 155, 166, 230–31, 244–45, 254–57, 260
Weber, Max, 1, 7, 213, 233; *The Protestant Ethic and the Spirit of Capitalism*, 213
Weil, Simone, 178, 322, 325
Wiblin, Ian, 111–12
Wilde, Marc de, 74, 80n15
Wills, David, 90
Winkler, Hartmut, 124n38
Wit, Theo de, 80n14, 81n22
Woodard, Ben, 249
Wriston, Walter, 131, 136

Yeats, William Butler, 6, 69, 79n1
Yuran, Noam, 219, 234n6

Zarmanian, Thalin, 74
Zelmanovitz, Leonidas, 234n6
Žižek, Slavoj, 5, 133, 187, 220, 225–26, 249, 251–54, 256
Zuckert, Rachel, 263n30

Notes on contributors

Arthur Bradley is Professor of Comparative Literature at Lancaster University. He works at the intersection of comparative literature, political theory, continental philosophy and theology. His most recent book is *Originary Technicity: The Theory of Technology from Marx to Derrida* (2011). He is currently working on a new project which is provisionally entitled *Unbearable Life: Genealogy of Nihilopolitics*.

Simon Critchley is Hans Jonas Professor at the New School for Social Research. His books include *Very Little...Almost Nothing* (1997), *Infinitely Demanding* (2007), *The Book of Dead Philosophers* (2009) and *The Faith of the Faithless* (2012). Recent works include a novella, *Memory Theatre*, a book-length essay, *Notes on Suicide*, and a book on David Bowie. He is series moderator of 'The Stone', a philosophy column in *The New York Times,* and co-editor of *The Stone Reader* (2016). He is also 50% of an obscure musical combo called Critchley & Simmons. *Ponders End*, their new album, was recently released.

Richard Dienst is the author of two books: *Still Life in Real Time: Theory after Television* (1994) and *The Bonds of Debt: Borrowing Against the Common Good* (2011), along with various essays on visual media and contemporary politics. He teaches theory in the Department of English at Rutgers University (New Brunswick).

Philip Goodchild is Professor of Religion and Philosophy at the University of Nottingham. His main areas of expertise are in continental, especially French, philosophy, and its relation to religion, as well as the philosophy of political economy. He has published several books, including *Gilles*

Deleuze and the Question of Philosophy (1996), *Deleuze and Guattari: An Introduction to the Politics of Desire* (1996), *Capitalism and Religion: The Price of Piety* (2002), *Theology of Money* (2007/2009), *Philosophy as a Spiritual Exercise* (2013), and *Religion and European Philosophy: Key Thinkers from Kant to Žižek* (2017, co-edited with Hollis Phelps).

Nicky Marsh is Professor of English Studies at the University of Southampton. Her publications include *Money, Finance and Speculation in Contemporary British Fiction* (2007), *Democracy in Contemporary U.S Women's Poetry* (2007), *Literature and Globalization: A Reader* (2011, co-edited with Liam Connell) and *Show me the Money: The Visual Image of Finance* (2014, co-edited with Peter Knight and Paul Crosthwaite).

Tom McCarthy is a novelist whose work has been translated into more than twenty languages. His books include *Remainder* (2005), which was recently adapted for cinema, *C* (2010), *Satin Island* (2015), and a work of criticism *Tintin and the Secret of Literature* (2006). In 2013 he was awarded the inaugural Windham-Campbell Prize for Fiction by Yale University.

Laurent Milesi is Tenured Professor of English Literature and Critical Theory at Shanghai Jiao Tong University and editor-in-chief of the journal *Word and Text – A Journal of Literary Studies and Linguistics*. He has edited *James Joyce and the Difference of Language* (2003) and published annotated translations of works by Jacques Derrida (*H. C. for Life, That Is to Say . . .*, 2006) and Hélène Cixous (*Zero's Neighbour*, 2010; *Philippines*, 2011; *Tomb(e)*, 2014).

Christopher John Müller is an Honorary Research Associate of the Centre for Critical and Cultural Theory, Cardiff University, and a Senior Associate Teacher at the Department of English, University of Bristol. He is the author of *Prometheansim: Technology, Digital Culture and Human Obsolescence* (2016) and further publications. His work draws on literature, philosophy and critical theory to address the manner in which technological and linguistic structures shape human perception, agency and interaction. He is also a translator of the writings of Günther Anders.

Benjamin Noys is Professor of Critical Theory at the University of Chichester. He is the author of *Georges Bataille: A Critical Introduction* (2000), *The Culture of Death* (2005), *The Persistence of the Negative: A Critique of Contemporary Theory* (2010), *Malign Velocities: Accelerationism & Capitalism* (2014), and editor of *Communization and Its Discontents* (2011). He is currently writing *Uncanny Life*, a critical discussion of the problems of the vital and vitalism in contemporary theory.

Mareile Pfannebecker is a Research Associate in Renaissance Literature and Critical Theory at the University of Strathclyde. She has published work on Shakespeare's drama and Renaissance travel writing.

Hollis Phelps is an assistant professor of religion at the University of Mount Olive, in Mount Olive, North Carolina (USA). He is the author of *Alain Badiou: Between Theology and Anti-Theology*, published by Routledge (2013). With Philip Goodchild, he is also the editor of *Religion and European Philosophy: Key Thinkers from Kant to Zizek*, also published by Routledge (2017).

Josh Robinson teaches contemporary poetry and literary and critical theory in the Cardiff University School of English, Communication and Philosophy and is an affiliated professor of the University of Haifa, Israel. They have co-edited *Marxism and the Critique of Value* (MCM', 2014) and *Contemporary Marxist Theory* (Bloomsbury, 2014). Their monograph, *Adorno's Poetics of Form*, is forthcoming in the SUNY Series in Contemporary Continental Philosophy in 2018.

Peter Sedgwick is Reader in Philosophy at Cardiff University. His publications include *Descartes to Derrida: An Introduction to European Philosophy* (2001), *Cultural Theory: The Key Concepts* and *Cultural Theory: The Key Thinkers* (both co-edited and co-authored with Andrew Edgar), *Nietzsche's Economy* (2007) and *Nietzsche's Justice* (2013).

Aidan Tynan is Lecturer in English literature at Cardiff University. He is the author of *Deleuze's Literary Clinic: Criticism and the Politics of Symptoms* (2012) and co-editor of *Deleuze and the Schizoanalysis of Literature* (2015). His current work is on the cultural significance of deserts and wastelands in the context of the environmental crisis.

Joseph Vogl is Professor of German Literature, Cultural and Media Studies at the Humboldt University in Berlin and Permanent Visiting Professor at Princeton University. His last publications are: *Kalkül und Leidenschaft. Poetik des ökonomischen Menschen* (2002), *Über das Zaudern* (2007) / *On Tarrying* (2011), *Soll und Haben. Fernsehgespräche* (2009, co-authored with Alexander Kluge), *Das Gespenst des Kapitals* (2010) / *The Specter of Capital* (2014), *Der Souveränitätseffekt* (2015) / *The Ascendancy of Finance* (2017).

Ian Wiblin is a photographer and filmmaker interested in the representation of place and its architecture in relation to real or imagined histories. He was Kettle's Yard Artist in Residence, University of Cambridge (1994/1995). He has shown work at The Photographers' Gallery, London, and elsewhere in Britain and internationally. Exhibitions include *Recovered Territory*, The New Art Gallery, Walsall (2007). His long-form video works – *Stella Polare* (2006) and *The View from Our House* (2013), made together with Anthea Kennedy – have been screened at various film festivals and venues, including the Whitechapel Gallery, London. He has written on photography considered in relation to architecture, film and performance. He teaches at the University of South Wales.

32957894R00206

Printed in Great Britain
by Amazon